International Crimes: Theories, Practice and Evolution

To my parents, Christian and Marie-Claude
and to my brothers, Antoine and Benjamin

International Crimes: Theories, Practice and Evolution

Caroline Fournet

CAMERON MAY
INTERNATIONAL LAW & POLICY

Published 2006 by Cameron May Ltd
Reprinted 2007

17 Queen Anne's Gate, London SW1H 9BU, UK.
Tel: +44 (0)20 7799 3636 Fax: +44 (0)20 7222 8517
email: enquiries@cameronmay.com
Website: http://www.lexmercatoria.org

ISBN 10: 1 905017 22 7
ISBN 13: 978 1 905017 22 5

Printed in Great Britain by Blissett Group

Table of Contents

Acknowledgments

This book being greatly inspired by my doctoral thesis, I wish to acknowledge the help I received all through my post-graduate research. In this respect, my first and deepest thanks go to my supervisor, Professor Malcolm N. Shaw Q.C. (University of Leicester). Not only was I able to benefit from his eminent academic skills, but I also received great help and moral support from him. I do not think I could ever thank him enough.

My most sincere thanks are also due to my external examiners on the doctoral thesis, Professor Robin C.A. White (University of Leicester) and Professor Christopher J. Greenwood C.M.G. Q.C. (London School of Economics). Their comments on my work have indeed been most helpful in helping transforming the thesis into a monograph.

From a more practical point of view, I of course want to thank the Faculty of Law of the University of Leicester for offering me a substantial Research Studentship which enabled me to pursue my research and complete the thesis, which has now turned into the present book. In thanking the Faculty of Law, I sincerely express my gratitude to the administrative staff, and most particularly to Mrs Jo Goacher, Mrs Holly Paisey and Mrs Dorothy Tomlinson, all of whom have always been extremely welcoming and very helpful. Finally, in the academic sphere, I wish to thank Professor Vaughan Lowe (All Souls College, Oxford) and Professor James Crawford (Lauterpacht Research Centre for International Law, Faculty of Law, University of Cambridge) for kindly inviting me to conferences held in their respective universities while I was still a student. Participation in such conferences has been a fulfilling experience, both personally and academically.

Regarding this particular book, I would also like to thank Shamsur Rahman, Commissioning Editor at Cameron May, who has been both enthusiastic and supportive about this project from the very beginning, and I truly and sincerely appreciate his help as well as his confidence in my work.

From a personal point of view, I would like to thank my friends and my greatest thanks go to Christophe and Karine for their incredible support even during the hardest and most difficult times. I would also like to thank Arnaud, Aurélia, Avo, Boudjelal, Cécile, Delphine, Dimitra, Floriane, Gilles, Julien, Salima, Valérie and Véronique. Their continuous friendship has been an essential help in the pursuance of my research. My deepest thanks also go to my family and notably to my maternal grandparents, Juliette and Paul Langlois, to my paternal grandparents, Georgette and Jean Fournet, as well as to my aunt and uncle, Marie-Christine and Dominique Jérôme, and to their children, Aurélie and Sylvain. Last but certainly not least, my most sincere thanks are due to my parents, Christian and Marie-Claude, and to my brothers, Antoine and Benjamin, for their love and support all through my life and my studies. I could not have done it without them and adequately acknowledging their help and appropriately thanking them is simply an impossible task.

Caroline I. Fournet
January 2006

Foreword

I was delighted to have been asked to provide a short introduction to this important book, written by Caroline Fournet, a former research student of mine. This work is based upon her thesis successfully submitted to the University of Leicester for a PhD, but has been updated and rewritten. Caroline was a talented and meticulous student, thoughtful and thorough and this book reflects those attributes.

Classical international law was founded upon the sovereignty and independence of states. The domestic jurisdiction of a state was sanctified and intervention prohibited. Within the jurisdiction of each state came competence under the domestic law to try crimes committed in the territory and, particularly under civil law systems, crimes committed by nationals. Thus crimes committed by non-nationals and outside of the territory of a state fell outside of the jurisdictional competence of that state. However, this classical conception has been under sustained challenge since the outbreak of the Second World War. Both at the international and the domestic level, moves have taken place to ensure that jurisdiction could be exercised with regard to certain egregious crimes, irrespective of where they were committed and the nationality of those committing them. Accordingly, international tribunals at one extreme have been established to deal with such crimes, while at the other, domestic courts have been enabled to try offences committed outside of the territory of the state in question. The globalisation of international crimes and jurisdiction proceeded apace.

At the international level, the seminal Nuremburg Tribunal established by the war-time Allies tried "major war criminals of the European Axis countries". Under the Charter of the Tribunal, its jurisdiction extended to crimes against peace, war crimes and crimes against humanity. The judgments of the Tribunal proved to be an indispensable precedent. Attempts to set up an international criminal court after the Second World War foundered. However, in the 1990s, the UN Security Council established by binding resolution two war crimes tribunals. The first tribunal was created in order to deal with the conflict taking place since 1991 in the territory of the Former Yugoslavia. The second was given the competence to prosecute persons responsible for serious violations of international humanitarian law committed in the territory of Rwanda and Rwandan citizens responsible for such violations committed in the territory of neighbouring States between 1 January

1994 and 31 December 1994. Finally, the Rome Statute establishing the International Criminal Court was adopted on 17 July 1998 and came into force on 1 July 2002. This has the jurisdiction with regard to war crimes, crimes against humanity, genocide and, once a definition has been agreed, aggression. This Court has commenced operations and is currently investigating situations brought to the attention of the Prosecutor by Uganda, the Central African Republic and the Democratic Republic of the Congo and the situation in Darfur referred to the Court by the Security Council.

In addition, many states have now adopted legislation empowering domestic courts to hear cases concerning the international crimes of torture, war crimes, crimes against humanity and genocide irrespective of the nationality of the alleged offender and irrespective of where the alleged offence took place. This is essentially the situation in the UK, for example, as a result of the Geneva Conventions Act 1957, the Genocide Act 1969 (now replaced by the International Criminal Court Act 2001), s. 134 of the Criminal Justice Act 1988 and the International Criminal Court Act 2001. The *Pinochet* litigation in the UK at the end of the 1990s proved to be a development of the utmost significance.

This surge forward in jurisdiction both at the international and domestic levels has focused attention upon the nature of international crimes. Dr Fournet's book comes into its own at this point. Clearly and authoritatively, it takes the reader through the evolution of the international crimes in question (crimes against humanity, genocide, war crimes and crimes against peace) carefully examining definitional and jurisdictional questions. The perspective adopted is founded upon a comprehensive and holistic approach with a particular emphasis upon crimes against humanity. Attention is drawn to defects arising out of definitional problems. Both state and individual responsibility for the commission of international crimes are covered and the book concludes with a significant consideration of jurisdictional issues both at the international and domestic level.

This book is likely to prove to be a significant work in an area of rapidly growing significance for both the international community and individual states.

Professor Malcolm N Shaw QC
The Sir Robert Jennings Professor of International Law
University of Leicester

March 2006

Table of Abbreviations

Additional Protocol I	Protocol Additional to the Geneva Conventions of 12 August 1949, and relating to the Protection of Victims of International Armed Conflicts, 8 June 1977
Additional Protocol II	Protocol Additional to the Geneva Conventions of 12 August 1949, and relating to the Protection of Victims of Non-International Armed Conflicts, 8 June 1977
AJIL	American Journal of International Law
American Convention on Human Rights	American Convention on Human Rights ('Pact of San José'), Organization of American States, 1969
Apartheid Convention	International Convention on the Suppression and Punishment of the Crime of Apartheid, United Nations, 1973
BYBIL	British Yearbook of International Law
cass. crim.	Cour de Cassation, Chambre Criminelle (France)
CCL No 10	Allied Control Council Law No. 10
Colum L Rev	Columbia Law Review

Commentary to Geneva Convention I	Pictet, Jean S. (ed), Commentary I Geneva Convention for the Amelioration of the Condition of the Wounded and Sick in Armed Forces in the Field, Geneva: International Committee of the Red Cross, 1952 (reprint 1995)
Commentary to Geneva Convention III	Pictet, Jean S. (ed), Commentary III Geneva Convention Relative to the Treatment of Prisoners of War, Geneva: International Committee of the Red Cross, 1960 (reprint 1994)
Commentary to Geneva Convention IV	Pictet, Jean S. (ed), Commentary IV Geneva Convention Relative to the Protection of Civilian Persons in Time of War, Geneva: International Committee of the Red Cross, 1958 (reprint 1994)
Crim L F	Criminal Law Forum
ECHR	European Convention for the Protection of Human Rights and Fundamental Freedoms, Council of Europe, 1950
EJIL	European Journal of International Law
Elements of Crimes	Report of the Preparatory Commission for the International Criminal Court, Part II: Finalised Draft Text on the Elements of Crimes, 2 November 2000, PCNICC/2000/1/Add 2
ESCOR	Economic and Social Council Official Records
F. 2d	Federal Reporter Second Series (United States)

F. 3d	Federal Reporter Third Series (United States)
F. Supp	Federal Supplement (United States)
F. Supp 2d	Federal Supplement Second Series (United States)
G. A.	General Assembly of the United Nations
GAOR	General Assembly Official Records
Geneva Convention I	Geneva Convention (I) for the Amelioration of the Condition of the Wounded and Sick in Armed Forces in the Field, 12 August 1949
Geneva Convention II	Geneva Convention (II) for the Amelioration of the Condition of Wounded, Sick and Shipwrecked Members of Armed Forces at Sea, 12 August 1949
Geneva Convention III	Geneva Convention (III) Relative to the Treatment of Prisoners of War, 12 August 1949
Geneva Convention IV	Geneva Convention (IV) Relative to the Protection of Civilian Persons in Time of War, 12 August 1949
Genocide Convention	Convention for the Prevention and Punishment of the Crime of Genocide, United Nations, 1948
HILJ	Harvard International Law Journal
HRLJ	Human Rights Law Journal
HRQ	Human Rights Quarterly
ICC	International Criminal Court

ICC Statute	Rome Statute of the International Criminal Court, 17 July 1998, UN Doc. A/CONF. 183/9
ICCPR	International Covenant on Civil and Political Rights, United Nations, 1966
ICJ	International Court of Justice
ICLQ	International and Comparative Law Quarterly
ICRC	International Committee of the Red Cross
ICTR	International Criminal Tribunal for Rwanda
ICTR Statute	Statute of the International Criminal Tribunal for Rwanda, in Security Council Resolution 955
ICTY	International Tribunal for the Prosecution of Persons Responsible for Serious Violations of International Humanitarian Law Committed in the Territory of the Former Yugoslavia since 1991 (also referred to as the International Criminal Tribunal for the Former Yugoslavia)
ICTY Statute	Statute of the International Criminal Tribunal for the Former Yugoslavia, in Security Council Resolution 808
ILC	International Law Commission
ILC 1954 Draft Code of Offences	1954 International Law Commission Draft Code of Offences Against the Peace and Security of Mankind, 28 July 1954, [1954] II *ILC Yearbook*
ILC 1991 Draft Code of Crimes	1991 Draft Code of Crimes Against the Peace and Security of Mankind,

	19 July 1991, [1991] II (2) *ILC Yearbook*
ILC 1996 Draft Code of Crimes	1996 International law Commission Draft Code of Crimes Against the Peace and Security of Mankind, 6 May-26 July 1996, [1996] II (2) *ILC Yearbook*
ILM	International Legal Materials
ILR	International Law Reports
ILQ	International Law Quarterly
IMT	International Military Tribunal at Nuremberg
IMT Charter	Charter of the International Military Tribunal, in Agreement for the Prosecution and Punishment of the Major War Criminals of the European Axis, 8 August 1945, 82 UNTS 279
IMTFE	International Military Tribunal for the Far East
JDI	Journal du Droit International
JICJ	Journal of International Criminal Justice
Law & Contemp Prob	Law and Contemporary Problems
LJIL	Leiden Journal of International Law
LNTS	League of Nations Treaty Series
LQR	Law Quarterly Review
Mich L Rev	Michigan Law Review
National Prosecutions	Post-Second World War prosecutions held in different states predi-

	cated on the Law of the IMT Charter, but based on national legislation and conducted before military tribunals, special tribunals and ordinary courts
NQHR	Netherlands Quarterly of Human Rights
NILR	Netherlands International Law Review
Nuremberg Judgment	Trial of the Major War Criminals before the International Military Tribunal (TMWC), 42 volumes, Nuremberg, 1947-49.
Nuremberg Principles	Principles of International Law Recognised in the Charter of the Nürnberg Tribunal and in the Judgment of the Tribunal, [1950] II *ILC Yearbook*
Nuremberg Subsequent Proceedings	Proceedings by the Allied Powers held pursuant to Control Council Law No 10. In [1950] Trials of War Criminals before the Nuremberg Military Tribunals Under Control Council Law No 10, 15 volumes, Washington: US department of the Army, Government Printing Office, 1946-49
PCIJ	Permanent Court of International Justice
RCADI	Recueil des Cours de l'Académie de Droit International
RGDIP	Revue Générale de Droit International Public
Ruhashyankiko Report	Study of the Question of the

	Prevention and Punishment of the Crime of Genocide, Study prepared by Mr Nicodème Ruhashyankiko, Special Rapporteur, United Nations Economic and Social Council, Commission on Human Rights, Sub-Commission on Prevention of Discrimination and Protection of Minorities, Thirty-first session, E/CN. 4/Sub. 2/416, 4 July 1978
SCOR	Security Council Official Records
S.C.R.	Supreme Court Reports (Canada)
The Raoul Wallenberg Compilation	Melander, Göran and Alfredsson, Gudmundur (eds), *The Raoul Wallenberg Compilation of Human Rights Instruments,* Martinus Nijhoff Publishers, 1997
Tokyo Charter	Charter of the International Military Tribunal for the Far East, 19 January 1946, *United States Treaties and Other International Acts Series* 1589.
Tokyo Trials	Trial of the Major War Criminals, Proceedings of the International Military Tribunal for the Far East at Tokyo, Compiled in Pritchard, John R. and Zaide, Sonia Magbanua (eds), *The Tokyo War Crimes Trial: Proceedings of the Tribunal,* Garland Publishing, 1981
Torture Convention	Convention against Torture and Other Cruel, Inhuman or Degrading Treatment or Punishment, United Nations, 1984
UDHR	Universal Declaration of Human Rights, United Nations, 1948
UN	United Nations

UN Charter	Charter of the United Nations, 1945
UN Convention on Statutory Limitations	Convention on the Non-applicability of Statutory Limitations to War Crimes and Crimes Against Humanity, United Nations, 1968.
UNTS	United Nations Treaty Series
US	United States Supreme Court Reports
Versailles Treaty	Treaty of Peace Between the Allied and Associated Powers and Germany, 28 June 1919, reprinted in Bevans, C.F., *Treaties and Other International Agreements of the United States of America 1776-1949, Vol 2,* 1970.
Whitaker Report	Review of Further Developments in Fields with which the Sub-Commission has been Concerned, Revised and updated report on the question of the prevention and punishment of the crime of genocide prepared by Mr B. Whitaker, United Nations Economic and Social Council, Commission on Human Rights, Sub-Commission on Prevention of Discrimination and Protection of Minorities, Thirty-eighth session, E/CN. 4/Sub. 2/1985/6, 2 July 1985
Yale L J	Yale Law Journal
YJIL	Yale Journal of International Law

Introduction

As recent events have highlighted, international criminal law is a fast-growing legal *corpus* which greatly evolved over the course of time, this evolution culminating in the adoption and subsequent entry into force of the Rome Statute of the International Criminal Court.[1] The development of international criminal law was mainly based on the development of its constitutive elements, namely, of the crimes falling under the concept of international criminal law and over which the International Criminal Court now has jurisdiction. It is precisely the evolution of these international crimes – crimes against humanity, genocide, war crimes and crimes against peace – which is at the heart of the present book. And, indeed, no matter the importance of their evolution, no matter their general recognition as crimes which should be prevented and punished, the fact is that these crimes are still perpetrated. If their continuous perpetration clearly demonstrates the failure of the international community actually to prevent them, it is also striking that, in most cases, the perpetrators will escape prosecution and go free and that, even when they are brought to justice, these prosecutions are more often than not unsatisfactory.

Accordingly, the purpose of this book is to address the defects of international criminal law, and thus of the definitions of the crimes it encompasses, in order to propose a new approach towards this particular legal field. Indeed, it seems that, although the legal tools and instruments to prosecute – and probably prevent – these 'core crimes' against international law from occurring actually exist, their enforcement and implementation generally remains illusory. The underlying reasoning of the present book is thus simple: why are the legal norms designed to prevent and prosecute these crimes ineffective? Why are they so scarcely applied? Why are these crimes not prevented and prosecuted? If political will is rightly seen as a decisive factor in implementing these norms, it is however only part of the answer. And indeed, law itself can be held responsible for its own defects. In other words, such instruments and legal norms are unapplied because inapplicable. Consequently, the aim of this book is to return somehow to the roots of the problem: law itself.

[1] Rome Statute of the International Criminal Court, 17 July 1998, UN Doc. A/CONF. 183/9; entry into force on 1 July 2002.

In order to highlight the intrinsic shortcomings of international criminal law and of the definitions of international crimes, this book will consider the evolution of these definitions in a rather comparative manner in order to assess which directions this evolution of the different crimes could – and ultimately should – take. In this respect, it may be pointed out from the outset that the most striking evolution was that of the notion of 'crimes against humanity'. As it will be analysed, 'crimes against humanity' went from an implicit recognition via the use of the expression 'laws of humanity' to an explicit legal acknowledgment but only as an accessory crime at Nuremberg to, finally, a crime which is now recognised as one of the 'core crimes' against international law. This fantastic evolution will be used all through this book as a model which, it is suggested, the other notions could follow and draw upon in order to become fully effective in terms of prosecution – and in some cases – prevention.

It has nonetheless to be stressed here that the point of this book is obviously not to equate these various crimes and to erase the existence of different international crimes from the legal sphere. On the contrary, the fact that these different crimes are legally recognised through their integration into different and specific instruments is both logical and desirable. By acknowledging these differences, law thus reflects different memories, histories and policies, all of which are embodied in different legal notions. This work is therefore not based on the presupposition that international crimes are malleable notions, and its purpose is certainly not to stretch the definition of crimes against humanity in order for it to encompass an irrelevant array of offences. Rather, it is to demonstrate that law has shown its limits and that the different instruments specific to the various crimes are highly questionable, notably due to some paralysing and defeating provisions, which impede their practical application.

As these four crimes against international law all have their own specificities and as they all correspond to different cultural, socio-political, historical and even moral realities, equating such crimes would annihilate these different origins and would empty them of their particular meaning. It is nonetheless perfectly true that advocating for an evolution of these crimes necessarily implies that their respective scope of application will be widened, but it must also be stressed that this broader conception will in no way affect their specificity and uniqueness, but that it will simply lead to better prevention and punishment.

This issue of uniqueness might notably be raised as regards the crime of genocide which, in the words of Dadrian, 'is today widely viewed as the ultimate crime in the evolution of modern human conflict'.[2] Still, the Genocide Convention, which is clearly the authoritative instrument on the subject,[3] contains serious shortcomings, as this work will subsequently highlight. As a matter of fact, despite its widely acknowledged significance and value – Schabas referred to it as the 'centrepiece in any discussion of the law of genocide'[4] – this Convention has been criticised on a number of grounds and definitions by scholars – whether legal scholars or social theorists – generally encompass 'a wider array of targeted groups, destructive actions and actual cases'.[5] Indeed, while Article II of the Genocide Convention contains a definition *stricto sensu* of the crime of genocide,[6] eminent scholars have emphasised the necessity of a broadly based definition,[7] notably due to the fact that 'genocide is a composite of different acts of persecution or destruction',[8] which thus requires a non-limitative definition. The new approach taken by this book is certainly not aimed at 'trivialising the horror of the real crime when it is committed',[9] by abusively proceeding to a total merging of all the different crimes. These crimes are inherently different and so they should remain. Nonetheless, it is precisely because genocide is one of the most odious crimes that its scope of *application* needs to be widened, that its scope of *protection* ought to be enlarged. The same reasoning applies to crimes against peace and war crimes respectively. As this necessary enlargement can only be achieved through the evolution of the definitions of such crimes, this book merely

[2] Dadrian, Vahakn N., 'The Secret Young-Turk Ittihadist Conference and the Decision for the World War I Genocide of the Armenians', (1993) 7 *Holocaust and Genocide Studies* 173.

[3] Indeed, its definition has been literally reproduced in subsequent major instruments, namely, the Statutes of the ICTY, the ICTR and the ICC.

[4] Schabas, William A., *Genocide in International Law – The Crimes of Crimes*, Cambridge University Press, 2000, p 3.

[5] Markusen, Eric, 'Genocide, Total War, and Nuclear Omnicide', in Charny, Israel W. (ed), *Genocide: A Critical Bibliographic Review, Volume Two*, Mansell, 1991, p 232. For scholarly definitions, see eg Huttenbach, Henry R., 'Locating the Holocaust on the Genocide Spectrum: Towards a Methodology of Definition and Categorization', (1988) 3 *Holocaust and Genocide Studies* 289-303.

[6] See Robinson, Nehemiah, *The Genocide Convention – A Commentary*, Institute of Jewish Affairs – World Jewish Congress, 1960, p 57.

[7] See notably Chalk, Frank, 'Definitions of Genocide and their Implications for Prediction and Prevention', (1989) 4 *Holocaust and Genocide Studies* 149-60.

[8] Lemkin Raphaël, *Axis Rule in Occupied Europe – Laws of Occupation, Analysis of Government, Proposals for Redress*, Carnegie Endowment for International Peace, Division of International Law, 1944, p 92.

[9] See Schabas, William A., n. 4 supra , p 114: 'Diluting the definition, either by formal amendment of its terms or by extravagant interpretation of the existing text, risks trivializing the horror of the real crime when it is committed.'

stresses that such evolution could follow that of crimes against humanity. As a matter of fact, the evolution of the notion of 'crimes against humanity' did not deprive these crimes of their meaning: if anything it enabled them to become part of international criminal law and to be acknowledged as international crimes universally condemned.

In any event, no matter how different these crimes all are, it must also be emphasised that they share similar features and overlap in a number of aspects. This legal interaction is indeed highlighted in this book through the analysis of the same definitional elements with respect to the different crimes. For instance, both the concepts of 'widespread and/or systematic action' as well as of 'grounds for commission', which are at the heart of the definition of crimes against humanity, are also definitional requirements for genocide and war crimes and even, to a certain extent, for crimes against peace, although these raise different questions due to the fact that, since Nuremberg, they have remained undefined and therefore not prosecuted. Furthermore, it might be recalled here that international crimes may also be called *delicti jus gentium,* which literally means 'crimes against humanity'. The fathers of international law – among which Grotius, Vattel and Gentili – have indeed referred to international crimes as 'crimes against mankind' and as crimes 'against the whole world', and have consequently qualified their perpetrators as 'enemies of the whole human family'[10]...or, in other words, as 'criminals against humanity'. Therefore, it is here contended that to reconsider genocide, war crimes and crimes against peace and to revisit their definitions in order to improve them through the model of 'crimes against humanity' would actually be in accordance with the roots of international criminal law, the concept of 'crimes against humanity' marking in fact the very beginning of international criminal law.

This book is based on the assumption that prosecutions for international crimes have remained much too rare and that, accordingly, change and improvement are necessary. Thus, even if the definition of crimes against humanity could still be seen as not definitely settled, it is here submitted that, compared with the other 'core crimes' against international law, they are sufficiently well-defined,[11] their scope of application is more appropriate and they therefore afford more guarantees of effective punishment. It is precisely this great evolution of the concept of 'crimes

[10] Ibid, p 3.

[11] Indeed, if under different instruments, the definition of crimes against humanity may vary, it will be shown throughout this work that these definitional differences have only little consequence in practice.

against humanity' which, it is argued, could and should serve as a basis for the evolution of the other crimes studied, in order to remedy to their ineffectiveness, both from a theoretical standpoint and from a practical perspective. Nonetheless, it might here be pointed out that, in some particular instances, the concept of 'crimes against humanity' might not be the one on which to base further evolution of the other crimes and the present book does expressly acknowledge these limits. Still, when such is the case, it is submitted that the definitions of international crimes should draw upon the most effective one among them, and not necessarily and systematically upon that of crimes against humanity. The aim of this work is not to globalise crimes against humanity but to consider international criminal law as a whole in which the different notions interact and should influence one another in order to ensure the effective implementation of the legal norms. The purpose of the present book is thus to demonstrate, through the example of the evolution undergone by the concept of 'crimes against humanity', that international criminal law is not a static legal *corpus*. It therefore could – and should – still evolve, precisely through the evolution of the international crimes it covers, evolution which would then lead to its legal harmonisation. In this context, the notion of 'crimes against humanity' could be used as an example to follow and to get inspiration from and, as this book will highlight, drawing upon the notion of 'crimes against humanity', while respecting the uniqueness of each of these crimes, might be a solution to ensure the implementation and effectiveness of international criminal law. In this respect, this book does not only deal with the theoretical understanding of these crimes: the aim behind this study and the proposal contained therein is to try and ensure their effective prevention and appropriate punishment. Because such international crimes 'can affect more directly the peace and security of humankind or shock human conscience',[12] accountability is a primary goal. One must recall that impunity is always seen as an approval, and thus as an incitement, which does nothing but to encourage the perpetrator to continue in his or her criminal attitude.

Accordingly, the first four chapters of this book explore the different international crimes, each chapter focusing on one crime. The aim of these chapters is to emphasise the similarities between these crimes, while still acknowledging their own individual specificity, in order to demonstrate that an evolution is not only necessary, but that it is also legally possible. Consequently, the analysis logically starts with the concept of 'crimes against humanity', as this concept subsequently generally serves as a model the other crimes could draw upon for

[12] Paust, Jordan J. et al., *International Criminal Law, Cases and Materials*, Carolina Academic Press, 2nd edn, 2000, pp 13-14.

definitional purposes in order to enforce, or reinforce, their effectiveness and applicability.

As these four chapters concentrate on individual criminal responsibility for the perpetration of these crimes, the fifth chapter could be seen as departing from the rest of the book as the focus therein is on state criminal responsibility. Nonetheless, it is here argued that such a concept should probably still be on the agenda in order fully to complete the definitions of each of these crimes and, in fact, in order to highlight their specificity as *international* crimes. In this respect, the notion of state criminal responsibility, far from being totally separated from that of individual criminal responsibility, is in reality yet another component of international crimes. The concept of international responsibility, it is here submitted, attaches both to the individual and to the state. Drawing upon the state responsibility, the conclusion explores the practicalities of prosecuting international crimes. Thus, as the whole work contemplates definitional issues which impede the application of international criminal law, the conclusion completes the theoretical study by analysing the practical feasibility of prosecuting international crimes as well as the jurisdictional rules and legal norms applicable to such crimes.

Ultimately, 'the existence of law-on-paper rights does not mean they exist in reality'.[13] Indeed, the impunity that has been accorded to perpetrators of international crimes reveals the impotence of the international community. The purpose of this book is thus to give meaning to the prohibition of international crimes by proposing a solution in order to ensure the effective application of the law. In 1946, Justice Jackson stated that he was 'consoled by the fact that in proceedings of this novelty, errors and missteps may also be instructive to the future'.[14] These missteps were mainly due to the fact that international criminal law was not yet widely accepted and acknowledged...but the question remains: have we learned anything from such errors?

---

[13] Kader, David, 'Progress and Limitations in Basic Genocide Law', in Charny, Israel W., *Genocide, A Critical Bibliographic Review, Volume Two*, Mansell, 1991, pp 141-42.
[14] Report of Robert H. Jackson, United States Representative to the International Conference on Military Trials, US Government Printing Office, 1949, p 440. Cited in Bassiouni, M. Cherif, *Crimes Against Humanity in International Criminal Law*, Kluwer Law International, 2nd edn (rev), 1999, p 576.

I. Crimes Against Humanity

> *C'est parce que l'humanité n'est pas suffisamment humaine, qu'il y a encore des actes ignobles qui échappent à la catégorie du crime contre l'humanité : plus s'élargira le domaine couvert par cette infraction, et plus l'espèce se rapprochera de cet état idéal où, unie contre le crime, elle pourra enfin proclamer que tout ce qui est inhumain lui est étranger.*
>
> Alain Finkielkraut[1]

If crimes against humanity are said to be as old as humanity itself,[2] the concept only appeared in a legal instrument at the end of the 19th century in the first Hague Convention of 1899 on Laws and Customs of War on Land, in which 'humanity' was invoked as a norm and 'the laws of humanity' were considered as being the mould of 'principles of international law'.[3] Subsequently, the notion re-emerged at the beginning of the 20th century in a declaration made by the Allied Powers during the First World War as regards the Armenian Genocide. Indeed, the term 'crimes against humanity' was used long before Nuremberg and its first recorded appearance is in a 1915 joint declaration of the governments of Great Britain, France and Russia describing the Turkish massacres of Armenians as 'crimes against humanity and civilisation'.[4] On 24 May 1915, the Allies thus condemned 'the tolerance and often [...] the support of the Ottoman authorities' in the massacres.

The Allied declaration was, for a large part, an act with political motives, close to the 19th century tradition of proclaiming the doctrine of humanitarian intervention to protect oppressed minorities. If the declaration, constantly repeated during the war, can be considered as a kind of precursor to the concept of 'crimes against humanity', subsequently used by the Nuremberg Charter,[5] such a precursor nonetheless remained, at the time without any effect and, if it did set forth general principles, it lacked all binding force. As victors who had obtained from their enemies a surrender with nearly no conditions, the

---

[1] Finkielkraut, Alain, *La Mémoire Vaine – Du Crime Contre l'Humanité*, Gallimard, Collection Folio Essais, 1998 (original 1989), p 84.

[2] See Graven, Jean, 'Les Crimes Contre l'Humanité', [1950] I RCADI 433.

[3] See Bassiouni, M. Cherif, *Crimes Against Humanity in International Criminal Law*, Martinus Nijhoff Publishers, 1992, pp 156-7.

[4] See Schwelb, Egon, 'Crimes Against Humanity', [1946] BYBIL 178-81.

[5] See Article 6(c) of the IMT Charter.

Allies did here let go a unique opportunity to set up, with their declaration, the principle of criminal responsibility for crimes against humanity. Instead, they abandoned all will to prosecute the individuals responsible for the genocide.[6]

In a report to the 1919 Preliminary Peace Conference, the majority of a special 15-membered Allied Commission – the Commission on the Responsibility of the Authors of the War and on Enforcement of Penalties –found that the Central Powers had committed numerous acts 'in violation of the established laws and customs of war and the elementary rules of humanity'.[7] The Turkish massacre of Armenians then received prominent attention but such an interest was only ephemeral. As a matter of fact, the two American members of the commission disagreed with such a finding and dismissed the concept of 'laws of humanity' as 'not the object of punishment by a court of justice' but rather as a question of 'moral law' without any 'fixed and universal standard'.[8] They further believed that these horrors were an internal matter not subject to the jurisdiction to other governments and that, therefore, the Allies could not legitimately punish them.[9] As a result, the first modern attempt to impute individual criminal responsibility for the commission of crimes against humanity failed. The Sèvres Treaty, signed by the representatives of the Ottoman Government, was never ratified while it included the lineaments of such a responsibility in its Article 230 which considered as an offence 'the massacres committed during the continuance of the state of war on territory which formed part of the Turkish Empire on 1 August 1914'.[10] Instead, it was replaced by the 1923 Treaty of Lausanne which, far from containing any such provision, granted amnesty to all the individuals who perpetrated such acts during 1914 to 1922.[11] The victors clearly preferred political benefit to the realisation of their promises and their principles.

[6] In the Turkish sphere, it must be emphasised that, in 1919-1920, a Special Turkish Military Tribunal judged the authors of such crimes against humanity. However, these legal proceedings failed as nationalist feelings rose against such trials. See generally Dadrian, Vahakn N., *Autopsie du Génocide Arménien*, Editions Complexe, 1995.
[7] See 'Commission on the Responsibility of the Authors of the War and on Enforcement of Penalties – Report Presented to the Preliminary Peace Conference, 29 March 1919', (1920) 14 *AJIL* 95-154.
[8] Ibid, p 118.
[9] See ibid, 'Annex II: Memorandum of Reservations Presented by the Representatives of the United States to the Report of the Commission on Responsibilities', (1920) 14 *AJIL* 127-51.
[10] Treaty of Peace Between the Allied Powers and Turkey (Treaty of Sèvres), signed at Sèvres, 10 August 1920, (Supp. 1921) 15 *AJIL* 235.
[11] See Treaty of Lausanne, 24 July 1924, (Supp. 1924) 18 *AJIL* 1-116.

At the end of the Second World War, faced with the horrors committed, the Allies were not to repeat their mistakes and, in the Charter of the International Military Tribunal set up which was set up to try high-ranking Nazis, the concept of crimes against humanity finally emerged in positive international law. [12]

The Charter was appended to the London Agreement of 8 August 1945; the Nuremberg Tribunal was thus established by a treaty, originally signed by the four major Allies and subsequently acceded to by nineteen states.[13] It defined the crimes the Allied were to prosecute in its Article 6 while Article 6 (c) gave a definition of the new notion of 'crimes against humanity' as being:

> [m]urder, extermination, enslavement, deportation, and other inhumane acts committed against any civilian population, before or during the war, or persecutions on political, racial or religious grounds in execution of or in connection with any crime within the jurisdiction of the Tribunal, whether or not in violation of the domestic law of the country where perpetrated.[14]

A. The emergence of crimes against humanity in international law

1. *Crimes against humanity and the principle of legality*

By creating a new crime and by simultaneously attaching to this legal creation individual criminal responsibility, the Nuremberg trials caused fierce and fervent debates – both before and after they took place – with respect to the principle of legality. The *nullum crimen, nulla poena sine lege praevia* principle, according to which there is no crime without pre-existing law, was invoked by the defendants who claimed that these crimes contravened this principle and that these trials were therefore illegal. As Bassiouni rightly observed:

[12] The Nuremberg Tribunal tried 22 Nazi German officials on three basic charges, namely, conspiring and ultimately launching an 'aggressive war', committing 'war crimes' and committing 'crimes against humanity'. Various German organisations and businesses were also indicted. As a matter of fact, the Leadership Corps of the Nazi Party, the Gestapo, the S.D., and the S.S. were found guilty, while the S.A., the Reich Cabinet and the General Staff and High Command of the German Armed Forces were acquitted. The trial lasted eleven months, from 4 November 1945 until 1 October 1946.

[13] These were Australia, Belgium, Czechoslovakia, Denmark, Ethiopia, Greece, Haiti, Honduras, India, Luxembourg, the Netherlands, New Zealand, Norway, Panama, Paraguay, Poland, Uruguay, Venezuela, and Yugoslavia.

[14] Bassiouni, M. Cherif, *Crimes Against Humanity in International Criminal Law,* Martinus Nijhoff Publishers, 1992, p 1.

> [i]t is ironic that the search for justice in accordance with a fair legal process led to the type of criticism which would not have occurred had such a process been eschewed in favor of summary court martial judgment and swift punishment.[15]

This defence is however definitely obsolete today and it might even be argued that this was in fact already the case at Nuremberg. And indeed, prior to Nuremberg, the Treaty of Sèvres of 10 August 1920, even if it never came into force, already stood as a clear proof that states condemned such crimes against humanity and that there existed some general principles applicable to all states, including Nazi Germany. Furthermore, if some authors maintain that the maxim *nullum crimen, nulla poena sine lege praevia* is a procedural safeguard against injustice, it may be argued that it is not a rule of law. Thus, in the words of Woetzel, 'since it is an ethical principle rather than a rule of law, it may be set aside if considerations of justice demand it'.[16] Similarly, Stone pointed out that '[w]here it has been adopted into a legal system, it is usually with exceptions and qualifications; and in many countries, including most British countries, it is not a *rule of law* at all'.[17] Today, such arguments are reinforced by the fact that the possibility of retroactive criminal law for the perpetration of international crimes is recognised at both the international and the regional levels.

For instance, Article 15 of the International Covenant on Civil and Political Rights which deals with the Prohibition of Retroactive Criminal Laws expressly makes an exception to the general principle in the following terms:

> 1. No one shall be held guilty of any criminal offence on account of any act or omission which did not constitute a criminal offence, under national or international law, at the time when it was committed. Nor shall a heavier penalty be imposed than the one that was applicable at the time when the criminal offence was committed. If, subsequent to the commission of the offence, provision is made by law

[15] Bassiouni, M. Cherif, '"Crimes Against Humanity": The Need for a Specialised Convention', (1994) 31 *Columbia Journal of Transnational Law* 472.
[16] Woetzel, Robert K., *The Nuremberg Trials in International Law With a Postlude on the Eichmann Case,* Stevens & Sons Limited, 1962, p 112.
[17] Stone, Julius, *Legal Controls of International Conflict – A Treatise on the Dynamics of Disputes – And War – Law,* Stevens & Sons Limited, Second Revised Impression, 1959, p 368. Emphasis in original.

for the imposition of a lighter penalty, the offender shall benefit thereby.

2. Nothing in this article shall prejudice the trial and punishment of any person for any act or omission which, at the time when it was committed, was *criminal according to the general principles of law recognized by the community of nations.* [18]

The exception embodied in Article 15 (2) of the International Covenant on Civil and Political Rights may also be found in Article 7 (2) of the European Convention on Human Rights which expressly states that:

> This Article shall not prejudice the trial and punishment of any person for any act or omission which, at the time when it was committed, was *criminal according to the general principles of law recognised by civilised nations.*[19]

Kelsen also maintained that an act may be punished as a crime if it was clearly *illegal in character* at the time of its commission.[20] It is obvious that the crimes perpetrated by the Nazis, which prompted the legal birth of the notion of crimes against humanity, were illegal *per se*. It is perfectly true that the law of the Nuremberg Charter was driven by the facts. It is also perfectly true that pre-existing law did not explicitly condemn such acts, but how could it? How could the law have foreseen what goes beyond human imagination and understanding? How could the law have predicted the horrors of the crimes committed? How could the law have guessed that such crimes were actually possible? In the words of Bassiouni, '[t]his was truly a situation so extreme that no law, however prescient, could have fantasized the horrors that occurred. It was truly a case so maximal that it was beyond foreseeability'.[21] In other words, justice required that such offences were to be tried and punished, and this is exactly what the Nuremberg trials aimed at achieving. In any event, the argument raised against the trials that

[18] International Covenant on Civil and Political Rights, United Nations, 1966. Emphasis added.

[19] European Convention for the Protection of Human Rights and Fundamental Freedoms, Council of Europe, 1950. Emphasis added.

[20] Kelsen, Hans, 'Will the Judgment in the Nuremberg Trial Constitute a Precedent in International Law?', (1947) 1 *ILQ* 165. It may also be noted here that in the *Llandovery Castle* case, the German Supreme Court at Leipzig ruled that an individual may be punished for violations of international law which may not have been defined as crimes, but which were clearly illegal in character. See Woetzel, Robert K., *The Nuremberg Trials in International Law With a Postlude on the Eichmann Case,* Stevens & Sons Limited, 1962, p 114.

[21] Bassiouni, M. Cherif, *supra* n 14, p 4.

they constituted an infringement of the principle of legality was soon dismissed and, with the Nuremberg trials, crimes against humanity emerged in the legal landscape and it rapidly became clear that they were here to stay.

2. *The precedent of Nuremberg confirmed*

In addition to the trials of the major criminals held at Nuremberg, the Allies prosecuted – or oversaw German prosecutions of – other Nazi leaders in the zones they occupied under Law No 10 of the Control Council for Germany. Under this law, promulgated on 20 December 1945 by the Control Council of the four Occupying Powers in Germany, 12 more trials of 185 important Nazi criminals were held at Nuremberg from 1946 to 1949. They are known as the 'Subsequent Proceedings of Nuremberg'. This law, unlike the Nuremberg Charter, was made pursuant to the supreme legislative authority of the Allies over Germany in view of that country's unconditional surrender[22] and it was not intended to be an international instrument but merely national legislation.[23] This law defined crimes against humanity in its Article II (c) as being:

> Atrocities and offences, *including but not limited to* murder, extermination, enslavement, deportation, imprisonment, torture, rape or other inhumane acts committed against any civilian population, or persecutions on political, racial or religious grounds, whether or not in violation of the domestic laws of the country where perpetrated.[24]

From the reading of this definition, one can notice the differences with Article 6 (c) of the Nuremberg Charter, as it defined crimes against humanity as *atrocities and offences*, as it contained the very broad expression 'included but not limited to' which extended the scope of the definition, and as it expressly provided that rape and imprisonment were unlawful acts while, in the IMT Charter, they were supposedly included in the expression 'other inhumane acts'.

Regarding the Far East, it must be recalled here that the International Military Tribunal for the Far East was established by the military order

---

[22] These trials were held by the Military Government of the American Military Tribunals. In the French zone of occupation, several trials of war criminals were also held at Rastatt by virtue of this law. See, eg *Roechling* case, National Prosecutions, in 14 *Nuremberg Subsequent Proceedings* 1097-143.

[23] Such legislation was not mandatory in the sense that, in their respective occupied zones, the Allies also applied their own military laws.

[24] Reprinted in Bassiouni, M. Cherif, *supra* n 14, p 35. Emphasis added.

of General MacArthur pursuant to his authority as Supreme Allied Commander for the Pacific. The 1946 Tokyo Charter was appended to a promulgation by General McArthur and, unlike the Nuremberg Charter, it was not part of a treaty nor of an agreement between the Allied forces.[25] In this instrument, crimes against humanity were defined slightly differently as both the phrase 'against any civilian population' and the religious grounds for commission of the crimes were omitted from its Article 5 (c):

> [m]urder, extermination, enslavement, deportation and other inhumane acts committed before or during the war, or persecutions on political or racial grounds in execution of or in connection with any crime within the jurisdiction of the Tribunal, whether or not in violation of the domestic law of the country where perpetrated.[26]

The next step was taken by the ILC which, following a request from the General Assembly, formulated the Nuremberg Principles in a Report entitled 'Principles of International Law recognized by the Charter of the Nuremberg Tribunal and the Judgment of the Tribunal'.[27] In its Principle VI(c), intrinsically equivalent to the Nuremberg Charter's definition, it defined crimes against humanity as:

> Murder, extermination, enslavement, deportation and other inhumane acts done against any civilian population, or persecutions on political, racial or religious grounds, when such acts are done or such persecutions are carried on in execution of or in connection with any crime against peace or any war crime.[28]

Subsequently, after numerous years of debate, the ILC completed the work on its Draft Code of Crimes which defined crimes against humanity by enumerating a rather broad list of acts and by stating that such crimes were:

> [a]ny of the following acts, when committed in a systematic manner or on a large scale and instigated or directed by a Government or by any organization or group:

[25] The parties to this agreement were the United States, the Republic of China, the United Kingdom, the USSR, Australia, Canada, France, the Netherlands, New Zealand, India and the Philippines. The trial began in May 1946 and the verdicts were returned 4-12 November 1948. See 'Editor's Note – The Tokyo Trials', in Bassiouni, M. Cherif (ed), *International Criminal Law, Volume III, Enforcement*, Transaction Publishers, Inc., 1987, pp 97-98.

[26] Bassiouni, M.Cherif, *supra* n 14, p 34.

[27] Reprinted in ibid, p 40.

[28] [1950] II *ILC Yearbook*.

(a) murder;
(b) extermination;
(c) torture;
(d) enslavement;
(e) persecution on political, racial, religious or ethnic grounds;
(f) institutionalised discrimination on racial, ethnic or religious grounds involving the violation of fundamental human rights and freedoms and resulting in seriously disadvantaging a part of the population;
(g) arbitrary deportation or forcible transfer of population;
(h) arbitrary imprisonment;
(i) forced disappearance of persons;
(j) rape, enforced prostitution and other forms of sexual abuse;
(k) other inhumane acts which severely damage physical or mental integrity, health or human dignity, such as mutilation and severe bodily harm.[29]

This disposition inexplicably deleted the requirement that the crimes had to be committed against a 'civilian population', but the deletion of the requirement of connection to other crimes was a major improvement. In this respect, it has to be stressed that the ICTY Statute went back to this requirement and defined crimes against humanity in its Article 5 as:

> [t]he following crimes when committed in armed conflict, whether international or internal in character, and directed against any civilian population:
> a) murder;
> b) extermination;
> c) enslavement;
> d) deportation;
> e) imprisonment;
> f) torture;
> g) rape;
> h) persecutions on political, racial and religious grounds;
> i) other inhumane acts. [30]

Interestingly, the ICTR Statute did not exactly reproduce the definition provided in that of the ICTY, and notably removed the nexus to armed

[29] ILC 1996 Draft Code of Crimes, [1996] II (2) *ILC Yearbook* 47.
[30] Reprinted in *The Raoul Wallenberg Compilation*, pp 584-85.

conflict requirement. As a matter of fact, its Article 3 defined crimes against humanity as:

> the following crimes when committed as part of a widespread or systematic attack against any civilian population on national, political, ethnic, racial or religious grounds:
> a) murder;
> b) extermination;
> c) enslavement;
> d) deportation;
> e) imprisonment;
> f) torture;
> g) persecution against any identifiable group or collectivity on political, racial, national, ethnic, cultural, rape;
> h) persecutions on political, racial and religious grounds;
> i) other inhumane acts.[31]

The most recent development – the ICC Statute – gives a broader definition of crimes against humanity in its Article 7 (1) which reads as follows:

> For the purpose of this Statute, 'crime against humanity' means any of the following acts when committed as part of a widespread or systematic attack directed against any civilian population, with knowledge of the attack:
> (a) murder;
> (b) extermination;
> (c) enslavement;
> (d) deportation or forcible transfer of population;
> (e) imprisonment or other severe deprivation of physical liberty in violation of fundamental rules of international law;
> (f) torture;[32]
> (g) rape, sexual slavery, enforced prostitution, forced pregnancy, enforced sterilization, or any other form of sexual violence of comparable gravity;

[31] Ibid, p 594.

[32] It is to be highly regretted that Article 7(2)(e) of the Statute mirrors Article 1 of the 1984 Torture's Convention by expressly recalling that torture does not cover 'pain or suffering arising only from, inherent in or incidental to, lawful sanctions'. Clearly, such a questionable formulation is an open door to the legal practice of torture.

(h) religious, gender as defined in paragraph 3, or other grounds that are universally recognised as impermissible under international law, in connection with any act referred to in this paragraph or any crime within the jurisdiction of the Court;
(i) enforced disappearance of persons;
(j) the crime of apartheid;
(k) other inhumane acts of a similar character intentionally causing great suffering, or serious injury to body or to mental or physical health.[33]

The reading of this provision clearly highlights the fact that, in its definition of crimes against humanity, the Rome Statute encompasses a wide array of different acts. In some respect, the statute does nothing but to acknowledge the legal qualification of certain crimes as crimes against humanity as provided for in prior instruments or in earlier case law, and this recognition and confirmation have to be welcomed as a step towards harmonisation of international criminal law as a whole. This harmonisation as regards the qualification of crimes as ones against humanity was indeed achieved in the statute with respect to both the crime of 'enforced disappearance' which had already been recognised as a crime against humanity, notably by the Inter-American Court of Human Rights,[34] as well as the crime of 'apartheid' which had also been qualified as such in Article 1(b) of the 1968 Convention on the Non-applicability of Statutory Limitations to War Crimes and Crimes Against Humanity and in Article 1 of the 1973 Convention on the Prevention and Suppression of Apartheid. Regarding the other crimes listed, and notably those constituting crimes of a sexual nature, the Rome Statute is also very progressive and its recognition of several of such offences in the definitional ambit of crimes against humanity is to be welcomed as the unequivocal – and long-lasted for – recognition of the gravity of such crimes.

From this overview of the different legal definitions of the notion of 'crimes against humanity', it is obvious that this concept evolved over the course of time. Even if the Nuremberg Charter definition will remain in history as being the first attempt to define the notion of 'crimes against humanity', this notion was indeed subjected to substantial changes in the post-Charter era and it must be stressed from the outset that such a concept still bears some ambiguities. The initial relevant legal

[33] Reprinted in Bassiouni, M. Cherif (ed), *The Statute of the International Criminal Court: A Documentary History*, Transnational Publishers, Inc., 1998, pp 41-42.
[34] See most particularly *Velasquez Rodriguez* case (Merits), (1988) 95 ILR 232 (29 July). For the general position of the United Nations, see eg UN Human Rights Committee, General Comment No. 20, regarding Article 7(15) ICCPR, UN Doc CCPR/C/21/Rev 1/ Add 3 (7 April 1992).

instruments on the matter, apart from the Nuremberg Charter, were the Tokyo Charter and the Allied Control Council Law No 10. Subsequently, the works of the International Law Commission also proved to be important landmarks in the development of the notion. More recently, the Statutes of the International Criminal Tribunals[35] as well as that of the ICC addressed the issue in a decisive manner. Moreover, one must not omit the role played by national courts and tribunals in the prosecution and punishment of crimes against humanity. Thus, all these instruments and the case law attached to them will be analysed in order to specify the meaning of crimes against humanity as they stand today.

The following study of the definitional elements of 'crimes against humanity' will indeed highlight the fact that, while crimes against humanity first emerged as an accessory crime of secondary importance, their evolution within the post-Charter legal instruments, culminating with the adoption of the Rome Statute of the ICC, unequivocally demonstrates their broad acceptation and overwhelming importance.

B. The connection with other crimes

The requirement of the connection with other crimes is a requirement which is specific to crimes against humanity – or so it was – as, initially, they could be qualified as such only when committed in connection with war crimes or crimes against peace. Thus, such requirement obviously does not apply – and never did – to these two latter crimes. As regards the crime of genocide, the Genocide Convention made it clear from the outset that such a crime could occur whether in time of peace or in time of war. As a matter of fact, Article I of the Convention reads as follows:

> The Contracting Parties confirm that genocide, *whether committed in time of peace or in time of war,* is a crime under international law which they undertake to prevent and to punish.[36]

In recognising the possibility of a genocide 'in time of war', the drafts men of the Convention proved realistic as history showed that the

[35] It is true that the definitions of crimes against humanity enshrined in the Statutes of the International Criminal Tribunals are not identical and, as Johnson pointed out, no explanation for such differences was given in the Security Council. See Johnson, Larry D., 'The International Criminal Tribunal for Rwanda', in Bassiouni, M. Cherif (ed), *International Criminal Law, Volume III: Enforcement*, Transnational Publishers, Inc., 2nd edn, 1999, p 555.

[36] For the full text of the Convention, see *The Raoul Wallenberg Compilation*, pp 575-78. Emphasis added.

existence of a conflict, whether internal or international, could more often than not be a decisive factor in the occurrence of a genocide. In his report on the crime of genocide, Whitaker did indeed acknowledge the fact that 'throughout recorded human history, war has been the predominant cause or pretext for massacres of national, ethnic, racial or religious groups'.[37]

The fact that both the Armenian Genocide and the Shoah occurred during a world war was certainly not a mere coincidence. As a matter of fact, the Turkish Military Tribunal, set up by the Ottoman Government in an attempt to punish the authors of the Armenian Genocide, also charged the Ittihad with exploiting the opportunity afforded by the war. In its main indictment, the Tribunal recognised 'the vile tricks and deceitful means' through which the Ittihad took Turkey into the First World War in order to carry out its hidden objectives while 'Europe was preoccupied with that war', and could never deter nor intervene.[38] Concerning the Shoah, as Aly recalled:

> [a]s amoral and racist as the anti-Jewish policies already were in 1933, the most important prerequisites to the Holocaust did not emerge until the war began. Far beyond the level reached in the first six years of Nazi dictatorship, the war promoted a non-public atmosphere, atomising individuals and destroying any ties they still had with religious and legal traditions.[39]

A number of scholars have indeed noted that warfare – and notably total warfare – provides conditions highly conducive to genocide. Indeed, most of them agree on the fact that the thought of committing large-scale massacres is initially amorphous and tentative. Turning that thought into action depends on developments which are very often crisis situations, such as war, and, notably, global war, which will serve as a screen, thus facilitating the transformation of these tentative ideas into plans of action. War then becomes the connecting link between the embryonic and implementing stages in the evolution of a genocide. For instance, Kuper stated that 'international warfare, whether between "tribal" groups or city states, or other sovereign states and nations, has been a perennial source of genocide'.[40] It is clear that the outbreak of First World War was an essential condition for the perpetration of the

[37] Whitaker Report, p 6, para 20.
[38] Ibid.
[39] See Aly, Götz, *'Final Solution': Nazi Population Policy and the Murder of the European Jews,* Edward Arnold, 1999, pp 1-2.
[40] Kuper, Leo, *The Prevention of Genocide,* Yale University Press, 1985, p 157.

Armenian Genocide. Similarly, Second World War provided both an opportunity and an incentive for the Nazis to attempt to definitely resolve the 'Jewish question'.

Markusen identified several aspects of warfare which contribute to genocide.[41] First, it does create a sense of direct threat within the states, threat which is then blamed not only on the external military enemy, but also on the targeted minority group. Secondly, it increases the vulnerability of the victim group, which becomes 'isolated, fragmented and nearly totally emasculated through the control of channel of communication, wartime secrecy, the various sections of the wartime apparatus, police and secret service, and the constant invocation of the principle of national security'.[42] Conversely, the perpetrating government and its agents become more powerful thanks to the centralisation of power which is necessary in time of war. Thirdly, the perpetrators can also use the mobilised military forces in the killing process, as this occurred in both the Armenian Genocide and the Shoah. Finally, warfare creates a climate of moral and psychological violence, which generates tolerance for brutality, particularly against groups designated by officials as dangerous enemies.

As previously stated, the IMT Charter marked the birth of the modern notion of crimes against humanity as Article 6 (c) was the first instance in positive international criminal law in which the specific terms 'crimes against humanity' were used. However, as previously mentioned, a critical compromise was made as crimes against humanity were defined only 'in connection with' other crimes. Indeed, the charter required a nexus with the other crimes over which the tribunal had jurisdiction, namely crimes against peace and war crimes.

It must be recalled here that, initially, Article 6 (c) was written with a semicolon after the word 'war' which meant that there were two types of crimes against humanity: some which could be qualified as such without any relationship with the two other crimes mentioned, and some – namely, persecutions – which could only be qualified as such if committed in relation to them. Nearly two months after the signature of the charter, a difference was discovered between the Russian text – with a comma after the word 'war' – and the English and French ones, which showed a semi-colon after this same word. On the basis of the Berlin Protocol of 6 October 1945, it was recognised that the proper version was the one with a comma. Such grammatical technique may

[41] Markusen, Eric, 'Genocide, Total War, and Nuclear Omnicide', in Charny, Israel W., *Genocide : A Critical Bibliographic Review, Volume Two*, Mansell, 1991, pp 229-47.
[42] Ibid, p 237.

seem a detail but, in reality, this substitution was of a great importance as the IMT then used it to give a restrictive interpretation of the notion of crimes against humanity: the requirement that these crimes be connected to some other crime within the jurisdiction of the tribunal became a limitation on all forms of crimes against humanity, and not only on persecutions. Thus, it became beyond any doubt that the qualification 'in execution of or in connection with any crime within the jurisdiction of the tribunal' applied to the whole paragraph. Consequently, the charter subjected crimes against humanity to a special condition: unlike crimes against peace and war crimes, both of which had an independent existence, crimes against humanity were 'accompanying' or 'accessory' crimes[43] to the first two and were punishable only if committed in connection with or in execution of the crimes of aggressive war or violations of the laws and customs of warfare. Furthermore, by negating the charter's definition 'before or during the war' clause, the tribunal limited the scope of Article 6 (c), limitation which resulted in the exclusion of all Nazi crimes committed before 1939. Consequently, the Tribunal Judgment stated:

> The Tribunal therefore cannot make a general declaration that the acts before 1939 were crimes against humanity within the meaning of the Charter as it has not been satisfactorily proved that they were done in execution of, or in connection with, any crime within the jurisdiction of the Tribunal.[44]

However, Woetzel believed that the Nuremberg definition did not deny this terrible reality but that it did not give the tribunal jurisdiction over such acts:

> The fact that the court only considered crimes committed in the period from 1939 to 1945 does not mean that only acts occurring during wartime can be considered crimes against humanity. It must be concluded that the court merely felt itself generally limited in its jurisdiction to cases occurring in connection with or during the war. It did not mean to qualify the nature of the acts, however, by stating this proviso.[45]

[43] See Robinson, Jacob, 'The International Military Tribunal and the Holocaust – Some Legal Reflections', (1972) 7 *Israel Law Review* 1-13.
[44] Bassiouni, M. Cherif, *supra* n 14, p 31.
[45] Woetzel, Robert K., *The Nuremberg Trials in International Law With a Postlude on the Eichmann Case*, Stevens & Sons Limited, 1962, p 180.

Similarly, Röling, who sat as a judge in the Tokyo Tribunal, believed that the requirement of the war nexus was jurisdictional and not definitional. He maintained that it did not narrow the scope of crimes against humanity; it only narrowed the Nuremberg and Tokyo Tribunals' jurisdiction. He indeed wrote that 'the connection did not restrict the scope of the crime, but only the scope of our jurisdiction'.[46]

The legal inconsistencies of the *stricto jure* definitions and the final judgment at Nuremberg did not remain unobserved.[47] Public opinion could not accept the fact that crimes against humanity were considered as such only if connected with other international crimes. Consequently, the Allied Control Council Law No 10 did not mention the expression 'in execution of or in connection with any crime within the jurisdiction of the Tribunal' and this lack of nexus offers some evidence that the Allies did not regard this link as necessary as a matter of custom. However, it must be noted that the wording of this law dealt with this issue not as fully as it would have been needed. Indeed, the Law was far from being an important landmark in the evolution of the concept of crimes against humanity as, under its preamble, it was meant to 'give effect' to the charter, while, under its Article I, the London Agreement was made an integral part thereof. As a result, a conflict emerged due to different provisions of the same law. One could have thought that the case-law under the Allied Control Council Law No 10 would have brought comprehensive solutions to this conflict but, in light of the cases analysed below, it is clear that no consensus position was reached.

The two following cases suggest that the nexus requirement had not been removed in practice. In the *Flick* case, the court acquitted the defendant of crimes against humanity for his acquisition of Jewish property before the war, finding itself without jurisdiction.[48] Similarly, in the *Ministries* case, the court discussed Bohle's activities against the Haavarah Agreement and stated:

> We are unable to see [...] that these transactions, which started in 1937, and were concluded in March 1938, were *so connected with the aggressive war and crimes against peace* as to render it reasonably certain that the measures had this in view.[49]

[46] Cassese, A. (ed), *B.V.A. Röling, The Tokyo Trial and Beyond, Reflections of a Peacemonger*, Polity Press, 1993, p 56.

[47] See Robinson, Jacob, *supra* n 13.

[48] *United States* v *Flick et al.*, Case No 5, Military Tribunal IV, 6 *Nuremberg Subsequent Proceedings* 1213.

[49] See *United States* v *Von Weizsaecker et al.*, Case No. 11, Military Tribunal IV, 12-14 *Nuremberg Subsequent Proceedings* 1-1096. Emphasis added.

In other words, the link was missing. As a result, the Court dismissed the count of crimes against humanity against officials in the Nazi Foreign Ministry and other bureaucracies, noting that the Allied Control Council Law N°10 was not meant to go any further than the Charter itself, which codified international law.[50]

Adopting an opposite stand, other cases suggested that the removal of the nexus requirement allowed for prosecutions for crimes not committed during the war. Thus, in the *Einsatzgruppen* case, the Court convicted the defendants for the large-scale execution of Jews in occupied Europe and in the Soviet Union,[51] without making any distinction as to *when* the murders occurred and held that:

> The International Military Tribunal, operating under the London Charter, declared that the Charter's provisions limited the Tribunal to consider only those crimes against humanity which were committed in the execution of or in connection with crimes against peace and war crimes. The Allied Control Council, in its Law No 10, removed this limitation so that the present Tribunal has jurisdiction to try all crimes against humanity as long known and understood under the general principles of criminal law.[52]

Also, in the *Justice* case, although the defendants were charged only with crimes committed during the war, the court noted the omission of the nexus language and seemed to suggest in *dicta* that it was legally unnecessary.[53] The uncertainty emanating from the legacy of these trials was further reinforced by the fact that, as the Allies chose to prosecute only crimes connected with the war, the Second World War cases fail to offer strong evidence of the necessity of the war nexus.

In a similar vein, Article 5 of the Tokyo Charter expressly stated that:

> The Tribunal shall have the power to try and punish Far Eastern war criminals who as individuals or as members of organizations are charged with *offences which include Crimes against Peace*.[54]

[50] Ibid, pp 112-17. Emphasis added.

[51] *United States* v *Ohlendorf et al.*, Case No 9, Military Tribunal II, 4 *Nuremberg Subsequent Proceedings* 499.

[52] Ibid., p 664.

[53] *United States* v *Altsoetter et al.*, Case No 3, Military Tribunal III, 3 *Nuremberg Subsequent Proceedings* 973-74 and 979-82.

[54] Article 5 of the IMTFE Charter. Emphasis added.

Thus, it made clear that the tribunal only had jurisdiction if persons were accused of having perpetrated offences which included crimes against peace. This exclusive provision explains why, at Tokyo, crimes against humanity were not explicitly applied. Still, the tribunal condemned the atrocities which were committed against civilian populations (most particularly in China) and found guilty of crimes against humanity several defendants among whom Hirota, Matsui and Muto.[55]

Subsequently, the ILC's 1954 Draft Code of Offences[56] completely emancipated crimes against humanity from any dependence to 'other offences defined in the Draft Code'.[57] When the Commission extensively re-examined the issue in 1996 and finally completed consideration on the Draft Code,[58] its Article 18 still did not require the nexus to other crimes.

Both Statutes of the International Criminal Tribunals also require the existence of certain conditions in order to qualify a crime as one against humanity. As regards the nexus to armed conflict, the ICTY Statute expressly maintained it by requiring that the acts be 'committed in armed conflict, whether international or internal in character'.[59] It is nonetheless true that, considering the temporal limitation to which the Tribunal is subjected,[60] the Security Council did not have to address a broader definition. As Johnson rightly pointed out, the nexus:

> [w]as not intended to reflect a general definition of crimes against humanity or alter the fact that such crimes may be committed in time of war or in time of peace. Rather, it was intended to make the crime specific to the Yugoslav context: an armed conflict which could, at different times, be characterised as being international, internal, or a combination of the two.[61]

Accordingly, the UN Secretary-General stressed that crimes against humanity are prohibited 'regardless of whether they are committed in

[55] Among the atrocities blamed on the Japanese officials was the so-called Rape of Nanking when Japanese soldiers slaughtered hundreds of thousands of Chinese civilians in Nanking in 1937.
[56] UN Doc A/1316.
[57] Article I of the 1954 Draft Code of Offences.
[58] 1996 Draft Code of Crimes, [1996] II (2) *ILC Yearbook*.
[59] Article 5 of the ICTY Statute.
[60] Article 8 of the ICTY Statute: as it was created by the Security Council as an enforcement measure, the Tribunal's jurisdiction is limited to the events occurring during the restoration of international peace and security.
[61] Johnson, Larry D., 'The International Criminal Tribunal for Rwanda', in Bassiouni, M. Cherif (ed.), *International Criminal Law, Volume III: Enforcement*, Transnational Publishers, Inc., 2nd edn, 1999, p 556.

an armed conflict, international or internal in character', thus suggesting that this limitation is not definitional but merely jurisdictional.[62] Moreover, in the *Tadić* case, the ICTY Appeals Chamber adopted the same position and held that:

> It is by now a settled rule of customary international law that crimes against humanity do not require a connection to international armed conflict. Indeed, as the Prosecutor points out, customary international law *may not require* a connection between crimes against humanity and any conflict at all. Thus, by requiring that crimes against humanity be committed in either internal or international armed conflict, the Security Council *may have defined* the crime in Article 5 more narrowly than necessary under customary international law.[63]

If one may notice the rather cautious approach of the Appeals Chamber in this ruling as it does not firmly reject the requirement of the connection to an armed conflict, it must be pointed out that the same Appeals Chamber, in the same case, unequivocally found that:

> The Prosecution is [...] correct in asserting that the armed conflict requirement is a *jurisdictional* element, not 'a substantive element of the *mens rea* of crimes against humanity' (ie not a legal ingredient of the subjective element of the crime).[64]

Similarly, in the *Blaškić* case, the trial chamber held that '[a]n armed conflict is not a condition for a crime against humanity but is for its punishment by the Tribunal'.[65] Such a position is however hardly satisfying as it can impede prosecution. For instance, in the *Tadić* case, the trial chamber expressly held that it required proof between the motives of the acts and the armed conflict, thus requiring additional elements than the ones expressly stated in its statute. In fact, it even went further than this and required proof that the defendant acted on the basis of non-personal motives. In other words, 'the act and the conflict must be related or, to reverse this proposition, the act must not be

[62] See Report of the Secretary-General Pursuant to Paragraph 2 of Security Council Resolution 808 (1993), UN Doc S/25704 and Annex (3 May 1993), para 47.

[63] See *Prosecutor* v *Tadić*, Case No. IT-94-1-AR72, Decision on the Defence Motion for Interlocutory Appeal on Jurisdiction, Appeals Chamber, 2 October 1995, para 141. Emphasis added.

[64] Ibid, para 249.

[65] *Prosecutor* v *Blaškić*, Case No IT-95-14, judgment, Trial Chamber I, 3 March 2000, para 66.

unrelated to the armed conflict, must not be done for purely personal motives of the perpetrator'.[66] As Van Schaack rightly pointed out, 'the requirement that the defendant act on the basis of other than personal motives threatens to revive the war nexus requirement by repackaging it in terms of the motivational state of the defendant'.[67] Fortunately, the Appeals Chamber subsequently held that:

> [t]here is nothing in Article 5 to suggest that it contains a requirement that crimes against humanity cannot be committed for purely personal motives [...], except to the extent that this condition is a consequence or a re-statement of the two conditions mentioned [ie 'that the acts of the accused must comprise part of a pattern of widespread or systematic crimes against a civilian population and that the accused must have known that his acts fit in such a pattern'].[68]

The ICTR Statute is totally silent on the matter and the nexus to armed conflict does not appear at all. It is true that this does not necessarily amount to an increase in the number of prosecutions for crimes against humanity committed outside the conflict as the tribunal only has jurisdiction over crimes committed in 1994, during which war was incessant.[69] Furthermore, as Meron rightly recalled, 'the Statute for Rwanda is predicated on the assumption that the conflict in Rwanda is a non-international armed conflict',[70] predication which might then explain the absence of the nexus requirement in the statute. Still, such an 'omission' might also be the sign that crimes against humanity can definitely be committed in time of peace.

The overwhelming majority of domestic systems retains the nexus to war crimes. For instance, the 1946 Chinese Statute criminalises several

[66] Van Schaack, Beth, 'The Definition of Crimes Against Humanity : Resolving the Incoherence', (1999) 37 *Columbia Journal of Transnational Law* 832-33. See *Prosecutor* v *Tadić*, Case No IT-94-1-T, opinion and judgment, Trial Chamber II, 7 May 1997, para.634.

[67] Van Schaack, Beth, ibid, p 840.

[68] See *Prosecutor* v *Tadić*, Case No. IT-94-1-A, judgment, Appeals Chamber, 15 July 1999, paras 248, 255, 271 and 272.

[69] See Meier Wang, Mariann, 'The International Tribunal for Rwanda : Opportunities for Clarification, Opportunities for Impact', (1995) 27 *Columbia Human Rights Law Review* 196-97. This author argued that 'the Statute's starting date of January 1, 1994, is artificially late given the explicit goal expressed by the Statute [...] to punish the perpetrators', even if 'the Tribunal may be able to introduce as evidence acts of planning, organization, and even implementation that occurred outside the period of January 1 to December 31, 1994, but that are nonetheless connected to crimes which were perpetrated during the Statute's designated time period'.

[70] See Meron, Theodor, 'International Criminalization of Internal Atrocities', (1995) 89 *AJIL* 556.

acts other than war crimes but with the requirement that they be committed 'before or during a period of hostilities against the Republic of China', thus suggesting a linkage to the war.[71] Similarly, the 1988 Australian War Crimes Statute, which specifically deals with Second World War criminals, requires that crimes against humanity be connected with an armed conflict to be qualified as such.[72] The United Kingdom's War Crimes Act of 1991[73] also maintains the temporal nexus to the second world conflict. Nevertheless, the above study of international criminal law seems to suggest that the requirement of the connection to other crimes has now been totally deleted. If it therefore appears that international criminal law does recognise crimes against humanity as being a totally independent offence, such an assertion must nonetheless be cautiously dealt with. As a matter of fact, even if 'war' is not expressly mentioned, the most recent definitions of crimes against humanity refer to 'a generalized and systematic attack',[74] thus indicating that the nexus to armed conflict is still implicitly required. This new requirement does not, however, necessarily imply a linkage to a war but rather refers to the scale – the number of victims – and the method – planned and systematic – in which the crimes are committed.

From this perspective, it can be safely asserted that roles have been inverted as crimes against humanity now have a wider temporal scope of application than war crimes. And, indeed, the main characteristic of war crimes is that their scope of application is necessarily restricted to armed conflicts. Nonetheless, as it will be subsequently analysed, the concept of war crimes should undergo a comparable evolution – and extension – than the concept of crimes against humanity and should cover crimes committed in international as well as in non-international armed conflicts. The evolution of crimes against humanity should thus represent a model that war crimes should draw upon in order to become a truly effective notion.

---

[71] Article II (3) of the Chinese Statute.

[72] Section 9 of the War Crimes Act 1991. See Triggs, Gillian, 'Australia's War Crimes Trials : All Pity Choked', in McCormack, Timothy L.M. and Simpson, Gerry J. (eds), *The Law of War Crimes, National and International Approaches*, Kluwer Law International, 1997, p 127.

[73] Evans, Malcolm D. (ed), *Blackstone's International Law Documents*, Blackstone Press Limited, 2nd edn, 1994, pp 407-8, c 13, §1(1).

[74] See Article 7 of the ICC Statute.

C. The widespread and/or systematic action

1. *The disjunctive requirements of widespread or systematic action*

The requirement as regards the large-scale or systematic character of crimes against humanity appeared in positive international law quite recently, although the premises of such a condition may be found in the initial phrase 'against any civilian population'. According to the Nuremberg Charter, crimes against humanity had to be committed against a 'population',[75] which meant that either their scale or their method qualified the nature of the atrocities. Similarly to the charter, the Allied Control Council Law required that crimes against humanity, in order to qualify as such, be committed 'against any civilian population'.[76] Subsequently, the 1996 Draft Code of Crimes expressly employed the terms 'in a systematic manner or on a large scale', thus understanding these requirements as non-cumulative. [77]

Both Statutes of the International Criminal Tribunals as well as that of the International Criminal Court follow the majority of the legal doctrine by requiring that these crimes are to be committed 'against any civilian population'.[78] In fact, Trial Chamber I of the ICTY, in the *Nikolić* case, defined crimes against humanity very narrowly by requiring that each type of crimes against humanity be directed against any civilian population, that each be organised *and* systematic, and not the work of an isolated individual, and that the crimes, considered as a whole, be of a certain scale and gravity.[79] Adopting a contrary view, Trial Chamber II, while interpreting the UN Secretary-General's Report on Article 5 of its statute[80] in the *Tadić* case, held that the requirement that acts be directed against a civilian population can be fulfilled if the acts are *either* widespread *or* systematic.[81] Subsequently, Trial Chamber II, again reading these requirements disjunctively, specified that the widespread or systematic requirement is to be appreciated on a case-by-case basis:

---

[75] Article 6(c) of the IMT Charter.

[76] Article II(c) of CCL No 10.

[77] Article 18 of the ILC 1996 Draft Code of Crimes, [1996] II (2) *ILC Yearbook* 47. Emphasis added.

[78] Article 5 of the ICTY Statute, Article 3 of the ICTR Statute, Article 7 (1) of the ICC Statute.

[79] *Prosecutor* v *Nikolić*, Case No. IT-94-2-R61, Review of the Indictment Pursuant to Rule 61 of the Rules of Procedure and Evidence, Trial Chamber I, 20 October 1995, para.26.

[80] UN Doc S/25704, para 48 (1993).

[81] *Prosecutor* v *Tadić*, Case No IT-94-1-T, opinion and judgment, Trial Chamber II, 7 May 1997, para.646.

> The widespread or systematic nature of the attack is essentially a *relative notion*. The Trial Chamber must first identify the population which is the object of the attack and, in light of the means, methods, resources and result of the attack upon this population, ascertain whether the attack was indeed widespread or systematic.[82]

Fortunately, the *Tadić* precedent was subsequently confirmed by Trial Chamber I in the *Blaškić* case:

> The 'widespread or systematic' character of the offence does not feature in the provisions of Article 5 of the Statute which mention only acts 'directed against any civilian population'. It is appropriate, however, to note that the words 'directed against any civilian population' and some of the sub-characterisations set out in the text of the Statute imply, both by their very nature and by law, an element of being widespread *or* organised, whether as regards the acts or the victims.[83]

It therefore reached the conclusion that:

> [t]here can be no doubt that inhumane acts constituting a crime against humanity must be part of a systematic *or* widespread attack against civilians.[84]

In the *Krstić* case, Trial Chamber I reconfirmed the *Tadić* ruling and affirmed that the attack must be 'widespread *or* systematic'.[85] More recently, the ICTY Appeals Chamber specified that 'only the attack, not the individual acts of the accused, must be widespread or systematic'.[86] It also reaffirmed that:

> The requirement that the attack be 'widespread' or 'systematic' comes in the alternative. Once it is convinced that either requirement is met, the Trial Chamber is not

[82] *Prosecutor* v *Kunarac et al.*, Case No IT-96-23 and IT-96-23/1, judgment, Trial Chamber II, 22 February 2001, para.430. Emphasis added.
[83] *Prosecutor* v *Blaškić*, Case No IT-95-14, judgment, Trial Chamber I, 3 March 2000, para 202. Emphasis added.
[84] Ibid. Emphasis added.
[85] *Prosecutor* v *Krstić*, Case No. IT-98-33, judgment, Trial Chamber I, 2 August 2001, para.482. See also *Prosecutor* v *Kunarac et al*, Case No. IT-96-23 and IT-96-23/1, Judgment, Trial Chamber II, 22 February 2001, para.410.
[86] *Prosecutor* v *Kunarac et al*, Case No. IT-96-23 and IT-96-23/1-A, judgment, Appeals Chamber, 12 June 2002, para 96.

> obliged to consider whether the alternative qualifier is also satisfied.[87]

Adopting a more explicit approach than the Yugoslav Statute, the Rwanda Statute expressly provided that the acts be committed 'as part of a widespread or systematic attack',[88] and, accordingly, the Rwanda Tribunal reads the requirement of widespread or systematic action disjunctively. In the *Akayesu* case as well as in the *Kayishema and Ruzindana* case, both Trial Chambers I and II of the ICTR made the widespread and/or systematic characteristics essential elements of the offence.[89] For instance, in the *Akayesu* case, Trial Chamber I unequivocally stated that it 'considers that it is a prerequisite that the act must be committed as part of a widespread or systematic attack and not just a random act of violence'.[90]

Finally, it may be pointed out that the Rome Statute also requires that the acts be committed 'as part of a widespread *or* systematic attack directed against any civilian population'.[91] The question of the disjunctive reading of the requirements of 'widespread' and 'systematic' is however still unsettled as the Statute subsequently defines the term 'attack' as 'a course of conduct involving the multiple commission of acts referred to in paragraph 1 against any civilian population, pursuant to or in furtherance of a State or organisational policy to commit such attack'.[92] For Schabas, '[i]t seems, therefore, that the term attack has both widespread *and* systematic aspects'.[93] The legacy of the Rome Statute on this matter is thus one of uncertainty and the question whether the attack needs to be both widespread and systematic in order for the crime to qualify as one against humanity is as yet not definitely solved.

2. *Crimes against humanity as isolated acts?*

In the Nuremberg Charter, crimes against humanity consisted of two separate clauses: murders and other acts against any civilian population on one hand, and persecutions on the other. It thus seemed that persecutions against isolated individuals were covered. Still, in the *Justice*

---

[87] Ibid, para 93.
[88] Article 3 of the ICTR Statute.
[89] *Prosecutor* v *Akayesu,* Case No ICTR-96-4-T, judgment, Trial Chamber I, 2 September 1998, paras 579-81, and *Prosecutor* v *Kayishema and Ruzindana,* Case No ICTR-95-1-T, judgment, Trial Chamber II, para 123.
[90] *Prosecutor* v *Akayesu, supra* n 89, para.579.
[91] Article 7(1) of the ICC Statute. Emphasis added.
[92] Article 7(2)(a) of the ICC Statute.
[93] Schabas, William A., *An Introduction to the International Criminal Court,* Cambridge University Press, 2001, p 36. Emphasis added.

case, the tribunal interpreted the language of Control Council Law No 10, which was also referring to acts 'against any civilian population', as precluding prosecutions for any isolated crimes.[94]

This dichotomy between the two types of crimes against humanity nonetheless appears to have vanished now that their definition is merely an enumeration of acts committed in a systematic manner or on a large scale, among which are listed murder and persecutions.[95] It thus seems that all the post-charter developments exclude isolated acts not part of a general policy, even if it may still be maintained that they include large-scale actions regardless of planning as well as small-scale ones if they are committed systematically.

Regarding this particular issue, an incoherence emerged in the case-law of the Yugoslavia Tribunal when the trial chamber held that the collective nature of crimes against humanity 'exclude[s] single or isolated acts which, although possibly constituting war crimes or crimes against national penal legislation, do not rise to the level of crimes against humanity',[96] before stating that:

> Clearly, a single act by a perpetrator taken within the context of a widespread or systematic attack against a civilian population entails individual criminal responsibility and an individual need not commit numerous offenses to be held liable. Although it is correct that isolated, random acts should not be included in the definition of crimes against humanity, that is the purpose of requiring that the acts be directed against a civilian *population* and thus '[e]ven an isolated act can constitute a crime against humanity if it is the product of a political system based on terror or persecution'[97].[98]

This inconsistency seems however to have been solved by the trial chamber itself in the same *Tadić* case when it specified that if the perpetrator acted while knowing that his acts 'were occurring on a

[94] See *United States* v *Altsoetter et al*, Case No 3, Military Tribunal III, 3 *Nuremberg Subsequent Proceedings*.
[95] See ILC 1996 Draft Code of Crimes, Article 5 of the ICTY Statute, Article 3 of the ICTR Statute and Article 7(1) of the ICC Statute.
[96] See *Prosecutor* v *Tadić*, Case No. IT-94-1-T, Opinion and judgment, Trial Chamber II, 7 May 1997, para 644.
[97] Henri Meyrowitz as quoted in the Report of ILC Special Rapporteur D. Thiam, [1986] II *ILC Yearbook*, UN Doc A/CN.4/466, para 89.
[98] See *Prosecutor* v *Tadić*, *supra* n 96, para 649. See also *Prosecutor* v *Mrkšić et al.*, Case No IT-95-13-R61, Review of Indictment Pursuant to Rule 61 of the Rules of Procedure and Evidence, Trial Chamber I, 3 April 1996, para.30.

widespread or systematic basis [...] that is sufficient to hold him liable for crimes against humanity'.[99] In other words, if the perpetrator has knowledge of the broader pattern of occurrence, a single act may qualify as a crime against humanity.[100] This formulation clearly increases the burden of proof for the prosecution which thus has to prove that the perpetrator knew of the widespread or systematic attack on a civilian population while committing his act. However, the appeal judges in the *Tadić* case lightened this burden of proof by holding that such knowledge could be inferred from the circumstances. It indeed maintained that:

> [i]t may be inferred from the words 'directed against any civilian population' in Article 5 of the Statute that the acts of the accused must comprise part of a pattern of widespread and systematic crimes directed against a civilian population and that the accused must have *known* that his acts fit into such a pattern.[101]

On this particular point, the case law of the ICTY seems settled as different trial chambers followed this path. For instance, in the *Vukovar Hospital* Decision, Trial Chamber I found that 'as long as there is a link with the widespread or systematic attack against a civilian population, a single act could qualify as a crime against humanity'.[102] In the same vein, in the *Kunarac* case, Trial Chamber II specified that:

> [o]nly the attack, not the individual acts of the accused, must be 'widespread or systematic'. A single act could therefore be regarded as a crime against humanity if it takes place in the relevant context.[103]

---

[99] *Prosecutor* v *Tadić*, Case No IT-94-1-T, opinion and judgment, Trial Chamber II, 7 May 1997, para.659.

[100] As Van Schaack notes, 'this two-tiered approach was substantially borrowed from the reasoning of the Canadian courts in *Regina v Finta*'. In the *Finta* case, the Court of Appeals hold that 'knowledge of the circumstances or facts which bring an act within the definition of a war crime or crime against humanity constitutes the mental component which must coexist with the prohibited acts to establish culpability for those acts'. See *Regina* v *Finta*, 92 D.L.R. 4th 1, 84 (Ont. C.A. 1992). See Van Schaack, Beth, 'The Definition of Crimes Against Humanity: Resolving the Incoherence', (1999) 37 *Columbia Journal of Transnational Law* 835-36.

[101] *Prosecutor* v *Tadić*, Case No. IT-94-1-A, Judgment, Appeals Chamber, 15 July 1999, para.248.

[102] *Prosecutor* v *Mrkšić et al.*, Case No. IT-95-13-R61, Review of the Indictment Pursuant to Rule 61 of the Rules of Procedure and Evidence, Trial Chamber I, 3 April 1996, para.30.

[103] *Prosecutor* v *Kunarac et al.*, Case No. IT-96-23 and IT-96-23/1, judgment, Trial Chamber II, 22 February 2001, para.431.

As regards the ICC Statute, this instrument is more explicit as, by adding the requirement that there should be a 'multiple commission of acts',[104] it clearly states that isolated acts are excluded from the definitional scope of crimes against humanity. Furthermore, it may be noted here that the possibility brought out by the Yugoslavia Tribunal of considering crimes against humanity as isolated acts if the perpetrator knew of the wider context of the attack seems to have been rejected by the Rome Statute which equates 'knowledge' with 'awareness' and which, from the reading of its Article 30 (3), suggests that such a mental element 'must be subjectively demonstrated, rather than merely inferable from circumstancial evidence'.[105]

As regards national legislation and practice, it must be pointed out that the situation is rather heterogeneous. For instance, the Canadian Statute, by referring to the concepts of 'population' or of 'group', does obviously express a requirement as to the scale of such crimes, being understood in terms of the number of victims. However, neither the Chinese nor the Australian Statutes mention large-scale or systematic acts.[106]

In the *Eichmann* case, the Israeli District Court easily conducted the trial on this matter of pattern of occurrence as the enormity of the defendant's crimes obviously corresponded to the criterion 'any civilian population' required by the Israeli Statute relative to crimes against humanity.[107] Consequently, in December 1961, Jerusalem's Tribunal found Eichmann guilty and sentenced him to death by hanging.[108] The French case law is also of interest here as, in the *Touvier* case, the Cour de Cassation held that even one single act could qualify as a crime against humanity, basing its qualification on the nature of the act rather than on its scale.[109]

The issue of the characteristics of crimes against humanity, in terms of their scale or of their systematic aspect, is thus tainted with uncertainty. Still, the previous developments did show that the correct reading of these two requirements is the non-cumulative one. In other words, acts need to be *either* systematic *or* widespread to qualify as crimes against

[104] See Article 7(2)(a) of the ICC Statute.

[105] Sadat Wexler, Leila, 'A First Look at the 1998 Rome Statute for a Permanent International Criminal Court : Jurisidiction, Definition of Crimes, Structure and Referrals to the Court', in Bassiouni, M. Cherif (ed), *International Criminal Law, Volume III : Enforcement*, Transnational Publishers, Inc., 2nd edn, 1999, pp 664-5.

[106] See Chinese Statute of 1946 and Australian War Crimes Act of 1988. For the latter, see Triggs, Gillian, 'Australia's War Crimes Trials : All Pity Choked', *in* McCormack, Timothy L.M. and Simpson, Gerry J. (eds), *The Law of War Crimes, National and International Approaches*, Kluwer Law International, 1997, p 127.

[107] See the Nazi and Nazi Collaborators (Punishment) Law, 5710/1950.

[108] Adolf Eichmann was executed on 31 May 1962.

[109] Judgment of 21 October 1993, cass. crim.

humanity. If this would appear to exclude isolated acts, the knowledge of the perpetrator of the broader context of commission of crimes against humanity could still qualify his or her own isolated act as a crime against humanity. Furthermore, it could here be argued that this knowledge could be automatically inferred due to the fact that the widespread or systematic commission of such crimes can hardly be disregarded or unknown. Clearly, the perpetrator of an isolated act will know of this wider context, context which in fact might have encouraged him or her in committing the crime. In other words, while isolated acts would not – and should not – be considered as crimes against humanity as they would not fulfil the requirements of widespread or systematic action, it is nonetheless here submitted that, if there is a wider pattern of commission of crimes against humanity, isolated acts should be considered as fitting in this pattern and should thus be qualified as crimes against humanity. The widespread or systematic characteristics of crimes against humanity would still remain as definitional elements, while the possibility of prosecuting *all* participants in the criminal enterprise would be increased.

D. Grounds for commission

Closely linked to the previous notion of systematic or mass action is the question of the reasons for the commission of the crime or, in other words, of whether the perpetrator acted because of some special characteristics of the victim.

The Nuremberg Charter listed two sets of crimes – murders and persecutions – and it appears that, if the motive is relevant in the case of persecutions, this is not the case as regards murders and the other enumerated acts. This 'bifurcation' makes sense in the way that some acts are so heinous and destructive that they are *per se* crimes while other acts are crimes because the perpetrator acted against the victim based on specific grounds, whether political, racial or religious. In this respect, it may be pointed out here that, at Nuremberg, the evidence overwhelmingly showed the Nazis' reasoning in the commission of all their crimes and the cases would have satisfied even a definition requiring specific motives for all acts.

The definition of crimes against humanity enshrined in the Tokyo Charter was substantially the same as the one given by the Nuremberg Charter. Nevertheless, at least one aspect was different. Indeed, Article 5 (c) did not make persecutions subject to religious grounds, certainly because the Nazi crimes against the Jews did not have a counterpart during the Asian conflict.

The ILC's position on the matter evolved. As a matter of fact, while the 1954 Draft Code made clear that grounds for commission were highly relevant,[110] the 1996 Draft Code referred to the 'bifurcation' contained in the Nuremberg Charter and thus eliminated this requirement except for 'persecutions' and 'institutionalised discrimination'.[111]

Similarly, the Statute of the Yugoslavia Tribunal made grounds for commission relevant only for persecutions and not for the other acts listed such as murder or extermination. Nevertheless, the Trial Chamber in the *Tadić* case held that the term 'population' implied that *all* the acts enumerated – and not only persecutions – had to be committed on discriminatory grounds to qualify as crimes against humanity,[112] while neither international customary law nor the statute of the tribunal itself require this. The requirement is a new one which was not recognised in the Nuremberg Charter, the Tokyo Charter, or in the ILC's Draft Codes. In fact, it was imposed by a decision of the Security Council as a limitation upon the jurisdiction of the Tribunal which stated that:

> Crimes against humanity refer to inhumane acts of a very serious nature, such as wilful killing, torture or rape, committed as part of a widespread or systematic attack against any civilian population on national, political, ethnic, racial or religious grounds.[113]

The tribunal itself recognised that it was departing from customary law, which did not require such intent. As Meron rightly noted:

> [t]here was no reason for the Tribunal to regard the more restrictive Report of the Secretary-General as gospel. This holding unnecessarily limits the scope of crimes against humanity; a decision to follow the Nuremberg jurisprudence would have been better.[114]

The risk contained in such a holding is that acts involving motives not expressly enumerated might be excluded from the definitional scope of crimes against humanity. However, the Appeals Chamber overruled this decision and subsequently held that:

---

110 See Article I of the 1954 Draft Code of Offences.

111 [1996] II (2) *ILC Yearbook* 47.

112 See *Prosecutor* v *Tadić*, Case No. IT-94-1-T, opinion and judgment, Trial Chamber II, 7 May 1997, paras 650-2.

113 Report of the Secretary-General Pursuant to Paragraph 2 of Security Council Resolution 808 (1993), UN Doc S/25704, para 48, 32 *ILM* 1173.

114 Meron, Theodor, 'War Crimes Law Comes of Age', (1998) 92 *AJIL* 465 n 16.

> The ordinary meaning of Article 5 makes it clear that this provision does not require all crimes against humanity to have been perpetrated with a discriminatory intent. Such intent is only made necessary for one sub-category of those crimes, namely 'persecutions' provided for in Article 5 (h).[115]

Nonetheless, when the statute of the Rwanda Tribunal was drafted, the definition of crimes against humanity was modified so as specifically to require that there be discrimination in the form of an 'attack against any civilian population on national, political, ethnic, racial or religious grounds'.[116] It thus greatly reduced the scope of crimes against humanity by requiring grounds for commissions for all offences and not only for persecutions. Such a narrow jurisdiction will definitely be an obstacle to the efficiency of the Tribunal because, in the words of Meron, this addition will make 'the burden of proving crimes against humanity more difficult to meet'.[117]

Fortunately, the ICC Statute went back to the Nuremberg 'bifurcation' and required grounds for commission only in the case of persecutions. Thus, all the other acts listed can be deemed crimes against humanity even if they are committed without any specific motive. It must however be stressed that Article 7 (1) (h) marks a step backwards in the definition of persecutions as it requires that persecutions be made 'in connection with any act referred to in this paragraph or any crime within the jurisdiction of the Court', thus adding a requirement which did not previously exist. With this formulation, the court will thus not be able to prosecute persecution *per se,* as it is not, in itself, considered in its statute as a crime against humanity.

As regards domestic legislation, it can be noted that, here again, practice differs from one state to another. Thus, the 1946 Chinese Statute requires some motivational element for all the acts[118] while the Australian Statute states that crimes against humanity must be committed 'in the course of political, racial or religious persecution', thus also making grounds for commission relevant for all offences.[119] Taking a different approach,

---

[115] See *Prosecutor* v *Tadić,* Case No. IT-94-1-A, Judgment, Appeals Chamber, 15 July 1999, para 283.

[116] Article 3 of the ICTY Statute.

[117] Meron, Theodor, 'International Criminalization of Internal Atrocities', (1994) 89 *AJIL* 557.

[118] Article II (3) of the Statute.

[119] Section 7 (3) of the Australian War Crimes Act. See Triggs, Gillian, 'Australia's War Crimes Trials : All Pity Choked', in McCormack, Timothy L.M. and Simpson, Gerry J. (eds), *The Law of War Crimes, National and International Approaches,* Kluwer Law International , 1997, p 128.

the 1987 Canadian War Crimes Statute merely declares that the crimes be committed 'against any civilian population or any 'identifiable group of persons', expression which might imply a necessary motivation against the 'identifiable group', although this requirement is far from being explicit.[120] Finally, the Israeli Statute also uses the bifurcated strategy of the Nuremberg Charter and therefore requires motivational elements only for persecutions.[121]

In the *Barbie* case, by its decision of 20 December 1985, the French Cour de Cassation found that Barbie had acted with the element of intent necessary for the qualification of crimes against humanity and thus highlighted the importance of grounds for commission by explicitly including political motivation among them.[122] Such a finding was most probably due to practical considerations as, if not considered crimes against humanity, crimes against members of the Résistance would have been qualified as war crimes, and would have remained unpunished due to the applicability, under French law, of statutory limitations to war crimes.[123] Had the court refused to extend the notion of crimes against humanity, and thus the pre-existing law, such crimes would have gone unpunished, just because they were committed for other motives than those expressly specified. Ultimately, because of the inherent dangers of requiring specific grounds for commission for *all* crimes against humanity, it is to be hoped that the return in the Rome Statute to the Nuremberg 'bifurcation' will remain and will thus definitively state the law on this issue.

[120] Section 7(3.76) of the Canadian Criminal Code. See Williams, Sharon A., 'Laudable Principles Lacking Application : The Prosecution of War Criminals in Canada', in McCormack, Timothy L.M. and Simpson, Gerry J. (eds), *The Law of War Crimes, National and International Approaches*, Kluwer Law International, 1997, p 161.

[121] Article 1(b) of the Nazi and Nazi Collaborators (Punishment) Law, Israel, 1950, 5710/1950.

[122] It can be noted here that the lower court had dismissed the case by arguing that crimes against humanity could not be directed against members of the Résistance since they did not form a racial or a religious group.

[123] It can nonetheless be asserted that crimes against Résistants were indeed crimes against humanity. Therefore, the debate surrounding the *Barbie* case regarding the application of the same legal qualification to both crimes against Jews and crimes against *Résistants* was based on a misunderstanding. If the crimes were indeed intrinsically different and should thus have been differently qualified, the problem was not that the court qualified crimes against Résistants as crimes against humanity, it was that it failed in qualifying crimes against Jews as genocide.

II. The Crime of Genocide

A. The widespread and/or systematic action: the genocidal pattern of conduct

If the widespread and/or systematic action element is one of the definitional requirements necessary to qualify a crime as one against humanity, this element is also central to the definition of genocide. Indeed, the requirement of widespread and/or systematic action is obviously present in the conventional definition of the crime which focuses on the 'intent to *destroy*, in whole or in part, a national, ethnical, racial or religious *group* as such'.[1] The use in this definition of the terms 'destroy' may easily be interpreted as referring to a systematic action taken against a 'group', while the very use of this latter expression is a direct reference to the number of victims. What is controversial as regards this definition is the convention's exhaustive enumeration of the acts it proscribes as well as its reference to the intent to destroy a group 'in whole' or 'in part', without defining the terms nor explaining the purpose of this distinction. And indeed, the issue of cultural genocide is of interest here, and this act should certainly be considered as an act of genocide, if only to serve as proof of the widespread and systematic action. Indeed, if the culture of a whole group is targeted, this is a clear demonstration that the very existence of this group is threatened.

1. *The exhaustive enumeration of acts of genocide*

The Genocide Convention proceeds to a restrictive list of acts of genocide. During the drafting of the text and the debates in the Sixth Committee, the question had been raised as whether to adopt an exhaustive or an illustrative definition of acts of genocide. The main argument in favour of the former was the respect of the fundamental principle in criminal law, that of *nulla poena sine lege*. It was thus maintained that no prosecution could occur for a crime not expressly specified. Furthermore, an illustrative list, it was argued, would leave states discretion as to the definition of acts of genocide, thus creating variations among the different countries.

It is however argued here that, in the case of genocide, an exhaustive enumeration of punishable acts is impossible because necessarily

[1] Article II of the Genocide Convention.

incomplete. History showed that human imagination in criminal behaviour is without limits. Thus, new means of perpetrating genocides might appear but will remain unpunished, because *not punishable,* under the charge of genocide even if they clearly *are* genocidal acts.

For instance, the issue of rape as an act of genocide has been widely discussed while the Convention does not even mention this crime. It is true that this crime is today addressed as a crime against humanity[2] or as a war crime.[3] Nevertheless, several authors have labelled rape, and notably forced impregnation, as genocide. By an extensive interpretation of Article II (d) of the Convention which incriminates 'measures intended to prevent births within the group', enforced pregnancy could amount to genocide. In fact, Wallimann and Dobkowski referred to the deliberate attacks on Muslim women as child bearers in Bosnia as 'gynocide'.[4] Also considering the 'ethnic cleansing' carried out by Serb forces in Bosnia, Goldstein rightly explained that forced impregnation prevented Bosnian births 'at least temporarily and in many cases permanently'.[5] Similarly, Bassiouni and Manikas demonstated that, in cases of rape, women might be considered unmarriageable and might thus be less likely to procreate and to bear a child of their own ethnicity.[6] It must also be noted here that, in the *Akayesu* case, the ICTR drew a parallel between rape and torture and held that rape and sexual violence 'constitute genocide in the same way as any other act as long as they were committed with the specific intent' required.[7] In the *Rutaganda* case, it was also recognised that rape accords with 'serious bodily and mental harm', as prohibited by Article II(b) of the convention.[8]

Another issue which is not contemplated in the Genocide Convention is that of 'ecocide', generally defined as the disruption or the destruction

---

[2] See Article 5(g) of the ICTY Statute; Article 3(g) of the ICTR Statute; Article 7(1)(g) of the ICC Statute.

[3] See Neier, Aryeh, *War Crimes – Brutality, Genocide, Terror, and the Struggle for Justice,* Times Books, 1998, pp 179-183 on the crime of rape as a war crime. It is also noticeable that the Statute of the ICC deals with the war crime of rape in its Article 8 (2) (b) (xxii).

[4] See Wallimann, Isidor and Dobkowski, Michael N. (eds), *Genocide and the Modern Age – Etiology and Case Studies of Mass Death,* Syracuse University Press, 2000, p xi.

[5] Cited in Neier, Aryeh, *supra* n.3, pp.187-88.

[6] Bassiouni, M. Cherif and Manikas, Peter, *The Law of the International Criminal Tribunal for the Former Yugoslavia,* Transnational Publishers, Inc., 1996, p 587.

[7] *Prosecutor* v *Akayesu,* Case No. ICTR-96-4-T, judgment, Trial Chamber I, 2 September 1998, para 731. For the first time, rapes and sexual violences were included among the acts of genocide, while they are not among those crimes listed in Article II of the Genocide Convention.

[8] *Prosecutor* v *Rutaganda,* Case No. ICTR-96-3-T, judgment, Trial Chamber I, paras 49-53.

of the environment, usually for military purposes.[9] Although it might appear that this crime should be addressed from the standpoint of war crimes, it must nonetheless also be stressed that threats to the integrity of the environment can endanger the survival of a group, and if such a behaviour is adopted in order to destroy the group, then it may well amount to genocide.

Finally, the problem of apartheid as an act of genocide was also debated. As a matter of fact, apartheid was examined in relation to the Genocide Convention by an Ad Hoc Working Group of Experts. The Working Group indeed 'defined the elements of apartheid which constitute the crime of genocide'.[10] Its report thus listed different practices of apartheid regarded as elements of genocide, and notably the institution of group areas, the regulations concerning the movement of Africans in urban areas, the deliberate malnutrition policy, the birth control policy, the imprisonment and ill-treatment of non-white prisoners and the killing of the non-white population.[11] If it is true that the adoption of the 1973 Apartheid Convention[12] subsequently solved the problem, it still remains that that, during more than 20 years, there has been a *vide juridique* as to the qualification of this crime because the Genocide Convention did not expressly mention it among its exhaustive list of punishable acts.[13]

The problem of the exhaustive enumeration of acts of genocide in the Genocide Convention was also considered by the ILC. As a matter of fact, in its 1954 Draft Code, it incorporated Article II of the Genocide Convention as Article 2 (10) of the Draft Code but with a significant modification. Article 2 (10) read as follows:

[9] The issue of ecocide was raised for the first time by Arthur Galston in 1970. See generally Falk, Richard A., 'Ecocide, Genocide, and the Nuremberg Tradition of Individual Responsibility', *in* Held, V., Morgenbesser, S., and Nagel, T. (eds), *Philosophy, Morality, and International Affairs,* Oxford University Press, 1974, pp 123-37.

[10] See the Study concerning the question of apartheid from the point of view of international penal law, UN Doc E/CN.4/1075.

[11] See the report of the Ad Hoc Working Group of Experts, UN Doc E/CN. 4/984/para 4.

[12] See Apartheid Convention. In its Article I, it defines apartheid as a crime against humanity. Although the crime of apartheid had already been qualified as a crime against humanity in the 1968 UN Convention on the Non-applicability of Statutory Limitations to War Crimes and Crimes Against Humanity, this instrument was not necessarily reflecting international customary law due to the fact that it only attracted forty-four ratifications, and it may be recalled here that France, Germany, the United Kingdom, China and the United States did not ratify it.

[13] The Group of Experts had indeed made a recommendation to the Commission on Human Rights to make specific proposals concerning a revision of the Genocide Convention, notably 'to make inhuman acts resulting from the policies of apartheid' punishable under that Convention. See UN Doc E/CN.4/984/Add.18 and UN Doc E/CN.4/1074, para 161.

> Acts by the authorities of a State or by private individuals committed with intent to destroy, in whole or in part, a national, ethnic, racial or religious group as such, *including* [...][14]

By this definition, the scope of genocide was broadened to include, besides the five acts enumerated by the convention, other acts which might destroy a protected group. However, this innovation did not last as the 1996 Draft Code of Crimes went back to the conventional definition in its Article 17. [15] Moreover, because the Statutes of the Ad Hoc Tribunals[16] as well as the Statute of the ICC[17] also reproduced Article II of the Genocide Convention, acts of genocide remain submitted to a restrictive approach. Furthermore, it is here interesting to note that, in analysing the elements of acts of genocide, the 'Elements of Crimes' adopted by the Preparatory Commission require that 'the conduct took place in the context of a manifest pattern of similar conduct against that group',[18] requirement clearly corresponds to that of widespread and/or systematic attack applicable to crimes against humanity. Therefore, the Preparatory Commission has acknowledged the fact that, similarly to crimes against humanity, these acts had to be committed as part of a widespread or systematic attack. Still, crimes against humanity have in this respect a wider scope of application as it seems that the expression used by the Preparatory Commission which requires a 'context of a manifest pattern of *similar conduct*' implies that the context must consist of the same acts of genocide, ie killing, *or* causing serious bodily or mental harm, *or* deliberately inflicting conditions of life calculated to bring about the physical destruction of the group, *or* imposing measures intended to prevent births, *or* forcibly transferring children of the group to another group. If the Rome Statute is to be interpreted in this extremely restrictive way, the court will only have jurisdiction over a genocidal conduct when the acts committed are the same.

2. *The distinction between genocide in whole and genocide in part*

Not only does the Genocide Convention prohibit a limited number of acts, it also recognises both genocide 'in whole' and genocide 'in part', thus raising the question as to what is really meant by genocide 'in whole' and genocide 'in part'. If the intent to destroy 'in whole' is an easy concept to understand, the intent to destroy 'in part' is more

14 [1954] II *ILC Yearbook*. Emphasis added.
15 [1996] II (2) *ILC Yearbook* 44.
16 Article 4 of the ICTY Statute, Article 2 of the ICTR Statute.
17 Article 6.
18 See Elements of Crimes, Article 6.

problematic, notably due to the fact that the Convention itself fails to provide any indication or clarification. Furthermore, the *travaux préparatoires* are equally vague and the draft convention submitted by the Secretary-General merely observed that 'the systematic destruction even of a fraction of a group of human beings constitutes an exceptionally heinous crime'.[19]

From the outset, it must be stressed that this definitional requirement of the crime of genocide actually relates to the intent of the genociders rather than to the genocidal action itself. As Tournaye rightly recalled: '[i]t is a not a matter of establishing whether all or part of a group was actually destroyed, but of ascertaining whether the perpetrators of the crime intended to destroy the group in whole or in part.'[20] Nonetheless, because this issue is closely linked to the widespread aspect of the crime, it will here be studied in relation with it. And indeed, an overview of the case law actually demonstrates that, far from ensuring a 'safety net' able to ensure the qualification of acts of genocide as such even in instances where the totality of the group was not destroyed, the conventional recognition of both genocide 'in whole' and genocide 'in part' led in practice to a distinction between two types of genocides artificially created and to questionable debates, to say the least, as to how many victims are required in order for a genocide to be qualified as such.

Accordingly, in a very good commentary on the convention, Robinson, referring to the *travaux préparatoires*, wrote that the number of victims had to be substantial, even if it was left to the courts to decide in each case whether 'the number was *sufficiently large*'.[21] Similarly, Whitaker, in his report on the convention, believed that the term 'in part' implied 'a *reasonably significant number*, relative to the total of the group as a whole, or else a significant section of a group such as its leadership'.[22] The caselaw of the International Criminal Tribunals shows the same inability to define properly the terms of the Convention. Thus, according to the ICTR, there must be a 'considerable number' of victims for the crime to qualify as genocide,[23] while the ICTY, adding to the confusion, referred to a 'substantial' part, although not necessarily a 'very important part'.[24]

[19] Draft Convention for the Prevention and Punishment of Genocide presented by the Secretary-General, 26 June 1947, UN Doc E/447, p 24.
[20] Tournaye, Cécile, 'Genocidal Intent Before the ICTY', (2003) 52 *ICLQ* 459.
[21] Robinson, Nehemiah, *The Genocide Convention – A Commentary*, Institute of Jewish Affairs – World Jewish Congress, 1960, p 58. Emphasis added.
[22] Whitaker Report, p 16, para.29. Emphasis added.
[23] *Prosecutor* v *Kayishema and Ruzindana*, Case No. ICTR-95-1-T, judgment, Trial Chamber II, 21 May 1999, para.97. Emphasis added.
[24] *Prosecutor* v *Jelisić*, Case No. IT-95-10-T, Judgment, Trial Chamber I, 14 December 1999, paras 81-82. Emphasis added.

It is here submitted that there cannot be genocide 'in whole' or genocide 'in part': either there is a case of genocide or there is not, but there is certainly no 'in-between category'. Some authors, such as Melson, found an easy way out and termed 'genocidal massacre' the partial destruction of a group. Needless to say that the problem remained the same, 'genocidal massacres' being nothing else than genocides 'in part'.[25] The convention here created confusion by not defining the terms it employs. As a result, the question may arise as to whether these two types of genocides are submitted to the same legal regime or if they are considered differently. In fact, some have argued that unless the goal was to kill *all* of a given people, the event was not 'really' genocide, or was a 'lesser genocide'. This has served for the basis for flagrant denials, such as the Turkish arguments that since many of the Armenians living in Istanbul were not killed, this was proof that there was no intent to kill *all* Armenians and thus no genocide.

It is obvious that this purely artificial distinction between genocide 'in whole' and genocide 'in part' is also very immoral. Clearly, such a distinction is based on the number of victims needed to qualify the acts as genocide. How many victims will a court need to consider their number *'sufficiently large'*? What is a *'reasonably significant number'* which will constitute genocide?

In this respect, the case law of the ICTY is particularly interesting as it does give some indication as to what is really meant by genocide 'in part'.

The first criterion which has been used by the ICTY in order to assess the commission of a genocide 'in part' is geographical. As a matter of fact, in the *Krstić* case, Trial Chamber I defined the term in relation with the geographical scale on which the crime had been perpetrated and found that 'the intent to eradicate a group within a limited geographical area such as the region of a country or even a municipality'[26] could amount to genocide, and the Appeals Chamber subsequently held that:

> The historical examples of genocide also suggest that the area of the perpetrators' activity and control, as well as the possible extent of their reach, should be considered. Nazi Germany may have intended only to eliminate Jews within Europe alone; that ambition probably did not

[25] Furthermore, as Smith rightly pointed out, 'sooner or later the *genocidal* is transformed into *genocide*'. See Smith, Roger W., 'Human Destructiveness and Politics: The Twentieth Century as an Age of Genocide', in Wallimann, Isidor and Dobkowski, Michael N. (eds), *supra* n 4, p 23.
[26] Ibid, paras 595-7.

> extend, even at the height of its power, to an undertaking of that enterprise on a global scale. Similarly, the perpetrators of genocide in Rwanda did not seriously contemplate the elimination of the Tutsi population beyond the country's borders. The intent to destroy formed by a perpetrator of genocide will always be limited by the opportunity presented to him. While this factor alone will not indicate whether the targeted group is substantial, it can - in combination with other factors – inform the analysis.[27]

Adopting a similar view, Trial Chamber III, in the *Sikirica* case, acknowledged the fact that that the destruction of part of the group living in a precise and limited geographical zone could amount to genocide, when this part of the group had been perceived by the genociders as a distinct entity to be targeted and subsequently exterminated as such:

> [t]he intent to destroy a multitude of persons belonging to a group may amount to genocide, even where these persons constitute only part of a group within a given geographical area: a country or a region or a single community.[28]

The second – more critical – criterion on which the ICTY has based its decision is the quantitative criterion. In the *Krstić* case, Trial Chamber I had to determine whether the genocidal intent existed while only men of military age were targeted and murdered and interestingly found that the killings of all military aged men amounted to genocide:

> The Bosnian Serb forces could not have failed to know, by the time they decided to kill all the men, that this selective destruction of the group would have a lasting impact upon the entire group. [...] By killing all the military aged men, the Bosnian Serb forces effectively destroyed the community of the Bosnian Muslims in Srebrenica as such and eliminated all likelihood that it could ever re-establish itself on that territory.[29]

In this particular case, the trial chamber used the concept of 'the group as a distinct entity' in order to assess the commission of genocide and

[27] *Prosecutor* v *Krstić*, Appeals judgment, 19 April 2004, para 13.
[28] *Prosecutor* v *Sikirica et al*, Case No IT-95-8, Judgment on Defence Motions to Acquit, Trial Chamber III, 3 September 2001, para.68.
[29] *Prosecutor* v *Krstić*, Case No. IT-98-33, Judgment, Trial Chamber I, 2 August 2001, paras 595-97.

this decision has to be welcomed as departing from a sordid mathematical approach. In this respect, the trial chamber further explained that:

> The Trial Chamber is therefore of the opinion that the intent to destroy a group, even if only in part, means seeking to destroy a *distinct part of the group* as opposed to an accumulation of isolated individuals within it. Although the perpetrators of genocide need not seek to destroy the entire group protected by the Convention, they must view the part of the group they wish to destroy as a *distinct entity* which must be eliminated as such. A campaign resulting in the killings, in different places spread over a broad geographical area, of a finite number of members of a protected group might not thus qualify as genocide, despite the high total number of casualties, because it would not show an intent by the perpetrators to target the very existence of the group as such. Conversely, the killing of all members of the part of a group located within a small geographical area, although resulting in a lesser number of victims, would qualify as genocide if carried out with the intent to destroy the part of the group as such located in this small geographical area. Indeed, the physical destruction may target only a part of the geographically limited part of the larger group because the perpetrators of the genocide regard the intended destruction as sufficient to annihilate *the group as a distinct entity* in the geographic area at issue. In this regard, it is important to bear in mind the total context in which the physical destruction is carried out.[30]

Nonetheless, only one month after the *Krstić* judgment, Trial Chamber III of the ICTY reached an opposite conclusion in the *Sikirica* case and by adopting a mathematical approach to the crimes committed, found that genocidal intent to destroy Bosnian Muslim or Bosnian Croats could not be inferred from the number of victims. Fortunately, the appeals chamber in *Krstić* confirmed the trial chamber's finding and held that the 'Trial Chamber's determination of the substantial part of the protected group [the Bosnian Muslims of Srebrenica] was correct.'[31]

The last – and probably even more problematic – criterion used by the ICTY is the qualitative criterion. In other words, the judicial

[30] Ibid, para 590. Emphasis added.
[31] *Prosecutor* v *Krstić, supra* n 27, para 23.

interpretation of the notion of 'substantial part' here lies on an elitist approach to victims of genocide. And, indeed, the case law shows that, for qualification purposes, 'substantial' has been equated with 'emblematic'.[32] In practical terms, this means that the elite of a group would be considered as a substantial part of this group.[33] In the *Jelisić* case, Trial Chamber I thus explained that:

> A targeted part of a group would be classed as substantial either because the intent sought to harm a large majority of the group in question or the most representative members of the targeted community. The Commission of Experts specified that '[i]f essentially the total leadership of a group is targeted, it could also amount to genocide. Such leadership includes political and administrative leaders, religious leaders, academics and intellectuals, business leaders and others – the totality *per se* may be a strong indication of genocide regardless of the actual numbers killed. A corroborating argument will be the fate of the rest of the group. The character of the attack on the leadership must be *viewed in the context of the fate or what happened to the rest of the group*. If a group has its leadership exterminated, and at the same time or in the wake of that, has a relatively large number of the members of the group killed or subjected to other heinous acts, for example deported on a large scale or forced to flee, the cluster of violations ought to be considered in its entirety in order to interpret the provisions of the Convention in a spirit consistent with its purpose'. Genocidal intent may therefore be manifest in two forms. It may consist of desiring the extermination of a very large number of the members of the group, in which case it would constitute an intention to destroy a group en masse. However, it may also consist of the desired destruction of a more limited number of persons selected for the impact that their disappearance would have upon the survival of the group as such. This would then constitute an intention to destroy the group 'selectively'. The Prosecutor did not actually choose between these two options.[34]

[32] *Prosecutor* v *Sikirica,* Motion for Acquittal Decision, para.77.
[33] *Prosecutor* v *Krstić, supra* n 29, paras 585-87.
[34] *Prosecutor* v *Jelisić,* Case No IT-95-10-T, Trial Chamber I, 14 December 1999, para 82. Emphasis in original.

Similarly, in the *Sikirica* case, Trial Chamber III subsequently found that:

> If the quantitative criterion is not met, the intention to destroy in part may yet be established if there is evidence that the destruction is related to a significant section of the group, such as its leadership.
>
> The Chamber finds persuasive the analysis in the *Jelisic* trial judgement that the requisite intent may be inferred from the 'desired destruction of a more limited number of persons selected for the impact that their disappearance would have upon the survival of the group as such'. The important element here is the targeting of a selective number of persons who, by reason of their special qualities of leadership within the group as a whole, are of such importance that their victimisation within the terms of Article 4(2)(a), (b) and (c) would impact upon the survival of the group, as such.[35]

This approach to the crime of genocide is very disturbing, and counting victims or relying on their social status in order to qualify the crime is extremely inappropriate. An act does not qualify as genocide according to the number of victims or to their profession or wealth. Rather, it is the deliberate and planned feature of the act that designates it as such. In this respect, it may be recalled here that, during the drafting of the convention, France suggested that the definition of genocide should be broad enough to include the murder of a single person.[36] Even if this proposal was dismissed, it is still interesting because it pointed out that the qualification of genocide does not rely on the number of deaths. Also, it has to be noted here that in the 'Elements of Crimes' adopted by the Preparatory Commission, it is specified that 'one or more persons' may be the victim of the crime of genocide.[37] It is true that this hypothesis certainly widens the definition of genocide as envisaged in the convention and it is most probable that the murder of an individual because of his belonging to a protected group would be qualified as a

---

[35] *Prosecutor* v *Sikirica et al*, Case No IT-95-8, judgment on Defence Motions to Acquit, Trial Chamber III, 3 September 2001, paras 76-77.

[36] UN Doc, 3 UN GAOR, Sixth Committee (1948), pp 91-92. See also Bryant, Bunyan, 'Substantive Scope of the Convention', in *Comment: The United States and the 1948 Genocide Convention, Part I*, (1975) 16 *HILJ* 686-98. During the drafting, the Ad Hoc Committee also expressed the view that the murder of an individual could be considered an act of genocide if it was part of a series of similar acts aimed at the destruction of the group to which the victim belongs. See Robinson, Nehemiah, *The Genocide Convention – A Commentary*, Institute of Jewish Affairs – World Jewish Congress, 1960, p 62.

[37] See Elements of Crimes, Article 6(a).

'racist murder' rather than as genocide. However, all genocides start by a single victim, and the question remains as to the qualification of this first particular murder in the event that the genocidal plan actually fails.

According to Drost:

> [b]oth as a question of theory and as a matter of principle nothing in the present [Genocide] Convention prohibits its provisions to be interpreted and applied to *individual cases* of murder by reason of the national, racial, ethnical or religious qualities of the *single victim* if the murderous attack was done with the intent to commit similar acts in the future and in connection with the first crime.[38]

It is here submitted that this interpretation of the Genocide Convention is legally correct. If an individual has been murdered as part of a plan of extermination of the group to which he or she belongs, this act should be considered as genocide, whether this plan succeeds or not. As a matter of fact, in section 6 of its 2002 Code of Crimes Against International Law,[39] German law:

> [n]ow explicitly states that a *single* genocidal act, such as a single killing or a single infliction of great bodily harm, may also constitute genocide if committed with genocidal intent (i.e. with the intent to destroy in whole or in part one of the groups referred to in the Convention). Thus, according to the German legislature, customary international law does not require that the genocidal act be committed as part of a systematic practice.[40]

Again, because such an individual act would have to be perpetrated with the specific genocidal intent in order to qualify as an act of genocide, it appears that the German law is more in phase with the concept of genocide than the Genocide Convention actually is. Ultimately, in the words of Miller, '[w]e must remind ourselves that the Holocaust was not six million. It was one, plus one, plus one'.[41]

---

[38] Drost, Pieter N., *The Crime of State – Penal Protection for Fundamental Freedoms of Persons and Peoples, Book II: Genocide – United Nations Legislation on International Criminal Law,* Leyden: A.W. Sythoff, 1959, p 85.
[39] Völkerstrafgesetzbuch
[40] Wirth, Steffen, 'Germany's New International Crimes Code : Bringing a Case to Court', (2003) 1 *JICJ* 151-68 at 156. Emphasis in original. Footnotes omitted.
[41] Miller Judith, *One by One, by One: Facing the Holocaust,* Simon & Schuster, 1990, p 287.

3. *Cultural genocide*

As regards the requirement of widespread or systematic action, cultural genocide is an extremely relevant issue as its occurrence also participates in demonstrating the large scale on which genocide is committed. It is true that the Genocide Convention excludes cultural genocide from its scope of application, and the only reference to it is in the incrimination of the forced transfer of children, as the cultural identity of the group might then be lost.[42]

Nonetheless, the convention's definition is here again more restrictive than the definitions proposed by the doctrine, and notably by Lemkin. As a matter of fact, he did identify 'genocide in the cultural field' which consisted of 'the prohibition or the destruction of cultural institutions and cultural activities, of the substitution of education in the liberal arts for vocational education, in order to prevent humanistic thinking, which the occupant considers dangerous because it promotes national thinking'.[43]

It must be stressed here that the initial draft of the convention – that of the Human Rights Division of the Secretariat – included cultural genocide among acts of genocide; it was there defined as the destruction of the specific characteristics of the persecuted groups by various means, such as forced exile, prohibition of the use of the national language, destruction of books, and similar acts.[44] The subsequent draft of the Ad Hoc Committee also dealt with cultural genocide in its Article III. The main argument raised in favour of the deletion of this article from the convention was that the concept was too indefinite to be included. Furthermore, the majority of representatives felt that the inclusion of cultural genocide would weaken the convention, aimed at preventing and punishing mass murder. It is perfectly true that the destruction of schools and churches cannot be compared with the physical destruction and the murder of a whole population. However, history shows that one does not go without the other, and that the destruction of cultural institutions is more often than not the first step towards physical genocide.[45]

[42] An example of such forced assimilation which may be seen as a genocidal policy is that of the 'stolen generation' of Aboriginals in Australia at the beginning of the 20th century.

[43] Lemkin, Raphaël, *Axis Rule in Occupied Europe – Laws of Occupation, Analysis of Government, Proposals* for *Redress,* Carnegie Endowment for International Peace, Division of International Law, 1944, pp xi-xii.

[44] UN Doc A/AC.10/41 and UN Doc A/362 (Appendix II).

[45] It can be noted here that Cambodia might be the only case where physical genocide was not accompanied by cultural genocide. As a matter of fact, the Khmer Rouge did

Continued

The destruction of a group's culture should be a matter of great concern for the international community as it is a definite sign that human rights violations, and even genocide, might follow. If the aim to prevent genocide is to be achieved, destruction of cultural symbols and institutions should be seriously looked into. For instance, the less than satisfying human rights situation in Tibet is highly reflected in the destruction of the Tibetan culture. Temples were designated victims for the Chinese perpetrators: from 1966 until the end of the Cultural Revolution, only 13 of the 6,259 places of Buddhist cult were still functioning. Many them had been completely razed and their treasures – including secular manuscripts, frescos, thanka (paintings), statues, and so forth – had been destroyed or stolen, and this in a systematic, methodical, calculated, planned and total way.[46] There was also a clear will to eradicate Buddhism and to annihilate Tibetan culture through the attempt, until 1979, to impose Chinese names to new-born Tibetan babies and to give Tibetan children a purely Chinese education. Since then, other methods have been used by the Chinese Government in order to eliminate Tibetan culture. Among other measures, the Chinese language was taught and spoken, names of historical figures and places were re-baptised, and Chinese products were truly invading Tibetan markets. It appears obvious that such attempts aim at denying the existence of the Tibetan culture, culture without which Tibetans as a group will disappear.

Like physical genocide, cultural genocide ultimately aims at the destruction of a group and should thus be included in the definition of the crime of genocide. As a matter of fact, the United Nations Sub-Commission on Human Rights has adopted a resolution in which the experts, representing 26 countries, expressed their worry as to the persisting violations of human rights in Tibet which 'threaten the distinctive identity of the Tibetan people on cultural, religious and national grounds'.[47]

The invasion of East Timor by Indonesia also brought into light the question of cultural genocide, at least until East Timor acceded to independence on 19 May 2002. As Dunn pointed out:

... not destroy the cultural heritage of Phnom Penh. According to Neier, 'Pol Pot's forces were like a neutron bomb, killing the people but leaving the buildings intact'. Neier, Aryeh, *War Crimes: Brutality, Genocide, Terror, and the Struggle for Justice*, Times Books, 1998, pp 119-20.

[46] During a liberalisation period, a Tibetan team found more than 32 tons of religious relics belonging to Tibet in Pekin. See generally Donnet, Pierre-Antoie, *Tibet, Mort ou Vif*, Gallimard, Collection Folio Actuel, 1992.

[47] Resolution of 23 August 1991.

> [i]t is very likely that 'Indonesation' of the territory, together with ongoing attempts to eliminate support for a separate Timorese state, if successful, will submerge Timorese culture and ultimately destroy it.[48]

As a matter of fact, the Indonesian authorities proceeded to the banning of traditional animistic cults and attempted to prohibit the use of the Portuguese language and of Tetum, the *lingua franca* spoken among the Timorese, as well as to promote Islam.[49] In the words of Dunn, 'the distinctive cultural identity of the people of this former Portuguese colony is at risk of being lost forever'.[50]

Dramatically, this list of examples is far from being exhaustive and one may also have in mind the cultural war against Sarajevo where historical heritage was deliberately destroyed. It is thus most likely that physical genocide is accompanied by cultural genocide. Indeed, the perpetrators seek to eradicate a group, to deny its existence, both physical and cultural. Genocide is, from the point of view of its perpetrators, the solution to annihilate a population and to eliminate its right to existence. Killing is not enough; all the traces of the group's existence also have to be erased. Its incrimination in the convention would have thus allowed for better prevention, as it could have served as a warning, but also as a tool for effective punishment. According to the ICTY, the proof of attacks directed against cultural institutions and monuments, committed in association with killing, may constitute an important element in establishing the existence of a genocidal intent:

> The Trial Chamber is aware that it must interpret the Convention with due regard for the principle *nullum crimen sine lege*. It therefore recognises that, despite recent developments, customary international law limits the definition of genocide to those acts seeking the physical or biological destruction of all or part of the group.[...] The Trial Chamber however points out that where there is physical or biological destruction there are often simultaneous attacks on the cultural and religious

48 Dunn, James, 'Genocide in East Timor', in Totten, Samuel, Parsons, William S. and Charny, Israel W. (eds), *Genocide in the Twentieth Century – Critical Essays and Eyewitness Accounts*, Garland Publishing, Inc., 1995, pp 357-58.

49 See Barbedo de Magalhaes, Antonio, *East Timor, Indonesian Occupation and Genocide*, President's Office, Oporto University, 1992, pp 36-37.

50 Dunn, James, 'East Timor : A Case of Cultural Genocide ?', in Andreopoulos George J. (ed), *Genocide : Conceptual and Historical Dimensions*, University of Pennsylvania Press, 1994, p 187. As East Timor became independent on 19 May 2002, it may be asserted that this genocide thus came to an end.

> property and symbols of the targeted group as well, attacks which may legitimately be considered as evidence of an intent to physically destroy the group. In this case, the Trial Chamber will thus take into account as evidence of intent to destroy the group the deliberate destruction of mosques and houses belonging to members of the group.[51]

Thus, even if it maintained that 'an enterprise attacking only the cultural or sociological characteristics of a human group [...] would not fall under the definition of genocide',[52] the trial chamber still recognised the existence of 'recent developments' towards the recognition of the crime of cultural genocide. In this respect, a recent German holding went in contradiction with international law by interpreting the term 'genocide' broadly. Indeed, the Federal Constitutional Court of Germany stated that:

> [T]he statutory definition of genocide defends a supra-individual object of legal protection, ie the *social* existence of the group [...] the intent to destroy the group [...] extends beyond physical and biological extermination [...] The text of the law does not therefore compel the interpretation that the culprit's intent must be to exterminate physically at least a substantial number of the members of the group.[53]

Also, it might be noted here that some scholars have considered interpreting the term 'to destroy' in the conventional definition of genocide so as to include cultural genocide. According to Schabas:

> [i]t can be argued that a contemporary interpreter of the definition of genocide should not be bound by the intent of the drafters back in 1948. The words 'to destroy' can readily bear the concept of cultural as well as physical and biological genocide, and bold judges might be tempted to adopt such progressive constructions.[54]

---

[51] *Prosecutor* v *Krstić*, Case No IT-98-33, Judgment, Trial Chamber I, 2 August 2001, para 580.

[52] Ibid. This finding was confirmed by the appeals chamber. See *Prosecutor* v *Krstić*, Case No IT-98-33-A, appeals judgment, 19 April 2004, para 25: 'The Genocide Convention, and customary international law in general, prohibit only the physical or biological destruction of a human group.'

[53] Federal Constitutional Court, 2 BvR 1290/99, 12 December 2000, para (III) (4) (a) (aa). Emphasis added. Cited in *Prosecutor* v *Krstić*, *supra* n 51, para 579.

[54] Schabas, William A., *An Introduction to the International Criminal Court*, Cambridge University Press, 2001, pp 31-32.

Ultimately, it might be asserted here that, whether there is a distinction between genocide 'in whole' and genocide 'in part', and whether cultural genocide is or is not recognised as proof of the widespread and systematic aspect of the action, the crime of genocide remains in any case one which is essentially both widespread and systematic. It is in fact its width and its 'systematicity' which gives it its specific meaning.

As we have previously seen, the definition of crimes against humanity is much more realistic in that it encompasses a wider array of different acts and, in that sense, the definition of genocide should draw upon that of crimes against humanity. By so doing, the notion of genocide would not lose its specific features, it would still remain a unique legal qualification, but it would not be submitted to an unduly limited approach and would provide for better prosecution of the crime of genocide by covering more punishable acts and by thus permitting the prosecution of different acts committed as part of a widespread or systematic attack.

B. Grounds for commission: the conventional selective protection of groups

The requirement of grounds for commission is not only one of the definitional elements of crimes against humanity, it is also omnipresent in the definition of the crime of genocide, this crime being perpetrated in order to destroy 'groups as such',[55] although the Genocide Convention is selective among the groups it would protect in whole or in part. As a matter of fact, the convention affords protection to *'national, ethnical, racial* [and] *religious'* groups. The first problem with this is that the convention does not provide for a definition of these groups. Thus, one can wonder what the differences are between a national, an ethnical and a racial group. And in fact, during the drafting of the Convention, some representatives argued that the terms 'racial' and 'ethnic' covered the same reality, as did the terms 'ethnic' and 'national'.[56] There was also a serious debate over the inclusion of religious groups, the Soviet representative arguing that these groups should be considered as

[55] Article II of the Genocide Convention.

[56] See 3 UN GAOR C.6 (75th meeting), pp 115-116, UN Doc A/633 (1948). *Cited in* Leblanc, Lawrence J., 'The United Nations Genocide Convention and Political Groups : Should the United States Propose an Amendment?', (1988) 13 YJIL 271. In this respect, Trial Chamber II of the ICTR gave a rather large definition of 'ethnic group', definition which could actually apply to the other groups enumerated in Convention: it was defined as a group 'whose members share a common language and culture; or, a group which distinguishes itself, a such (self identification); or, a group identified as such by others, including perpetrators of the crimes (identification by others)'. *Prosecutor* v *Kayishema and Ruzindana*, Case No. ICTR-95-1-T, Judgment, Trial Chamber II, 21 May 1999, para 98.

subgroups of national groups.[57] Moreover, the use of the term 'racial' is ambiguous as it is obvious that the concept of 'race' is nothing less than a fantasy inherited from the previous centuries. According to Margolin, the concept of race only exists from the point of view of those who intend to define it as, in reality, there is no race.[58]

In the *Akayesu* case, the tribunal acknowledged such a shortcoming of the Genocide Convention as it had to resort to a most improbable interpretation of the convention and found that the conventional scope of protection was meant to apply to 'permanent and stable' groups.[59] Indeed, Tutsis did not fit in any of the groups described as they were not really a different ethnical group compared with the Hutus: they shared the same language and probably the same culture.[60] According to Destexhe, there 'were certainly distinguishable *social categories* in existence before the arrival of the colonisers, but the differences between them were not based on ethnic or racial divisions'.[61] He further found that the colonisers reinforced the antagonism between Hutus and Tutsis which 'has since become absorbed by the people themselves'.[62] Nevertheless, the trial chamber forced an interpretation in order to qualify the facts as genocide; had it not, the Rwanda mass killings would not have qualified as genocide!

The case of Cambodia is also perfectly illustrative of the ambiguities of the conventional definition of the crime of genocide. As Van Schaack pointed out, 'a close reading of the Genocide Convention leads to a surprising and worrisome conclusion'.[63] Indeed, although the Cambodia massacre perpetrated by the Khmer Rouge (1975-1978) is widely defined as genocide,[64] most of the acts committed are in reality not covered by

[57] See Report of the Ad Hoc Committee on Genocide, 3 UN ESCOR Supp. 6, UN Doc E/794 (1948), p 6.

[58] Margolin, Jean-Louis, 'Cambodge : Au :Pays du Crime Déconcertant', in Stéphane Courtois et al., *Le Livre Noir du Communisme – Crimes,Terreur, Répression*, Robert Laffont, Collection Pocket, 1997, pp 898-900.

[59] *Prosecutor* v *Akayesu*, Case No ICTR-96-4-T, Judgment, Trial Chamber I, 2 September 1998, para 515.

[60] See Destexhe, Alain, *Rwanda and Genocide in the Twentieth Century*, Translated by Alison Marschner, Pluto Press, 1995, p 36: 'The Hutu and the Tutsi cannot even correctly be described as ethnic groups for they both speak the same language and respect the same traditions and taboos. It would be extremely difficult to find any kind of cultural or folkloric custom that was specifically Hutu or Tutsi.'

[61] Ibid. Emphasis added.

[62] Ibid.

[63] Van Schaack, Beth, 'The Crime of Political Genocide: Repairing the Genocide Convention's Blind Spot', (1997) 106 *Yale L J* 2261.

[64] See eg the opinion of Beres who sees, among the instances of genocide committed since the Second World War, the Cambodian case as 'being, perhaps, the most far-reaching and abhorrent'; Beres, Louis René, 'Justice and Realpolitik: International Law and the Prevention of Genocide', (1988) 33 *American Journal of Jurisprudence* 133.

the convention. Thus, some of the crimes committed by the Khmer Rouge would fall within the scope of the convention[65] while others would not, because the victims did not constitute a national, ethnic, racial, or religious group.[66] As a matter of fact, some authors argue that 'confusing mass killing of the members of the perpetrator's own group with genocide is inconsistent with the purpose of the Convention, which was to protect national minorities from crimes based on ethnic hatred'.[67] In this case, what some refer to as 'auto-genocide'[68] falls out of the scope of the convention.[69] If this is so, the atrocities committed by the Khmer Rouge in Cambodia against members of their own group do not amount to genocide. Indeed, in its 1999 report, the Group of Experts for Cambodia stated that:

> [w]hether the Khmer Rouge committed genocide with respect to part of the Khmer national group turns on complex interpretative issues, especially concerning the Khmer Rouge's intent with respect to its non-minority-group victims.[70]

As a result, the Group of Experts did not take position on the issue, and considered that the matter should be dealt with by the courts if Khmer

[65] The Khmer Rouge did indeed commit genocide against a religious group – the Buddhists – and against ethnic groups: the Vietnamese community was entirely eradicated, while members of the Chinese and of the Muslim Cham communities were massacred.

[66] For an analysis of the Cambodian massacre, see Van Schaack, Beth, *supra* n 63, 2269-72.

[67] See Schabas, William A., *Genocide in International Law – the Crimes of Crimes*, Cambridge University Press, 2000, p 120.

[68] See UN Doc E/CN.4/SR.1510: A report to the UN Human Rights Commission noted that the mass murder which had occurred in Cambodia was comparable with the depredations of the Nazis and that it represented 'nothing less than autogenocide'. The term 'autogenocide' has also been used by some scholars. However, it might be confusing as it could imply a suicidal attitude.

[69] In this respect, crimes against humanity have a far wider scope of application as the requirement is that they must be committed 'against any civilian population'. In the *Tadić* case, the trial chamber explained that '[t]he inclusion of the word 'any' makes it clear that crimes against humanity can be committed against civilians of the same nationality as the perpetrators or those who are stateless, as well as those of a different nationality'. *Prosecutor* v *Tadić*, Case No IT-94-1-T, Opinion and Judgment, Trial Chamber II, 7 May 1997, para.939. As regards war crimes, it seems that, although their scope extends to victims of the same nationality than the perpetrators, there are however some restrictive conditions. For instance, the *Tadić* appeals chamber held that 'even if in the circumstances of the case the perpetrators and the victims were to be regarded as possessing the same nationality, Article 4 [of Geneva Convention IV] would still be applicable. Indeed, *the victims did not owe allegiance to (and did not receive the diplomatic protection of) the State* (the FRY) on whose behalf the Bosnian Serb armed forces had been fighting'. Had the victims owed such allegiance (or had they received such diplomatic protection), Article 4 [of Geneva Convention IV] would not have been considered as applicable. *Prosecutor* v *Tadić*, Case No. IT-94-1, Judgment, Appeals Chamber, 15 July 1999, para 169. Emphasis added.

[70] UN Doc E/CN.4/SR.1510.

Rouge officials were charged with genocide against the Khmer national group.[71] Such an interpretation of the Convention thus leads to absurd results.

Nevertheless, it is arguable that this position is wrong according to the Convention itself, which expressly confers protection to 'national' groups, thus including cases of 'auto-genocide'.[72] Furthermore, such a reading of the text omits the fact that the majority of a population might also be a victim of genocide. In his report, Whitaker observed that a victim group can constitute either a minority or a majority.[73] He thus concluded that 'the definition does not exclude cases where the victims are part of the violator's own group' and that, accordingly, the Cambodian massacres were a clear case of genocide 'even under the most restricted definition'.[74] According to Schabas: 'the label "group" is flexible, enabling the convention to apply without question to the destruction of entities that may not qualify as "minorities".'[75]

Ultimately, as the convention does not provide for detailed definitions in its provisions, it leaves the states parties significant discretion as to the groups which are protected. As a matter of fact, 'defining the groups more precisely was presumably left to the implementing legislation which parties to the Convention are to adopt in accordance with Article V'.[76] As a result, 'different states have varying definitions of protected groups and problems could arise in interpreting and applying the Convention'.[77]

Because the convention proceeds to a limitative list of the groups which deserve protection, it seems to suggest that some groups are less worthy of protection than others and that genocide against these groups could

[71] Report of the Group of Experts for Cambodia Established Pursuant to General Assembly Resolution 52/135, UN Doc A/53/850, UN Doc S/1999/231, annex, para 65. In this respect, it remains to be seen whether the internationalised domestic tribunal in Cambodia which was set up to prosecute the crimes committed by the Khmer Rouge will qualify such offences as genocide. See generally Linton, Suzannah, 'New Approaches to international justice in Cambodia and East Timor', (2002) 84 *International Review of the Red Cross* 93-119.

[72] See also Hannum, Hurst, 'International Law and Cambodian Genocide : The Sounds of Silence', (1989) 11 *HRQ* 107: 'nothing in the *travaux préparatoires* is contrary to or incompatible with the proposition that the Khmer people of Kampuchea constitute a national group within the meaning of Article II.'

[73] Whitaker Report, p 16, para 29.

[74] Ibid, p 16, para 31.

[75] Schabas, William A., *Genocide in International Law – the Crimes of Crimes,* Cambridge University Press, 2000, p 108.

[76] LeBlanc, Lawrence J., 'The United Nations Genocide Convention and Political Groups: Should the United States Propose an Amendment?', (1988) 13 *Yale Journal of International Law* 271-72.

[77] Ibid.

be acceptable. Furthermore, the fact that the convention protects the enumerated groups *'as such'* also gives rise to serious problems. Indeed, genocidal actions may be taken against any national, ethnical, racial or religious group, but the application of the convention to them can easily be impeded by the claim that they are not being proceeded against as members of one of these groups *'as such'*, but as members of other groups which are not protected by the Convention. In other words, perpetrators are here provided with a defence to a charge of genocide, as they could use the pretext of oppressing other groups to persecute groups conventionally protected. In this respect, Robinson rightly wrote that 'the destruction of ethnic, racial, or religious groups under the guise of "political groups" would be an obvious violation of the Convention'.[78] Such an assertion is perfectly true but remains completely theoretical. Indeed, such a manipulation of truth will be impossible to prove. Furthermore, it is arguable that the international community of states will find this very convenient as it will give them a perfect excuse not to condemn the mass killings, let alone to intervene.

The *travaux préparatoires* of the convention show that the exclusion of political and social groups from Article II provoked more debate than any other aspect of the text. At the time of the drafting, pressure was put on states to ratify the convention on the ground that genocide was being committed behind the Iron Curtain, while the convention would in fact not apply to such cases! Indeed, the Soviet Union and its communist satellites only had to invoke the fact that their victims were political enemies in order to avoid punishment. Thus, the religious persecutions which took place in Czechoslovakia, Hungary and Bulgaria on the ground that the clergy were enemies of the state would be a clear example of the meaninglessness of the convention in such cases. Van Schaack explained this contradiction by the 'imperative to avoid having the Convention inculpate Stalin's purges' of the Kulaks during the late 1920s and early 1930s.[79] Dramatically, such an imperative was respected as, under this exclusion, for many years Stalin's extensive mass-murders of ethnic groups in the Soviet Union were not acknowledged as genocide.

During the drafting, delegates suggested that, where acts fell outside the scope of the definition because the victims did not belong to one of the groups enumerated, the offence 'could also constitute crimes against humanity when committed against members of other groups, including

[78] Robinson, Nehemiah, *The Genocide Convention – A Commentary*, Institute of Jewish Affairs – World Jewish Congress, 1960, pp 61-62.
[79] For a description of these purges, see Kuper, Leo, *Genocide : Its Political Use in the Twentieth Century*, Yale University Press, 1981, pp 146-50.

social and political groups'.[80] In other words, the delegates did acknowledge the fact that genocide was indeed possible against other groups than those expressly cited, but estimated that these groups did not deserve the protection of the Genocide Convention, which was then more efficient than the one offered by the concept of crimes against humanity. One has to remember that, at the time, it was not clear whether crimes against humanity could be qualified as such if they were committed in time of peace, the IMT having ruled that crimes against humanity had to be connected with war.[81] As a result, the numerous groups excluded from the conventional scope of application were left without any protection, and the draftsmen of the convention proved very hypocritical in suggesting that they could be protected through the apparently broader concept of crimes against humanity. One could argue that this problem is now completely solved due to the fact that it has been recognised that crimes against humanity could also occur in time of peace, and that this latter concept now definitely has a wider scope of application.[82] In this respect, it might be noted that the ICTR Statute indirectly acknowledged the reality of genocide committed on political grounds, as such grounds were actually added in its definition of crimes against humanity, in order to allow for the prosecution of acts against Hutu opponents, which are not covered by the convention.[83]

In any case, this distinction among groups is still highly questionable. In the words of Donnedieu de Vabres:

> [g]enocide is an odious crime, regardless of the group which falls victim to it [...], the exclusion of political groups might be regarded as justifying genocide in the case of such groups.[84]

Although this might be an extreme – and wrong – interpretation as crimes against political groups are excluded from the conventional sphere of protection rather than 'justified' and as such crimes would still qualify as crimes against humanity, it still remains that there is no reason why genocide against some groups should be considered as a crime against humanity, and not as genocide. If genocide is happening, then the adequate term must be used to describe the criminal acts.

[80] Report of the Ad Hoc Committee on the Establishment of an International Criminal Court, UN Doc A/50/22, pp 12-13, para 61.
[81] See *supra* I A.
[82] Ibid.
[83] See Article 3 of the ICTR Statute.
[84] UN Doc E/447, p 22.

It has been argued that the exclusion of 'political groups' from the scope of the convention was due to the fact that such groups were neither stable nor permanent.[85] For instance, LeBlanc accepted the exclusion of political groups because of the 'difficulty inherent in selecting criteria for determining what constitutes a political group' and because of 'their instability over time'.[86] However, such an argument is far from being convincing. Indeed, apart from the so-called racial groups, the other groups enumerated in the convention do not appear to be stable or permanent.[87] In fact, one day after the adoption of the Genocide Convention, the General Assembly adopted the UDHR, of which Articles 15 (2) and 18 expressly recognise the rights to change nationality as well as religion respectively.[88] Furthermore, history showed that political opinion or belonging to a social group could be seen as a permanent feature of a given individual. Thus, if we take the example of Cambodia, the Khmer Rouge believed that some social groups were globally criminal, that they were criminal by nature, *per se*, and that this 'crime' was transmitted to spouses as well as to descendants,[89] through a '*hereditarisation*' of the acquired social features. In the words of Kuper, 'past political affiliation can be as ineradicable a stigma, and as irrevocable a warrant for murder as racial or ethnic origin'.[90]

Another reason given in order to justify the exclusion of political groups from the convention's scope of application was the 'right of the State to protect itself',[91] to respond to disturbing elements in its own country. Such an argument is obviously highly immoral as it expressly recognises the possibility for the state to commit genocide in order to repress political opposition and to take action against subversive elements. Should it be recalled that genocide is never justifiable or admissible? As Lane rightly pointed out the elimination of political groups from the convention:

[85] During the Ad Hoc Committee's debates, Lebanon's representative argued that political groups were far less stable in character than the other groups mentioned (UN Doc E/AC.25/SR.4, p 10), while China's representative questioned the fact that political groups 'had neither the stability nor the homogeneity of an ethnical group'. He further stated that 'there was a risk of bringing about a confusion between the idea of political crime and that of genocide' (UN Doc E/AC.25/SR.3, pp 5-6).

[86] LeBlanc, Lawrence J., 'The United Nations Genocide Convention and Political Groups: Should the United States Propose an Amendment?', (1988) 13 *YJIL* 292.

[87] This is certainly why the ICTR has been seen as giving a wrong interpretation of the Convention in the *Akayesu* case by resorting to the 'stable and permanent group' concept. *Prosecutor* v *Akayesu*, Case No. ICTR-96-4-T, Judgment, Trial Chamber I, 2 September 1998, para 515.

[88] Article 15(2) provides that 'No one shall be [...] denied the right to change his nationality' and Article 18 that 'Everyone has the right to [...] freedom to change his religion'.

[89] Children were deemed to be 'dangerous' until the third generation.

[90] Kuper, Leo, *The Prevention of Genocide*, Yale University Press, 1985, p 127.

[91] LeBlanc, Lawrence J., *supra* n 86.

> [c]reates a serious loophole in the Convention's scheme, for not only does it leave unprotected political groups *per se*, but also suggests that the mass killing of protected groups may be justifiable for political reasons. This is of particular concern in the Cambodian setting, where the alleged mass killing had been directed to a large extent at the regime's middle-class constituency.[92]

Again, we here have to disagree with Lane in that the exclusion of political groups from the conventional ambit does not justify their extermination. The conventional restrictions have an impact on the legal qualification of the crime but not on its recognition and acknowledgment as a crime.

In any event, it appears clear that none of the reasons brought forward in order to justify the conventional selective protection of groups are valid. As a matter of fact, political groups are excluded from the conventional sphere of protection on the grounds that they are neither stable nor permanent, and that they may represent a threat to a government's authority. If this was so, why would entire families be completely eradicated?[93] Why would children be murdered? How can someone honestly believe that a child can have so strong a political opinion that he or she should be killed for it?[94]

From the *travaux préparatoires* of the convention, it is obvious that such a shortfall is due to political reasons, notably the desire to insulate political leadership from scrutiny and liability. As Kuper rightly noted, 'the real issue was the freedom of governments to dispose of political opposition without interference from the outside world'.[95] As Van Schaack pointed out, the exclusion of political groups in the convention results 'in a legal regime that insulates political leaders from being charged with the very crime that they may be most likely to commit: the extermination of politically threatening groups'.[96]

---

[92] Lane, Eric, 'Mass Killings by Governments : Lawful in the World Legal Order ?', (1979) 12 *New York University International Law and Politics* 261-62.

[93] Whole families were indeed executed during the Indonesian anti-communist genocide, as well as in Soviet Russia under the Stalinist regime, and in Cambodia under Pol Pot's regime.

[94] There was in fact a Jewish child imprisoned in Drancy in May 1944 under this mention: 'Boy, 18 months, terrorist'. The horror of genocide clearly has no limit. See de Fontette, François, *Histoire de l'Antisémitisme*, Presses Universitaires de France, Collection Que Sais-Je?, p 111.

[95] Kuper, Leo, *The Prevention of Genocide*, Yale University Press, 1985, p 16.

[96] Van Schaack, Beth, *supra* n 63, p 2268.

Once again, the argument of state sovereignty had the lead over that of Justice. Indeed, it can easily be argued that most states would never had ratified the Convention had it extended protection to political groups, even if it can already be pointed out that some national laws do recognise genocide committed on political grounds.[97] Nonetheless, during the drafting, some representatives feared that the inclusion of political groups in Article II might jeopardise support for the Convention in many states. In other words, states wanted to keep a possibility to commit genocide against their own citizens. As a result, Article II of the Genocide Convention embodies a regime which ensures disparate protection to victims of genocide on completely arbitrary grounds. It also leads, as previously mentioned, to the wrong understanding that some acts were somehow justified and legalised by omission. For instance, in the words of Chalk, the exclusion of political and social groups from the protection of the Genocide Convention means:

> [i]gnoring the 15 to 20 million Soviet civilians liquidated as 'class enemies' and 'enemies of the people' between 1920 and 1939; [...] neglecting the roughly 300,000 mentally impaired and mentally ill Germans and others murdered by the Nazis as 'life unworthy of life'; [...] overlooking the thousands of homosexuals killed by the Nazis because of their sexual orientation; [...] disregarding the million of more Khmer murdered by the State and the Communist party of Kampuchea in the years from 1975 to 1978.[98]

If this statement is only partially true as some of the acts referred to by Chalk were in fact not genocide but rather crimes against humanity, it still is that 'membership to social categories had proven lethal to millions of human beings'.[99] Some scholars tried to resolve this situation by introducing the notion of 'politicide', meaning genocide on a political basis and thus covering the killings of members of political groups.[100] The term 'sociocide' could also be used to designate genocide on a social basis. However, this is not a proper solution as it does not answer the question whether these killings are or are not genocide. In the affirmative, then the word 'genocide' should be employed. Furthermore,

[97] See *infra*.

[98] Chalk, Frank, 'Redefining Genocide', in Andreopoulos G.J. (ed), *Genocide: Conceptual and Historical Dimensions*, University of Pennsylvania Press, 1997, p 50.

[99] Chalk, Frank, 'Definitions of Genocide and their Implications for Prediction and Prevention', (1989) 4 *Holocaust and Genocide Studies* 150-51.

[100] Professor Paust even proposed a new draft convention on the Crime of Politicide. See Fein, Helen, 'Genocide : A Sociological Perspective', (1990) 38 *Current Sociology* 11. See also Harff, Barbara and Gurr, Ted Robert, 'Victims of the State: Genocides, Politicides and Group Repressions since 1945', (1990) 1 *International Review of Victimology* 23-41. They distinguish between two categories of genocides and four types of politicides.

the introduction of new words only complicates existing int law by creating numerous distinctions which completely e notion of its meaning.

Moreover, one can really wonder why the convention does not include political groups while other major instruments include the category of political groups among the protected ones. Indeed, the prohibition of crimes against humanity as defined by Article 6(c) of the IMT Charter prohibits persecutions on '*political*, racial or religious grounds'.[101] Article I of the Convention relating to the Status of Refugees provides for protection of individuals from persecution on account of 'race, religion, nationality, membership in a particular *social* group, or *political* opinion'.[102] In other words, the Genocide Convention here creates 'an internally inconsistent human rights regime'.[103] The prohibition of genocide against political groups is also expressed in various national legislations, thus allowing for prosecutions in this case. This is expressly the case in Ethiopia[104] and in Costa Rica.[105] In Peru, the prohibition includes 'social groups', and, by extension, political ones. [106] Finally, in France and in Romania, the protection is broader and the definition provides a 'catch all' category: while the French Penal Code refers to 'un groupe déterminé à partir de tout autre critère arbitraire',[107] the Romanian one prohibits the destruction of a 'collectivity'.[108]

According to Chalk and Jonassohn, 'the wording of the Convention is so restrictive that not one of the genocidal killings committed since its adoption is covered by it'.[109] In fact, it could also be held that not one of the genocides ever committed is covered by the convention. As a matter of fact, it could be argued that the Armenians, seen as a political threat in the Ottoman Empire, were a political group, and thus that their extermination was not genocide. In fact, such an absurd conclusion could also be drawn from the Shoah itself, as the Jews were considered as 'enemies of the Reich'.[110] Moreover, it is not entirely sure that Jews

[101] Emphasis added.
[102] Article 1 (A) (2) of the 1951 Convention relating to the Status of Refugees. Reprinted in *The Raoul Wallenberg Compilation* 347-359. Emphasis added.
[103] Van Schaack, Beth, *supra* n 63, p.2283.
[104] Article 281 of the Ethiopian Penal Code (1957).
[105] Article 373 of the Costa Rican Penal Code. Also, Article 127 of the Costa Rican Penal Code Project (1998) offers an extremely wide protection as the definition of genocide covers gender, age, political, sexual, social, economic and civil groups.
[106] Article 319 of the Peruvian Penal Code (1998).
[107] Article 211-1 of the Nouveau Code Pénal.
[108] Article 356 of the Romanian Socialist Republic Penal Code (1976).
[109] Chalk, Frank and Jonassohn, Kurt, *The History and Sociology of Genocide – Analyses and Case Studies,* Yale University Press, 1990, p 11.
[110] Adolf Eichmann himself argued that he had always called Jews 'enemies of the Reich'. See Arendt, Hannah, *Eichmann à Jérusalem – Rapport sur la Banalité du Mal,* Gallimard, Collection Folio-Histoire, 1997 (original 1966), p 81.

could be seen as an ethnic, racial, religious or national group. As Sartre stated:

> [l]a communauté juive n'est ni nationale, ni internationale, ni religieuse, ni ethnique, ni politique: c'est une communauté quasi historique [...] Ce corps quasi historique ne saurait être considéré comme un élément étranger dans la société.[111]

Furthermore, in the words of Drost:

> [a] convention on genocide cannot effectively contribute to the protection of certain described minorities when it is limited to particular defined groups [...] it serves no purpose to restrict international legal protection to some groups; firstly, because the protected members always belong at the same time to other unprotected groups.[112]

Dramatically, the opinion of the French representative during the drafting of the convention proved to be prophetic. He had indeed warned that 'whereas in the past crimes of genocide had been committed on racial or religious grounds, it was clear that in the future they would be committed mainly on political grounds'.[113] Events since the adoption of the Genocide Convention did show that political groups are targeted for genocide in many countries. As a matter of fact, the Whitaker Report acknowledged the importance of such killings and proposed to include them in an additional optional protocol. This would already be a first step towards the protection of other groups than those expressly cited in Article II of the Convention.[114]

Political and social groups are not the only groups 'omitted' in the Genocide Convention. Indeed, while the atrocities of the Second World

[111] Sartre, Jean-Paul, *Réflexions sur la Question Juive*, Gallimard, Collection Idées, 1954, p 176.

[112] Drost, Pieter N., *The Crime of State – Penal Protection for Fundamental Freedoms of Persons and Peoples, Book II: Genocide – United Nations Legislation on International Criminal Law*, A.W. Sythoff, 1959, pp 122-3. Kuper also noted this interweaving of the political with the racial, ethnic, or religious massacres, notably due to the fact that 'in situations of group conflict, the internal divisions become politicized, and political division tends more and more to coincide with ethnic (or racial and religious) origin. Thus political mass murders and the ethnic factor become interwoven, raising difficult problems of classification'. See Kuper, Leo, *The Prevention of Genocide*, Yale University Press, 1985, p 127.

[113] UN ECOSOC, Session 7, 26 August 1948, p 723. On the contrary, the Swedish representative curiously stated that 'it seemed that all States could guarantee that limited measure of protection [against physical destruction] to political groups'. See UN Doc A/C.6/75, p 114.

[114] See Whitaker Report, p 19, para 37.

War provided the stimulus for the convention, nothing is said about the mentally-ill who were exterminated by the Nazis, or about the homosexuals who were also victims of persecutions and murders. The purpose here is not to go into the debate whether these crimes were genocide or crimes against humanity – and it is in fact most probable that they were crimes against humanity rather than genocide due to the lack of 'hereditarisation', or 'racialisation', of the specific features of victims, 'hereditarisation', or 'racialisation', which constitutes the specific element of the crime of genocide. And, indeed, the crime of genocide lies precisely in the transmissibility of the individual features of the victims to their descendants, thus leading directly to the destruction of the targeted group as a whole. Nonetheless, it is still submitted here that, even if at the time of the drafting these subject matters were taboos, we are now in the 21st century, and it is about time to recognise the potential vulnerability of other groups than those expressly listed in the Convention.

In any event, as Schabas rightly stated, 'determining the meaning of the groups protected by the Convention seems to dictate a degree of subjectivity. It is the offender who defines the individual victim's status as a member of a group protected by the Convention'.[115] This subjective approach was upheld by Trial Chamber I of the ICTY in the *Krstić* case in which it found that the protected group could be qualified 'by using as a criterion the stigmatisation of the group, notably by the perpetrators of the crime, on the basis of its perceived national, ethnical, racial or religious characteristics'.[116] More recently, in the *Blagojević and Jokić* case, the trial chamber confirmed this position and found that 'the correct determination of the relevant protected group has to be made on a case-by-case basis, consulting both objective and subjective criteria.'[117]

Thus, it is in fact the perpetrator of the genocide himself or herself who identifies the group as such, often by giving it a false identity, and who then may, or may not, decide to afford the group he or she aims at annihilating the protection of the convention ... as well as the possibility to be himself or herself prosecuted! Needless to say that, in such circumstances, the perpetrator will do everything to avoid punishment, simply by arguing that the targeted group is not among those

[115] Schabas, William A., *Genocide in International Law – The Crimes of Crimes*, Cambridge University Press, 2000, p 109.

[116] *Prosecutor* v *Krstić*, Case No IT-98-33, Judgment, Trial Chamber I, 2 August 2001, para 557. The chamber nonetheless observed that objective criteria, and notably 'the socio-historic context which [the group] inhabits', must also be identified in order to qualify the relevant group. Ibid.

[117] *Prosecutor* v *Blagojević and Jokić*, Case No IT-02-60-T, Judgment, Trial Chamber I, 17 January 2005, para 667.

enumerated in the convention. According to Chalk and Jonassohn, 'potential perpetrators have taken care to victimise only those groups that are not covered by the Convention's definition'.[118]

We will here conclude by regretting the fact that the absence of several groups from the Genocide Convention's sphere of protection:

> [h]as unfortunately had the effect of diverting discussion from what to do to deter or remedy a concrete situation of mass killings into a debilitating, confusing debate over the question of whether a situation is 'legally' genocide.[119]

Ultimately, it must be acknowledged that '[t]he world cannot afford to ignore this form of genocide simply because most of its victims were not selected as members of racial, religious, or ethnic groups'.[120] Here again, grounds for commission being seen more extensively in the case of crimes against humanity, the definition of the crime of genocide should be inspired by that of crimes against humanity. Further, Trial Chamber I of the ICTY, in the *Krstić* case, actually identified the similarities between grounds for commission in the context of crimes against humanity and in the context of genocide:

> [t]he limitation to certain types of 'group' as defined in the crime of genocide is far more specific than the 'civilian population' defined in the crimes against humanity. The requirement in Article 5 that the crimes be part of a widespread or systematic attack against a civilian population is comprised within the genocide requirement that there be an intent to destroy a specified type of group.[121]

Nevertheless it has to be acknowledged that the trial chamber probably erred in this assertion as totally operating a merge between the two types of crimes might hold the risk of deleting their specific features and, as Mettraux observed:

> A protected 'group' under the genocide regime differs from a 'population' for the purpose of crimes against humanity. A population may contain several protected groups, and a

[118] Ibid.

[119] Hawk, David, as cited in Chalk, Frank, 'Definitions of Genocide and their Implications for Prediction and Prevention', (1989) 4 *Holocaust and Genocide Studies* 151.

[120] Chalk, Frank and Jonassohn, Kurt, *The History and Sociology of Genocide - Analyses and Case Studies*, Yale University Press, 1990, p 407.

[121] *Prosecutor* v *Krstić*, Case No IT-98-33, Judgment, Trial Chamber I, 2 August 2001, para 682.

> widespread and systematic attack upon a civilian population may have no discriminatory effect upon any particular protected group that forms part thereof. The attack could, for instance, have been directed against a certain civilian population which is not distinguishable on national, ethnic, racial or religious grounds from the attacking side.[122]

This position was in fact upheld by the Appeals Chamber of the ICTR itself in the *Musema* case:

> Genocide requires proof of an intent to destroy, in whole or in part, a national, ethnical, racial or religious group; this is not required by extermination as a crime against humanity. Extermination as a crime against humanity requires proof that the crime was committed as a part of a widespread or systematic attack against a civilian population, which proof is not required in the case of genocide.[123]

In order to avoid emptying both the notions of crimes against humanity and of genocide of their respective meanings by equating their definitional elements, it is here submitted that the scope of the prohibition of genocide should be extended. This could notably be achieved, as suggested earlier, through the adoption of an illustrative list of protected groups. Consequently, the prohibition of genocide would become truly effective as it would in fact apply to cases of ... genocide. In that sense, the definition of genocide would draw upon that of crimes against humanity by similarly covering a wider array of groups, without however losing its specificity as enshrined in the notion of 'group' rather than of 'civilian population'. Indeed, the uniqueness of the crime of genocide lies on the arbitrary definition of the group made by the genociders themselves, on their *racialisation* by the perpetrators of the genocide and, precisely because the law cannot penetrate the evil mind, because it cannot foresee or predict any future artificial qualification of the group, it cannot be effective if it exhaustively lists the potential vulnerable groups. Thus, an extension of the groups covered by the prohibition of genocide would not deprive the crime of its specificity; it would simply make its definition applicable.

[122] Mettraux, Guénaël, *International Crimes and the Ad Hoc Tribunals*, Oxford University Press, 2005, p 332.

[123] *Prosecutor* v *Musema*, Case No ICTR-96-13-A, Judgment, Appeals Chamber, 16 November 2001, para 366.

C. The specificity of genocide: the intent requirement

The real difference between crimes against humanity and genocide is the very particular intent which gives the crime of genocide all its specificity. In the context of crimes against humanity, no specific intent is required. What is needed is knowledge that the crimes are committed within the context of a widespread or systematic attack against a civilian population. In fact, according to the case law of the ICTY's Appeals Chamber, as long as the accused knew that the crimes were related to an attack on a civilian population, such an act could qualify as a crime against humanity.[124]

For the purposes of the present book, which is to redefine international criminal law in order to enhance its applicability and application, the genocidal intent is precisely what distinguishes the crime of genocide from any other crimes. Thus, while the definition of genocide should, as previously stressed, draw upon the notion of crimes against humanity with respect to all its other definitional requirements, the specific and particular intent should remain the differentiating factor between crimes against humanity and genocide.

The different acts covered by the Genocide Convention constitute only one element of the crime of genocide, the other element is a very specific criminal intent: those acts constitute genocide only if committed with 'the *intent* to destroy in whole or in part, a national, ethnical, racial, or religious groups, as such'.[125] The reference to 'intent' in the convention indicates that not only must the offender have meant to engage in the conduct or to cause the consequences of his or her conduct, he or she must also have had a 'specific intent' or *dolus specialis*. Indeed, it appears from the debates during the drafting of the text that the drafters chose the intent to destroy the group as the distinctive element in genocide.[126] The draftsmen thus wanted clearly to distinguish 'the international crime of genocide from the municipal crime of homicide'.[127] As a result, if such a specific intent is not established, the act remains punishable

[124] *Prosecutor* v *Tadić*, Case No. IT-94-1-A, Judgment, Appeals Chamber, 15 July 1999, para 121. See also *Prosecutor* v *Kupreškić*, Case No. IT-95-16, Judgment, Trial Chamber II, 14 January 2000, para 550.

[125] Article II of the Genocide Convention. Emphasis added.

[126] 3 UN GAOR, Sixth Committee, 89-97 (1948). Cited in Bryant, Bunyan, 'Substantive Scope of the Convention' in 'Comment: The United States and the 1948 Genocide Convention, Part I', (1975) 16 *HILJ* 692.

[127] Ibid. In this respect, Robinson also pointed out that 'from the viewpoint of the minority groups, which are or may be exposed to acts described in the Convention, it makes a great difference whether those who commit these acts against them are prosecuted on that basis or only on the basis of ordinary violations of the criminal code'. See Robinson, Nehemiah, *The Genocide Convention – A Commentary*, Institute of Jewish Affairs – World Jewish Congress, 1960, pp 33-34.

but not as genocide. Schabas believes that it may be classified as a crime against humanity.[128] In fact, echoing the District Court of Jerusalem in the *Eichmann* case,[129] the ILC also noted that, where the specific intent cannot be established, the crime may still meet the conditions to qualify as a crime against humanity, namely, that of persecution.[130]

In the *Akayesu* case, Trial Chamber I of the ICTR pointed out that 'intent is a mental factor which is difficult, even impossible, to determine', adding that, without confession of the accused, intent can only be 'inferred from a certain number of presumptions of fact'.[131] Applying this to the case, the trial chamber found that it was possible to infer the genocidal intent of the accused.

The position of the ICTY seems however to be different and it may be pointed out here that the difficulties proving the genocidal intent as to the crimes committed in Kosovo led to the abandonment of the charge of genocide in the indictment of Milošević. Similarly, in the *Jelisić* case, Trial Chamber I of the ICTY considered that the prosecution had failed to prove the genocidal intent beyond reasonable doubt and thus unanimously acquitted the accused for the charge of genocide. Fortunately, the ICTY Appeals Chamber subsequently recognised that 'the Trial Chamber erred in law'[132] and unequivocally held that 'this evidence [on the record that was presented by the prosecution during the appeal] and much more of a similar genre in the record could have provided the basis for a *reasonable chamber* to find beyond a *reasonable doubt* that the respondent had the intent to destroy the Muslim group'.[133] Even though the appeals chamber decided that there should not be a retrial in this case,[134] its express reference to the notion of *reasonableness* in the assessment of evidence in cases of alleged genocide is to be welcomed. [135] This reasonableness concept might indeed be used as a useful criterion on which judges will be able to rely in order to induce the genocidal intent and the perpetration of genocide from factual evidence.

[128] Schabas, William A., *Genocide in International Law – The Crimes of Crimes,* Cambridge University Press, 2000, p 214.
[129] *Attorney-General of the Government of Israel* v *Eichmann,* 36 ILR 18 (Israel District Court – Jerusalem, 1961), para 25.
[130] Report of the ILC on the Work of Its Forty-Eighth Session, 6 May-26 July 1996, UN Doc A/51/10, p 87.
[131] *Prosecutor* v *Akayesu,* Case No ICTR-96-4-T, Judgment, Trial Chamber I, para 523. Already in his 1985 Report, Whitaker suggested that 'a court should be able to infer the necessary intent from sufficient evidence'. See Whitaker Report, p 19, para 39.
[132] See *Prosecutor* v *Jelisić,* Case No IT-95-10-A, Appeal Judgment, Appeals Chamber, 5 July 2001, para.75.
[133] Ibid, para 68. Emphasis added.
[134] Ibid, para 77.
[135] Ibid, para 68.

The *Jelisić* case illustrated the difficulty of proving that a given commander specifically intended to destroy a particular group. However, the principle of command responsibility might facilitate the prosecution of a commander when his or her subordinates have committed genocide. It is true that the convention is silent on the subject but the ICC Statute clearly established the responsibility of commanders and other superiors in its Article 28.[136]

Proving the specific genocidal intent in the case of obedience to superior orders is however more problematic. As the Genocide Convention is yet again silent on this matter, it could be argued that such a defence is permissible in the case of genocide. Nonetheless, the prohibition of the defence of superior orders has now been clearly established. Indeed, the ILC's 1954 Draft Code of Offences excluded this defence in its Article 4, while its 1996 Draft Code of Crimes excluded it in its Article 5. Similarly, Article 7 (4) of the ICTY Statute and Article 6(4) of the ICTR Statute rejected this defence, even if it still 'may be considered in mitigation of punishment'. Finally, it was also rejected by the Rome Statute in its Article 33, even though this equivocal provision is far from being satisfying as it still lists circumstances in which the person accused might be relieved. According to this Article:

> 1. The fact that a crime within the jurisdiction of the court has been committed by a person pursuant to an order of a government or of a superior, whether military or civilian, shall not relieve that person of criminal responsibility unless:
>   (a) the person was under a legal obligation to obey orders of the government or the superior in question;
>   (b) the person did not know that the order was unlawful; and
>   (c) the order was not manifestly unlawful.
> 2. For the purposes of this article, orders to commit genocide or crimes against humanity are manifestly unlawful.

The wording of this Article is all the most problematic as, although paragraph 2 unequivocally recognises the illegality of orders to commit genocide, thus excluding any exception to criminal responsibility in such cases, it still seems that the two exceptions contained in sub-paragraphs (a) and (b) could still be admissible even in cases of genocide.

[136] Previously, Article 7(3) of the ICTY Statute and Article 6(3) of the ICTR Statute had established the criminal responsibility of a superior.

If this is so, it would be a great step backwards compared with the trend started at Nuremberg and subsequently adhered to by all major instruments.

The real problem with the conventional requirement of a specific intent is that, if such intent cannot be proved, the persecutors will have to be acquitted of the charge of genocide. Genociders may thus easily deny the commission of genocide by simply arguing that the required intent to destroy a group in whole or in part was lacking and absent.[137] It may be recalled here that, during the drafting of the convention, France as well as the Soviet Union were both concerned about this issue and about the danger that the definition of the intentional element might be too narrow and might thus result in acquittals.[138] Some scholars also identified this risk of acquittals: as Lane wrote, 'the requirement of intent adds a subjective factor to the definition and thus potentially provides an escape from responsibility for mass killing'.[139]

To remedy this inextricable situation, recognition of a crime of 'negligent genocide' or 'genocide in the second degree' has been proposed.[140] Nevertheless, this solution is hardly satisfying as it is based on the completely incoherent proposal that genocide could be committed by negligence, carelessness or imprudence, and as it thus totally erases the fact that genocide is intentional *per se.* Instead of giving a solution to this problem, this suggestion would totally empty the notion of genocide of its meaning and purpose, and would render this horrendous crime somehow ridiculous and absurd. There cannot be genocide without

[137] For instance, in *Genocide in Paraguay,* Arens provided great evidence that genocide was committed against the Aché Indians. However, the Paraguayan Government however claimed that there was no 'intent to destroy' and that therefore genocide was not being committed. Cited in LeBlanc, Lawrence J., 'The intent to destroy groups in the Genocide Convention: The proposed US understanding', (1984) 78 *AJIL* 380.

[138] UN Doc A/C.6/SR.73 (Chaumont, France ; Morozov, Soviet Union).

[139] Lane, Eric, 'Mass Killings by Governments: Lawful in the World Legal Order ?', (1979) 12 *New York University International Law and Politics* 262. He also referred to Drost who wrote that 'measures resulting in the partial or total destruction of a group but taken without the intention of such purpose and result do not fall under the definition and therefore do not constitute acts of genocide under the Convention'. See Drost, Pieter N., *The Crime of State – Penal Protection for Fundamental Freedoms of Persons and Peoples, Book II: Genocide – United Nations Regulation on International Criminal Law,* A.W. Sythoff, 1959, p 82.

[140] Lippman, Matthew, 'The Drafting of the 1948 Convention on the Prevention and Punishment of the Crime of Genocide', (1985) 3 *Boston University International Law Journal* 1-62. See also Clark, Roger S., 'Does the Genocide Convention go Far Enough ? Some thoughts on the nature of criminal genocide in the context of Indonesia's Invasion of East Timor', (1981) 8 *Ohio Northern University Law Review* 328: 'the Genocide Convention should be expanded to include negligent as well as reckless everyday genocide within its ambit.'

intention; this is just not possible.[141] Thus, the convention should not be criticised for not including unintentional or negligent genocide, as it does not exist.

Ultimately, it has to be acknowledged that genocidal intent is best revealed in initiatives that actually have genocidal results. As Bryant rightly pointed out:

> [u]nless the intent were express, [...] the intent to destroy the group could be difficult or impossible to prove, except in those instances where the mere number of people of the group affected was significant. Practically speaking, then, the number of victims may be of evidentiary value with respect to proving the necessary intent.[142]

Indeed, intent can be inferred mainly from concrete results together producing the genocide.[143] Thus, genocidal intent can be very difficult to prove, and there is thus a real risk of seeing a crime of genocide being wrongly qualified as a crime against humanity because the specific intent could not be proved. A positive step has nonetheless been taken by the ICTY which, drawing upon the knowledge requirement in the context of crimes against humanity and thus using the concept of 'knowledge', has stated that 'the offender is culpable [of genocide] because *he knew or should have known* that the act committed would destroy, in whole or in part, a group'.[144] Even if this has remained an isolated sentence, it is true that it could lead the way to the recognition of indirect means to prove the genocidal intent, by, in fact, bringing together the notions of genocide and of crimes against humanity while still acknowledging the criminal state of mind of the crime's perpetrator.[145]

[141] See Chalk, Frank, 'Definitions of Genocide and their Implications for Prediction and Prevention', (1989) 4 *Holocaust and Genocide Studies* 189: 'genocide is primarily a crime of state and empirically it has not been true that it appears without intent.'

[142] Bryant, Bunyan, 'Substantive Scope of the Convention' in 'Comment: The United States and the 1948 Genocide Convention, Part I', (1975) 16 *HILJ* 692.

[143] In this respect, it might be noted that Article III of the Genocide Convention incriminates 'conspiracy to commit genocide', thus making punishable the anticipation of the crime of genocide itself. However, Article 25 of the ICC Statute on individual criminal responsibility expressly restricts this offence by providing that the planning and organising of genocide not followed by the commission of the crime is not a crime the ICC will be able to prosecute. It is to be hoped that the court will nonetheless use the factual evidence emerging from such a planning and organising in order to prove the genocidal intent.

[144] *Prosecutor* v *Akayesu*, Case No. ICTR-96-4-T, Judgment, Trial Chamber I, 2 September 1998, para.519. Emphasis added.

[145] As opposed to the recognition of 'reckless' genocides.

D. Filling in the gaps of the Genocide Convention

The previous developments have highlighted the failures of the Genocide Convention. This instrument indeed contains some serious shortcomings and, due to its very narrow sphere of protection, its application in practice is extremely limited. The question which thus arises is whether a convention on genocide was itself desirable. Far from being a new one, this question had already been raised during the drafting of the Genocide Convention. As a matter of fact, on 20 November 1947, the Sixth Committee adopted a draft resolution on genocide which made a recommendation to the Economic and Social Council to study this question.[146] During the drafting in the Sixth Committee, this point was also debated as the representative of the Union of South Africa doubted whether a convention, as contemplated, would be practicable and effective.[147] Sir Shawcross, the representative of the United Kingdom, was also very critical of the idea of a convention and stated that:

> [i]t was a complete delusion to suppose that the adoption of a convention of the type proposed, even if generally adhered to, would give people generally a greater sense of security or would diminish the dangers that at present existed of persecution on racial, religious, or national grounds.[148]

He further noted that genocide was already a crime under international law, as a consequence of the IMT judgment, and thus believed that a convention would defeat the purpose it sought to achieve because the failure to ratify by some states would undermine the claim that it stood for universally accepted principles.[149]

On the other hand, some expressed the view that the crime of genocide was to be dealt with in a convention as, 'under the Nuremberg law, genocide is not an international crime if not committed in connection with or during war'.[150] If this was true at the time, this argument is now completely obsolete, the required nexus between war and crimes against humanity having been abolished,[151] and the crime of genocide having been recognised in time of war as well as in time of peace.[152]

---

[146] UN Doc A/510.
[147] UN Doc A/C.6/SR.64/p 2.
[148] UN Doc A/C.6/SR.64/p 9.
[149] UN Doc A/C.6/SR.39 (Shawcross, United Kingdom).
[150] Tillott, Charles W., Chairman of the Section of International and Comparative Law of the American Bar Association. Cited in Robinson, Nehemiah, *The Genocide Convention – A Commentary*, Institute of Jewish Affairs – World Jewish Congress, 1960, p 45.
[151] See *supra* I A.
[152] Article I of the Genocide Convention.

One of the biggest problems caused by a convention is that its application necessarily depends on ratification. The Convention, adopted on 9 December 1948, entered into force three years later, on 12 January 1951. A convention will indeed only apply to the states which have ratified it, international agreements being only binding on the parties to them. Thus, assuming that such a convention was enforceable, such enforcement could only be directed against contracting Parties. Still today, the Genocide Convention only has 132 States Parties, 'a rather unimpressive statistic when compared with the other major human rights treaties of the United Nations system which, while considerably younger, have managed to approach a more general degree of support by the nations of the world'.[153]

Furthermore, the application of the convention may vary from one state to another, depending on when a particular state has ratified it. For instance, the United States of America became a party to the Convention only on 25 November 1988 ... 40 years after its adoption! The United Kingdom also waited for as long as 22 to finally to accede the Genocide Convention, as it felt that every aspect of the crime was already covered by domestic laws.[154] Also, it may be noted here that the French Penal Code only included the definition of genocide in March 1994.[155]As a result, some judges had declared themselves incompetent as regards crimes committed in Rwanda.[156]

In other words, the punishment of the crime of genocide depends on whether the perpetrator state has ratified the convention or not. It is true that the outlawing of genocide is now part of international customary law, and that, as such, it should also apply to non-parties to the Genocide Convention. Similarly, it might well be argued that Article VIII of the Genocide Convention applies to both States Parties and non-parties, as it states that:

[153] Schabas, William A., *Genocide in International Law – The Crimes of Crimes*, Cambridge University Press, 2000, p 4. He compares the state of ratification of the Genocide Convention with that of the 1989 Convention on the Rights of the Child (191 States parties), of the 1965 International Convention for the Elimination of all Forms of Racial Discrimination (153 States Parties), of the 1979 Convention for the Elimination of Discrimination Against Women (163 States Parties), and of the 1949 Geneva Convention relative to the Protection of Civilians (187 States Parties).

[154] The United Kingdom became a party to the Convention on 30 January 1970.

[155] See Article 211-1 of the Nouveau Code Pénal.

[156] See *RSF* v *Mille Collines*, Cour d'Appel de Paris, 6 November 1995 ; *Dupaquier et al* v *Munyeshyaka*, Cour d'Appel de Nîmes, 20 March 1996. The Cour de Cassation subsequently overruled the lower courts' findings and held that French courts could have jurisdiction over acts falling within the jurisdiction of the ICTR. See cass. crim. 6 janvier 1998. Reproduced in (1998) 3 *RGDIP* 825-832.

> Any Contracting Party may call upon the competent organs of the United Nations to take such action under the Charter of the United Nations as they consider appropriate for the prevention and suppression of acts of genocide or any of the other acts enumerated in Article III.[157]

As Professor Kunz noted, 'although only Contracting Parties can invoke [Article VIII] of the Convention, United Nations are called to intervene'.[158] However, this does not render the convention binding upon non-parties as Article VIII is merely a reminder of the powers of the United Nations to act and, so far, international practice has shown that such an allegation has remained purely theoretical.

A convention raises another serious problem, that of the reservations and understandings which undermine the scope of the ratifying states' obligations under this convention.[159] As regards the Genocide Convention, this problem is further aggravated by the complete silence of the convention on that matter. Furthermore, the *travaux préparatoires* are not very explicit on the subject. Consequently, the question of the permissibility of reservations was submitted to the ICJ for an advisory opinion. In its opinion of 21 May 1951, the court laid down a new principle, namely, that of compatibility of the reservation with the object and purpose of the treaty.[160] Subsequently, the General Assembly passed Resolution 598(VI) which recommended that States Parties be guided by the court's advisory opinion.[161] As Nehemiah Robinson rightly pointed out, the difficulty with the advisory opinion is that 'it leaves the "decision" concerning the compatibility to the various parties'.[162] Furthermore, the advisory opinion does not provide for any means of

[157] It must be noted here than Myanmar formulated a reservation as regards Article VIII and excluded its application to the Union of Burma.

[158] Kunz, Josef L., 'The United Nations Convention on Genocide', (1949) 43 *AJIL* 738-46.

[159] On the 132 States parties to the Convention, 29 have formulated reservations, but 10 of these have since been withdrawn. Still, it might be noted here that the United States attached an understanding to its instrument of ratification which provides that 'the term "intent to destroy, in whole or in part, a national, ethnical, racial or religious group, as such" appearing in Article II means the specific intent to destroy, in whole or *in substantial part*, a national, ethnic, racial or religious group as such by the acts specified in Article II'. Emphasis added. See the reservations to the Genocide Convention: www.unhchr.ch/html/menu3/b/treaty1gen.htm. According to LeBlanc, because the understanding contradicts the ordinary meaning of the phrase, it 'thus takes on the character of a reservation, which could lead to justifiable objections by other States parties'. LeBlanc, Lawrence J., 'The Intent to Destroy Groups in the Genocide Convention: The Proposed U.S. Understanding', (1984) 78 *AJIL* 382.

[160] *Reservations to the Convention on the Prevention and Punishment of the Crime of Genocide*, Advisory Opinion, [1951] ICJ Reports 15-30 (28 May).

[161] Resolution of 12 January 1952.

[162] Robinson, Nehemiah, *The Genocide Convention – A Commentary*, Institute of Jewish Affairs – World Jewish Congress, 1960, pp 38-9.

reconciliation in case a reservation generates different views as to its compatibility with the Convention.[163] It merely stated that:

> [i]f a party to the Convention objects to a reservation which it considers to be incompatible with the object and purpose of the Convention, it can in fact consider that the reserving State is not a party to the Convention.[164]

Such a statement can have very dangerous results as many states may consider that one or more states are in fact not parties to the convention, which, in the crucial matter of genocide, could be catastrophic. It seems that some states reacted by not officially objecting to a reservation, which is probably the only solution, even if it is certainly not satisfying.[165]

In any case, it is here submitted that, despite the position of the ICJ, reservations should not be allowed in such crucial matters as genocide. In the words of Judge Alvarez, in a dissenting opinion urging that the Genocide Convention cannot admit any reservations, such conventions as that on genocide:

> [b]y reason of their nature and of the manner in which they have been formulated, constitute an indivisible whole. Therefore, they must not be made the subject of reservations, for that would be contrary to the purposes at which they are aimed, namely, the general interest and also the social interest.[166]

1. *The prohibition of genocide as a peremptory norm of international law* (**jus cogens**)

The outlawing of genocide has frequently been qualified as a universal and peremptory norm of international law.[167] In the words of Judge Elihu Lauterpacht:

[163] See ibid.

[164] *Reservations to the Convention on the Prevention and Punishment of the Crime of Genocide*, Advisory Opinion, [1951] ICJ Reports 29 (28 May).

[165] Robinson, Nehemiah, *supra* n 162, pp 38-39. Robinson illustrated this point by reference to the Canadian position concerning the reservations of the communist states. Being aware of the fact that, even if Canada objected to these reservations, some states will still maintain that they were compatible with the convention. Canada ratified the convention without reference to the reservations, which legally means that it accepted them.

[166] *Reservations to the Convention on the Prevention and Punishment of the Crime of Genocide*, Advisory Opinion, dissenting opinion of M. Alvarez, [1951] ICJ Reports 53 (28 May).

[167] See eg Van Schaack, Beth, 'The Crime of Political Genocide: Repairing the Genocide Convention's Blind Spot', (1997) 106 *Yale L J* 2259-91.

> the prohibition of genocide [...] has generally been accepted as having the status not of an ordinary rule of international law but of *jus cogens*. Indeed the prohibition of genocide has long been regarded as one of the few undoubted examples of *jus cogens*.[168]

Clearly, the prohibition of genocide as embodied in the Genocide Convention is widely accepted, and it has been indeed reproduced in several authoritative instruments.[169] Thus, it seems that it is the conventional outlawing of genocide which is part of *jus cogens*. Nevertheless, it may also be argued that a broader *jus cogens* prohibition of genocide existed prior to the adoption of the Genocide Convention, and that the latter has in fact replaced, and is inconsistent with, the broader *jus cogens* norm. The problem here is that, with the convention, the outlawing of genocide finds itself unduly restricted. This restriction of an existing peremptory norm is highly questionable, and it may thus be ascertained that it is this previous norm which should apply. As Van Schaack rightly argued:

> [t]he Genocide Convention is not the sole authority on the crime of genocide. Rather, a higher law exists. The prohibition of genocide represents the paradigmatic *jus cogens* norm, a customary and peremptory norm of international law from which no derogation is permitted.[170]

The prohibition of genocide can indeed be traced back prior to the adoption of the convention[171] and to the Nuremberg trials when, in the reference to the extermination of any civilian population, genocide was included among crimes against humanity. For instance, already in October 1933, at the Fifth International Conference for the Unification

[168] *Application of the Convention on the Prevention and Punishment of the Crime of Genocide*, Further Requests for the Indication of Provisional Measures, Separate opinion of Judge Lauterpacht, [1993] ICJ Reports 440, para.100 (13 September).

[169] See Article 4 of the ICTY Statute, Article 2 of the ICTR Statute, Article 6 of the ICC Statute.

[170] Van Schaack, Beth, *supra* n 167, 2261.

[171] It might be recalled here that, in Article I of the convention, 'The Contracting Parties *confirm* that genocide [...] is a crime under international law', thus implying the existence of a prior rule. (Emphasis added). In this respect, see the *Eichmann* case in which the Israeli Supreme Court emphasised the existence of the crime of genocide in international law prior to the Genocide Convention, *Attorney-General of the Government of Israel* v *Eichmann*, 36 ILR 277 (Israel Supreme Court, 1962). The court also dismissed an objection by the defendant that he could not be tried for genocide since the Genocide Convention was not in effect at the time of his acts. The court maintained that anyone would know that such acts were legally and morally wrong. Ibid p 282. The UN Secretariat also acknowledged that this was not 'the first time that a convention has been concluded on a matter on which rules of common law already exist'. See UN Doc E/AC.25/3 (1948).

of Penal Law held in Madrid, Lemkin had identified the crime of barbarity which would amount to the actual notion of genocide and he defined it as 'oppressive and destructive actions directed against individuals as members of a national, religious, or racial group'.[172] The fact is, genocide has *always* been illegal, genocide is illegal *per se,* it did not become illegal thanks to the ratification of a Convention, it is illegal in itself. As Beres rightly noted, '[g]enocide is a modern word for an old crime'.[173] So much so that, already in 1947, Lemkin had noted that 'no great difficulties are involved in this field [legislation on genocide] since genocide is a composite crime and consist of acts which are themselves punishable by most existing legislation'.[174] As pointed out in the report of the Committee on Peace and Law through the United Nations, what is left of the convention 'is a code of domestic crimes which are already denominated in all countries as common law crimes.'[175] But if the outlawing of genocide is definitely a *jus cogens* norm, it does not mean that such a norm is embodied in the Genocide Convention or that this convention is of a peremptory character.

First, as the rather small number of States Parties to the Convention suggests, it is far from certain that this instrument has acquired value of *jus cogens*. In this respect, Sir Shawcross was completely correct when he expressed the fear that a convention would defeat the purpose it sought to achieve, because the failure to ratify by some states would undermine the claim that it stood for universally accepted principles.[176] Similarly, Lane pointed out that to consider the Genocide Convention as international common law is a position which 'must be regarded sceptically in light of the reaction of many States which, despite the convention's compelling motivation and unassuming legal nature, have refused to ratify it. This refusal is inconsistent with the international common law characterisation'.[177]

Secondly, it must here be recalled that the convention is not a permanent one and it is thus arguable that the draftsmen of the convention did not intend to generate a *jus cogens* norm. Indeed, the convention was concluded for a period of 10 years with the provision that 'it shall

[172] Lemkin, Raphaël, *Axis Rule in Occupied Europe – Laws of Occupation, Analysis of Government, Proposals for Redress,* Carnegie Endowment for International Peace, Division of International Law, 1944, p 91.
[173] Beres, Louis René, 'Justice and Realpolitik : International Law and the Prevention of Genocide', (1988) 33 *American Journal of Jurisprudence* 123-4.
[174] Lemkin, Raphaël, 'Genocide as a Crime Under International Law', (1947) 41 *AJIL* 150.
[175] Cited in Finch, George A., 'The Genocide Convention', (1949) 43 *AJIL* 735.
[176] UN Doc A/C.6/SR.39 (Shawcross, United Kingdom).
[177] Lane, Eric, 'Mass Killings by Governments: Lawful in the World Legal Order?', (1979) 12 *New York University International Law and Politics* 263-264.

thereafter remain in force for successive periods of five years for such Contracting Parties as have not denounced it'.[178] Also, the convention contains a highly unusual provision for a multilateral convention in its Article XV. As a matter of fact, if, as a result of denunciations, the number of parties to the Convention should become less than 16, the whole convention shall cease to remain in force. Thus, the convention's existence could be easily challenged, while it should have been an authoritative and permanent instrument of protection of human rights. In the words of Drost:

> It shocks the juristic conscience to realize that under the positive law of the Convention genocide is conceived an international crime for an indefinite and uncertain period yet delimited in definite and certain terms of time. The legislators established genocide as a crime under the law of nations on a temporary basis. Under the Convention genocide is considered a crime for the time being. Admittedly, this notion does not refer to the moral nature of the act but, legally speaking, this 'old crime under a new name' may possibly disappear from the international statute book.[179]

Thirdly, the fact that reservations to the Convention are permitted might indicate that its provisions are not customary law. As a matter of fact, in the *North Sea Continental Shelf* cases, the ICJ noted that:

> [s]peaking generally, it is a characteristic of purely conventional rules and obligations that, in regard to them, some faculty of making unilateral reservations may, within certain limits, be admitted; whereas this cannot be so in the case of general or customary law rules and obligations which, by their very nature, must have equal force for all members of the international community, and cannot therefore be the subject of any right of unilateral exclusion exercisable at will by anyone of them in its own favour.[180]

Thus the court concluded that where customary law figures in a convention, it will generally be among the provisions where the right

[178] Article XIV of the Genocide Convention. See Schwelb, Egon, 'Some Aspects of International Jus Cogens as Formulated by the International Law Commission', (1967) 61 *AJIL* 955.

[179] Drost, Pieter N., *The Crime of State – Penal Protection for Fundamental Freedoms of Persons and Peoples ; Book II : Genocide – United Nations Legislation on International Criminal Law,* A.W. Sythoff, 1959, p 134.

[180] *North Sea Continental Shelf* cases, judgment, [1969] ICJ Reports 38-39, para.63 (20 February).

of unilateral reservation is not conferred or is excluded.[181] Clearly, this is not the case of the Genocide Convention as, even if the convention is silent on the matter, the ICJ itself found that reservations were permissible.[182]

Ultimately, as the ICJ ruled in the *Military and Paramilitary Activities in and Against Nicaragua* case, the fact that principles 'have been codified or embodied in multilateral conventions does not mean that they cease to exist and to apply as principles of customary law, even as regards countries that are parties to such conventions'.[183] As a matter of fact, already during the drafting of the convention, the UN Secretariat addressed the issue of the interplay between the *jus cogens* prohibition of genocide and the convention and stated that 'common law retains its full force for the States which have not signed the convention'.[184] Considering the fact that the *jus cogens* prohibition of genocide is broader than the conventional one, this might lead to the absurd situation where a non-ratifying state has in fact more obligations and duties than the States Parties to the convention.

Prior to the adoption of the Genocide Convention, the General Assembly had adopted Resolution 96(I), which reads as follows:

> Genocide is a denial of the right to existence of entire human groups, as homicide is the denial of the right to live of individual human beings; such denial of the right of existence shocks the conscience of mankind, results in great losses to humanity in the form of *cultural* and other contributions represented by these human groups, and is contrary to moral law and the spirit and aims of the United Nations.
>
> Many instances of such crimes of genocide have occurred when racial, religious, *political and other groups* have been destroyed, entirely or in part.
>
> The punishment of the crime of genocide is a matter of *international concern.* [185]

[181] Ibid, p 39, para 63.
[182] *Reservations to the Convention on the Prevention and Punishment of the Crime of Genocide*, Advisory Opinion, [1951] ICJ Reports 15-30 (28 May).
[183] *Military and Paramilitary Activities in and against Nicaragua*, Jurisdiction and Admissibility, Judgment, [1984] ICJ Reports 424 (26 November).
[184] UN Doc E/AC.25/3 (1948).
[185] G.A. Resolution 96(I), UN Doc A/231, (11 December 1946). Emphasis added.

Because the definition of genocide is here broader than the one embodied in the convention, the question arises as to the value of the resolution and of the prohibition it contains. As it is a resolution of the General Assembly, Resolution 96(I) is not a source of binding law. However, it seems that Resolution 96(I) did nothing less than codify an existing peremptory norm of international law. As the ICJ held in 1996:

> The Court notes that General Assembly resolutions, even if they are not binding, may sometimes have normative value. They can, in certain circumstances, provide evidence important for establishing the existence of a rule or the emergence of an *opinio juris*. To establish whether this is true of a given General Assembly resolution, it is necessary to look at its content and the condition of its adoption; it is also necessary to see whether an *opinio juris* exists as to its normative character. Or a series of resolutions may show the gradual evolution of the *opinio juris* required for the establishment of a new rule.[186]

Thus, the General Assembly Resolution 96 (I) can reflect the *opinio juris* of states, especially as it was adopted unanimously and without debate. It is widely acknowledged now that the way states vote in the General Assembly constitutes evidence of state practice and of state understanding of the law. Furthermore, it could also be asserted that, as regards General Assembly resolutions adopted unanimously, 'no question arises as to the legal validity and obligatory nature of General Assembly resolutions, for each State casting a vote could be regarded as bound by that expression of opinion'.[187] Moreover, it has been cited frequently in subsequent instruments and judicial decisions, thus reinforcing the claim that it codifies a customary principle. For example, the United States Military Tribunal cited General Assembly Resolution 96(I) on four occasions and stated that: 'The General Assembly is not an international legislature, but it is the most authoritative organ in existence for the interpretation of world opinion.'[188] The significance of Resolution 96(I) was also enhanced by the statement of the ICJ in its advisory opinion on the *Reservations to the Genocide Convention* case:

> The origins of the Convention show that it was the intention of the United Nations to condemn and punish

[186] *Legality of the Threat or Use of Nuclear Weapons*, Advisory Opinion, [1996] ICJ Reports 254-255, para 70 (8 July).
[187] Green, Leslie C., 'New Trends in International Criminal law', (1981) 11 *Israel Yearbook on Human Rights* 19-20.
[188] *United States* v *Alstoetter et al*, Case No 3, Military Tribunal III, 3 *Nuremberg Subsequent Proceedings* 983.

> genocide as 'a crime under international law' involving a denial of the right of existence of entire human groups, a denial which shocks the conscience of mankind and results in great losses to humanity, and which is contrary to moral law and to the spirit and aims of the United Nations. The first consequence arising from this conception is that the *principles underlying the Convention* are principles which are recognized by civilized nations as binding on States, *even without any conventional obligation.*[189]

This statement illustrates the fact that the convention is not necessarily the decisive element in the outlawing of genocide, as it seems clear that the 'principles underlying the Convention [...] which are binding on States' are these very principles found in Resolution 96 (I). Thus, the court's statement supports the idea that it is the crime of genocide *as defined in the Resolution* which is outlawed as a matter of custom. This does not imply that the General Assembly has legislative power or that the resolution is a source of international law because it only put in a written form the pre-existing peremptory norm. It is indeed arguable that, with the Nuremberg precedent which dealt with genocide as a crime against humanity, 'the prohibition of genocide was already an established principle of international law'.[190] Thus, while for many writers, treaties constitute the most important sources of international law as they require the express consent of the contracting parties, it seems that the court, on its reasoning on the legal prohibition of genocide, did not only rely on the positive element of recognition by states, but also on the underlying moral considerations of the prohibition. The fact is here that states unanimously gave their consent to Resolution 96(I), and, as the representative of Czechoslovakia, Mr. Zourek, stated during the drafting of the Convention:

> although the General Assembly could not by a resolution adopt new rules of law, its resolutions could nevertheless reaffirm already existing laws; as such they would be binding upon the Members, particularly if they were unanimously adopted.[191]

[189] *Reservations to the Convention on the Prevention and Punishment of the Crime of Genocide*, Advisory Opinion, [1951] ICJ Reports 23 (28 May). Emphasis added.

[190] Ragazzi, Maurizio, *The Concept of International Obligations Erga Omnes*, Oxford : Clarendon Press, 1997, p 94.

[191] Cited in Robinson, Nehemiah, *The Genocide Convention – A Commentary*, Institute of Jewish Affairs – World Jewish Congress, 1960, pp 55-6. According to Schwarzenberger, the resolution can be interpreted as creating estoppel, thus a rule of evidence which prevents future denials of the previous statement. See Schwarzenberger, Georg, 'International Jus Cogens?', (1965) 43 *Texas Law Review* 474.

Some would argue that the resolution was adopted hastily and that there is little recorded debate on some important questions, such as the inclusion of political groups within the definition. Furthermore, some important issues were reconsidered and revised during the debates on the convention in 1947 and 1948. Thus, a part of the doctrine believes that 'much caution is advised with respect to claims that Resolution 96(I) constitutes a codification of customary law'.[192] On the contrary, it may also be argued that the fact that there is little recorded debate on the inclusion of political groups means that there was no debate on the question, that it appeared logical to protect them, and that their deletion from the convention was purely due to political considerations which were clearly out of place considering such a crucial issue. Furthermore, it appears that, on this particular point, a considerable number of states took the approach of Resolution 96(I) in their domestic legislation.[193] It is thus probable that, compared to the Genocide Convention, Resolution 96 (I) resembles more domestic provisions on the prohibition of genocide and therefore provides clear evidence of state opinion and practice.

Similarly, it may be argued that the modifications in the convention were also made because of political arrangements. Such modifications would then be contrary to the concept of *jus cogens.* In the *Reservations to the Genocide Convention* case, the ICJ identified one of the accepted meanings of *jus cogens* seen as a 'public order of the international community' made up of principles and rules of 'such vital importance to the international community as a whole that any unilateral action or any agreement which contravenes these principles can have no legal force':[194]

> The Convention was manifestly adopted for a purely humanitarian and civilizing purpose. It is indeed difficult to imagine a convention that might have this dual character to a greater degree, since its object on the one hand is to safeguard the very existence of certain human groups and on the other to confirm and endorse the most elementary principles of morality. *In such a convention the contracting States do not have any interests of their own;* they merely have, one and all, a common interest, namely, the

192 Schabas, William A., *Genocide in International Law – The Crimes of Crimes,* Cambridge University Press, 2000, pp 45-46.

193 See *supra.*

194 Mosler, Hermann, 'The International Society as a Legal Community', [1974] IV *RCADI* 34. In this respect, see Article 53 of the 1969 Vienna Convention on the Law of Treaties according to which a treaty which is contrary to an existing rule of *jus cogens* is void *ab initio.*

> accomplishment of those high purposes which are the *raison d'être* of the convention. Consequently in a convention of this type one cannot speak of individual advantages or disadvantages to States, or of the maintenance of a perfect contractual balance between rights and duties. The high ideals which inspired the Convention provide, by virtue of the common will of the parties, the foundation and measure of all its provisions.[195]

Verdross also wrote that the criterion for rules having the character of *jus cogens* 'consists in the fact that they do not exist to satisfy the needs of the individual states but the higher interest of the whole international community'.[196] It is however most likely that, in defining and writing the prohibition of genocide, states have interpreted 'international community' as 'international community of states' rather than as 'mankind'. As Bull rightly pointed out, 'agreements reached among States are notoriously the product of bargaining and compromise rather than of any consideration of the interests of mankind as a whole'.[197] Clearly, the Genocide Convention was a political compromise which considered the interests of states and the protection of state sovereignty rather than the overriding interests of humanity as a whole. With the Convention, there is a risk of a 'weakened international law' or of an international law 'enfeebled by its own norms'.[198] The obvious illustration of this is the difference between General Assembly Resolution 96 (I) and the convention itself, and it is most probable that the prohibition of genocide as following from natural law was reproduced in Resolution 96(I) of the General Assembly,[199] the Genocide Convention being in fact inconsistent with the broader *jus cogens* norm.

Thus, it is here submitted that it is not the convention-based prohibition but the one embodied in Resolution 96(I) which should apply.[200] Then, and only then, will the peremptory norm be respected and will the

[195] *Reservations to the Convention on the Prevention and Punishment of the Crime of Genocide* Advisory Opinion, [1951] ICJ Reports 23 (28 May). Emphasis added.
[196] Verdross, Alfred, '*Jus Dispositivum* and *Jus Cogens* in International Law', (1966) 60 *AJIL* 55.
[197] Cited in Christenson, Gordon A., '*Jus Cogens* : Guarding Interests Fundamental to International Society', (1988) 28 *Virginia Journal of International Law* 589-90.
[198] Carrillo Salcedo, Juan Antonio, 'Reflections on the Existence of a Hierarchy of Norms in International Law', (1997) 8 *EJIL* 587.
[199] On the General Assembly Resolutions as a new source of international law, see Gomez Robledo, Antonio, 'Le *Ius Cogens* International : Sa Genèse, Sa Nature, Ses Fonctions', [1981] III *RCADI* 176-79.
[200] See Article 53 of the 1969 Vienna Convention on the Law of Treaties. In fact, it is arguable that, because the Genocide Convention unduly restricts the *jus cogens* norm, it is in fact contrary to it. As a result, the convention could be considered void.

definition of the crime of genocide be satisfying. Indeed, as a result of the application of the broader *jus cogens* norm, political and other groups would be recognised as possible targets of genocide and the principle of universal jurisdiction, which also seemed to have been the intention of Resolution 96 (I), would cease to raise any doubts. In fact, the ILC, in its 1996 Report on the Draft Code of Crimes, had already acknowledged 'the character of the crime of genocide as a crime under international law for which *universal jurisdiction existed as a matter of customary law*'.[201] As its work is evidence of state practice and as its drafts may constitute evidence of custom, this clearly indicates the importance and relevance of Resolution 96 (I).

Applying the broader *jus cogens* norm would remedy to the most important shortcomings of the Genocide Convention. It has nonetheless to be acknowledged here that we are faced with a paradox. Indeed, while a Convention might prove counter-productive and self-defeating notably because it necessarily relies on ratification, a written norm is still essential in the prevention and punishment of human rights violations. The arguments raised against the Nuremberg trials are indeed a constant reminder of the necessity to respect the *nulla crimen sine lege* principle in order to avoid criticism, no matter how inappropriate, to say the least, it was. As we have argued, such a norm was put down on paper in Resolution 96 (I), but it might still be maintained that General Assembly resolutions have no binding force even if they are declaratory of international law. Therefore, the best way of securing prevention and punishment of genocide would most probably be to revise the existing definition, although the necessary consent of states would hold the great risk of, yet again, letting sovereignty have the lead over the requirements of justice. In other words, the effectiveness of the prohibition of genocide – through its re-definition – ultimately depends upon the good will of states ... or, in other words, upon the willingness of the primary perpetrators of genocide.[202]

2. *Genocide and crimes against humanity*

The first Special Rapporteur on genocide believed that 'the 1948 Convention can only be considered a point of departure in the adoption of effective international measures to prevent and punish genocide'; he

[201] 1996 Draft Code of Crimes, [1996] II (2) *ILC Yearbook* 29. Emphasis added. Thus, Article 8 of the Draft Code 'extends national court jurisdiction over the crime of genocide set out in Article 17 to every State party to the Code'. Ibid. See also Van Schaack, Beth, 'The Crime of Political Genocide: Repairing the Genocide's Convention's Blind Spot', (1997) 106 *Yale L J* 2277-80.
[202] See *infra*.

thus proposed 'to examine the possibility of fresh international measures for effective prevention and punishment of genocide'.[203] Similarly, in its report on genocide, Whitaker acknowledged the fact that 'certainly in its present form, the Convention must be judged to be not enough. Further evolution of international measures against genocide is necessary and indeed overdue'.[204] Sibert went even further when he wrote that if effectiveness is preferred to spectacular text, it will be necessary 'to start again right from the beginning a work which is no more than the first step on an arduous road leading to absolute respect for the most sacred rights of mankind'.[205]

Such a step could be achieved through the concept of crimes against humanity. Indeed, although the crime of genocide is different from crimes against humanity, it still has to be recognised that Nuremberg dealt with genocide as a crime against humanity. Far from being a revolutionary suggestion, starting from the notion of crimes against humanity to redefine genocide would thus be nothing than a return to the roots. As a matter of fact, genocide has been generally acknowledged as a species, as a particular form, of crimes against humanity so much so that it is the concept of crimes against humanity itself which led to the adoption of the Genocide Convention.[206] In the words of Professor Clark:

> [t]he establishment of the doctrine of crimes against humanity [...] paved the way for subsequent development of other offences of international concern. It led directly to the definitions of genocide and the crime of apartheid and less directly to the development of a whole package of international crimes.[207]

In preparation for the debate on the Secretariat's draft, France circulated a memorandum 'on the subject of genocide and crimes against humanity' which challenged the use of the term 'genocide', calling it a useless and even dangerous neologism. France preferred to approach the problem of extermination of racial, social, political or religious groups from the standpoint of crimes against humanity.[208] During the second

[203] Ruhashyankiko Report, p 120, para 440.
[204] Whitaker Report, p 37, para 71.
[205] Sibert, Marcel, *Traité de Droit International Public, Volume I*, Librairie Dalloz, 1951, pp 445-46.
[206] See Brownlie, Ian, *Principles of Public International Law*, Clarendon Press, 4th Edn, 1990, p 562.
[207] Clark, Roger S., 'Crimes Against Humanity at Nuremberg', in Ginsburgs, George and Kudriavtsev, V.N. (eds), *The Nuremberg Trial and International Law*, Martinus Nijhoff Publishers, 1990, pp 198-99.
[208] UN Doc A/AC.20/29.

session of the General Assembly, the heart of the issue was whether to consider genocide as a variety of crime against humanity, or to treat it as a distinct form of criminal behaviour. During the debates in the Ad Hoc Committee, France was the most insistent about the linkage between genocide and crimes against humanity, while others firmly believed that the concepts had to be made distinct and separate. France had urged that the preamble described genocide as 'a crime against humanity',[209] but this was rejected by the Ad Hoc Committee, which chose instead to characterise it as 'a crime against mankind'.[210] According to the final report of the Committee, its members 'categorically opposed the expression "crimes against humanity" because, in their opinion, it had acquired a well-defined legal meaning in the Charter of the Nuremberg Tribunal'.[211]

It is true that crimes against humanity were still widely believed to be crimes that could only be committed during armed conflict, a consequence of the Nuremberg jurisprudence. Taking an opposite approach, the draftsmen of the convention proceeded to the 'equalisation of acts committed in peace or war'[212] in Article I, and this constituted at the time a major innovation. However, it is now admitted that crimes against humanity also occur in time of peace, and thus a distinction between genocide and crimes against humanity cannot be made from the standpoint of 'time of war or time of peace'.[213]

It is further argued that the major dissimilarity between genocides and crimes against humanity is that genocides require a specific intent to destroy a *group* as such, while crimes against humanity do not necessarily involve offences or persecutions against groups. Nonetheless, as previously stressed, the intent requirement in the context of genocide is in fact not a dissimilarity between crimes against humanity and genocide. Rather, it constitutes the *differentiating factor* between crimes against humanity and genocide, which is not the same thing.

Furthermore, some cases of crimes against humanity clearly show that these crimes too are committed against individuals because of their belonging to a targeted group. As a matter of fact, the case law of the international tribunals seems to suggest that the distinction between

209 UN Doc E/AC.25/SR.20, p 7.
210 UN Doc E/794/, p 2.
211 Ibid, p 3.
212 Robinson, Nehemiah, *The Genocide Convention – A Commentary*, Institute of Jewish Affairs – World Jewish Congress, 1960, pp 56-7.
213 Ruhashyankiko Report, p 107, para 392. See *supra* I A.

these two crimes is vanishing, notably due to the facts that 'persecutions', which are crimes against humanity, require the same 'specific intent' than the crime of genocide. Thus, in the *Kupreškić* case, Trial Chamber II of the ICTY held that:

> [P]ersecution as a crime against humanity is an offence belonging to the same *genus* as genocide. Both persecution and genocide are crimes perpetrated against persons that belong to a particular group and who are targeted because of such belonging. [...] [F]rom the viewpoint of *mens rea*, genocide is an extreme and most inhuman form of persecution. To put it differently, when persecution escalates to the extreme form of wilful and deliberate acts designed to destroy a group or part of a group, it can be held that such persecution amounts to genocide.[214]

It also found that:

> Persecution is one of the most vicious of all crimes against humanity [...] Persecution is only one step away from *genocide – the most abhorrent crime against humanity* – for in genocide the persecutory intent is pushed to its uttermost limits through the pursuit of the physical annihilation of the group or of members of the group[215]

Nonetheless, it must also be acknowledged that, departing from these findings, Trial Chamber I of the ICTY subsequently indicated that:

> The [Genocide] Convention thus seeks to protect the right to life of human groups, as such. This characteristic makes genocide an exceptionally grave crime and distinguishes it from other serious crimes, in particular persecution, where the perpetrator selects his victims because of their membership in a specific community but *does not necessarily* seek to destroy the community as such.[216]

---

[214] *Prosecutor* v *Kupreškić et al*, Case No IT-95-16, Judgment, Trial Chamber II, 14 January 2000, para.636.

[215] Ibid., para.751. Emphasis added. See also *Prosecutor* v *Krstić*, Case No. IT-98-33, Judgment, Trial Chamber I, 2 August 2001, para 684 ; *Prosecutor* v *Nikolić*, Case No IT-94-2, Initial Indictment, 4 November 1994, para 24. See also Article 17 of the ILC 1996 Draft Code, in the commentary of which the ILC stated that genocide as currently defined corresponds to the second category of crimes against humanity established under Article 6(c) of the Nuremberg Tribunal's Statute, namely the crimes of persecution. [1996] II (2) *ILC Yearbook* 44.

[216] *Prosecutor* v *Krstić*, Case No. IT-98-33, Judgment, Trial Chamber I, 2 August 2001, para 553. Emphasis added.

Although this statement seems to be in contradiction with the earlier findings of Trial Chamber II, it must nevertheless be pointed out that Trial Chamber I is rather cautious in establishing the distinction between persecution and genocide. The use of the terms 'not necessarily' indeed implies that persecution can 'seek to destroy the community as such'. In other words, persecutions could be seen as nothing but individualised genocidal acts which would qualify as genocide if their number actually increases. In this respect, it must be recalled here that

> The persecution policy against the Jews commenced with non-violent measures, such as disfranchisement and discriminations against their religion, and the placing of impediments in the way of success in economic life. It moved rapidly to organised mass violence against them, physical isolation in ghettos, deportation, forced labour, mass starvation and extermination. [217]

As previously stressed, relying on the number of victims to assess whether genocide has been committed or not is taking an immoral but also wrong path. As a matter of fact, it is most probable that persecutions pertain to the definitional scope of the crime of genocide rather than to that of crimes against humanity. Indeed, how would the persecutions against the European Jews be qualified had the Nazi genocidal plan failed to generate the adequate number of deaths? By relying yet again on the number of victims to qualify an act – by essence genocidal – as an act of genocide, the law of persecutions, surrounded with uncertainty, is symptomatic of the striking resemblances these two crimes actually share. It is also highly representative of the current incapacity of international criminal law to provide for satisfactory definitions of the crimes it actually covers.

Nevertheless, in spite of the similarities between the notions of genocide and of crimes against humanity, it must be borne in mind that similarity does not mean identity. In this respect, Drost's affirmation that these two offences 'do overlap to a great extent and, generally speaking, the two crimes as comprehensively understood correspond completely with each other',[218] seems exagerated. Similarly, Glaser erred in considering it indisputable that crimes against humanity and genocide:

[217] Justice Robert Jackson, *Opening Speeches of the Chief Prosecutors,* The Trial of German Major War Criminals by the International Military Tribunal Sitting at Nuremberg, Germany, 20 November 1945, pp 14 and 18. Cited in Mettraux, Guénaël, *International Crimes and the Ad Hoc Tribunals,* Oxford University Press, 2005, p 336.

[218] Drost, Pieter N., *The Crime of State – Penal Protection for Fundamental Freedoms of Persons and Peoples ; Book II: Genocide – United Nations Legislation on International Criminal Law,* A.W. Sythoff, 1959, p 196.

> fall within the same category, or, in other words, belong to the one and the same class of acts [...] [T]he essential differences between crimes against humanity and genocide is not so much objective as subjective, in that it relates to the motives of the perpetrator. The same act – for example, murder – may be, or rather may be described as, either a crime against humanity or an act of genocide, depending on the motives of the person committing it; if his aim is to eliminate the victim because of the latter's race, religion or political beliefs, with no other intent, his act constitutes a crime against humanity, whereas if committed with intent to destroy, in whole or in part, a national, ethnic, racial or religious group, it will be qualified as genocide. It follows that genocide, too, is by its nature simply a crime against humanity, and indeed an aggravated crime against humanity. Accordingly, it would seem more correct from the standpoint both of logic and of method to regard genocide as simply an *aggravated* case of crimes against humanity. The aggravation lies simply in the additional intent which is characteristic of genocide.[219]

It has indeed to be stressed that such assertions are to be handled with great care because they do omit the facts that genocides and crimes against humanity are different and that, even if they share striking similarities, they are not identical. It is thus submitted here that, rather than equating the notions of genocide and of crimes against humanity, the definition of genocide should be revised by drawing upon the definition of crimes against humanity and by considering it as a model for evolution.

By legally acknowledging the similarities between the concept of 'crimes against humanity' and that of 'genocide', while still specifying the difference between these two notions as regards the mental element required, international criminal law could make a great step forward. By drawing upon the definition of crimes against humanity to fill the

[219] Glaser, Stefan, *Droit International Pénal Conventionnel*, 1970, p 109. Emphasis in original. See also Destexhe, Alain, *Rwanda and Genocide in the Twentieth Century*, translated by Alison Marschner, Pluto Press, 1995, p 4: 'genocide is a crime on a different scale to all other crimes against humanity and implies an intention to completely exterminate the chosen group. Genocide is therefore both the gravest and the greatest of the crimes against humanity.' Furthermore, it can be recalled here that, when Special Rapporteur Thiam produced a substantially revised set of draft articles in 1986 [UN Doc A/CN.4/398 (1986)], the ILC gave it a favourable welcome 'first because it places genocide first among the crimes against humanity'. See Report of the Commission on the Work of its Forty-First Session, UN Doc A/CN.4/SER.A/1989/Add.1 (Part 2), p 59, para 160.

gaps of the conventional definition of genocide, international criminal law might just start to achieve the aims set forth in the Genocide Convention itself, notably in terms of adequate prosecution and of effective punishment, thus putting an end to the culture of impunity generally surrounding the crime of genocide and contributing, through deterrence, to the prevention of the crime.

The purpose of this proposal is certainly not to empty the notion of genocide of its meaning and of its uniqueness. In fact, far from erasing the special features of international crimes, the present suggestion would probably reinforce their specificity. Indeed, due to the incapacity of the Genocide Convention adequately to cover the crime of genocide, it is the notion of crimes against humanity itself which has been trivialised. As we have previously stressed, in order to 'preserve' the notion of genocide, several scholars have adopted the view that elements which were not embodied in the Genocide Convention could nevertheless be considered as crimes against humanity.[220] Clearly, such a proposal would transform the notion of crimes against humanity into a 'catch-all' category into which every genocidal act that would not fit in the conventional restrictive ambit would fall into. This is of course a very inappropriate way of dealing with international crimes and of finding effective solutions for prevention and punishment as the whole system would then lack credibility. Thus, the whole purpose of the previous developments was to give meaning to the prohibition of the crime of genocide by proposing a solution in order to ensure the effective prevention and prosecution of such a crime.

[220] See *supra* II B.

III. War Crimes

A. The widespread and/or systematic action: the distinction between international and non-international armed conflicts

The requirement of large scale and systematic action is logically fulfilled in the case of war crimes as war is *per se* a widespread and systematic action against one's enemy. In this respect, war crimes are thus similar to crimes against humanity. Still, a few remarks need to be made as regards international humanitarian law, and notably as regards the categorical – though often artificial – distinction it draws between international and internal armed conflicts. These remarks do not affect the fact that all types of conflicts are widespread and systematic actions, but they do highlight some serious shortcomings of international humanitarian law, and thus the need for change. Indeed, it must be pointed out here that the four Geneva Conventions of 1949 apply only to international conflicts. In other words, they are not applicable in the majority of conflicts which have occurred since their entry into force. As Aldrich wrote:

> [r]eality can be messy, and armed conflicts in the real world do not always fit neatly into the two categories – international and noninternational – into which international humanitarian law is divided.[1]

Further, an overview of the different conflicts which occurred since the end of the Second World War overwhelmingly shows that these conflicts are, in their great majority, internal and that they cause more and more injuries among civilians.[2] Thus, between 1945 and 1970, 82 conflicts out of 97 were internal; in 1995, 35 conflicts out of 38 were internal and this was also the case for 15 conflicts out of the 24 which occurred in 2001.[3]

Far from being of a purely theoretical interest, the study of the distinction between international and non-international armed conflicts and the legal consequences attached to the characterisation of a given conflict is of great significance in practice.

---

[1] Aldrich, George H., 'The Laws of War on Land', (2000) 94 *AJIL* 62.
[2] See *infra*.
[3] See Garapon, Antoine, *Des Crimes qu'on ne Peut ni Punir ni Pardonner – Pour une Justice Internationale*, Paris: Editions Odile Jacob, 2002, p 118.

1. The 1949 Geneva Conventions

The Geneva Conventions form part of what are generally known as the laws and customs of war, breaches of which are commonly called 'war crimes'. In the history of the laws and customs of war, the Geneva Conventions were the first instruments to incorporate a coherent system of rules for the repression of violations of its provisions. It must be noted from the outset that the 1949 Geneva Conventions create criminal liability only for violations committed in international armed conflicts. Unequivocally, the ICRC stated that 'according to International Humanitarian Law *as its stands today*, the notion of war crimes is limited to situations of international armed conflict'.[4]

Indeed, even if common Article 1 requires the respect of the conventions 'in all circumstances', it is clear that it was not the intention behind these words to refer to non-international conflicts.[5] Rather, they refer to just and unjust wars, to aggressive wars and to wars of self-defence, and mean that the application of the conventions does not depend on the character of the conflict.[6] Practically, this means that, in cases of non-international armed conflicts, only common Article 3 and Additional Protocol II, which only provide for very basic protections, will be applicable.

Still, common Article 3 is referred to as 'the guiding principle common to all the Geneva Conventions', from which 'each of them derives the essential provision on which it centres'.[7] As it ensures the application of the rules of humanity, common Article 3 is often referred to as a 'convention in miniature',[8] or 'mini-convention'.[9] It does indeed set forth a number of minimum standards which are to be respected in conflicts of a non-international nature. Among those acts which 'are and shall remain prohibited at any time and in any place whatsoever' are

[4] 'Some Preliminary Remarks by the International Committee of the Red Cross on the Setting Up of an International Tribunal for the Prosecution of Persons Responsible for Serious Violation of International Humanitarian Law Committed on the Territory of the Former Yugoslavia' (22 February 1993), reprinted in Morris,Virginia and Scharf, Michael, *An Insider's Guide to the International Criminal Tribunal for the Former Yugoslavia,* 1995, p. 391. Emphasis added.

[5] See Commentary to Geneva Convention *I* 26-27.

[6] It may be noted here that the same expression is repeated in Article 1 (1) of Additional Protocol I.

[7] See Commentary to Geneva Convention *I* 23. The essential provisions referred to are the following: Article 12 in Convention I, Article of Convention II, Part II (Articles 12-16) of Convention III and Article 27 of Convention IV.

[8] Ibid., p. 48.

[9] Sandoz, Yves, Swinarski, Christophe, Zimmermann, Bruno (eds), *Commentary on the Additional Protocols of 8 June 1977 to the Geneva Conventions of 12 August 1949,* International Committee of the Red Cross, Martinus Nijhoff Publishers, 1987, p 1319.

'violence to life and person, in particular murder of all kinds' and 'the carrying out of executions without previous judgment pronounced by a regularly constituted court, affording all the judicial guarantees which are recognized as indispensable by civilised nations'. The former UN Assistant Secretary-General for Human Rights has noted that these 'fundamental prescriptions' have 'universal validity'.[10] Interestingly, in the *Nicaragua* case, the International Court of Justice held in its ruling that common Article 3 was compulsory for all states, whether or not they had ratified or adhered to the 1949 Geneva Conventions.[11] It also found that common Article 3, even if only applicable to non-international armed conflicts, also states customary law applicable to international armed conflicts.[12] It thus considered that certain rules stated therein:

> [c]onstitute a minimum yardstick, in addition to more elaborate rules which are also to apply to international conflicts; and they are rules which, in the Court's opinion, reflect what the Court in 1949 called 'elementary consideration of humanity'.[13]

Nonetheless, in spite of its extreme importance, it should be recalled that common Article 3 does not offer a clear definition of the notion of non-international armed conflicts, even if they do have some distinctive features to these conflicts compared to international ones, such as the legal status of the entities opposing each other. According to Torrelli:

> [v]olontairement, l'article 3 ne définit pas la notion de 'conflit armé' , afin de ne pas donner à l'Etat l'occasion de trouver des alibis pour ne pas l'appliquer. Les tensions ou les troubles intérieurs ne sont cependant pas considérés comme entrant dans cette catégorie. Dès lors, en pratique, c'est à l'Etat qu'il appartient de dire où cesse le simple maintien de l'ordre face à un désordre et où commence le conflit armé![14]

---

[10] Van Boven, 'Distinguishing Criteria of Human Rights', in Vasak, K. and Alston, P. (eds), *International Dimensions of Human Rights*, 1982, p. 5. Cited in Hannum, Hurst, 'International Law and Cambodian Genocide : The Sounds of Silence', (1989) II *HRQ* 127.

[11] *Military and Paramilitary Activities in and against Nicaragua*, Merits, [1986] ICJ Reports 113-115, paras 218-20 (27 June).

[12] Ibid.

[13] Ibid. See generally Meron, Theodor, 'The Geneva Conventions as Customary Law', (1987) 81 *AJIL* 348-70.

[14] Torrelli, Maurice, *Le Droit International Humanitaire*, Presses Universitaires de France, Collection Que Sais-Je?, 1985, p. 30.

It is true that a definition of internal armed conflicts appears in Article 1 of Additional Protocol II, but the difficulties of reaching a compromise during the Diplomatic Conference of 1974-1977 led to certain ambiguities. Indeed, the necessity to 'reassure' states, which were required to give increased humanitarian guarantees, led to the narrowing of the scope of application of Additional Protocol II. The result was a restrictive definition which covers only conflicts of major importance, as only these can fulfil the conditions set up by this definition. First, the conflict has to occur on the territory of a State Party. Secondly, it has to oppose the armed forces of the state to dissident armed forces or to organised armed groups which must fulfil three cumulative conditions: to have a responsible commandment, to control a part of the territory and to be able to lead military, continuous and concerted operations and to apply the Additional Protocol. If the requirement of a commandment is normal as it allows for the establishment of a differentiating criterion with acts of sporadic and unorganised violence, the adjunction of the other conditions marks a step back to the old concept of 'belligerency': the adversary of the state must indeed reunite all the elements constitutive of the state, namely, an organisation, a territory and a population. Thus, the rules of the Additional Protocol may only apply to conflicts which have the features of an inter-state conflict.

From a practical standpoint, this means that there are situations of non-international armed conflicts in which only common Article 3 will apply, the level of organisation of the dissident groups being insufficient for Additional Protocol II to operate. A perfect example of this absurd situation was given by the ICJ in the *Nicaragua* case, as it contrasted the conflict between the *contras* and the Sandinista Government with that between the United States and Nicaragua. The first, as internal, was governed by common Article 3 only, while the second, as international, fell under the rules of international conflicts.[15] Furthermore, as Meier Wang rightly noted:

> [t]he protections [provided for by common Article 3 and Protocol II] *only* become applicable to a situation once it is categorized as a non-international armed conflict, and getting to that point of applicability can prove close to impossible. On the one hand, opinions vary greatly as to when an internal strife reaches a grave enough level for the provisions of Common Article 3 or Protocol II to apply. Protocol II has been interpreted to demand a conflict with a higher degree of violence than Article 3 demands, but

[15] *Military and Paramilitary Activities in and against Nicaragua*, Merits [1986] ICJ Reports 114 (27 June).

> even Common Article 3's commentary has suggested a 'high threshold of violence' before it necessarily applies. On the other hand, states have predictably been unwilling to acknowledge that events in their own countries might fit the description of 'non-international armed conflict.[16]

Finally, it may be pointed out here that, according to Article 1(2) of Additional Protocol II, international humanitarian law is not applicable in situations of internal violence and tensions,[17] which are thus not governed by any rules. [18] It seems therefore that, due to the artificial distinction drawn by international humanitarian law between internal and international conflicts, the former are left with few rules and regulations, and the crimes which might be committed during these conflicts will more often than not be left unpunished. Indeed, one of the legal advisers of the ICRC wrote that international humanitarian law 'applicable to non-international armed conflicts does not provide for international penal responsibility of persons guilty of violations'.[19] It has also been asserted that the normative customary law rules applicable in non-international armed conflicts do not encompass the criminal element of war crimes. In its final report, the UN War Crimes Commission for Yugoslavia was categorical on this matter:

> The content of customary law applicable to internal armed conflict is debatable. As a result, in general [...] the only offences committed in internal armed conflicts for which universal jurisdiction exists are 'crimes against humanity' and genocide, which apply irrespective of the conflicts' classification.[20]

[16] Meier Wang, Mariann, 'The International Tribunal for Rwanda: Opportunities for Clarification, Opportunities for Impact', (1995) 27 *Columbia Human Rights Law Review* 219-20.

[17] Sassoli, Marco and Bouvier, Antoine A., *How Does Law Protect in War? Cases, Documents and Teaching Materials on Contemporary Practice in International Humanitarian Law*, International Committee of the Red Cross, 1999, pp 89-90.

[18] The ICTR applied the criteria of the intensity of the conflict and of sufficient organisation of the parties to the conflict in order to distinguish between internal armed conflicts and internal disturbances and tensions, but with little precision as to the definition of such criteria. See *Prosecutor* v *Akayesu*, Case No ICTR-96-4-T, Judgment, Trial Chamber I, 2 September 1998, paras 620-1. Also, the ICTY has used the criterion of 'aim and objective' of the parties to a conflict, but failed to elaborate on its substance. See *Prosecutor* v *Delalić et al*, Case No. IT-96-21-T, Judgment, Trial Chamber II *quater*, 16 November 1998, para 224.

[19] Plattner, Denise, 'The Penal Repression of Violations of International Humanitarian Law Applicable in Non-International Armed Conflicts', [1990] *International Review of the Red Cross* 414.

[20] UN Doc S/1194/674, annex, para 42 (1994).

Nevertheless, recent developments have shown the possibility of prosecuting war crimes in internal conflicts, without having to find some sort of linkage to an international war, through reliance on special statutes and customary international law. As noted by Meron:

> *Until very recently,* the accepted wisdom was that neither common Article 3 [...] nor Protocol II [...] provided a basis for universal jurisdiction, and that they constituted, at least on an international plane, *an uncertain basis for individual criminal responsibility*. Moreover, it has been asserted that the normative customary law rules applicable in noninternational armed conflicts do not encompass the *criminal* element of war crimes.[21]

2. *The International Criminal Tribunals and their case law*

The similarities between the Statutes of the two International Tribunals do not exclude some differences, and notably as regards their material jurisdiction, both tribunals having to deal with crimes committed in two conflicts of a different nature, one being internal and the other international, and thus subject to different legal principles. In other words, even if facts are similar, the applicable legal rules are different. Indeed, the crimes committed in Rwanda are subject to common Article 3 and to Additional Protocol II, while those perpetrated in the former Yugoslavia are subject to the provisions of the 1949 Geneva Conventions, Additional Protocol I, and the laws and customs of war.

a. The Statute of the ICTR

In contrast to that of the ICTY, the Statute of the ICTR was drafted on the assumption that the conflict in Rwanda was non-international. Thus, it explicitly gives the tribunal jurisdiction over serious violations of common Article 3 of the Geneva Conventions and of Additional Protocol II. Indeed, by allowing the tribunal to prosecute persons who have committed serious violations of common Article 3 of the Geneva Conventions and of Additional Protocol II, Article 4 of the Statute provides a safety net which is seen as the statute's greatest innovation. A report by the UN Secretary-General recognised that:

> Article 4 of the Statute includes violations of Additional Protocol II, which, as a whole, has not yet been universally

[21] Meron, Theodor, 'International Criminalization of Internal Atrocities', (1995) 89 *AJIL* 559. Emphasis added.

> recognised as part of customary international law, and for the first time criminalises common Article 3...[22].

Furthermore, Article 4 of the ICTR Statute draws a non-exclusive list of violations which derives both from Article 4 of Additional Protocol II[23] and from common Article 3. Because this list is merely illustrative, the tribunal is empowered to apply other provisions of Protocol II as well.[24]

As previously studied, neither common Article 3 nor Additional Protocol II are generally found to apply to conflict situations, and are therefore often not considered effective international humanitarian standards. Furthermore, none of these provisions specifically provide for the international criminal responsibility of a person who commits the acts listed as prohibited. However, in light of the atrocities committed in Rwanda, the trend to regard these instruments as bases for individual criminal responsibility was accentuated. Indeed, after having determined that the conflict in Rwanda constituted a non-international armed conflict, the Independent Commission of Experts on Rwanda asserted that common Article 3 and Additional Protocol II,[25] as well as the principle of individual criminal responsibility in international law,[26] were applicable.[27] Accordingly, the ICTR Statute considered violations of common Article 3 and of Additional Protocol II as criminal offences. Still, as Meron rightly noted:

> [t]he Rwanda Statute contains no provisions paralleling Article 3 of the Yugoslavia Statute, which grants the Tribunal jurisdiction over violations of the Fourth Hague Convention and annexed Regulations. This omission reflects the accepted wisdom, which unfortunately denies war crimes a place in internal conflicts.[28]

b. The Statute of the ICTY

As regards war crimes, the ICTY's subject matter jurisdiction covers rules of international humanitarian law which are applicable to international armed conflicts and are declaratory of customary law. As a matter of fact, there were valid reasons to consider the entire

[22] UN Doc S/1995/134, para 12 (1995).
[23] The 'Fundamental guarantees' clause.
[24] See Meron, Theodor, *supra* n.21, pp 558-59.
[25] See UN Doc S/1194/1125, annex, paras 90-93 (1994).
[26] See ibid, paras 125-28.
[27] Meron, Theodor, *supra* n 21, p 561.
[28] Ibid, p 574.

Yugoslavian conflict as international, and therefore subject to the rules on international wars. In fact, according to Meron, 'the statute of the tribunal constitutes a determination that the conflicts in Yugoslavia are international in character'.[29] Also, the UN War Crimes Commission shared the view that the conflicts in Yugoslavia were international and thus that all the laws of war, including the rules governing war crimes, were applicable:

> [T]he character and complexity of the armed conflicts concerned, combined with the web of agreements on humanitarian issues the parties have concluded among themselves, justify an approach whereby it applies the law applicable in international armed conflicts to the entirety of the armed conflicts in the territory of the former Yugoslavia.[30]

Furthermore, the fact that the UN Secretary-General emphasised that the tribunal should apply 'only those rules of international customary law applicable to international armed conflicts'[31] could be seen as an indication that the facts pertain to the field covered by the rules on such conflicts. Finally, another element demonstrating the international character of these conflicts is the fact that foreign states recognised Slovenia, Croatia and Bosnia-Herzegovina, which were also admitted to the United Nations.

The facts and the caselaw of the ICTY, however, showed that the situation in the Balkan region was not as easily qualified. Indeed, the conflicts in Yugoslavia, and especially in Bosnia-Herzegovina, were in fact mixed internal-international conflicts.[32] In this respect, the approaches taken in the *Tadić* and *Celebići* cases should be analysed here as they were diametrically opposed. In *Tadić*, the trial chamber held that the civilian victims (Bosnian Muslims and Bosnian Croats) could not be regarded as protected persons within the meaning of the Fourth Geneva Convention, because they were not in the hands of a party – of which they were not nationals – to an armed conflict: they were in the hands of Bosnian (Serb) nationals. Furthermore, it found that the *de facto* agent standard applied to trigger the Geneva Conventions and

[29] Meron, Theodor, supra n 29, p 81-82.
[30] Interim Report of the Commission of Experts Established Pursuant to Security Council Resolution 780 (1992), UN Doc S/25274, Annex I, para 45 (1993).
[31] Report of the Secretary-General Pursuant to Paragraph 2 of Security Council Resolution 808 (1993), UN Doc S/25704 and Annex (3 May 1993), paras 33-37.
[32] Meron, Theodor, 'War Crimes in Yugoslavia and the Development of International Law', (1994) 88 *AJIL* 81.

that, as the Bosnian Serb army was not a *de facto* agent of Serbia, Serbia was not a party to the conflict. As a consequence, the grave breaches provisions of the Geneva Conventions recognised in Article 2 of the ICTY Statute did not apply.[33]

Reaching a different conclusion in the *Celebići* case, while addressing incidents that occurred in 1992 and involved Bosnian Serb victims and perpetrators linked to the Bosnian Government, the trial chamber held that:

> [s]hould the conflict in Bosnia and Herzegovina be international, the relevant norms of international humanitarian law apply throughout its territory until the general cessation of hostilities, unless it can be shown that the conflicts in some areas were separate internal conflicts, unrelated to the larger international armed conflict.[34]

Having found that the conflict was international,[35] the trial chamber asserted that Article 2 of the ICTY Statute, which covers 'grave breaches' of the Geneva Conventions, was applicable and held that the victim group (Bosnian Serbs) should be regarded as protected persons who did not share the nationality of their Bosnian Muslim and Bosnian Croat captors.[36]

Fortunately, the ICTY caselaw now seems settled as, in the final *Tadić* appeals judgment, the appeals chamber, applying the 'overall control' test, held that there was an international conflict and thus that the 'grave breaches' regime of the 1949 Geneva Conventions applied.[37] It also specified that the victims were 'protected persons' under the meaning of the Fourth Geneva Convention.

In any case, the issue of conflicts qualification had already become less significant with the crucial decision reached by the Appeals Chamber in the *Tadić* case, as it found that leading principles of international humanitarian law apply to both sorts of conflicts.[38] It is true that these specific principles and rules for *international* armed conflicts are not

[33] *Prosecutor* v *Tadić*, Case No IT-94-1-T, Opinion and Judgment, Trial Chamber II, 7 May 1997, paras 607-8.
[34] *Prosecutor* v *Delalić et al*, Case No. It-96-21-T, Judgment, Trial Chamber II *quater*, 16 November 1998, para 209.
[35] Ibid, para 214.
[36] Ibid, para 265.
[37] *Prosecutor* v. *Tadić*, Case No IT-94-1-A, Judgment, Appeals Chamber, 15 July 1999, paras 115-45.
[38] See *Prosecutor* v *Tadić*, Case No. IT-94-1-AR72, Decision on the Defence Motion for Interlocutory Appeal on Jurisdiction, Appeals Chamber, 2 October 1995, para 91.

transposed *verbatim* into the laws of *internal* armed conflicts. Thus, it is unclear whether certain provisions apply to both. As Meron rightly emphasised:

> [w]hether the conflicts in Yugoslavia are characterized as internal or international is critically important. The fourth Hague Convention of 1907, which codified the principal laws of war and served as the normative core for the post-World War II war crimes prosecutions, applies to international wars only. The other principal prong of the penal laws of war, the grave breaches provisions of the Geneva Conventions and Protocol I, is also directed to international wars. Violations of common Article 3 of the Geneva Conventions, which concerns internal wars, do not constitute grave breaches giving rise to universal criminal jurisdiction. Were any part of the conflict deemed internal rather than international, the perpetrators of even the worst atrocities might try to challenge prosecutions for war crimes or grave breaches, but not for genocide or crimes against humanity.[39]

Nonetheless, in *Tadić*, the appeals Chamber ruled that some atrocities committed in internal conflicts were universal crimes, i.e. crimes for which an international court can summon individuals to account. Indeed, while it reluctantly held that Article 2 of the ICTY Statute could only apply within the framework of international armed conflicts since the Geneva Conventions themselves were so limited, the Appeals Chamber nonetheless indicated that a change in customary law may be occurring so that the grave breaches system may eventually operate regardless of whether the armed conflict is international or internal.[40] As a matter of fact, the *Celebići* trial chamber had opined that there was a possibility that customary law had already reached the stage of development referred to by the appeals chamber.[41] Furthermore, in the *Kordić* and *Cerkez* case, Trial Chamber III took note of the *dicta* of the appeals chamber and of the *Celebići* Trial Chamber on this question.[42]

Most importantly, in the same *Tadić* case, the appeals chamber held that Article 3 of the Statute, which deals with violations of the law or customs

[39] Meron, Theodor, *supra* n 29, p.80.

[40] *Prosecutor* v. *Tadić*, *supra* n 38, paras 83-84.

[41] *Prosecutor* v. *Delalić et al.*, Case No. IT-96-21-T, Judgment, Trial Chamber II *quater*, 16 November 1998, para.202.

[42] *Prosecutor* v *Kordić and Cerkez*, Case No IT-95-14/2-PT, Decision on the Joint Defence Motion to Dismiss the Amended Indictment for Lack of Jurisdiction Based on the Limited Jurisdictional Reach of Articles 2 and 3, Trial Chamber III, 2 March 1999, para 15.

of war, did apply to internal armed conflicts, as it functions 'as a residual clause designed to ensure that no serious violation of international humanitarian law is taken away from the jurisdiction of the international tribunal'.[43] It accordingly stated that:

> A State-sovereignty-oriented approach has been gradually supplanted by a human-being-oriented approach. Gradually the maxim of Roman law *hominum causa omne jus constitutum est* (all law is created for the benefit of human beings) has gained a firm foothold in the international community as well. It follows that in the area of armed conflict the distinction between interstate wars and civil wars is losing its value so far as human beings are concerned. Why protect civilians from belligerent violence, or ban rape, torture or the wanton destruction of hospitals, churches, museums or private property, as well as proscribe weapons causing unnecessary suffering when two sovereign States are engaged in war, and yet refrain from enacting the same bans or providing the same protection when armed violence has erupted 'only' within the territory of a sovereign State? If international law, while of course duly safeguarding the legitimate interests of States, must gradually turn to the protection of human beings, it is only natural that the aforementioned dichotomy should gradually lose its weight.[44]

Furthermore, even if it was argued on behalf of Tadić that the tribunal's jurisdiction was confined under Article 3 of its Statute to war crimes committed during international armed conflicts and that the Balkan conflict was purely internal, the tribunal's broad definition of 'armed conflict' extended customary law to cover the treatment of rebels, at least when they are both 'armed' and 'organised':

> [A]n armed conflict exists whenever there is resort to armed force between States or protracted armed violence between governmental authorities and organized armed groups or between such groups within a State. International humanitarian law applies from the initiation of such armed conflicts and extends beyond the duration of hostilities until a general conclusion of peace is reached; or, in the case of internal conflicts, a peaceful settlement is achieved. Until that moment, international humanitarian law continues

[43] *Prosecutor* v. *Tadić, supra* n 38, para 91.
[44] Ibid, para 97.

> to apply in the whole territory of the warring States or, in the case of internal conflicts, the whole territory under the control of a party, whether or not actual combat takes place there.[45]

In the words of Orentlicher, the appeals chamber of the ICTY hereby 'rendered one of the most important rulings on war crimes since the Nuremberg judgment'.[46] This decision indeed confirmed the applicability of some principles of the Hague Law to non-international armed conflicts as well as the criminalization of violations of common Article 3 of the Geneva Conventions in such conflicts. As a matter of fact, the chamber unequivocally stressed that 'customary international law imposes criminal liability for serious violations of Common Article 3'.[47] For Aldrich, the tribunal thus 'explosively expanded the customary law applicable to noninternational armed conflicts'.[48]

Clearly, the *Tadić* case blurred the distinction between the distinctive features of international and non-international conflicts respectively, and such a conclusion is to be welcomed as perpetrators of atrocities in internal wars should not be treated more leniently than those engaged in international wars. In the words of Robertson:

> [t]he individuals responsible for any widespread pattern of barbarity [...] should be indictable and the charges against them should not depend on technical legal characterization of the nature of the background conflict.[49]

Still, notwithstanding this great step forward in the prosecution of crimes committed in internal armed conflicts, it might be noted that the scope of application of common Article 3 of the Geneva Conventions might be reduced due to the addition of a new requirement. Indeed, in the recent *Kunarac* case, Trial Chamber II, while enumerating the general requirements for the application of common Article 3, held that:

> It would appear to the Trial Chamber that common Article 3 would also require some *relationship to exist between a perpetrator and a party to the conflict.* Since, in the present case, the three accused fought on behalf of one of the parties to

[45] Ibid, para 70.
[46] Orentlicher, Diane F., 'Internationalizing Civil War', in Cooper, Belinda (ed), *War Crimes – The Legacy of Nuremberg*, TV Books, 1999, p. 154.
[47] *Prosecutor* v *Tadić, supra* n 38, para. 464.
[48] See Aldrich, George H., 'The Laws of War on Land', (2000) 94 *AJIL* 60-61.
[49] Robertson, Geoffrey QC, *Crimes Against Humanity – The Struggle for Global Justice*, Penguin Books, 2000, p 383.

> the conflict, the Trial Chamber does not need to determine whether such a relationship is required, and if so, what the required relationship should be.[50]

It is true that the trial chamber is here very cautious in its finding and raises the question of such a relationship between a perpetrator and a party to the conflict without answering it. It is to be hoped that, if reconsidered, the question will be answered in the negative; if not, there is a real danger to see the prosecution and punishment of violations of common Article 3 greatly restricted as, in times of mixed conflicts, proving this particular relationship might be a difficult task.

3. *The Rome Statute of the International Criminal Court*

It may be noted from the outset that the Rome Statute considers that the widespread or systematic action requirements are not inherent elements of war crimes but rather 'factors which should be taken into account by the prosecutor in determining whether or not to commence investigations against particular potential accused'.[51] This disposition seems nontheless unnecessary as, as previously mentioned, war crimes are always part of a widespread or systematic action as they are committed during war, which is itself a widespread and systematic action.

The Rome Statute of the ICC 'expands the traditional definition of war crimes to include crimes committed in internal conflicts'.[52] Still, it operates a distinction between war crimes perpetrated in international conflicts and in internal ones. As a matter of fact, there are 34 crimes listed for international conflicts and only 16 for internal ones. In other words, this means that the 18 other crimes 'omitted' in the statute are not considered serious enough to be prosecuted by the Court as war crimes. Furthermore, the ICRC noted that, as regards internal conflicts, some crimes remain absent from Article 8(2)(c), among which slavery and the crimes consisting in deliberately hungering the civilian population, in using certain weapons, in deliberately causing extended,

[50] *Prosecutor* v *Kunarac et al*, Case No IT-96-23 and IT-96-23/1, Judgment, Trial Chamber II, 22 February 2001, para 407. Emphasis added. It can be noted here that, subsequently, the appeals chamber remained silent on this particular point and merely reiterated the well-settled requirement that the acts be closely related to the armed conflict. *Prosecutor* v. *Kunarac et al.*, Case No. IT-96-23 and IT-96-23/1-A, Judgment, Appeals Chamber, 12 June 2002, paras 55-65.

[51] Article 8 of the ICC Statute. It may also be noted that the ILC 1996 Draft Code of Crimes established a questionable hierarchy of gravity between 'ordinary ' war crimes and war crimes committed in a systematic manner or on a large scale, only the latter being considered as a crime against the peace and security of mankind.

[52] Kirsch, Philippe, 'Keynote Address', (1999) 32 *Cornell International Law Journal* 438.

durable and grave damages to the natural environment, as well as in executing minors and pregnant women. In the words of Spieker, these gaps 'weaken the system of individual criminal responsibility in non-international armed conflicts considerably'.[53]

Also, it may be noted that Article (2)(f) limits the court's jurisdiction as regards situations of internal armed conflicts by requiring that such conflicts be 'protracted between the governmental authorities and organized armed groups or between such groups'. In this respect, Cassese analysed Article 8 of the Rome Statute in a very pertinent manner. He indeed pointed out that:

> Certain of the substantive provisions may be considered retrogressive in the light of existing law. These include: the distinction between international and internal armed conflicts, needlessly perpetuated in Article 8; an insufficient prohibition of the use in armed conflict of weapons that cause unnecessary suffering or are inherently indiscriminate; the excessively cautious criminalisation of war crimes offences.[54]

Notwithstanding the inherent weaknesses of the Rome Statute, it is to be hoped that the trend towards effective prosecution and punishment of crimes committed in internal conflicts will continue. In the words of Aldrich:

> At the close of the twentieth century, we see – remarkably – in the context of criminal prosecution, an astounding growth of the law applicable to noninternational armed conflicts.[55]

B. Grounds for commission: the distinction between combatants and civilians

> *War, as it becomes more and more total, annuls the differences which formerly existed between armies and civilian populations in regard to exposure to injury and danger.*
> Max Huber [56]

[53] Spieker, Heike, 'The International Criminal Court and Non-International Armed Conflicts', (2000) 13 *LJIL* 425.
[54] Cassese, Antonio, 'The Statute of the International Criminal Court: Some Preliminary Reflections', (1999) 10 *EJIL* 144.
[55] See Aldrich, George H., 'The Laws of War on Land', (2000) 94 *AJIL* 60-61.
[56] Commentary to Geneva Convention IV 5.

In the context of war crimes, the requirement of grounds for commission is also fulfilled. Indeed, the crimes committed are clearly directed at certain particular targets, namely, the military adversaries. Nonetheless, the case of war crimes needs to be studied in more depth as the *jus in bello* – the laws of warfare – draws a fundamental distinction between combatants and civilians (ie non-combatants). In essence, under international law, war is supposed to be waged exclusively between combatants, while injury to civilians ought to be kept to a minimum. Thus, Article 48 of Additional Protocol I confirmed as a 'basic rule', pertaining to international customary law, the duty to differentiate at all times between civilians and combatants. Still, such a distinction is blurred in practice and:

> [i]t is reported that in World War I, five percent of casualties were civilian. Today, 80 percent of casualties are civilian, and these are mostly women and children who are often deliberately targeted as a terror tactic.[57]

Indeed, a look at the statistics demonstrates that conflicts generate an increasing number of civilian casualties. In the course of the 20th century, international conflicts were responsible for 35 millions victims while internal wars cause 150 million victims.[58]

Still, no matter which category an individual will fall into, the requirement of grounds for commission is fulfilled. Whether considered as combatants or as non-combatants, the victims of wars are targeted because of their belonging to the enemy camp. In practice, the distinction made by international humanitarian law means that the level of protection of an individual will vary. Thus, the protection of combatants require that they enjoy certain rights as prisoners of war once they have been captured and disarmed, that they are to be safeguarded against execution or deliberate injury when they are *hors de combat* because they have been wounded or they have surrendered, that certain weapons, such as poisonous gases, may not be used against them. However, next to this category of 'privileged' combatants, the *jus in bello* establishes that of unlawful (or 'unprivileged') combatants,[59] who are denied the privileges of prisoners of war. Practically, this means that they may be prosecuted and punished for any act defined as criminal by the enemy's domestic penal code, if committed by them prior to capture.[60] This distinction is an artificial one as, in practice, no clear

[57] Kirsch, Philippe, 'Keynote Address', (1999) 32 *Cornell International Law Journal* 441-42.
[58] See Horowitz, Irving Louis, *Taking Lives. Genocide and State Power*, 1997.
[59] Dinstein, Yoram, 'The Distinction Between Unlawful Combatants and War Criminals', *in* Dinstein,Yoram (ed), *International Law at a Time of Perplexity – Essays in Honour of Shabtai Rosenne*, Martinus Nijhoff Publishers, 1989, p 103.
[60] Ibid, p 104.

distinction is possible. This was recently illustrated by the case of Taliban fighters and members of Al Qaeda detained by the Americans in Guantanamo Bay, none of whom were granted the status of 'prisoners of war' as they were seen as 'irregular combatants'. Still, a distinction was drawn between Taliban prisoners, to whom the Geneva Conventions apply, and Al Qaeda members, to whom these do not, Al Qaeda being a terrorist organisation and not a state. [61]

Furthermore, it can also be noted here that, under Article 4 (A) (2) of Geneva Convention III, to qualify as lawful combatants, members of organised resistance movements and other irregular forces must fulfil the condition of 'having a fixed distinctive sign recognisable at a distance', which is however a requirement not always easy to respect, to say the least. For instance, it seems clear that, during the Second World War, no such distinctive sign could have been adopted by the freedom fighters.

As regards non-combatants, their protection became of international concern with the 1949 Fourth Geneva Convention which provides that they should be protected against deliberate or indiscriminate attacks, reprisal killings, seizure as hostages, starvation or deportation, destruction of their cultural objects and places of worship. Before 1949, in the words of Lemkin, '[t]he Hague Regulations deal[t] with the sovereignty of a State, but [were] silent regarding the preservation of the integrity of a people'.[62] However, according to eminent commentators, Convention IV is above all concerned with the protection of civilians against arbitrary action by the enemy, and not against the whole series of dangers which threaten them in wartime.[63] Furthermore, its Article 4, which deals with protected persons, provides for some noticeable exceptions in its paragraph 2 and excludes from the conventional scope of protection '[n]ationals of a State which is not bound by the Convention', '[n]ationals of a neutral State who find themselves in the territory of a belligerent State, and nationals of co-belligerent States'.[64] The most regrettable provision still remains its Article 5 which expressly allows for derogations in the case of individuals 'suspected of or engaged in activities hostile to the security of the State',[65] or 'detained as a spy or saboteur, or as a person under definite suspicion of activity hostile to the security of the Occupying

[61] See Murphy, Sean D. (ed), 'Decision Not to Regard Persons Detained in Afghanistan as POWs', (2002) 96 *AJIL* 475-80.

[62] Lemkin, Raphaël, *Axis Rule in Occupied Europe – Laws of Occupation, Analysis of Government, Proposals for Redress*, Carnegie Endowment for International Peace, Division of International Law, 1944, p. 90.

[63] See Commentary to Geneva Convention IV 11.

[64] See Article 4(2) of Geneva Convention IV.

[65] Article 5(1) of Geneva Convention IV.

power'.[66] It is true that this disposition also provides that '[i]n each case, such persons shall nevertheless be treated with humanity',[67] but Article 5 still holds the risk of having a category of civilian internees who will be denied the normal conventional treatment and their conditions of detention will be almost impossible to supervise.[68]

In the context of the Rome Statute, it is to be deplored that Article 8(2)(b)(iv) poses some new conditions for the repression of indiscriminate attacks against civilians, civilian goods or the environment. First, the attack must be deliberate. Secondly, its author must know that it will cause excessive damages regarding the military advantage. Furthermore, the use of the expression 'overall military advantage' implies that it will most probably be appreciated more in function of the general armed context than in function of the losses and damages caused by the given attack.

The major problem with these distinctions is that they leave an in-between category, the freedom fighters, with hybrid protection, even if it might be stated here that several General Assembly resolutions declared that they should benefit from the status of prisoners of war.[69] Still, it seems extremely artificial to draw such a clear-cut distinction. This situation can be perfectly illustrated by the case of the Jewish freedom fighter during the Second World War as the question arises whether he was persecuted, and ultimately murdered, because he was a Jew or because he was a freedom fighter. The French Cour de cassation was faced with this issue in the *Barbie* case, where it admitted that crimes committed against members of the Résistance were crimes against humanity.[70] Thus, the crime was defined no longer by the nature of the victim but by the nature of the act and the ideological identity of its author. This finding led to the fortunate recognition that crimes committed against members of the Résistance were actually crimes against humanity and not war crimes. Indeed, had this not been the case, the crimes committed against Résistants could not have been punished, war crimes being submitted to statutory limitations in French domestic law.[71]

[66] Article 5(2) of Geneva Convention IV.
[67] Article 5(3) of Geneva Convention IV.
[68] See Commentary to Geneva Convention I 58.
[69] Res 2383 (XXIII), 7 November 1968 ; Res 2508 (XXIV), 21 November 1969 ; Res 2547 (XXIV), 11 December 1969 ; Res 2652 (XXV), 3 December 1970 ; Res 2678 (XXV), 9 December 1970 ; Res 2707 (XXV), 14 December 1970 ; Res 2795 (XXVI); Res. 2796 (XXVI) 10 December 1971 ; Res 2871 (XXVI), 20 December 1971 ; Res 3103 (XXVIII), 12 Dec 1973.
[70] See *Barbie* case, *Fédération Nationale des Déportés et Internés Résistants et Patriotes et Autres* v *Barbie*, cass. crim., 20 December 1985. Reprinted in (1986) 90 *RGDIP* 1024.
[71] See *infra*.

In the *Vukovar Hospital* decision, the ICTY used the definition of crimes against humanity set forth in the *Barbie* case so as to find that crimes against humanity applied equally whether the victims were members of a resistance movement or civilians:

> Although according to the terms of Article 5 of the Statute of this Tribunal combatants in the traditional sense of the term cannot be victims of a crime against humanity, this does not apply to individuals who, at one particular point in time, carried out acts of resistance. As the Commission of Experts, established pursuant to Security Council Resolution 780, noted 'it seems obvious that Article 5 applies first and foremost to civilians, meaning people who are not combatants. This, however, should not lead to any quick conclusions concerning people who at one particular point in time did bear arms [...]' Information of the overall circumstances is relevant for the interpretation of the provision in a spirit consistent with its purpose.[72]

As regards the position of the ICTY on this particular matter, it might be pointed out that if, in the *Tadić* judgment, it made it clear that crimes against humanity could be committed only against a 'civilian population', it nonetheless construed broadly this expression and stated that:

> The presence of those actively involved in the conflict should not prevent the characterization of a population as civilian and those actively involved in a resistance movement *can* qualify as victims of crimes against humanity.[73]

This finding is however extremely cautious. Not only did the trial chamber seem to suggest, rather than affirm, that crimes against humanity *can* be committed against members of a resistant movement, but it also further restricted this possibility by holding that 'although crimes against humanity must target a civilian population, individuals who *at one time* performed acts of resistance *may in certain circumstances* be victims of crimes against humanity'.[74]

[72] *Prosecutor* v *Mrkšić et al.*, Case No. IT-95-13-R61, Review of the Indictment Pursuant to Rule 61 of the rules of Procedure and Evidence, Trial Chamber I, 3 April 1996, para 29. For the report of the Commission of Experts, see UN Doc S/1994/674, para 78.
[73] *Prosecutor* v *Tadić*, Case No. IT-94-1-T, Opinion and Judgment, Trial Chamber II, 7 May 1997, para 643. Emphasis added.
[74] Ibid. Emphasis added.

In the 21 century, it is about time to recognise that combatants are human beings before being combatants and they should obviously be covered by the prohibition of crimes against humanity. In this respect, the commentators of the First Geneva Convention had stated that:

> The principle of respect for human personality, which is at the root of all the Geneva Conventions [...] is concerned with persons, not as soldiers but as human beings.[75]

If international humanitarian law really is concerned by human beings, it seems logical that *all* human beings, whether combatants or civilians, be awarded the exact same standard of protection, and this may only be achieved through the continuation of the evolution of the concept of war crimes. To this end, the concept of 'civilian population' in the law of crimes against humanity should be used by international humanitarian law to remedy to its defects and to thus recognise that victims of war crimes and of crimes against humanity can be both combatants and non-combatants.

C. Revisiting war crimes

> *Le crime de guerre n'étant pas autre chose qu'un crime contre l'humanité, adapté, dans ses modalités, aux circonstances particulières que les hostilités font naître.*
>
> Henri Donnedieu de Vabres[76]

Unlike other international crimes, such as the crime of genocide which is embodied in one main instrument, or crimes against peace which have so far remained undefined, war crimes constitute the object of numerous different instruments. Bassiouni has indeed found that:

> [t]he category of war crimes contains 71 relevant instruments dating from 1854 to 1998. There are also 35 other applicable instruments from 1868 to 1998 that have been classified, in accordance with the methodology employed, under other categories of crimes.[77]

[75] Cited in Von Sternberg, Mark R., 'A Comparison of the Yugoslavian and Rwandan War Crimes Tribunals : Universal Jurisdiction and the "Elementary Dictates of Humanity"', (1996) XXII *Brooklyn Journal of International Law* 149.

[76] Donnedieu de Vabres, Henri, 'Le Procès de Nuremberg devant les Principes Modernes du Droit Pénal International', [1947] I *RCADI* 521.

[77] Bassiouni, M. Cherif, 'The Sources and Content of International Criminal Law: A Theoretical Framework', in Bassiouni M. Cherif (ed.), *International Criminal Law, Volume I: Crimes*, Transnational Publishers, Inc., 2nd edn, 1999, p 69.

Nonetheless, it is arguable that this enormous amount of legal norms has some major side-effects. As a matter of fact, the multiplication of provisions certainly creates complications as to the rules to be applied to a particular case, and might ultimately impede effective prosecution. To avoid such a risk, it is here submitted that war crimes should draw upon the concept of crimes against humanity in order to have a more comprehensive body of international law, in which no crimes go unpunished. As the following developments will highlight, this proposal would not be incoherent nor would it contradict existing international law, notably as the two crimes share major similarities and as the notion of crimes against humanity could serve as an inspirational model for a redefinition of war crimes which would remedy to the existing shortcomings of their current legal understanding.

1. *Acknowledging the similarities of criminal acts*

The notion of war crimes and the concept of crimes against humanity both prohibit the same type of acts. As a matter of fact, the Nuremberg Charter and judgment highlighted the extreme similarities between war crimes and crimes against humanity. Indeed, the judgment unequivocally noted that 'from the beginning of the war in 1939 war crimes were committed on a vast scale, which were also crimes against humanity'.[78]As Schwelb rightly pointed out:

> [u]nder the [Nuremberg] Charter the notions of 'war crimes' and 'crimes against humanity' overlap and most war crimes are also crimes against humanity, while many crimes against humanity are simultaneously war crimes.[79]

The broad approach adopted by the Nuremberg Tribunal definition allowed it to generally avoid distinguishing between these two types of crimes.[80] According to Bassiouni:

> The confusion between war crimes and crimes against humanity could also be seen in the Tribunal's judgment which did not distinguish between war crimes and crimes against humanity. The assumption was that they saw no need to do so because crimes against humanity included war crimes committed against civilian populations. [According to article 6 (c), crimes against humanity could be committed against "any civilian populations", and by

[78] *Nuremberg* Judgment 254.

[79] Schwelb, Egon, 'Crimes Against Humanity', (1946) 23 *BYBIL* 179-80.

[80] See McAuliffe de Guzman, Margaret, 'The Road from Rome: The Developing Law of Crimes against Humanity', (2000) 22 *HRQ* 347.

> the terms of article 6 (b), war crimes could be committed against 'civilian populations of or in occupied territory'. The latter population is included in the former]. This was reflected in the case of the sixteen defendants who were charged with and tried for both the commission of war crimes and crimes against humanity; each was found guilty of both charges or innocent of both charges.[81]

Subsequently, the 1949 Geneva Conventions and their Additional Protocols did 'incorporate certain components of crimes against humanity by including them among activities prohibited to belligerents in conflicts of an international character'.[82] Such an overlap between the two notions can easily be explained by the facts that these two crimes share the same roots and that both were generated by the wider concept of 'laws of humanity', which is omnipresent in international humanitarian law.[83] As Bassiouni rightly recalled:

> [t]he seeds of the Charter's 'Crimes Against Humanity' provision were planted in the Preambles of the First Hague Convention of 1899 on the Laws and Customs of War and expanded in the Fourth Hague Convention of 1907, and in their annexed Regulations Respecting the Laws and Customs of War on Land. The Preamble of the two conventions used the term 'laws of humanity' and they based their normative prescriptions on these unarticulated values.[84]

The fact that international humanitarian law and crimes against humanity apply to the same types of acts has also been acknowledged by the Commission of Experts for Yugoslavia:

---

[81] Bassiouni, M. Cherif, 'Crimes Against Humanity', in Bassiouni, M. Cherif (ed.), *International Criminal Law, Volume III: Enforcement*, Transnational Publishers, Inc., 1987, p 57.

[82] Bassiouni, M. Cherif, *supra* n 77, p 575. See eg common Articles 50, 51, 130 and 147 of the Four 1949 Geneva Conventions. However, these provisions apply only to certain contexts and to certain protected persons.

[83] See, for instance, the Martens clause, as embodied in the preamble of the 1899 First Hague Convention for the Peaceful Adjustment of International Disputes, The Hague, 29 July 1899, reprinted in (1907) 1 *AJIL* 107, in the preamble of the 1907 Fourth Hague Convention Respecting the Laws and Customs of War on Land, 18 October 1907, reprinted in International Committee of the Red Cross, *International Law Concerning the Conduct of Hostilities – Collection of Hague Conventions and Some Other International Instruments*, International Committee of the Red Cross, revised and updated edition, 1996, p 13, in Article 1 (2) of Additional Protocol I and in the preamble of Additional Protocol II.

[84] Bassiouni, M. Cherif, *supra* n 81, p 535.

> In the context of crimes against humanity, it is relevant to observe that the same kind of prohibited acts listed in common article 3 (relevant conflicts not of an international character) in the four Geneva Conventions of 1949, and in Protocol II to the Geneva Conventions are mere codifications of elementary dictates of humanity.[85]

Most recently, this overlap appeared within the provisions of the Rome Statute, in which there are strong similarities between crimes against humanity and war crimes. As Dinstein noted:

> Some offences (like rape) are simply duplicated in both definitions of war crimes and crimes against humanity, and at one point (forced pregnancy) there is a cross-reference from one definition to another. One can therefore anticipate a dramatic increase in the number of instances in which the same set of circumstances will be categorised simultaneously as a war crime and a crime against humanity.[86]

Thus, it seems that the legal frontiers between war crimes and crimes against humanity are vanishing, due to the fact that these two qualifications cover the same prohibited acts. There should therefore be no legal obstacle impeding the application of the wider definitional elements of crimes against humanity to war crimes. In this respect, Green went even further as he suggested that 'grave breaches' should be qualified as crimes against humanity:

> In so far as grave breaches under the Conventions and Protocol I are concerned, [...] all of these fall within the general umbrella of crimes against humanity, with the greater including the lesser. To employ this term rather than 'grave breaches' overcomes any difficulty arising from the fact that a particular offences charge does not fall within the Convention definition. Moreover, while Article 3 common to the Conventions makes no reference to enforcement or punishment, since the offences listed clearly amount to crimes against humanity it is entirely proper to define them as such. Defining them as crimes against humanity overcomes any difficulty which may be raised on behalf of a defendant contending that, as the Article is

[85] Final Report of the Commission of Experts Pursuant to Security Council Resolution 780, UN SCOR, 49th Sess., Annex, 82, UN Doc S/1994/674 (1994).
[86] Dinstein, Yoram, 'Crimes Against Humanity After Tadic', (2000) 13 *LJIL* 393.

> silent and the offence charged is not listed in the grave breaches Article, there is no means of proceeding against him, despite the gravity of his offences.[87]

In a response to Green, Fenrick considered that such a theory was premature because 'the content of the crimes against humanity concept is as yet too skeletal to provide a satisfactory replacement'.[88] He also argued that:

> Attacks which are directed against legitimate military objectives and which do not cause excessive incidental civilian casualties cannot be crimes against humanity because they do not meet the requirement that they be directed against the civilian population. Lawful, but regrettable, incidental, but not disproportionate, civilian casualties caused in the course of an attack directed against a legitimate military objective should not be converted into the victim group of crimes against humanity charge by creative recategorisation.[89]

The purpose of the present developments is not necessarily to go as far as Green does, at least not yet, and it is true that replacing 'grave breaches' with 'crimes against humanity' might be premature in light of the law as it stands today. Nonetheless, it must equally be acknowledged that war has changed and that its new features should mean that civilian casualties are not a necessary corollary of war. Indeed, armed forces do now have extremely precise weapons which should greatly reduce the cost of civilian lives. If an attack directed against a military objective harms and kills civilians, it is arguable that it is not purely 'incidental'.

2. *Enhancing the concept of war crimes*

a. *Enforcing the non-applicability of statutory limitations*

Until the adoption of the Rome Statute of the ICC, the principal international instrument dealing with the issue of the applicability – or, rather, non-applicability – of statutes of limitations to international crimes was the 1968 United Nations Convention on Statutory

---

87 Green, Leslie C., 'Grave Breaches' or Crimes Against Humanity?', (1998) 8 *Academy Journal of Legal Studies* 20.
88 See Fenrick, William J., 'Should Crimes Against Humanity Replace War Crimes?', (1999) 37 *Columbia Journal of Transnational Law* 785.
89 Ibid.

Limitations. This Convention is a self-explanatory treaty which assumes both that there is a duty to punish such offences and that this duty cannot be attenuated by the passage of time. The main problem with this convention, which entered into force on 11 November 1970, is that it has only 44 states parties, and it is noticeable that France, Germany, the United Kingdom, China and the United States are not among them.[90] It is also striking that no South American country is a party to this convention, while these states are well-known refuges for former Nazis. From a practical standpoint, the fact that Argentina is not a party to this convention combined with the fact that, under Argentinian law, crimes against humanity are subject to statutory limitations, would have caused any demand of extradition in the *Eichmann* case to fail. According to Ratner and Abrams :

> In light of the UN Convention's limited acceptance and the extensive range of domestic legal approaches on the issue, it is difficult to conclude that *mandatory* non-applicability of statutes of limitations has yet entered the realm of custom. The willingness of many states to eliminate such prescription and the negotiation of the 1968 Convention do, however, support the view that international law at least *permits* states to eliminate statutes of limitations for crimes against humanity and war crimes.[91]

Domestic legislation with respect to statutory limitations differs widely. For instance, the 1993 Belgian law provides for universal jurisdiction and non-prescriptibility for war crimes, crimes against humanity and genocide.[92] In Germany, however, the application of statutory limitations is prohibited for genocide and murder but not for war crimes.[93] In France, crimes against humanity are the only crimes not submitted to statutory limitations and, therefore, as in Germany, statutory limitations do apply in the case of war crimes. [94] These statutes of limitations may have dramatic consequences in practice as their application might lead to the impunity of the perpetrators of the most terrible crimes. In fact, in August 1996, an Italian court acquitted Priebke,

[90] It might be noted here that the European Convention on the Non-Applicability of Statutory Limitations to Crimes Against Humanity and War Crimes, adopted by the Council of Europe on 25 January 1974, never entered into force.

[91] Ratner, Steven R . and Abrams, Jason S., *Accountability for Human Rights Atrocities in International Law – Beyond the Nuremberg Legacy*, Oxford University Press, 2nd edn, 2001, pp 143-4.

[92] Loi relative à la répression des violations graves du droit international humanitaire, 10 February 1999.

[93] German Penal Code, as modified in 1979, s 78.

[94] See Article 213-15 of the Nouveau Code Pénal.

a former S.S. captain responsible for the massacre of 335 civilians in Italy in 1944, based on the Italian Penal Code which provides that statutes of limitations apply, unless the crimes lead to life imprisonment sentences.[95]

The temporal issue is highly relevant in the case of war crimes, due to the more frequent application of statutes of limitations to them rather than to crimes against humanity. Thus, in this respect also, allowing war crimes to 'imitate' crimes against humanity would be of great interest and this may be perfectly illustrated by the case of France where, as previously mentioned, crimes against humanity are the only crimes not subjected to statutory limitations.[96]

The issue of statutes of limitations was central to the *Barbie* case as the application of these statutes to war crimes would have necessarily implied that Barbie would have had to be acquitted for the crimes he committed against members of the Résistance. Faced with the necessity to avoid the collective outrage an acquittal would have caused, the Cour de cassation fortunately requalified these crimes as crimes against humanity, through an extension of their scope of application. Had it not, Barbie's crimes against the Résistants would have remained unpunished. In any event, it can here be pointed out that such a decision was in fact legally correct as crimes against Résistants were indeed crimes against humanity and not war crimes. It is true that by applying the same qualification to both the crimes perpetrated against members of the Résistance and the crimes committed against Jews, also qualified in the *Barbie* case as crimes against humanity, the legacy of the trial is far from satisfactory as there was no recognition of the specificity of the different crimes and of the different victims. What the court should have done is to qualify crimes against Résistants as crimes against humanity and crimes against Jews as genocide. Had it done so, the question of statutory limitations would have never been raised – genocide being included in the prohibition of statutes of limitations – and the crimes would have retained their specificity through their adequate qualification.

---

[95] Article 157 of the Italian Penal Code. See Military Court of Rome, 1 August 1996. Subsequently, the Court of Cassation held that the principle of non-applicability of statutory limitations to war crimes and crimes against humanity was a *jus cogens* norm. The Appellate Military Court confirmed this judgment on appeal and Priebke was sentenced to life imprisonment.

[96] Article 213-5 of the Nouveau Code Pénal reads : 'L'action publique relative aux crimes prévus par le présent titre [crimes contre l'humanité], ainsi que les peines prononcées sont imprescriptibles.'

The question of statutory limitations arose again in France and regained actuality through the debates surrounding the crimes committed in Algeria during the war of decolonisation and the possibility to prosecute them.[97] As it appears that – very conveniently for the French authorities – the crimes perpetrated during this war, and notably the systematic and planned actions of torture as well as the massive killings of civilians, are to be considered as war crimes, their perpetrators will escape prosecution and punishment. Had statutory limitations not been applicable to war crimes, as is the case for crimes against humanity, the criminals will not have been able to evade justice. It is nonetheless submitted here that the crimes perpetrated during this conflict were in fact crimes against humanity, and not war crimes, and should thus never have been submitted to statutes of limitations in the first place. It can in fact be safely asserted that, in this context, the qualification of these crimes as war crimes is in fact a highly political decision, this qualification necessarily impeding prosecution of the criminals due to the applicability of statutes of limitations. This argument is further reinforced by the fact that these crimes were also covered by the 1968 law of amnesty – here again a political manoeuvre – in order to ensure that they never could be prosecuted. And even if it was demonstrated that amnesties should not be recognised in the case of international crimes, the ultimate obstacle to the prosecution of the crimes perpetrated in Algeria would be the Code Pénal itself. Indeed, under French law, the actual definition of crimes against humanity does not apply to crimes committed before 1994, date of entry of the New Penal Code, unless they are related to the Second World War. In other words, under the French legislation, the only crimes against humanity which were perpetrated before 1994 were, again very conveniently, those committed by the Axis Powers or their accomplices. Law and historical truth do not necessarily go hand in hand, to say the least.

Considering international criminal law as it stands today, the problem of statutory limitations appears to have been definitively solved with the adoption and entry into force of the Rome Statute of the ICC. Its Article 29 indeed eliminated all doubts by unequivocally affirming that 'the crimes within the jurisdiction of the Court shall not be subject to any statute of limitations'. It is thus to be hoped that this will pave the way for the recognition of a new international legal rule which will in turn trigger harmonisation among the various domestic legal systems.

[97] See eg Thoraval, Armelle, 'Criminel de guerre ou contre l'humanité', *Libération*, 4 May 2001.

b. Confirming the seriousness of war crimes

The proposal that the concept of war crimes should draw upon that of crimes against humanity and use it as a model for further evolution would ultimately contribute in affirming the importance and seriousness of war crimes. For instance, such evolution would uphold the value of war crimes as international crimes and would, in the future, prevent such rulings as that of Trial Chamber I of the ICTR in the *Kambanda* case, where it held that:

> The Chamber has no doubt that despite the gravity of the violations of Article 3 common to the Geneva Conventions and of the Additional Protocol II thereto, they are considered as *lesser crimes* than genocide or crimes against humanity.[98]

The debate over the gravity of war crimes as compared to that of crimes against humanity also occurred within the ICTY where the judges have been divided on whether crimes against humanity were more serious than war crimes, and on whether the same criminal conduct should entail a heavier penalty if characterised as a crime against humanity. This issue arose in the *Erdemović* case in which the defendant, accused of participating in the killing of civilians, pleaded guilty to the charge of murder as a crime against humanity, but dismissed the alternative charge of murder as a war crime. He was sentenced to 10 years of imprisonment and immediately appealed on the ground that his guilty plea was not informed. He then repleaded guilty but to the charge of murder as a war crime and saw his sentence reduced to five years of imprisonment.[99] In his separate and dissenting opinion, Judge Li rightly questioned the assertion that a crime against humanity is necessarily more serious than a war crime and wrote that:

> [t]he gravity of a criminal act, and consequently the seriousness of its punishment, are determined by the intrinsic nature of the act itself ant by its classification under one category or another. Take the present case: the Appellant killed 70 to one 100 innocent civilians. Whether his criminal act is classified under crimes against humanity or war crimes, the harm done to individuals and society is

[98] *Prosecutor* v *Kambanda,* Case No ICTR 97-23-S, Judgment and Sentence, Trial Chamber I, 4 September 1998, para 14. Emphasis added. In fact, the ICTR established a precise hierarchy among crimes and held that genocide 'constitutes the crime of crimes'. Ibid, para 16.

[99] *Prosecutor* v *Erdemović,* Case No IT-96-22, Appeal of Sentencing Judgment, Appeals Chamber, 7 October 1997.

> exactly the same, neither an iota more nor less. Then, why should he be punished more severely if his criminal act is subsumed under crimes against humanity and not war crimes?[100]

The issue had, in fact, already arisen in the *Tadić* case when Trial Chamber II found that:

> A prohibited act committed as part of a crime against humanity, that is with an awareness that the act formed part of a widespread or systematic attack on a civilian population, is, all else being equal, a more serious offence than an ordinary war crime. This follows from the requirement that crimes against humanity be committed on a widespread or systematic scale, the quantity of the crimes having a qualitative impact on the nature of the offence which is seen as a crime against more than just the victims themselves but against humanity as a whole.[101]

In this particular case, the appeals chamber however departed from its previous position adopted in the *Erdemović* case and took 'the view that there is no legal distinction between the seriousness of a crime against humanity and that of a war crime'.[102] According to Judge Shahabuddeen:

> Under existing law, which the Tribunal has to apply, there is no principle that, all things being equal, a crime against humanity is more serious than a war crime and that the same act charged as the former has to be punished more severely than if charged as the latter. Today's judgment is in conformity with existing law: it does not recognise such a principle.[103]

[100] Ibid. See Separate and Dissenting Opinion of Judge Li, para 19.
[101] *Prosecutor* v *Tadić*, Case No IT-94-1, Sentencing Judgment, Trial Chamber II, 14 July 1997, para.73. Trial Chamber II reaffirmed this in *Prosecutor* v *Tadić*, Case No IT-94-1, Sentencing Judgment, Trial Chamber II, 11 November 1999, para 28.
[102] *Prosecutor* v *Tadić*, Case No IT-94-1-A and IT-94-1-A *bis*, Judgment in Sentencing Appeals, Appeals Chamber, 26 January 2000, para 69. See also *Prosecutor* v. *Furundžija*, Case No IT-95-17/1, Judgment, Appeals Chamber, 21 July 2000, paras 240-3; *Prosecutor* v. *Delalić et al*, Case No IT-96-21, Judgment, Appeals Chamber, 20 February 2001, para 41 ; *Prosecutor* v *Kunarac et al*, Case No IT-96-23 and IT-96-23/1, Judgment, Trial Chamber II, 22 February 2001, para 891.
[103] *Prosecutor* v *Tadić*, Case No IT-94-1-A and IT-94-1-A *bis*, Judgment in Sentencing Appeals, Appeals Chamber, 26 January 2000, Separate Opinion of Judge Shahabuddeen. See also *Prosecutor* v *Tadić*, Case No IT-94-1, Sentencing Judgment, Trial Chamber II, 11 November 1999, Separate Opinion of Judge Robinson. For an opposite view, see ibid, Separate Opinion of Judge Cassese.

In this respect, an analysis of admissible defences in the context of war crimes also demonstrates that war crimes – and, for that matter, crimes against peace – are generally considered as less 'important' than crimes against humanity and genocide.

First, regarding reprisals, understood as the retributive practices of a state against another state or its nationals in order to force it to respect the international regulation of armed conflicts, international law excludes them as admissible defences for the perpetration of crimes against humanity and genocide. The situation is however far from being as clear with respect to war crimes and crimes against peace. And indeed, according to the UN Charter, 'armed reprisals are prohibited unless they qualify as an exercise of self defence under Article 51' of the UN Charter.[104] In other words, reprisals are not excluded as a defence in the context of war crimes and crimes against peace, recent events having shown that self-defence might be subjectively interpreted by states in order to justify aggression.[105] It may also be recalled here that Article 31 (1) (c) of the ICC Statute also questionably states that, in the case of war crimes, self-defence may be a cause of exoneration of responsibility when used to defend property. Not only does this provision extends the notion of self-defence to the protection of property, but it also artificially distinguishes between war crimes on one side and crimes against humanity and genocide on the other, for which protection of property can never be invoked as a defence. According to David, this provision is 'a Pandora's box that is rigorously incompatible with the law of armed conflict',[106] and that it is nothing less than a violation of *jus cogens* which is accordingly null and void pursuant to the Vienna Convention on the Law of Treaties.[107]

Secondly, it may be recalled here that the defence of military necessity is still accepted as a justification of acts which could easily be qualified as war crimes. For instance, this defence is admitted even in the cases of 'extensive destruction and appropriation of property',[108] as well as of 'wanton destruction of cities, towns or villages, or devastation'.[109]

Thirdly, the provision of the Rome Statute with respect to the defence of superior orders also takes the direction of a 'devaluation' of the notion

[104] Dinstein, Yoram, *War, Aggression and Self-Defence,* Cambridge University Press, 3rd edn, 2001, p. 195 and generally pp. 194-203.
[105] See *infra* IV.
[106] Cited in Schabas, William A., *An Introduction to the International Criminal Court,* Cambridge University Press, 2001, p 90.
[107] Ibid.
[108] Article 2(d) of the ICTY Statute and Article 8 (2) (a) (iv) of the ICC Statute.
[109] Article 3(b) of the ICTY Statute.

of war crimes. Indeed, while the Nuremberg and Tokyo Charters, the Allied Control Council Law No 10 and both Statutes of the International Criminal Tribunals adopted the principle of absolute liability, thus always rejecting the defence of obedience to superior orders, Article 33 of the Rome Statute questionably adopted the conditional liability approach, thus departing from customary international law, and this without any justifiable reasons.[110] In fact, unlike other legal instruments, it does not exclude categorically this defence and it draws a distinction between crimes against peace and war crimes on one side and crimes against humanity and genocide on the other. As it expressly states that 'orders to commit genocide or crimes against humanity are manifestly unlawful',[111] it simultaneously and automatically suggests, by opposition, that orders to commit crimes against peace and war crimes are not always manifestly unlawful. Thus, if the person 'was under a legal obligation to obey orders of the Government or the superior in question',[112] if he or she 'did not know that the order was unlawful',[113] and if '[t]he order was not manifestly unlawful' which remains, under the Statute, a possibility as regards war crimes and crimes against peace,[114] he or she will be relieved of criminal responsibility. What Article 33 implies is that orders to commit crimes against peace and war crimes may not be manifestly unlawful, while Article 8 of the Statute, which gives an exhaustive list of war crimes, clearly covers acts which are undoubtedly crimes. How can an order to commit such acts not be manifestly unlawful? As Cassese rightly recalled, according to customary international law, any order to commit an international crime – regardless of its classification – is illegal and thus may not be urged in defence.[115] He further considered that:

> Given the specificity of Article 8, one fails to see under what circumstances the order to commit one of the crimes listed therein may be regarded as not manifestly unlawful, i.e. if nothing else, it would be 'manifest' in the text of the Rome Statute itself [...] On this score [...] Article 33 must be faulted as marking a retrogression with respect to existing customary law.[116]

[110] According to Gaeta, this new approach is due to the concern of the United States to protect their servicemen on the battlefield from international criminal responsibility if they obey orders in order to carry out military operations. See Gaeta, Paola, '*The Defence of Superior Orders : The Statute of the International Criminal Court* versus *Customary International Law*, (1999) 10 *EJIL* 189.

[111] Article 33(2) of the ICC Statute.

[112] Article 33(1)(a) of the ICC Statute.

[113] Article 33(1)(b) of the ICC Statute.

[114] Article 33(1)(c) of the ICC Statute.

[115] Cassese, Antonio, 'The Statute of the International Criminal Court: Some Preliminary Reflections', (1999) 10 *EJIL* 157.

[116] Ibid. See also Gaeta, Paola, *supra* n 110, pp 172-91.

It is here symptomatic that the Rome Statute provides that, unlike crimes against humanity and genocide which would always be considered as serious enough to trigger the jurisdiction of the court, some war crimes could be seen as falling outside its competence, notably if they were not 'committed as part of a plan or policy or as part of a large-scale commission of such crimes'.[117] If war crimes were to be subjected to the same legal rules than those applicable to crimes against humanity, this harmonisation would ensure their effective prosecution and punishment, simply by excluding the admissibility of some defences and by recognising that war crimes are serious enough to be dealt with in The Hague.

Finally, it must here be recalled that, in order to satisfy some states, and notably France, which required more protection for their military forces against possible prosecutions, Article 124 allows any state to decline the court's jurisdiction over war crimes for seven years renewable. [118] In other words, the Statute here explicitly provides for the possible exclusion of the court's jurisdiction over war crimes, and this for an unlimited period of time. This real 'licence to kill' in complete impunity is all the most shocking and, here again, it shows the utility of drawing upon the definition and legal regime of crimes against humanity as, in their case, there is no 'opt-out' clause with respect to the jurisdiction of the court. This legal manoeuvre would defeat the numerous impediments to the prosecution of war crimes and would thus allow for their effective punishment, the provisions specifically applicable to war crimes being clearly defective.

Ultimately, it is to be hoped that the time will soon come when war crimes will be recognised as nothing but crimes against humanity committed in times of war, whether international or non-international. Clearly, the acts listed as constituting war crimes are nothing other than crimes against humanity and, if the great improvement made after Nuremberg was the recognition that crimes against humanity could be perpetrated in time of peace, it should also be remembered that they can equally be committed in times of war.

[117] Article 8 of the ICC Statute. But see *supra* where it is submitted that war crimes are always committed as part of a widespread attack, and that they are also always perpetrated as part of a plan or policy.
[118] See generally Bourdon, William and Duverger, Emmanuelle, *La Cour Pénale Internationale – Le Statut de Rome*, Editions du Seuil, Collection Points Essais, 2000, pp 296-300.

IV. Crimes Against Peace: From 'the supreme international crime' to Legal Oblivion

In 1946, the Nuremberg Tribunal described crimes against peace as 'the supreme international crime, differing only from other war crimes in that it contains within itself the accumulated evil of the whole'.[1] Although the illegality of crimes against peace, understood here as primarily referring to the crime of aggression, is perhaps the most fundamental norm of modern international law and although its prevention is the chief purpose of the United Nations,[2] such a recognition and a general condemnation of these crimes did not come easily. As a matter of fact, the debates surrounding the respect of the principle of legality by the Nuremberg Tribunal clearly showed that the criminal nature of these acts was still controversial at the end of the Second World War. Subsequently, one would have thought the horrors committed following the waging of the Nazi aggressive war would have generated a tremendous interest for these crimes, accompanied by a clear and determinate will to prosecute them. Astonishingly, the exact opposite happened: since Nuremberg and Tokyo, there has been no such prosecution. The 'supreme crime' against international law clearly seems to have become obsolete, notably due to the fact that the international community has proved totally unable to define these crimes.

Accordingly, the following developments will focus on the evolution of the notion of crimes against peace, from its emergence as an international crime to its subsequent decline. As with no definition there can be no prosecution, the aim of these developments will be to highlight the advantages, notably in terms of prosecution and punishment, of considering crimes against peace as specific crimes against humanity.

A. The emergence of crimes against peace as international crimes

By opposition to the *jus ad bellum*, or the law governing the starting of war, modern international law has witnessed the emergence and evolution of the notion of *jus contra bellum* – or law against war – which, in fact, gradually replaced the *jus ad bellum*. Such

---

[1] *Nuremberg* judgment 186.
[2] See Article 1 of the UN Charter.

transformation was launched by the movement for the 'outlawry of war' and culminated in the punishment of individuals for crimes against peace at Nuremberg.[3]

Indeed, even before the outbreak of the First World War, several international instruments aimed at outlawing war, through the imposition of restrictions and limitations on the right of states to use armed force, were adopted. For instance, the Convention for the Pacific Settlement of International Conflicts at the First Hague Conference of 1899 restricted the right of recourse to war, as the nations thereby agreed 'before an appeal to arms [...] to have recourse, as far as circumstances allow, to the good offices or mediation of one or more friendly powers'. Similarly, the 1907 Second Hague Convention respecting the Limitation of the Employment of Force for the Recovery of Contract Debts participated in the evolution of the concept. It is nonetheless in the aftermath of the first world conflict that the idea actually to criminalise the fact of waging a war emerged.

1. *The abortive attempt of the Versailles Treaty*

At the end of the First World War, at the Paris Conference held on 18 January 1919, a Commission on the Responsibility of the Authors of the War and the Enforcement of Penalties was appointed in order to study such matters as the origins of – and culpability for – the conflict, the offences against the laws and customs of war in its conduct, as well as the constitution of a tribunal to try the accused. Due to opening clashes, it had to divide its work among three sub-committees, the second of which dealt with responsibility for the war, and concluded that, due to the 'purely optional character of the institutions at The Hague for the maintenance of peace,[4] [...] a war of aggression may not be considered as an act directly contrary to positive law'.[5] Furthermore, it found that proving the different responsibilities linked to the authorship of the war would be an extremely difficult task due to the 'difficult and complex problems which might be more fitly investigated' by historians and statesmen than by a court.[6] Subsequently, the Commission concluded

[3] See Woetzel, Robert K., *The Nuremberg Trials in International Law – With a Postlude on the Eichmann Case*, Stevens & Sons Limited, 1962, p 140.
[4] Here referring to the International Commission of Inquiry, Mediation and Arbitration.
[5] 'Commission on the Responsibility of the Authors of the War and on Enforcement of Penalties' (1920) 14 *AJIL* 118. See Glueck, Sheldon, *The Nuremberg Trial and Aggressive War*, Kraus Reprint Co., 1971 (original, 1946), pp 15-16. See also Willis, James F., *Prologue to Nuremberg – The Politics and Diplomacy of Punishing War Criminals of the First World War*, Greenwood Press, 1982, p 73.
[6] 'Commission on the Responsibility of the Authors of the War and on Enforcement of Penalties' (1920) 14 *AJIL* 118. See Glueck, Sheldon, *The Nuremberg Trial and Aggressive War*, Kraus Reprint Co, 1971 (original, 1946), pp 15-16.

that, notwithstanding these 'culpable acts', and this 'high-handed outrage [...] committed upon international engagements, deliberately, and for a purpose which cannot justify the conduct of those who were responsible', it was 'of opinion that no criminal charge can be made against the responsible authorities and individuals on the special head of these breaches of neutrality'.[7] Nevertheless, even if it failed to qualify the treaty-violating acts of aggression as crimes'which the public conscience reproves and which history will condemn',[8] the Commission still declared to be 'desirable that, for the *future, penal sanctions* should be provided for such grave outrages against the elementary principles of international law'.[9]

Subsequently, the feeling that aggressive war was a criminal act started to emerge, notably among politicians. Thus, proposing to bring the Kaiser to trial'solely for the violation' of the treaty guaranteeing the neutrality of Belgium, Lloyd George stated that '[w]ar between nations is justifiable in conformity with the precedents. But an aggression without provocation, without any grievance against the country attacked, committed because it was convenient to cross her territory and in spite of a solemn engagement treated like a scrap of paper is an *indisputable crime*'.[10]

As a consequence, the Treaty of Versailles called for the trial by an international military tribunal of the Kaiser – the Supreme German Commander – for what was to be termed, in Article 6 (a) of the Nuremberg Charter, 'crimes against peace'.[11] Article 227 of the Versailles Treaty thus established the personal responsibility of a commander-in-chief.[12] As Green correctly pointed out, 'by the Treaty of Versailles, it was decided to proceed not against an individual who had committed war crimes himself, but, reviving the views of Vattel, to proceed against the head of State who was held responsible for having launched the War'.[13]

---

[7] Ibid.
[8] Ibid.
[9] Ibid.
[10] Council of Four Meeting, April 8, 1919, Cited in Willis, James F., *supra* n 5, p 79. Emphasis added.
[11] Bassiouni, M. Cherif Bassiouni, *Crimes Against Humanity in International Criminal Law*, 2nd edn (rev), p 425.
[12] Article 227 of the Treaty of Versailles reads as follows: 'The Allied and Associated Powers publicly arraign William II of Hohenzollern , formerly German Emperor, for a supreme offence against international morality and the sanctity of treaties (...)'.
[13] Green, Leslie C., *New Trends in International Criminal Law*, (1981) 11 *Israel Yearbook on Human Rights* 14-15.

Article 231 of the Versailles Treaty – also referred to as a 'war-guilt' clause – clearly affirmed the responsibility of Germany and of its allies for the waging of the aggressive war, thus implying that the contracting parties had actually agreed on the qualification of war as an illegal act.[14] And in fact, the responsibility of Germany was further stated in Articles 232 and following of the Treaty, which provided for Germany's obligation to repair the losses and damages caused to the Allied Powers.

Thus, the Versailles Treaty, by reference to the aggressive war waged by Germany and its allies, not only foresaw the obligation of these states to repair the damages caused, but also considered as 'punishable' the individuals who perpetrated such acts in their quality of organs of the State. Furthermore, the Treaty recognised the jurisdiction of courts and tribunals, other than those of the responsible states and individuals, over such acts. In this respect, the Versailles Treaty departed from International Law at the time, notably regarding the 'acts of state' doctrine as well as the traditional rules in matters of judicial competence.

Although, at the end of the war, the Netherlands gave the Kaiser asylum on the grounds that, as a Head of State, he had committed a political act for which he was immune from prosecution, the fact is that the states parties to the Versailles Treaty linked the war of aggression launched by Germany and its allies not only with the international responsibility of the aggressive states, but also with the personal accountability of the individuals who could thus be tried by courts and tribunals of foreign states.[15]

2. *The efforts of the inter-war period*

a. The League of Nations

In the inter-war period, Article 10 of the Covenant of the League of Nations was at the heart of collective security as the member states of the League undertook 'to respect and preserve as against external aggression the territorial integrity and existing political independence of all Members of the League'. It also stated that '[i]n case of any such aggression or in case of any threat or danger of such aggression the Council shall advise upon the means by which this obligation shall be

[14] Similar clauses appeared in Article 177 of the Treaty with Austria and Article 161 of the Treaty with Hungary. See Jorgensen, Nina H.B., *The Responsibility of States for International Crimes,* Oxford University Press, p. 9.
[15] See Starace Vincenzo, 'La Responsabilité Résultant de la Violation des Obligations à l'égard de la Communauté Internationale', [1976] V *RCADI* 284-285.
[16] Reproduced in Evans, Malcolm D. (ed), *Blackstone's International Law Documents,* 2nd edn, Blackstone Press Limited, 1994, pp 1-8 at 3.

fulfilled',[16] and thus seemed to prohibit wars of aggression. Article 11 of the League Covenant did not in itself impose obligations on any state nor did it provide for any sanctions but it nonetheless granted the Council the power to intervene in cases of war, threat of war, or rupture of the friendly relations between states. Nevertheless, from its very beginning, the Council found itself paralysed by disabling procedural rules attached to its functioning. And indeed, if it could intervene, both contestant states were given the right to be present and vote on the Council, which had to be unanimous in its decisions. As a guilty state would obviously never vote for sanctions to be imposed against itself, the role of the Council was bound to be heavily restricted, if not to say non-existent.[17]

Furthermore, even if it must be acknowledged that the covenant did establish an elaborate set of procedures aimed at restricting the recourse to force, it still allowed for it, notably in cases where one party would refuse to comply with the decision of the settlement.[18] As Woetzel explained, Articles 10 to 16 of the League of Nations Covenant:

> imposed certain conditions which had to be fulfilled before war could be waged. But it was still possible for states legally to wage war, in spite of this net of obligations. The practical effect of the Covenant in international law was to further the distinction between legal and illegal wars, or wars waged after the fulfilment of the legal prerequisites and those launched as aggressive actions. This, as should be noted, is very different from the distinction between just and unjust wars, since a state could conceivably wage a legal war without just cause against a member of the League, if it had previously complied with formal, procedural requirements of the Covenant.[19]

The League Covenant was far from representing the only attempt to try and restrict the use of force and recourse to war during this period, and several other attempts were made in order to clarify and refine the *jus ad bellum*. Consequently, several instruments were drafted or adopted under the League's auspices, and aggression was increasingly being referred as an 'international crime'.[20]

---

[17] See Stone, Julius, *Aggression and World Order – A Critique of United Nations Theories of Aggression*, Stevens & Sons Limited, London, 1958, p 28.
[18] See Article 12 of the covenant.
[19] Woetzel, Robert K, *The Nuremberg Trials in International Law – With a Postlude on the Eichmann Case*, Stevens & Sons Limited, 1962, p 142.
[20] Ibid, pp 142-5.

For instance, Article 1 of the 1923 Draft of a 'Treaty of Mutual Assistance', prepared by the League, the 'High Contracting Parties solemnly declared that aggressive war is an international crime and severally undertake that no one of them will be guilty of its commission'.[21] This Draft Treaty however failed to go beyond the definition of 'aggression' as an 'international crime' and to provide for efficient restrictions regarding recourse to force.

The Geneva Protocol for the Peaceful Settlement of International Disputes was probably the most comprehensive effort of the League of Nations to define aggression. It was unanimously adopted by 48 delegations on 2 October 1924 and was subsequently signed by 19 governments. Its preamble condemned wars of aggression as international crimes by expressly asserting 'that a war of aggression constitutes a violation of international solidarity and an *international crime*', and expressed the willingness 'of ensuring the repression of *international crimes*'.[22] Its Article 2 also stated that the nations were obligated 'in no case to resort to war' and specified that, in the event of a state resorting to war rather than accepting the compulsory arbitration of the dispute, this state would be considered as an aggressor against whom members of the League would be required to impose sanctions, unless the Council of the League unanimously decided otherwise.

If the use of the terms 'international crime' on two occasions, although only in the preamble, is certainly significant, the comments of Politis and Benes, two statesmen involved in the drafting of the protocol, show no intention of attributing to these terms the meaning attributed to them now. Nonetheless, according to Glueck, this protocol 'did express the strong attitude of leading jurists and statesmen of most of the nations of the world regarding both the illegality and the criminalism of aggressive war'.[23] And indeed, it must be recalled here that Article 2 of the protocol sought to limit the cases allowing resort to war to two defined cases: defence from aggression and use of force authorised by a competent organ of the League. Unfortunately, the protocol failed to receive the number of ratifications necessary to enter into force.

Also in 1924, the Draft Treaty of Disarmament and Security declared in its Article 1 that 'aggressive war is an international crime', while its

[21] Records of the Fourth Assembly, Plenary Meetings, League of Nations, *Official Journal*, Sp Supp. No 13 (1923), p 154 and p 403. See Gross, Leo, 'The Criminality of Aggressive War', (1947) XLI *The American Political Science Review* 210-11, and Glueck, Sheldon, *supra* n 5, p 28.
[22] League of Nations, *Official Journal*, Sp. Supp. No 23 (1924), p 225. Emphasis added.
[23] Glueck, Sheldon, *supra* n 5, p 30.

Article 2 stated that a 'State engaging in war for other than purposes of defence commits the international crime described in Article 1'.[24]

Furthermore, on 24 September 1927, the Assembly of the League adopted a resolution which explicitly declared that 'war of aggression [...] is [...] an international crime', and that 'all wars of aggression are, and shall always be prohibited'. The Assembly also unequivocally held 'that a war of aggression can never serve as a means of settling international disputes and is, in consequence, an international crime.'[25] According to Gross, this resolution 'is regarded as a further link in the chain of events which are said to have contributed to the formation of an international custom to regard aggressive war as an international crime'.[26]

b. *The 1928 Kellogg-Briand Pact*

Following these abortive attempts to impose additional restrictions on the *jus ad bellum*, another effort was made during the interwar period to regulate the right of states to go to war. This was the General Treaty for Renunciation of War as an Instrument of National Policy, often referred to as the Pact of Paris or the Kellogg-Briand Pact.[27] The nations who signed or adhered to it unconditionally renounced for the future to use war as a policy instrument. Although it is true that no sanctions were provided by the pact and that no specific machinery was set up for the settlement of differences between states. Wright nonetheless explained that:

> The concert of the nations evidenced by the Pact had the sanction of being embodied in a Treaty, the most formal testimony to its binding force. As a treaty or agreement it only bound the nations which were parties to it. But it may be regarded from a different aspect. It is evidence of the acceptance by the civilized nations of the principle that war is an illegal thing. This principle so accepted and evidenced, is entitled to rank as a rule of International Law. It may be that before the Pact the principle was simply a

[24] Records of the Fifth Assembly, Meetings of the Committee, Minutes of the Third Committee, *League of Nations Official Journal*, Sp Supp. No 26, 1924, Annex 4, p 169.
[25] League of Nations, *Official Journal*, Sp Supp No 54, 1927, p 155.
[26] Gross, Leo, 'The Criminality of Aggressive War', (1947) XLI *The American Political Science Review* 214.
[27] General Treaty for Renunciation of War as an Instrument of National Policy (Kellogg-Briand Pact) 94 LNTS 57. The pact was signed on 27 August 1928 by over 60 states, including all the great powers, and it entered into force on 24 July 1929. Interestingly enough, it is technically still in force today.

> rule of morality, a rule of natural as contrasted with positive law. The Pact, which is clear and specific, converts the moral rule into a positive rule comparable to the laws and customs of war, and like these laws and customs binding on individuals since the principle that individuals may be penally liable for particular breaches of International Law is now generally accepted.[28]

Under the Pact, the signatories declared 'in the names of their respective peoples that they condemn recourse to war for the solution of their international controversies, and renounce[d] it as an instrument of national policy in their relations with one another.'[29] They further agreed 'that the settlement or solution of all disputes or conflicts of whatever nature or of whatever origin they may be, which may arise among them, shall never be sought except by peaceful means.'[30] Hence, unlike the League Covenant which permitted the recourse to war in certain circumstances, the Kellogg-Briand Pact totally and expressly outlawed the resort to war, without any exception. It was nonetheless generally recognised by the parties to the pact that recourse to war would be permissible in the case of self-defence as well as when it was authorised by the League Council in accordance with the provisions of the covenant. In these cases, resort to the use of force would not constitute war 'as an instrument of *national* policy' – which was expressly prohibited by Article 1 of the pact – but 'as an instrument of *international* policy',[31] which remained lawful.

But, unlike the Geneva Protocol, the Kellogg-Briand Pact entered into force and was widely regarded by states as authoritative. Still, this treaty contained serious shortcomings. First, it only explicitly outlawed 'war',[32] and, thus, failed to restrict the use of force short of war. Secondly, since the Kellogg-Briand Pact did not define the concept of self-defence, this notion remained subject to interpretation, and its regime of permissibility was thus left unclear. Thirdly, as Dinstein observed, the use of the words 'national policy' in the prohibition contained in the

[28] Wright, 'War Crimes Under International Law', (1946) 62 *LQR* 50-51.
[29] Article 1.
[30] Article 2.
[31] Dinstein, Yoram, *War, Aggression and Self-Defence,* 3rd edn, Cambridge University Press, 2001, p 79. Emphasis added.
[32] In this respect, Woetzel pointed out that '[i]t has been said that the Kellogg-Briand Pact "outlawed" war; this is technically incorrect, however, since there existed no rule in international law prior to the Pact which permitted war'. See Woetzel, Robert K., *The Nuremberg Trials in International Law With a Postlude on the Eichmann Case,* Stevens & Sons Limited, 1962, pp 145-46.

pact could imply that other motives behind the recourse to war could be permissible and legal. Dinstein indeed argued that 'the 'national policy' formula gave rise to the interpretation that other wars – in pursuit of religious, ideological and similar (not strictly national) goals – were also permitted'.[33] States could thus easily claim that the wars they were waging were not in contradiction with the provisions of the pact and were thus permissible.

Nonetheless, these defects did not impede the pact from playing an important role during the inter-war development of the *jus contra bellum*. First, it led to further efforts to reaffirm and clarify the obligation not to resort to aggressive war. Indeed, during the inter-war period, numerous treaties reiterating this obligation were concluded, among which several 'non-aggression pacts' as well as the 1933 Convention on the Definition of Aggression. Secondly, diplomats and leaders from several states considered the pact as a source of legal obligation. For instance, even after the Second World War had begun, Germany, Italy and Japan were condemned for violations of the pact. As late as 1941, American Secretary of War Stimson spoke of the 'vital change' that 'was made in the system of international law' by the ratification of the pact. As Clark Arend and Beck pointed out:

> [i]t would seem that despite the failure of the Pact to prevent the war, the idea of prohibiting aggressive war had been indelibly planted in the minds of modern world leaders. This idea would surface again after the war in the form of Article 2 (4) of the UN Charter.[34]

Finally, it must be recalled here that the Pact of Paris made no distinction between aggressive, defensive, or other kinds of war. Rather, it renounced all wars. Secretary of State Kellogg thus stated that 'from the broad standpoint of humanity and civilization, all war is an assault upon the stability of human society, and should be suppressed in the common interest'.[35]

---

[33] Dinstein, Yoram, *War, Aggression and Self-Defence*, Cambridge University Press, 1988, p 82.

[34] Clark Arend, Anthony and Beck, Robert J., *International Law and the Use of Force – Beyond the UN Charter Paradigm*, Routledge, 1993, p 24.

[35] Note to the French ambassador, 27 February 1928. Publication of the Department of State entitled *Notes Exchanged Between the United States and Other Powers on the Subject of a Multilateral Treaty for the Renunciation of War*, Washington, Government Printing Office, 1928, in Finch, George A., 'The Nuremberg Trial and International Law', (1947) XLI *AJIL* 30.

Subsequently, other instruments were adopted. Thus, also in 1928, the Sixth International Conference of American States held at Havana adopted two resolutions: the Resolution on Arbitration and Conciliation in which these states expressed 'that they condemn[ed] war as an instrument of national policy in their mutual relations' and the Resolution on Aggression in which they stated 'that war of aggression constitutes an international crime against the human species', and that 'all aggression is considered illicit and as such is prohibited'.[36] Furthermore, the International Conference of American States on Arbitration and Conciliation held in Washington in 1928-1929 adopted the 'General Convention of Inter-American Conciliation', which, in spite of the fact that it focused exclusively on arbitration and conciliation without making any attempt at implementing the condemnation of war, still expressed in its preamble the desire 'to demonstrate that the condemnation of war as an instrument of national policy in their mutual relations [...] constitutes one of the fundamental bases of inter-American relations'. In the words of Hughes, the American delegate in the Committee on Arbitration:

> We are not here to add to international law. We are not here to codify international law. We are not here to create, we have no power to create, additional rights under international law. We have no power to impose upon any state additional duties under international law. We are simply providing means for pacific settlement. [37]

The Anti-War Treaty on Non-Aggression and Conciliation signed at Rio de Janeiro on 10 October 1933 condemned in its preamble 'wars of aggression and territorial acquisitions that may be obtained by armed conquest', and, in its Article 1, the contracting parties 'solemnly declare[d] that they condemn wars of aggression in their mutual relations or those with other states'.[38] This treaty, commonly known as the Saavedra Lamas Pact, is the American counterpart to the Kellogg-Briand Pact and, although it was generally presented as an 'improved Kellogg-Briand Pact', such improvement attached to the means to achieve the

[36] According to Gross, it did 'not appear from the official Report of the American Delegation to that Conference that any particular importance or legal meaning was attached to the condemnation of war or to the declaration that it constituted an international crime' ['Report of the Delegates of the USA to the Sixth International Conference of American States", US Govt Printing Office (1928), p 26]. See Gross, Leo, 'The Criminality of Aggressive War', (1947) XLI *The American Political Science Review* 215.

[37] 'Proceedings of the International Conference of American States on Conciliation and Arbitration', Washington, 10 December 1928 – 5 January 1929, US Govt Printing Office (1929), p 614. See Gross, Leo, *supra* n 36, pp 215-16.

[38] (1936) 906 *US Treaty Series*. See Gross, Leo, *supra* n 36, pp 216-17.

peaceful settlement of international disputes rather than to the concept of individual criminal responsibility.

Finally, it must be recalled here that a number of treaties, known as the London Conventions, were concluded between the Soviet Union and neighbouring states, such as the Convention for the Definition of Aggression of 3 July 1933 between Russia and Afghanistan, Estonia, Latvia, Persia, Romania and Turkey. According to Glueck:

> The fact that the contracting Parties to a treaty have agreed to render aggressive war illegal does not necessarily mean that they have decided to make its violation an international crime.[39][...] These solemn expressions [...] may be regarded as powerful evidence of the existence of a widely prevalent custom among civilized peoples sufficient to energize a juristic climate favorable to the regarding of a war of aggression as not simply 'unjust' or 'illegal' but downright *criminal*.[40]

But the trend towards the outlawry of war was short-lived and, in the words of Stone, '*Inter arma silent definitiones* might be a significant maxim for the decade of muted debate on the definition of aggression from 1935 to 1945'.[41]

3. *Nuremberg and crimes against peace*

a. Crimes against peace and the principle of legality

The idea of charging the Nazis with the crime of starting the Second World War was controversial at the time and has remained so ever since. For the Americans, crimes against peace were the chief offence of the Nazis, and the criminality of aggressive war needed to be enshrined in international law. But starting a war had not been regarded as criminal up to that time. The Kellogg-Briand Pact of 1928, which outlawed war, only rendered aggression an *illegal* act for states, not a *criminal* act for which *individuals* could be tried.

> Nonetheless, even if 'the French resisted the concept for this reason',[42] while the Soviets 'were concerned about criminalising aggressive war given their invasions of

[39] Glueck, Sheldon, *supra* n.5, p. 21.
[40] Ibid. at 34.
[41] Stone, Julius, *Aggression and World Order – A Critique of United Nations Theories of Aggression*, Stevens & Sons Limited, 1958, p 46.
[42] Ratner, Steven, ' Crimes against Peace', in Gutman, Roy and Reiff, David (eds), *Crimes of War – What the Public Should Know*, W.W Norton& Company Ltd, 1999, P 109.

> Finland and annexation of parts of Poland',[43] 'the American view prevailed – though the Tribunal's jurisdiction was limited to *Axis* aggression – leading to the conviction of high-ranking Nazis for crimes against peace'.[44]

As the tribunal famously stated:

> The charges in the Indictment that the defendants planned and waged aggressive wars are charges of the utmost gravity. War is essentially an evil thing. Its consequences are not confined to the belligerent States alone, but affect the whole world. To initiate a war of aggression, therefore, is not only an international crime; it is the supreme international crime differing only from other war crimes in that it contains within itself the accumulated evil of the whole.[45]

The tribunal also held that Article 6(a) of the London Charter, which dealt with crimes against peace, was declaratory of modern international law, which regards war of aggression as a grave crime,[46] and that:

> The Charter is not an arbitrary exercise of power on the part of the victorious Nations, but in the view of the Tribunal, as will be shown, it is the *expression of international law existing at the time of its creation*; and to that extent is itself a contribution to international law. [47]

This pronouncement instigated much criticism at the time, but, in the words of Dinstein, 'it is virtually irrefutable that present-day international law reflects the Judgment'.[48] Also, even if the tribunal unequivocally stated that, due to the criminalisation of crimes against peace in the charter, it was 'not strictly necessary to consider whether and to what extent aggressive war was a crime before the execution of the London Agreement',[49] it still relied on several relevant instruments, namely, the 1899 Hague Convention, the 1907 Convention for Pacific Settlement of International Disputes and the accompanying Convention Relative to Opening of Hostilities, the Versailles Treaty, the Treaties of Mutual Guarantees, Arbitration and Non-Aggression entered into by

[43] Ibid.
[44] Ibid. Emphasis in original.
[45] *Nuremberg Judgment* 186.
[46] Ibid., pp. 219-23.
[47] Ibid., p. 189. Emphasis added.
[48] Dinstein, Yoram , 'The Distinctions between War Crimes and Crimes Against Peace', *in* Dinstein, Yoram and Tabory, Mala (eds), *War Crimes in International Law*, Martinus Nijhoff Publishers, 1996, p. 2.
[49] *Nuremberg* judgment 190.

Germany Conventions of Arbitration and Conciliation also entered into by Germany, and, most importantly, the 1928 Kellogg-Briand pact. Indeed, the tribunal quoted the text of the Pact, binding sixty-three nations, including Germany, Italy and Japan at the outbreak of the war in 1939, and referred to the analogous situation of the Hague Convention, violation of which created individual criminal liability, in order to find that the result was to make the waging of aggressive war illegal and those committing the act criminally liable.[50] The tribunal also cited various draft treaties, and resolutions of the League of Nations and of the Pan-American Organization declaring aggressive war a crime and added that:

> All these expressions of opinion, and others that could be cited, so solemnly made, reinforce the construction which the Tribunal places upon the Pact of Paris that *resort to a war of aggression is not merely illegal, but is criminal.* The prohibition of aggressive war demanded by the conscience of the world, finds its expression in the series of Pacts and Treaties to which the Tribunal has just referred.[51]

As regards the pact, it found that:

> The nations who signed the Pact or adhered to it unconditionally *condemned recourse to war* for the future as an instrument of policy, and expressly renounced it. After the signing of the Pact, any nation resorting to war as an instrument of national policy breaks the Pact. In the opinion of the Tribunal, the solemn renunciation of war as an instrument of national policy necessarily involves the proposition that *such a war is illegal in international law*; and that those who plan and wage such a war, with its inevitable and terrible consequences, are committing a *crime* in so doing. War for the solution of international controversies undertaken as an instrument of national policy certainly includes a war of aggression, and such a war is therefore outlawed by the Pact.[52]

The judgment argued that, even if the pact did not expressly state that such wars were crimes and did not appoint any courts for the trial of the aggressor:

---

[50] Ibid, pp 218-19.
[51] Ibid, p 220. Emphasis added.
[52] Ibid, p 191. Emphasis added.

> it must be remembered that international law is not the product of an international legislature, and that such international agreements as the Pact of Paris have to deal with general principles of law, and not with administrative matters of procedure. The law of war is to be found not only in treaties, but in the customs and practices of states which gradually obtained universal recognition, and from the general principles of justice applied by jurists and practised by military courts. This law is not static, but by *continual adaptation* follows the needs of a changing world.[53]

The Nuremberg Subsequent Proceedings confirmed the position of the IMT that crimes against peace had a basis in international law. Thus, the court in the *Ministries* case stated that 'aggressive wars and invasions have since time immemorial, been a violation of international law, even though specific sanctions were not provided'.[54] The same court also found the main legal basis for crimes against peace in the Kellogg-Briand Pact and, as far as individual liability was concerned, it declared that:

> Those who plan, prepare, initiate, and wage aggressive wars and invasions, and those who knowingly, consciously, and responsibly participate therein violated international law and may be tried, convicted, and punished for their acts.[55]

As a concluding remark to this overview of the position of the Nuremberg Tribunal on the issue of crimes against peace and of the respect of the principle of legality, it might be suggested that the arguments previously brought in favour of the emergence of crimes against humanity[56] could also be raised here. In the words of Röling:

> [t]he dreadfulness of World War II made us realise the necessity of preventing wars in the future. [...] [T]he conviction was carried that to plan and initiate aggressive war was a crime. This conviction signified a revolution in legal thought. It introduced in international law the concept

[53] Ibid, p 221. Emphasis added.
[54] *United States* v *Von Weizsaecker et al*, Case No 11, Military Tribunal IV, 12-14 *Nuremberg Subsequent Proceedings* 319.
[55] Ibid, pp 321-22. See also *United States* v *Von Leeb et al*, Case No 12, Military Tribunal V, 10-11 *Nuremberg Subsequent Proceedings* 487-491.
[56] See I A.

> of individual criminal responsibility for the maintenance of a minimum standard of human behavior, as formulated in some essential rules of the law of nations.[57]

Thus, even if it is perfectly true that criminal individual responsibility for crimes against peace was a 'creation' of Nuremberg, it obviously may be argued that this was perfectly legitimate. Furthermore, it is to be admitted that the findings of the Nuremberg Tribunal and the new principles it established were nothing less than the logical consequence of the efforts made during the inter-war period and of the favourable climate towards outlawry of war. Ultimately, as Baxter rightly states:

> the very fact that it [the Tribunal] has declared that the Pact is evidence of customary international law gives that proposition all the force commanded by a pronouncement of an international tribunal – whether right or wrong.[58]

In any case, these considerations did not prevent the tribunal from charging – and punishing – the war criminals with crimes against peace as it held that:

> In the first place, it is to be observed that the maxim *nullum crimen sine lege* is not a limitation of sovereignty, but is *in general* a principle of justice. To assert that it is unjust to punish those who in defiance of treaties and assurances have attacked neighboring states without warning is obviously untrue, for in such circumstances, the attacker must know that he is doing wrong, and so far from it being unjust to punish him, it would be unjust if his wrong were allowed to go unpunished.[59]

With this holding, the tribunal unequivocally established the principle of individual criminal responsibility for crimes against peace. As in the case of crimes against humanity, justice required that such offences were tried and punished.

---

[57] Röling, Bert V.A., 'The Nuremberg and the Tokyo Trials in Retrospect', in Bassiouni, M. Cherif and Nanda, Ved P. (eds), *A Treatise on International Criminal Law, Volume I: Crimes and Punishment*, Charles C. Thomas Publisher, 1973, p 603.
[58] Baxter, R.R., 'Multilateral Treaties as Evidence of Customary International Law', (1965/1966) 41 *BYBIL* 279.
[59] *Nuremberg* judgment 219. Emphasis added.

b. *Individual criminal responsibility for crimes against peace*

The issue of intent is highly relevant in the case of crimes against peace as it appears that such intent can only exist if the perpetrator of such a crime is in a superior position. It is true that, along with its Far-East counterpart at Tokyo, Nuremberg still remains the only instance where the accused were charged with crimes against peace and that its case-law is thus the only valid precedent one can rely on. Article 6 (a) of the Nuremberg Charter categorised 'planning' for, 'preparation' for, or 'participation' in a common plan or conspiracy for the accomplishment of a 'war of aggression as a crime against international peace'. It should be stressed here that this category of crimes carried criminal responsibility only for involvement in wars of aggression and not for participation in aggressive acts short of war. Therefore, while such acts could be described as threats of aggression, the Nuremberg Charter criminalised only those acts which could amount to threats to commit a war of aggression, and not mere threats to commit aggressive acts short of war.[60]

> Thus, at Nuremberg, emphasis was put on the preparation, initiation and waging of an aggressive war. However, the interpretation of the Nuremberg Tribunal narrows the meaning of the words 'planning' and 'preparation' to activities intended by the individual to contribute to the 'initiation' of a war which he knows will be 'aggressive', and it narrows the word 'waging' to activities intended by the individual to win such a war. [...] The planning, preparation, initiation and waging must be related to an actual or concretely planned war which the individual believes has been, or is about to be, initiated for aggressive purposes in the sense that the hostilities do, or would, constitute the international delinquency of aggressive war [...] Even if this intent was aggressive, he would still be immune from liability if he acted in pursuance of a lawful act of State, that is if in fact the war was not aggressive. He is not guilty unless both in his intention and in international law the war was, or would be, aggressive.[61]

As a matter of fact, the tribunal found that Schacht's financial and armament building activity, which he terminated in November 1937

[60] McCormack, Timothy L. H. and Simpson, Gerry J., 'The International Law Commission's Draft Code of Crimes against the Peace and Security of Mankind : An Appraisal of the Substantive Provisions', (1994) 5 *Crim L F* 27.
[61] Wright, Quincy, 'The Law of the Nuremberg Trial', (1947) 49 *AJIL* 67.

when he discovered Hitler's intention to resort to aggressive war, was not 'preparation' of aggressive war. Thus, despite the facts that he was responsible for the rapid rearmament of Germany after 1933 and that he 'was in a peculiarly good position to understand the true significance of Hitler's frantic rearmament, and to realise that the economic policy adopted was consistent only with war as its object',[62] the tribunal found that:

> [r]earmament of itself is not criminal under the Charter. To be a crime against peace under article 6 it must be shown that Schacht carried out this rearmament as part of the Nazi plans to wage aggressive wars.[63]

Similarly, the tribunal also found that Fritzche's propaganda activity aimed at supporting collective morale during the war was not inconsistent with the defensive intent this defendant claimed to have had. It may here be noted that an American tribunal, in the *High Command* case, found that 'in the intent and purpose for which it [the war] is planned, prepared, initiated and waged is to be found its lawfulness or unlawfulness', and that '[a]s long as there is no aggressive intent, there is no evil inherent in a nation making itself militarily strong'.[64]

In fact, the Nuremberg Subsequent Proceedings are all the more interesting here as, while focusing on the issue of criminal responsibility, they put the emphasis on the personality of the accused charged with crimes against peace. For instance, in the *High Command* case, the tribunal ruled that the criminality of aggressive war attached only to 'individuals at the policy-making level',[65] and was contingent on the actual power of the individual to 'shape or influence' the war policy of his country.[66] Similarly, in the *I.G. Farben* case, another tribunal declared that only those individuals in the execution of policies are to be held liable for crimes against peace.[67] Subsequently, the ILC stated that only 'high-ranking military personnel and high State officials' could be guilty of waging war of aggression,[68] while both its 1991 and 1996 Draft Codes also restricted the circle of potential perpetrators to leaders and organisers.[69]

[62] *Nuremberg* judgment 106.
[63] Ibid.
[64] *United States* v *Von Leeb et al*, Case No 12, Military Tribunal V, 10-11 *Nuremberg Subsequent Proceedings* 762.
[65] Ibid, p 486.
[66] Ibid, pp 488-89.
[67] *United States* v *Krauch et al*, Case No 6, Military Tribunal VI, 7-8 *Nuremberg Subsequent Proceedings* 1124-25.
[68] ILC Report , Second Session, [1950] II *ILC Yearbook* 376.
[69] 1991 Draft Code of Crimes, [1991] II (2) *ILC Yearbook* 95-96, and 1996 Draft Code of Crimes, [1996] II (2) *ILC Yearbook* 42-43.

However, if the existence of such a limited 'circle of potential perpetrators' was justifiable at the time due to the fact that only high-ranking individuals could launch an aggressive war, such a restriction now seems inappropriate. Indeed, the development of new and cheaper means of warfare gives the possibility to plain individuals, and not only to official policy-makers, to initiate an aggressive war and to 'shape or influence' not only the war policy of their own country, but also that of many other states. By including crimes against peace among crimes against humanity, the limitation as to the perpetrators of these crimes would disappear and, therefore, prosecution for crimes against peace might become possible.

B. Defining crimes against peace

In the spring of 1945, the delegates of 49 states met in San Francisco to draft the Charter of the United Nations. In this charter, these delegates pledged their determination 'to save succeeding generations from the scourge of war, which twice in [their] lifetime [had] brought untold sorrow to mankind'.[70] From then on, the struggle to achieve peace worldwide has been the essential purpose of the United Nations. However, facts clearly show that international peace has remained utopian and thus suggest a need for change and improvement, notably due to the fact that the existing instruments on the issue fall short of satisfactorily defining the crime itself. Indeed, if the UN Charter provides for a general prohibition of the use of force,[71] it nonetheless fails to define the term 'aggression', thus raising many unanswered questions, and notably whether only wars of aggression are seen as international crimes, or if this incrimination also covers acts of aggression.[72] So far, the main achievement on the issue was made by the General Assembly which, after a 20 year project to define aggression, finally completed its task in resolution 3314.[73] According to the General Assembly, '[a] war of aggression is a crime against international peace',[74] and, unlike other acts of aggression short of war, is an international crime. As the Resolution was however intended as a guide for the Security Council and not as a definition for judicial use, it only deals with aggression by states, and not with the crimes of individuals. Due to the failure of the Resolution to provide for a legally binding definition

[70] See preamble of the UN Charter.
[71] Article 2(4) of the UN Charter.
[72] See generally Stone, Julius, *Aggression and World Order – A Critique of United Nations Theories of Aggression*, Stevens & Sons Limited, 1958, pp 43-95.
[73] Resolution on the Definition of Aggression 1974, adopted without a vote, 14 December 1974, GAOR, 29th Session, Supp 21. Its Article 1 defines 'aggression' as 'the use of armed force against the sovereignty, territorial integrity or political independence of another State'.
[74] Article 5(2) of the resolution.

of aggression for the purpose of determining individual criminal responsibility, such as a dfinition remains non-existent. In this context, it is to be highly deplored that the draftsmen of the ICC Statute missed this opportunity to fill in this gap as the Rome Statute only mentions 'aggression' with absolutely no precision whatsoever.

As a matter of fact, one of the important compromises at Rome was the decision to include the crime of aggression within the subject-matter jurisdiction of the Court. Indeed, as it is the international crime which, by its very nature, is the most political, states never wanted to be bound by a definition, in order to keep a power of appreciation on a case by case basis regarding the political opportunity to qualify an aggressor as such.

Not surprisingly, the inclusion of the crime of aggression in the Rome Statute has been a contentious issue since the beginning of the process. States opposed to the inclusion of aggression emphasised that there is no legally binding definition of that crime for the purpose of determining individual criminal responsibility.[75] Thus, the Statute provides for the Court's jurisdiction over crimes against peace only if and when states formally amend that Statute to add a definition of the crime and the conditions for the exercise of jurisdiction. Still, Article 5 (2) of the Statute is a reminiscence of the willingness of states not to be subjected to the court's jurisdiction:

> The Court shall exercise jurisdiction over the crime of aggression once a provision is adopted *in accordance with Articles 121 and 123* defining the crime and setting out the *conditions* under which the Court shall exercise jurisdiction with respect to this crime. Such a provision shall be *consistent with the relevant provisions of the Charter of the United Nations.*[76]

By making a direct reference to Articles 121 and 123, this Article provides that it is only after a period of seven years from the date of entry into force of the Statute, that an Assembly of States Parties or a Review Conference will be able to adopt an amendment providing for the definition of the crime of aggression. Also, such an amendment will only, according to Article 121(5), 'enter into force for those States Parties which have accepted the amendment'. It is thus probable that, if an

[75] Report of the Preparatory Committee on the Establishment of an International Criminal Court, Volume I, Proceedings of the Preparatory Committee March-April, August 1996, UN GAOR, 51st Session, Supp No 22, para 70, UN Doc. No A/5/22 (1996).
[76] Article 5(2) of the ICC Statute. Emphasis added.

amendment is ever adopted, its scope of application will be rather limited: states simply have to refuse the amendment to prevent the court from exercising its jurisdiction over this crime.

Furthermore, by emphasising the importance of the UN Charter, this Article is a reminder that the Security Council remains the responsible organ to 'determine the existence of any threat to the peace, breach of the peace, or act of aggression'.[77] The problem here is that, due to the absence of definition of the crime, the Security Council remains free as to whom is to be qualified as an 'aggressor'. Indeed, the charter leaves the determination of aggression to the Security Council in each case as it arises, and provides no criteria for reaching decisions, over which the permanent members have a right of veto. In other words, it is most probable that these Permanent Members have here reaffirmed their willingness to be able to interfere in – and thus, if necessary, to prevent – any qualification of aggression. As a result, it is doubtful that individuals who occupy leadership positions in the administration of a permanent member will be tried. With this provision, Security Council leaders, and most probably their nationals, are here afforded immunity for the commission of the crime of aggression. As Schwebel rightly argued:

> If a body like the Security Council has complete freedom of action in its determination of an act of aggression, it is liable to take arbitrary action, responsive to political rather than legal considerations. [78]

Clearly, the Rome Statute gives a preponderant role to the Security Council,[79] and this role might greatly impede the independence of the court by unduly restricting its jurisdiction over the crime of aggression. Indeed, '[i]f the Security Council is the arbiter of situations of aggression, would this mean that the court can only prosecute aggression once the council has pronounced on the subject?'[80]

Thus, there is a real risk that, if the ICC ever has jurisdiction over crimes against peace, such jurisdiction will remain purely theoretical. If such

[77] Article 39 of the UN Charter.
[78] Schwebel, S.M., 'Aggression, Intervention and Self-Defence in Modern International Law', [1972] II *RCADI* 425.
[79] On the preponderant role of the Security Council, see also Article 16 of the ICC Statute.
[80] Schabas, William A., *An Introduction to the International Criminal Court*, Cambridge University Press, 2001, p. 27.

crimes were generally considered as crimes against humanity, this risk would be avoided, the court having a clearly established jurisdiction over the latter. Furthermore, this requalification would remedy to the problem inherent to the notion of crimes against peace, namely, their lack of definition due to the *impossibility* of a definition...which ultimately resulted in the disappearance of prosecutions for such crimes since the Second World War trials.

Indeed, one has to remember that 'the definition of aggression is one of the most politically oriented operations in a field where politics always plays some role'.[81] Thus, every single definition, or proposal in order to define, the crime of aggression will clearly be influenced by political considerations. Furthermore, the determination of aggression rests on the facts and motives of the particular case, thus rendering undesirable a definition. In the words of Sir Gerald Fitzmaurice:

> one and the same act may be aggression or may be the reverse if committed from different motives and in different circumstances [...] An enumerated definition could...do little more than list a number of acts which are fairly obvious cases of aggression, if committed without adequate justification [...] The whole problem is to determine when certain acts are justified and, therefore, are not aggressive, and when they are not justified, and therefore, are aggressive [...] This determination [...] cannot be achieved by a priori rules laid down in advance.[82]

He also pointed out that:

> an incomplete list would be extremely dangerous because it would almost inevitably imply that other acts not listed did not constitute aggression. States would thus be encouraged to commit the acts not listed, because, prima facie at any rate, they would not be regarded as acts of aggression. In addition, the existence of an incomplete list would show potential aggressors how to accomplish their aims without actually being branded as aggressors, for they would keep their acts within the precise letter of the

81 Hazard, John N., 'Why Try Again to Define Aggression?', (1968) 62 *AJIL* 703.
82 Fitzmaurice, G., 'The Definition of Aggression', [1952] *ICLQ* 140.

> definition and then claim that they were technically justified.[83]

Thus, if from a purely legal point of view a definition would be desirable in order to fulfil the requirements of the principle of legality, and thus to avoid criticism if prosecution for such crimes were to occur, it however appears that, on practical grounds, such a definition could have some major side-effects. In any case, it can be reasonably asserted that, in the light of the impossibility to reach a consensus on a definition during the drafting of the Rome Statute, the likelihood of a definition is very doubtful. On the other hand, this situation of complete impunity for criminals against peace cannot continue. If crimes against peace were generally seen as a sub-category of crimes against humanity, if they were thus included in the list of criminal acts pertaining to crimes against humanity, the problem of defining the crime would be avoided and prosecution would become possible.

In this respect, it might also be pointed out that the confusion and uncertainty as to the definition of crimes against peace was well illustrated by the legal discussion following the terrorist attacks of 11 September 2001 and notably by the debate around the question whether these attacks amounted to the waging of an aggressive war.[84] This legal uncertainty and confusion could clearly be avoided if crimes against peace were considered as crimes against humanity as this would at least provide them with a legal definition.

Furthermore, this legal manoeuvre could also constitute the first step towards considering terrorism as a crime against humanity.[85] This

---

[83] Sir Gerald Fitzmaurice, cited in the Report by the Secretary-General of the United Nations on the Question of Defining Aggression, General Assembly: Official Records: Seventh Session, Annexes, Agenda item 54, UN Doc A/2211, 3 October 1952, p 57. Cited in Schwebel, S.M., 'Aggression, Intervention and Self-Defence in Modern International Law', [1972] II *RCADI* 424.

[84] See Pellet, Alain, 'No, This is not War !', *in The Attack on the World Trade Center : Legal Responses – Discussion Forum*, EJIL website, October 2001. See also Cassese, Antonio, 'Terrorism is also Disrupting Some Crucial Legal Categories of International Law', (2001) 12 *EJIL* 993-1001 and Cassese, Antonio, 'Créons des Tribunaux Internationaux!', *Courrier International* No 583, January 2002, p 29. Suggesting that these acts amounted to an 'armed attack' was NATO's reaction which invoked Article 5 of the Washington Treaty according to which an armed attack against one or more allies in Europe or North America shall be considered as an attack against all. See NATO, Article 5, Treaty of Washington, 4 April 1949, reprinted in 34 UNTS 243.

would, here as well, prevent the unresolved questions of how to legally qualify the particular acts.[86] It was precisely the lack of definition of the crime of terrorism which impeded its inclusion in the Rome Statute, even if, through the adoption of an amendment, its future incorporation has not been ruled out. Still, it is here maintained that an easier way to actually make terrorism a crime under the Statute without having to resort to amendments which always take time and which are also more often than not the result of compromises –not always beneficial in terms of prosecution an punishment of a crime – would be to consider terrorism as a crime against humanity.[87] Clearly, the attacks of 11 September 2001 were nothing else:

> In view of their advance planning, large-scale nature and intentionally targeting of thousands of innocent civilians, there can be little doubt indeed that these attacks meet the description of 'widespread or systematic attack against any civilian population' in the *chapeau* of Article 7 of the Rome Statute and carry the features of 'murder', 'extermination' or 'other inhumane acts', as included in the list of crimes within the purview of crimes against humanity.[88]

This re-categorisation of crimes against peace – including terrorism – as crimes against humanity would not be a legal incongruity as, in reality, these crimes share the same definitional elements. As a matter of fact, the widespread action requirement is fulfilled in both the case of crimes against peace – waging an aggressive war will scarcely be a small-scale act – and of terrorism which is becoming global and which

---

[85] Several authors agree with this proposal. See Byers, Michael, 'Terrorism, The Use of Force and International Law after 11 September', (2002) 51 *ICLQ* 413; Schrijver, Nico, 'Responding to International Terrorism: Moving the Frontiers of International Law for 'Enduring Freedom'?', (2001) XLVIII *NILR* 289; Drumbl, Mark A., 'Judging the 11 September Terrorist Attack', (2002) 24 HRQ 336-8. Also, both the U.N. Secretary-General and the U.N. High Commissioner for Human Rights have identified the attacks as 'crimes against humanity'. See Press releases, 18 October 2001, www.un.org.

[86] The crime of terrorism shares with that of aggression the fact that, for years, the international community has tried unsuccessfully to arrive at a common definition of terrorism, notably due to obvious political issues. See generally Paust, Jordan J. et al, 'Terrorism', *International Criminal Law, Cases and Materials,* Carolina Academic Press, 2nd edn, 2000, pp 995-1012.

[87] During the drafting of the Rome Statute, some states, and notably, Algeria, India, Sri Lanka and Turkey proposed that terrorism be considered as a crime against humanity. See A/C.183/C.1/L.27.

[88] Schrijver, Nico, 'Responding to International Terrorism : Moving the Frontiers of International Law for 'Enduring Freedom'?', (2001) 48 *NILR* 289.

might now be on the verge of becoming systematic. Further, both these crimes also fulfil the element of grounds for commission as they both target a 'civilian population', as the war on Iraq or the terrorist attacks sadly illustrate. It thus seems that the embodiment of these two offences within the concept of crimes against humanity would remedy to the numerous lacunae of the definitions – or non-definitions – of these crimes. In the words of Warren R. Austin, Chief Delegate of the United States, in his opening address to the UN General Assembly on 30 October 1946:

> Besides being bound by the law of the United Nations Charter, twenty-three nations, members of this Assembly, including the United States, Soviet Russia, the United Kingdom and France, are also bound by the law of the Charter of the Nuremberg Tribunal. That makes *planning or waging a war of aggression a crime against humanity* for which individuals as well as nations can be brought before the bar of international justice, tried and punished.[89]

[89] *The New York Times*, 31 October 1946. Cited in Wright, Quincy, 'The Law of the Nuremberg Trial', (1947) 41 *AJIL* 38. Emphasis added.

V. The State and International Crimes

As the title unequivocally indicates, the following developments focus on the concept of state action in the perpetration of international crimes and thus depart – although, as we will see, only partly[1] – from the previous chapters of the present book which dealt with individual criminal responsibility. Furthermore, the subsequent analysis will also go beyond the concept of state direct responsibility for international crimes and will explore issues of state moral responsibility in connection with the prevention of such crimes.

The purpose of this development is not to contemplate the issue of international crimes committed by states within the context of the work of the International Law Commission and of its effort to codify and develop the law on this issue. And indeed, Draft Article 19 of the ILC Draft Articles on State Responsibility dealt with the notion of state crimes and Draft Article 19(2) unequivocally stated that:

> An interntionally wrongful act whcih results from the breach by state of an international obligation so essential for the protection of fundamental interests of the international community that its breach is recongized as a crime by that community as a whole constitutes an international crimes.[2]
>
> Nontheless when the question of international crimes by states was revisited, the concept of 'crime' was totally deleted in favour of that of 'serious breach by a State of an obligation.'[3] Notwithstanding the disappearance of the notion of 'crime' from the ILC's Draft Articles on Responsibility of States for internationally Wrongful Acts, the following development will still address this notion which, as it will be demonstrated, has yet to be satisfactorily solved.

---

[1] See *infra* V B.

[2] [1976] II *ILC Yearbook* 95-6.

[3] See [2001] Report of the International Law Commission on the work of its Fifty-third session, Official Records of the General Assembly, Fifty-sixth session, Supplement No 10 (A/56/10), ch IV.E.1.

A. The perpetration of international crimes: the legal responsibility of the criminal state?

1. *State participation in the perpetration of international crimes*

In the context of international crimes, yet another definitional – and often critical – element is required: the governmental involvement in the commission of the acts. As Bassiouni rightly pointed out, international crimes are either 'the product of "state-action" or the result of a "state-favouring policy" by commission, or as a result of a lack of state enforcement, that ranges from permissiveness to purposeful omission'.[4] However, he also stated, and rightly so, that:

> In all cases, individuals commit crimes. What is called 'state action' and 'state-favouring policy' does not alter the fact that one or more individual authors are involved. The characterizations of 'state action' and 'state-favouring policy' refer to collective decision-making and actions by individuals who develop a policy or who execute a policy or carry out acts which constitute international crimes under color of legal authority. Decision-makers are usually few in comparison to the entire apparatus of government, let alone to the entire population of a state [...] The invocation of the concept of state responsibility is, however, a symbolic act by the international community to stigmatise regimes that engage in internationally proscribed policies and conduct, irrespective of the effective results of the stigmatisation in altering the internationally proscribed behaviour.[5]

The idea that only individuals can commit crimes can be found as early as 1923, when the PCIJ held that 'States can act only by and through their agents and representatives'.[6] In the same vein, Justice Jackson, in his opening statement at Nuremberg, stated:

> While it is quite proper to employ the fiction of responsibility of a state or corporation for the purpose of

[4] Bassiouni, M. Cherif (ed.), *International Criminal Law, Volume I: Crimes*, Transnational Publishers, Inc., 2nd edn, 1999, p 27.
[5] Ibid, pp 27-8.
[6] German Settlers in Poland, PCIJ No.6, at 22 (1923). Cited in Bassiouni, M. Cherif, *Crimes Against Humanity in International Criminal Law*, Kluwer law International, 2nd edn (rev), 1999, p 269.

> imposing a collective liability, it is quite intolerable to let such a legalism become the basis of personal immunity.[7]

At Nuremberg, the tribunal also famously stated that '[c]rimes against international law are committed by men, not by abstract entities, and only by punishing individuals who commit such crimes can the provisions of international law be enforced'.[8] The tribunal neither denied nor admitted the criminal responsibility of states, but based itself on the principle of individual responsibility. Still, as Friedlander rightly observed, '[t]he victorious allies in both world wars treated the defeated states as criminal entities'.[9] He further explained that:

> Despite the impossibility of placing the German state in the dock at Nuremberg, Germany was on trial with its major war criminals. There can be no doubt that the allies intended to punish the German nation as well as its captured leaders. The Yalta Conference meetings, declarations, and documents are replete with references to the 'dismemberment of Germany', sizeable reparations, and enforced disarmament.[10]

It is true that state responsibility is a highly political issue which was thus eluded by the Nuremberg Tribunal which instead concentrated on individual criminal responsibility. In the words of Bassiouni:

> 'Nuremberg' focused on individual criminal responsibility for conduct that was the product of state policy and for which collective responsibility and state responsibility could have been assessed. Those who established the IMT were careful to avoid the notions of state and collective responsibility, except with respect to criminal organization, namely the S.S., S.D., and S.A. The simple reason is that these governments did not want to establish a principle that could one day be applied to them.[11]

[7] Jackson, Robert H., *The Nürnberg Case*, Cooper Square Press, Inc., 1972, pp. 88-89.
[8] *Nuremberg* judgment 565-66.
[9] Friedlander, Robert A., 'Problems of Enforcing International Criminal Law', in Bassiouni, M. Cherif (ed), *International Criminal Law, Volume III : Enforcement*, Transnational Publishers, Inc., 1987, p 15.
[10] Ibid.
[11] Bassiouni, M. Cherif, 'The "Nuremberg Legacy", in Bassiouni, M. Cherif (ed.), *International Criminal Law, Volume III: Enforcement*, Transnational Publishers, *Inc.*, 2nd edn, 1999, p 210.

In the *Eichmann* case, the court was less cautious and unequivocally stated that '[a] State that plans and implements a 'final solution' cannot be treated as *par in parem*, but only as a gang of criminals'.[12]

As regards the crimes studied in the present book, it seems clear that they all are the product of state policy in the sense that they all rely on the state apparatus, or on an organisation which has the same features than the state apparatus, in order to be committed. In other words, state action – or policy – corresponds to an objective reality in the commission of international crimes. History has indeed show that crimes against humanity and genocide needed an organisational policy in order to be perpetrated while crimes against peace and war crimes, because directly linked to a war, also rely on the state apparatus in order to be committed.

The purpose of the following developments is not to put into question the existence of the concept of state action as an objective element in the commission of international crimes. Rather, it is to analyse whether state action is – or is to be – considered as a legal component of the above-mentioned crimes or if it should merely be regarded as an evidentiary tool for their qualification and prosecution. In this respect, it may be pointed out that the particular case of war crimes will not be studied in this chapter as in their case the question does not really arise. Indeed, all armed conflicts being by definition nothing but policies conducted by one or more states – or by an organisation or even by an organised group of individuals – war crimes are always the direct consequences of this policy. In any event, from a legal point of view, state action *per se* is not required in order to qualify a war crime as such: what is required for this qualification is the existence of a conflict, from which state action or organisational policy may then be induced. The matter is nonetheless far less settled in the case of crimes against humanity, genocide and even crimes against peace.

a. State crimes against humanity

The analytical study of the definition of crimes against humanity shows that the question whether the qualification of a crime as such requires

[12] *Attorney-General of the Government of Israel* v *Eichmann*, 36 ILR 46 (Israel District Court – Jerusalem, 1961). Cited in David, Eric, 'L'actualité juridique de Nuremberg', in Centre de Droit International de l'Institut de Sociologie de l'Université Libre de Bruxelles (Centre Henri Rolin) et Fondation Auschwitz – Stichting (Centre d'Etudes et de Documentation), *Le Procès de Nuremberg – Conséquences et Actualisation*, Actes du Colloque International, Université de Bruxelles, 27 Mars 1987, Editions Bruylant, Editions de l'Université de Bruxelles, 1988, p 144. The Israeli court here rejected the acts of state doctrine which lies in the principle *par in parem non habet jurisdictionem*, according to which a sovereign state cannot prosecute another sovereign state.

the existence of a state policy or of some form of organisational policy has yet to be definitely settled.

From a purely historical point of view, facts clearly indicate that, until now, the commission of crimes against humanity primarily relied on the state apparatus. Thus, already in their joint declaration of 1915, the Allies acknowledged this reality by condemning the 'new crimes of *Turkey*', and by stating that members of the government or their responsible agents would be tried.[13] Similarly, it must be recalled that the Nazis used the state apparatus and bureaucracy in order to achieve their horrendous crimes. Indeed, as soon as he obtained dictatorial powers over Germany, Hitler focused his attention on what he would do about the Jews and, by 1935, the violence of the Nazi anti-Semitism was channelled into law. A series of laws were unanimously adopted at the annual Congress at Nuremberg. These laws, termed the 'Nuremberg Laws', made anti-Semitism legal. In other words, persecutions against Jews became legal, and this was nothing else than the policy of the German Nazi State.

In this respect, it may be recalled here that the IMT Charter gave the tribunal the authority to punish persons '*acting in the interests of the European Axis countries*, whether as individuals or as members of organizations'.[14] It is true that the Allied Control Council Law remained silent on the matter but it may be still be noted that most of the individuals tried under it were governmental officials. However, in the cases of the German industrialists who took advantage of the Nazi policies, the American courts adopted a looser standard and found defendants guilty based on their conduct towards the victims without requiring any connection with state policy.[15]

Since then, this looser standard seems to have been the one adopted in international law as the ICTY Statute does not mention state policy in its definition of crimes against humanity.[16] The matter gave nonetheless rise to debate within the Yugoslavia Tribunal before being finally settled by the appeals chamber. In the *Tadić* case, Trial Chamber II clearly stated that crimes against humanity need not be associated with a formal state policy against a civilian population but held that proof of an informal policy carried out by non-state actors was sufficient.[17] Subsequently, instead of requiring state action, the *Tadić* decision reached

[13] See Schwelb, Egon, 'Crimes Against Humanity', [1946] *BYBIL* 178-81.
[14] See Article 6 of the IMT Charter. Emphasis added.
[15] See generally *Nuremberg Subsequent Proceedings*.
[16] Article 5 of the ICTY Statute.
[17] See *Prosecutor* v *Tadić*, Case No. IT-94-1, Opinion and Judgment, Trial Chamber II, 7 May 1997, paras 653-54.

the quite reasonable conclusion that crimes against humanity could be committed by non-state entities in *de facto* control of a particular territory.[18] Nonetheless, even if the trial chamber specified that 'it need not be the policy of a state'[19] and that 'such a policy need not be formalized and can be deduced from the way in which the acts occur',[20] it still recognised that crimes against humanity could only be committed when there was a policy to commit such acts. Similarly, in the *Nikoliæ* case, Trial Chamber I, while identifying 'three distinct components' in the concept of crimes against humanity, found that:

> the crimes must, to a certain extent, be organised and systematic. Although they need not be related to a policy established at State level, in the conventional sense of the term, they *cannot* be the work of isolated individuals alone.[21]

Nevertheless, the ICTY Appeals Chamber subsequently departed from these findings and finally settled the tribunal's jurisprudence on this issue by reaching the conclusion that the existence of a plan or policy does not constitute a legal element of crimes against humanity. According to the appeals chamber, it is more an evidentiary tool which can be used in order to prove that the acts were directed against any civilian population or that the attack was widespread or systematic. In the *Kunarac* appeal judgment, the appeals chamber unequivocally held that:

> [...] neither the attack nor the acts of the accused needs to be supported by any form of 'policy' or 'plan'. There was nothing in the Statute or in customary law at the time of the alleged acts which required proof of the existence of a plan or policy to commit these crimes. As indicated above, proof that the attack was directed against a civilian population and that it was widespread or systematic, are legal elements of the crime. But to prove these elements, it is not necessary to show that they were the result of the existence of a policy or plan. It may be useful in establishing that the attack was directed against a civilian population and that it was widespread or systematic (especially the latter) to show that there was in fact a policy or plan, but it may be possible to prove these things by reference to

[18] Ibid, para.654.
[19] Ibid, para.655.
[20] Ibid, para.653.
[21] *Prosecutor* v *Nikolić*, Case No IT-94-2-R61, Review of Indictment Pursuant to Rule 61 of the Rules of Procedure and Evidence, Trial Chamber I, 20 October 1995, para 26. Emphasis added.

> other matters. Thus, *the existence of a policy or plan may be evidentially relevant, but it is not a legal element of the crime.*[22]

Supporting the ICTY Appeal Chamber's position is the fact that the Statute of the Rwanda Tribunal makes no reference to state action in its definition of crimes against humanity.[23] In this instance, this implies that, although many crimes were committed by persons not associated with a recognised state, the Security Council – most probably evidencing state practice – considered that these individuals still had to be tried for crimes against humanity. Although the events in Rwanda clearly showed that some form of organisation was needed in order to perpetrate the crime – such as propaganda through the media – and that the criminal factions had *de facto* control over the country's institutions and media, the wording of the ICTR Statute nonetheless acknowledges the fact that state action is not to be considered as a definitional element of crimes against humanity.

Also illustrating the ICTY Appeal Chamber's assertion that no such requirement exists under customary international law is state practice. As a matter of fact, this requirement is not mentioned in any of the national legislations pre-cited in this work.[24]

Nevertheless, it is doubtful that the decision reached by the ICTY's Appeals Chambers finds any support in the work of the International Law Commission which has a settled – and different – position on the issue. Indeed, the 1954 Draft Code made state action highly relevant, and so did the 1996 Code which mentioned acts 'instigated or directed by a government or by any organization or group'.[25] The Commission's own commentary expressly stated that this also involves private groups and criminal gangs committing systematic or mass human rights violations.

More importantly, the Rome Statute of the ICC also departed from the ICTY case law and become the first legal instrument to require a 'state or organisational policy' in the definition of crimes against humanity.[26]

[22] *Prosecutor* v *Kunarac et al*, Case No IT-96-23 and IT-96-23/1-A, Judgment, Appeals Chamber, 12 June 2002, para 98. Emphasis added. It may be noted here that this position of the appeals chamber was largely foreseeable since the *Jelisić* genocide case. *Prosecutor* v. *Jelisić*, Case No. IT-95-10-A, Judgment, Appeals Chamber, 5 July 2001, para 48. See *infra*.

[23] Article 3 of the ICTR Statute.

[24] However, see *Regina* v *Finta*, [1994] 1 S.C.R. 701, Supreme Court of Canada, 24 March 1994. In this case, the Supreme Court of Canada found that the national statute implied the connection between crimes against humanity and governmental action.

[25] Article 18, [1996] II (2) *ILC Yearbook* 47.

[26] Article 7(2)(a).

In this respect, the ICC Statute is a major step backwards. Such a requirement might indeed contain the risk that massive human rights violations committed by non-state actors would fall outside the definitional scope of crimes against humanity. Even if it may be argued that the use of the term 'organizational' prevents such an absurd result from occurring,[27] the formulation of the Preparatory Commission in the 'Elements of Crimes' is in this respect all the more confusing. Indeed, while the Commission introduced yet another restriction by interpreting 'policy to commit such attack' as requiring 'that the State or organization *actively promote or encourage* such an attack against a civilian population',[28] in a footnote attached to its interpretation of Article 7, the Commission also provided that '[s]uch a policy may, in exceptional circumstances, be implemented by a deliberate failure to take action, which is consciously aimed at encouraging such attack'.[29] It is to be hoped that the ICC will overcome this contradiction and that, even if it applies its statute and thus ignores the *Kunarac* decision, it will at least follow the *Tadić* jurisprudence, according to which 'if the acts occur on a widespread or systematic basis that demonstrates a policy to commit those acts, whether formalised or not'.[30]

This aspect of the Rome Statute is to be highly regretted as, not only is the conclusion reached by the ICTY Appeals Chamber legally correct, it is also the most reasonable. While it is very true that, more often than not, crimes against humanity will need the state apparatus for their commission as only the state – or another organisation usurping the functions of a state – will have the means and resources necessary to perpetrate them,[31] the element of state action should be dealt with great caution and should be considered as an evidentiary element and not as a definitional one.

In this respect, the French experience may be seen as perfectly illustrating the danger of requiring state action in order to characterise

[27] However, some authors however held that the term 'organisational' is ambiguous and if interpreted as a *mens rea* requirement contains the risk of limiting prosecution to high level perpetrators. In this context, culpability for crimes against humanity would then depend on the perpetrator's knowledge that he or she is acting pursuant to a policy. See, eg, McAuliffe de Guzman, Margaret, 'The Road from Rome: The Developing Law of Crimes Against Humanity', (2000) 22 *HRQ* 371.

[28] Elements of Crimes, Article 7, Introduction (3). Emphasis added.

[29] Ibid.

[30] *Prosecutor* v *Tadić*, Case No IT-94-1, Opinion and Judgment, Trial Chamber II, 7 May 1997, para 653.

[31] See Bassiouni, M. Cherif, *Crimes Against Humanity in International Criminal Law*, Martinus Nijhoff Publishers, 1992, pp 248-49: crimes against humanity are 'collective crimes which cannot be committed unless they are part of a given state's policy because their commission requires the use of the state's institutions, personnel and resources in order to commit, or refrain from preventing the commission of, specific crimes described in Article 6(c)'.

a crime as one against humanity. Indeed, not only did the French courts consider the existence of state action as a definitional element of crimes against humanity, but they also added a restrictive condition and required that this state be a state practising a policy of ideological supremacy and that the crimes be committed on behalf of such state.[32] In other words, the notion of crimes against humanity found itself unduly enclosed with one particular state policy: Nazism. The consequences of such a finding was that there could be no crimes against humanity without Nazism and that, therefore, no subsequent complaints for crimes against humanity could ever be filed, notably as to the crimes committed in Algeria by the French army in the 1950s and 1960s.[33]

The Cour de Cassation subsequently confirmed this position in the *Touvier* case, as it stated that the authors or accomplices of crimes against humanity were only punishable if they had acted on the account of a European Axis Power, thus again linking crimes against humanity with the crimes committed by the Axis Powers.[34] When the case was referred to the Cour d'Appel de Versailles, the Cour upheld the finding of the Cour de Cassation and unequivocally stated that:

> Aux termes du Statut du Tribunal militaire international de Nuremberg et de son interprétation jurisprudentielle, seule la politique d'un pays européen de l'Axe est susceptible d'être incriminée de crimes contre l'humanité.[35]

When the case came back before the Cour de Cassation in 1993, the Cour again made a strictly historical reading of the notion of crimes against humanity. It thus confirmed that only the policy of a European Axis Power was liable to be incriminated with crimes against humanity and declared that Touvier's responsibility was engaged only because he was an accomplice in a crime against humanity ordered by a European Axis Power.[36]

The French judges made a restrictive interpretation of the Nuremberg Charter which was completely wrong. Instead of referring themselves to the Nuremberg judgment, they referred themselves to the

[32] *Barbie* case : *Fédération Nationale des Déportés et Internés Résistants et Patriotes et Autres* v. *Barbie*, cass. crim., 20 December 1985. Reprinted in (1986) 90 *RGDIP* 1024.
[33] See *supra*.
[34] *Touvier* case, cass. crim., 27 November 1992, [1993-II] JCP 21.977.
[35] Arrêt de la Chambre d'accusation de Versailles, 2 June 1993.
[36] Touvier was found guilty and condemned to life imprisonment on 20 April 1994, cass. crim., 20 April 1994. He died in prison in July 1996.

motivations of the draftsmen of the charter and made of Nuremberg a law of circumstances, relative to the sole crimes committed by the European Axis Powers during a precise period of time which was now over. In no case should the judges have based their decisions on a time limit, to a given conflict and to specific authors defined by their nationality as neither international law nor domestic law impose such restrictions. This absurd case law could have terrible consequences as no crimes committed today would be qualified as crimes against humanity because they obviously would be exterior, in time and circumstances, to the European Axis Powers.

By emphasising state action as regards particular states, French courts artificially restricted the scope of crimes against humanity and, as a result, there could be no crimes against humanity without Axis Powers. Fortunately, the 1994 French New Penal Code now provides for a broad definition of crimes against humanity which obviously would apply outside the particular context of the Second World War. Still, the notion of crimes against humanity cannot apply to acts committed between 1945 – the end of the Second World War – and 1994 – the date of entry into force of the New Penal Code – and this is clearly an inadmissible *vide juridique*.

The French experience thus clearly highlights the legal risks embodied in the notion of state action as a legal requirement for a crime against humanity to be qualified as such. Nonetheless, if it is indeed submitted here that state action should not be regarded as a definitional element of crimes against humanity but merely as an evidentiary tool, it must also be stressed that this should not in any case be an obstacle to the recognition of state responsibility for such crimes. In this respect, the French case law is rather symptomatic: by artificially modifying the notion of crimes against humanity, the French courts very conveniently avoided the question whether the French state had been an autonomous author of crimes against humanity and, as such, whether it was responsible for their commission.[37] In the *Touvier* case, the Cour de cassation indeed decided, regardless of the historical truth, that Touvier was an accomplice in a crime ordered by the Nazis. It was thus a Nazi collaborator who was charged with – and condemned for – crimes against humanity, and not a member of Vichy France's police: the Milice. In the case of crimes against humanity committed during the Second World War, the facts overwhelmingly show that the entire French State

[37] This case law may also be explained by the desire of the French courts to avoid any complaint for crimes against humanity committed in another context than the Second World War from being filed, and thus to avoid having to recognise the responsibility of the French state in other occurrences.

was a criminal state and the deletion of the state action requirement must never preclude a state from being held responsible for the commission of crimes against humanity.

b. Genocide as a state crime

The state action requirement in the context of genocide raises the exact same questions than in the context of crimes against humanity. Nonetheless, from a legal perspective, the situation might here be more settled, notably since the *Jelisiœ* case before the ICTY in which Trial Chamber I found that the draftsmen of the Genocide Convention:

> [d]id not deem the existence of an organisation or a system serving a genocidal objective as a legal ingredient of the crime.[38]

Subsequently, the appeals chamber unequivocally confirmed this finding and held that:

> *The Appeals Chamber is of the opinion that the existence of a plan or policy is not a legal ingredient of the crime* [of genocide]. However, in the context of proving specific intent, the existence of a plan or policy may become an important factor in most cases. The evidence may be consistent with the existence of a plan or policy, or may even show such existence, and the existence of a plan or policy may facilitate proof of the crime.[39]

For the same reasons than the ones analysed in respect of crimes against humanity, this position, as reflecting customary international law, is legally correct. Nevertheless, the fact that state action is not a legal element of the crime of genocide must not in any instance imply that states cannot be recognised responsible for the commission of this crime as this would clearly be nothing but a legal nonsense. Although it is theoretically correct that one single individual could commit genocide, through the use of a deadly virus aimed at contaminating a designated group for example, this hypothesis has so far remained purely theoretical. Strictly all the genocides committed so far have been crimes organised by a state or by an organisation with all the characteristics and features of a state.

[38] *Prosecutor* v *Jelisić*, Case No IT-95-10-T, Judgment, Trial Chamber I, 14 december 1999, para 100.

[39] *Prosecutor* v *Jelisić*, Case No IT-95-10-A, Appeal Judgment, Appeals Chamber, 5 July 2001, para 48.

It is thus submitted here that, although state action or policy is not a definitional component of the crime of genocide, the issue of state responsibility in the commission of the crime should nonetheless cease to be put into question. If genocide is committed and if a state – or any other organisation – is involved in its commission, the responsibility of this state – or organisation – should be recognised. In this respect, it must be highly regretted that the Genocide Convention does not deal properly with the crime of genocide as one *potentially* committed by the state. Even though its Article IX expressly mentions 'the responsibility of a State for genocide', the whole approach of the Convention is that of individual crime and not of a crime which *could be* instigated by governments.[40] This is all the more surprising as the involvement of the state in the commission of genocide was recognised in Resolution 180 (II), in which the General Assembly stated that genocide was an international crime with national and international responsibilities for individuals as well as for states.[41] Furthermore, during the drafting of the Convention itself and the debates in the Sixth Committee, the Belgian representative stated that genocide could not be committed without the collaboration or the connivance of the governments.[42] Also, in the *Kayishema and Ruzindana* case, the trial chamber of the Rwanda tribunal held that 'it is virtually impossible for the crime of genocide to be committed without some direct involvement on the part of the state given the magnitude of this crime'.[43]

According to Ago, former Special Rapporteur on state responsibility, the Genocide Convention 'failed to do the very thing that needed to be done: namely, to make clear that genocide is a State crime and should result in sanctions against the State'. He thus regarded:

> [a]s totally inadequate to have made a Convention on a matter such as genocide at the end of World War II, in which all that is required for governments to punish those who actually carried out the acts of genocide. Can one really believe that, if a genocide has taken place on the territory

[40] See Finch, George A., 'The Genocide Convention', (1949) 43 *AJIL* 733: the crime of genocide properly defined is 'inherently one committed at the instigation or with the complicity of the States'. See also Horowitz who defined genocide as '*a structural and systematic destruction of innocent people by a state bureaucratic apparatus*'. Horowitz, Irving Louis, *Genocide, State Power and Mass Murder*, Transaction Books, 2nd edn, 1977, p 18 Emphasis in original.

[41] Resolution 180(II), 20 November 1947.

[42] See Robinson, Nehemiah, *The Genocide Convention – A Commentary*, Institute of Jewish Affairs – World Jewish Congress, 1960, pp 25-26.

[43] *Prosecutor* v *Kayishema and Ruzindana,* Case No ICTR-95-1-T, Judgment, Trial Chamber II, 21 May 1999, paras 93-94.

> of a given State, this has happened without the connivance of the higher authorities of that State? And can one expect that those authorities will be willing to punish the individuals or State agencies that carried out the genocide?[44]

For Horowitz, 'genocide is always and everywhere an *essentially political decision*',[45] which:

> [m]ust be conducted with the approval of, if not direct intervention by, the *state apparatus*. Genocide is mass destruction of a special sort, one that reflects some sort of political support base within a given ruling class or national grouping.[46]

In the same vein, Fein defined genocide as 'organised *state murder*',[47] stressing that it is a 'calculated crime',[48] while Jonassohn and Chalk hold that 'twentieth-century genocide was increasingly becoming a case of the *state* physically liquidating a group of its own citizens'.[49]

The fact that the Genocide Convention gives jurisdiction to the ICJ necessarily implies state responsibility as this court only deals with states. Indeed, the International Court of Justice had to deal with the issue of genocide notably in the *Application of the Genocide Convention* case, where it 'observe[d] that the reference in Article IX to "the responsibility of a State for genocide or for any of the other acts enumerated in Article III", does not exclude any form of State responsibility'.[50] It thus did not rule out the possibility that a state could be held directly responsible for the crime of genocide.

---

[44] Ago, R., 'Remarks on Some Classes of Crimes by States', in Weiler, Cassese and Spinedi (eds), *International Crimes of State – A Critical Analysis of the ILC's Draft Articles 19 on State Responsibility*, Walter de Gruyter, 1989, p 215.

[45] Horowitz, Irving Louis, *Genocide, State Power and Mass Murder*, Transaction Books, 2nd edn, 1977, p 38. Emphasis added.

[46] Ibid., p. 16. Emphasis added. See also Horowitz, Irving Louis, *Taking Lives – Genocide and State Power*,4th edn, Transaction Publishers, 1997, p 12.

[47] Fein, Helen, 'Genocide: A Sociological Perspective', (1990) 38 *Current Sociology* 8. Emphasis added.

[48] Ibid.

[49] Jonassohn, Kurt and Chalk, Frank, 'A Typology of Genocide and Some Implications for the Human Rights Agenda', in Walliman, Isidor and Dobkowski, Michael N. (eds), *Genocide and The Modern Age – Etiology and Case Studies of Mass Death*, Syracuse University Press, Edition 2000, p 8.

[50] *Application of the Convention on the Prevention and Punishment of the Crime of Genocide*, Preliminary Objections, Judgment, [1996] ICJ Reports 616, para 32 (11 July).

At least until 1 July 2002, date of entry into force of the ICC Statute, the conventional elimination of the principle of universal enforcement and the failure to establish an international criminal court meant that the Convention relied only on the states on the territories of which the crime of genocide had been committed to prosecute such a crime. According to Fein:

> [t]he Genocide Convention has an intrinsic disabling provision. By making the signatories responsible for punishing genocide (and incitement to genocide), it relied on the State – the organization which is most often the perpetrator of genocide – to sanction its own crime.[51]

Practice clearly showed that domestic enforcement was at best illusory: genocide, as a government policy, will not be subjected to the jurisdiction of any national court, at least while the offending government is in power.[52] In the words of Schwarzenberger:

> the whole convention is based on the assumption of virtuous governments and criminal individuals, a reversal of the truth [...] Thus, the Convention is unnecessary where it can be applied [...] and inapplicable where it may be necessary".[53] Ultimately, because genocide is committed, as a general rule, by the State or with its complicity, leaving genocide prosecution to the domestic courts may only ensure impunity.[54]

[51] Fein, Helen, *supra* n 45, p 3.

[52] As regards Germany, it is interesting to note that, due to the prohibition of retroactive laws, Nazi crimes were prosecuted not as crimes against humanity or as genocide but as murder. Consequently, the punishment was not as severe as it should have been. For example, on the twenty individuals tried during the Auschwitz trial which opened in Frankfurt on 20 December 1963, only six were condemned to life emprisonment, while three others were acquitted. See Pendas, Devin O., '"Auschwitz, Je ne savais pas ce que c'était", Le Procès d'Auschwitz à Francfort et l'Opinion Publique Allemande', in Brayard, Florent (ed), *Le Génocide des Juifs entre Procès et Histoire, 1943-2000*, Editions Complexe, 2000, pp 79-111. However, it must also be stressed here that in the case of Rwanda, more than 120,000 alleged participants in the genocide were jailed after the Rwandan Patriotic Front came into power. It is true that many of the leaders escaped, but most of those who were indicted by the International Criminal Tribunal were apprehended. As a matter of fact, they could not obtain protection, let alone immunity, in their own country as they were defeated mainly by Tutsis from Uganda, the children of Rwandan refugees from previous massacres.

[53] Schwarzenberger, Georg, *International Criminal Law, Volume I*, Stevens & Sons Limited, 3rd edn, 1957, p 143. He also refers to the Convention as being 'an insult to the intelligence'. Ibid.

[54] Schabas, William A., *Genocide in International Law – The Crimes of Crimes*, Cambridge University Press, 2000, p 346.

Furthermore, because the convention does not provide for any details or definitions in its provisions, States Parties are left with great discretion as to the definition of the crime and as to the scope of application of the convention. As a result, the convention, instead of creating a universal system of prevention and punishment of the crime of genocide, generated a heterogeneous system which varies from one country to another. In fact, Article V provides that:

> The Contracting Parties undertake to enact, in accordance with their respective Constitutions, the necessary legislation to give effect to the provisions of the present Convention and, in particular, to provide effective penalties for persons guilty of genocide or any of the other acts enumerated in Article III.

With this Article, the obligation of states to enact relevant legislation is quite weak. The use of the term 'necessary' leaves to the states the power to decide whether or not they ought to enact legislation. Furthermore, it does not impose any time limit within which the legislation has to be put into effect, thus providing states with an excuse for endlessly postponing such an enactment. Many states, among them Canada, Norway and Australia, thought that their existing legislation was sufficient. Moreover, some states also believed that genocide was unlikely to occur on their own territory. Thus, Article V does not establish uniform measures to be taken by all the States Parties. In the words of Sibert, 'Article V opens an "abyss" which threatens to wreck the whole value of the Convention'.[55] Consequently, legislation on genocide varies, and so does the punishment of this crime. It is true that insufficient legislation or penalties could constitute violations of Article IX which deals with state responsibility. Until today, however, such a remedy has remained purely theoretical. As a result, the convention has been almost totally ineffective in securing punishment of the crime. As Kuper noted:

> the consequences are particularly absurd in the case of domestic [ie internal] genocide. The effect of the present procedures is that in most cases of domestic genocide, governments would be required to prosecute themselves.[56]

He further stated that 'the performance of national courts in the punishment of genocide is thus hardly impressive'.[57] In this respect, it

[55] Sibert, Marcel, *Traité de Droit International Public*, Paris, 1951. Cited in Robinson, Nehemiah, *The Genocide Convention – A Commentary*, Institute of Jewish Affairs – World Jewish Congress, 1960, p 76.
[56] Kuper, Leo, *The Prevention of Genocide*, Yale University Press, 1985, p 102.
[57] Ibid, p 174.

is also incomprehensible that the Genocide Convention does not even mention the question of reparation or redress ... and thus completely omits and forgets the victims of this most terrible crime. It was argued during the drafting that responsibility other than criminal would be out of place in such a document.[58] However, Article V could have expressly imposed on states an obligation to provide for damages in their legislation. It must be noted that the Whitaker Report did recommend the inclusion of a provision for a state's responsibility for genocide together with reparations.[59] Ultimately:

> [w]hether one applies the test of the number of genocides that have run their seemingly uninhibited course since the adoption of the Convention, or the test of the prosecutions for genocide during the same period, it is impossible to escape the conclusion that the Convention has been quite ineffective.[60]

As a concluding remark, it may be pointed out that all the above developments overwhelmingly show the importance of state action in the commission of genocide and, historically speaking, it is very true that genocide has primarily been a state crime. Nonetheless, as noted from the outset, it still is theoretically possible for one single individual to commit genocide and state action should thus be seen as a potential factor in the commission of the crime rather than as a necessary requirement for its qualification. In this respect, it is worth noting that Trial Chamber I of the ICTY has recognised the possibility that genocide could be perpetrated on an individual basis and found that:

> The murders committed by the accused are sufficient to establish the material element of the crime of genocide and it is *a priori* possible to conceive that the accused harboured the plan to exterminate an entire group without this intent having been supported by any organisation in which other individuals participated. (...) [T]he drafters of the [Genocide] Convention did not deem the existence of an organisation or a system serving a genocidal objective as a legal ingredient of the crime. In so doing, they did not discount the possibility of a lone individual seeking to destroy a group as such. [61]

---

[58] UN Doc A/C.6/SR.95, pp 11 ff.
[59] Whitaker Report, p.26 , para.54.
[60] Kuper, Leo, *supra* n 54, p. 17.
[61] *Prosecutor* v *Jelisić*, Case No IT-95-10-T, Judgment, Trial Chamber I, 14 December 1999, para 100.

To consider state action as a legal component of the crime of genocide would constitute a retrospective definition of the crime which would apply to the genocides already committed. It would indeed freeze the definition in time: if the state action requirement would undoubtedly be met in the case of all previous genocides, this might not be the case in the future. The risk enshrined in the state action requirement is too great to be taken. Consequently, the position adopted in the *Jelisiæ*case was legally correct.[62] In this respect, it may be recalled here that the conclusion reached by the ICTY's Appeals Chamber as regards the state action requirement was rigorously the same in the contexts of both genocide and crimes against humanity.[63] This case law had to be welcomed, not only because it reflected customary international law, but also because it symbolised a trend towards adopting a unified – and thus coherent – legal regime to be applied to both these crimes. By departing from the ICTY's precedent as regards crimes against humanity, and thus from customary international law, the ICC Statute represents a serious obstacle to the unequivocal harmonisation achieved by the ICTY.[64]

c. *State crimes against peace*

Historically speaking, it seems clear that individual responsibility for involvement in an aggressive war has always been contingent upon state action. Indeed, all the crimes against peace ever committed have so far relied on state – or on organisational – action for their perpetration. Nonetheless, as with genocide, it is theoretically possible – mostly if we consider the new modern means of warfare – for a crime against peace to be committed by one single individual. Consequently, state – or any organisational – action should not be regarded as a legal ingredient of crimes against peace as those crimes committed on an individual basis would then fall out of the ambit of the definition. This approach was the one taken at Nuremberg as the Nuremberg Charter was concerned exclusively with individual criminal responsibility. Indeed, its Article 6 read as follows:

> The Tribunal established by the Agreement referred to in Article 1 hereof for the trial and punishment of the major war criminals of the European Axis countries shall have

[62] See *Prosecutor* v *Jelisić*, Case No IT-95-10-A, Appeal Judgment, Appeals Chamber, 5 July 2001, para.48.
[63] See *Prosecutor* v *Kunara et al*,Case No IT-96-23 and IT-96-23/1-A, Judgment, Appeals Chamber, 12 June 2002, para 98.
[64] See Article 7 (2) (a) of the ICC Statute as well as Elements of Crimes, Article 7, Introduction (3).

> the power to try and punish persons who, acting in the interests of the European Axis countries, whether as individuals or as members of organizations, committed any of the following crimes.
>
> The following acts, or any of them, are crimes coming within the jurisdiction of the Tribunal for which there shall be individual responsibility:
>
> (a) CRIMES AGAINST PEACE: namely, planning, preparation, initiation or waging of a war of aggression, or a war in violation of international treaties, agreements or assurances, or participation in a common plan or conspiracy for the accomplishment of any of the foregoing;[65]

Subsequently however, during the debates within the General Assembly on the definition of aggression, a Six-Power draft definition, proposed by Australia, Canada, Italy, Japan, the United Kingdom and the United States, stated that:

> Any act which would constitute aggression by or against a State likewise constitutes aggression when *committed by a State or other political entity* delimited by international boundaries or internationally agreed lines of demarcation against any State or other political entity so delimited and not subject to its authority.[66]

The idea that crimes against peace are state crimes is further reinforced by the fact that a state is 'responsible', in the sense that it is obliged to make reparation, for injuries resulting from its unlawful engagement in hostilities, to other states and to individuals. By extension, if the launching of a war, aggressive or not, is the product of state action, the crimes committed during this war, and thus war crimes, are also a result of state action or policy. Indeed, it seems obvious that, similarly to the launching of a war, the conduct of a war also requires organisation, resources and structures which, if they are not those of a state, are similar to them. In fact, in this context also, the law recognises the responsibility of the state as it is made responsible for injuries resulting from the violation of the laws of war by its armed forces. This is a well-recognised principle of customary international law which already

[65] IMT Charter, Article 6.

[66] See Report of the Special Committee on the Question of Aggression, UN GAOR, Twenty-Seventh Session, Supp No 19, UN Doc A/8719. Emphasis added.

figured in Article 3 of the 1907 Fourth Hague Convention.[67] In this respect, Wright wrote that:

> The aggressor should make reparation for all losses of life and property resulting from its military operations, all of which were in violations of its obligations under international law, while states engaged in defense or enforcement action must make reparation only for injuries resulting from breaches of the law of war, including breaches by their armed forces. States engaged in enforcement action may, however, escape liability for certain acts in violation of the normal rules of war and neutrality in case these acts were authorized by the United Nations.[68]

As with both crimes against humanity and genocide, the concept of state – or organisational – involvement in the commission of crimes against peace does correspond to the reality of the facts, at least from a retrospective viewpoint. Nonetheless, in their case also, state – or organisational – action should not be regarded as a legal component of their definition as it would hold the great risk of limiting their definitional scope to the type of crimes committed in the past. As with crimes against humanity and genocide, the ambit of the definition of crimes against peace should remain wide enough to embody new types of crimes.

If the definitional element of state action is a common feature shared by all the international crimes studied in the present book, it still remains a highly controversial issue. Indeed, what exactly would be the consequences of declaring a state criminal? How could the criminal state be adequately punished without punishing the citizens of that state? How could the concept of state criminal responsibility work without its questionable corollary of collective responsibility? According to Dominicé, the actions which will be taken in order to punish the criminal state will affect 'women, children and innocent people [...] Punishment will bring pain to innocents much more than those responsible in government, who, in many ways, will escape.'[69] Furthermore, the punishment of the criminal state will generally entail

[67] 1907 Fourth Hague Convention, Article 3.
[68] Wright, Quincy, 'The Outlawry of War and the Law of War', (1953) 47 *AJIL* 374.
[69] Dominicé, C., 'The Need to Abolish the Concept of Punishment', in Weiler, Cassese and Spinedi (eds), *International Crimes of State – A Critical Analysis of the ILC's Draft Article 19 on State Responsibility*, Walter de Gruyter, 1989, pp 257-58 at 258.

the punishment of this state's population, population which, more often than not, was the victim of the international crimes perpetrated.

International criminal law is thus faced here with an insurmountable paradox. Indeed, while it is arguable that it is precisely the state ingredient that will turn a crime into an international crime, it must also be recognised that prosecuting and punishing the criminal state will prove difficult, if not impossible. However, international criminal law did not completely abandoned the notion of state involvement in the perpetration of international crimes, and has in fact indirectly recognised it through the responsibility of those individuals who symbolise and represent the state.

2. *Beyond the abstract entity: back to individual criminal responsibility*

C'est en vain que l'on tentera de transformer un ordre visant à l'extermination de millions d'innocents en un acte d'Etat afin de décharger de leur crime ceux qui ont donné l'ordre et ceux qui l'ont exécuté.

Léon Poliakov [70]

a. Responsibility of heads of states

The issue here is that of the responsibility of heads of states and it might be recalled that the first removal of this immunity concerned the crime of aggression and appeared in the treaty of Versailles,[71] but it did not go any further than its mere inclusion in the treaty as the Kaiser was not tried. The Nuremberg Charter also provided for the principle of Heads of States' responsibility for crimes against peace, war crimes and crimes against humanity but, by the time the trials took place, both Hitler and Mussolini had died and, thus, no prosecutions in this regard could occur. However, it may be noted that the Tokyo Charter was silent on the responsibility of Emperor Hirohito.

Subsequently, in the Nuremberg Principles, the ILC clearly stated that:

> The fact that a person who committed an act which constitutes a crime under international law acted as Head of State or responsible Government official does not relieve him from responsibility under international law.[72]

[70] Poliakov, Léon, *Le Procès de Jérusalem – Juger Adolf Eichmann*, Calmann-Lévy, 1963 (reprint 1999), p 271.
[71] Article 227 of the Versailles Treaty.
[72] Nuremberg Principles, Principle III.

In its 1996 Draft Code of Crimes, the Commission maintained this position and Article 7 reads as follows:

> The official position of an individual who commits a crime against the peace and security of mankind, even if he acted as head of State or Government, does not relieve him of criminal responsibility or mitigate punishment.[73]

The post-charter legal developments all proceeded to the removal of this immunity, although it may be noted here that the Genocide Convention does not expressly exclude it. Following the rule that monarchs could not be prosecuted under the basic laws of the respective countries, the draftsmen only rejected the immunity of 'constitutionally responsible rulers, public officials or private individuals'.[74] This intentional omission has impeded effective prosecution. Indeed, since the adoption of the convention, there have only been two domestic prosecutions of heads of states for the crime of genocide, that of Pol Pot and his deputy prime minister in Cambodia,[75] and that of Macias and some of his collaborators in Equatorial Guinea[76] in August and September 1979 respectively. Moreover, if one could argue that a dictator would certainly be considered as a 'responsible ruler' and could thus be prosecuted under the convention, one must not forget that states are entitled to formulate reservations as regards Article IV.[77]

Fortunately, other international instruments are less equivocal and reject such immunity. Still, practice in this respect remains extremely rare even if, clearly, international tribunals seem to be more willing to prosecute heads of states than national courts. In fact, the ICTY did not hesitate to indict Milosević for the crimes perpetrated by the Serbs in

[73] ILC 1996 Draft Code of Crimes, [1996] II (2) *ILC Yearbook* 26.

[74] Article IV of the Genocide Convention. However, both statutes of the Ad Hoc Tribunals and the ICC Statute excluded this immunity. See Article 7(2) of the ICTY Statute, Article 6 (2) of the ICTR Statute, and Article 27 of the ICC Statute.

[75] Both were found guilty *in abstentia* by a people's revolutionary tribunal. See generally Kiernan, Ben (ed.), *Genocide and Democracy in Cambodia – The Khmer Rouge, the United Nations and the International Community*, Monograph Series 41 / Yale University Southeast Asia Studies, 1993.

[76] Macias was convicted and executed. See generally International Commission of Jurists, *The Trial of Macias in Equatorial Guinea : The Story of a Dictatorship, Report submitted by Alejandro Artucio*, International Commission of Jurists, 1978.

[77] In fact, the Philippines formulated such a reservation : 'the Philippine Government does not consider the said article, therefore, as overriding the existing immunities from judicial processes guaranteed to certain public officials by the Constitution of the Philippines'. See Ruhashyankiko Report, p 40. It must be noted that, on accession, Finland had also made a reservation regarding Article IV, but it withdrew it on 5 January 1998.

Kosovo,[78] Croatia[79] and Bosnia-Herzegovina.[80] For the first time, a head of state in exercise was accused of crimes against humanity, grave breaches of the Geneva Conventions, violations of the laws or customs of war and, for Bosnia-Herzegovina, of genocide against the Bosnian Muslim and the Bosnian Croat populations. In other words, the ICTY found no legal obstacle impeding the indictment for the most serious international crimes of Milosević, President of the Federal Republic of Yugoslavia.

However, the position of the ICJ is much more ambiguous on the matter as it recently ruled that, in the absence of relevant treaty provisions, a minister for foreign affairs enjoys complete immunity from criminal jurisdiction as a matter of custom and

> [a]ccordingly concludes that the functions of a Minister for Foreign Affairs are such that, throughout the duration of his or her office, he or she when abroad enjoys full immunity from criminal jurisdiction and inviolability. That immunity and that inviolability protect the individual concerned against any act of authority of another State which would hinder him or her in the performance of his or her duties.[81]

It is true that this case concerned a minister for foreign affairs and not a head of state but it is still interesting here as the court clearly proceeded 'from a mere analogy with immunities for diplomatic agents and Heads of State'.[82] This case had its origins in an international arrest warrant issued *in abstentia* in April 2000, by a Belgian investigating judge, against the then minister for foreign Aaffairs of the Congo, MrYerodia Ndombasi. This warrant accused him of having made public speeches which incited to racial hatred, and thus charged him with grave breaches of the 1949 Geneva Conventions and of the Additional Protocols, as well as with crimes against humanity. In its application instituting proceedings, the Congo asked the court to declare that Belgium should annul that warrant. It contended that the investigating judge was not entitled to hold himself competent in respect of the offences in question by relying on a universal jurisdiction not recognised by international law. It also argued that the charges had been brought

[78] *Prosecutor* v *Milošević et al*, Case No IT-99-37-I, Initial Indictment, 22 May 1999, First Amended Indictment, 29 June 2001, and Case No IT-99-37-PT, Second Amended Indictment, 16 October 2001.

[79] *Prosecutor* v *Milošević*, Case No IT-01-50-I, Initial Indictment, 8 October 2001.

[80] *Prosecutor* v *Milošević*, Case No IT-01-51-I, Initial Indictment, 22 November 2001.

[81] *Arrest Warrant* case, ICJ, General List No 121, 14 February 2002, para 54.

[82] Ibid, Dissenting Opinion of Judge Van Den Wyngaert, para 14.

in defiance of the immunities enjoyed by incumbent ministers for foreign affairs.[83] It is however to be deplored that, in the subsequent proceedings, the Congo relied only on the second argument and that, accordingly, the Court did not rule on the first one.[84]

Despite the fact that, from mid-April 2001, Mr Yerodia Ndombasi no longer held any ministerial office, the court rejected Belgium's objection that there was no longer a 'concrete case',[85] and recalled that its jurisdiction was determined at the time that the act instituting proceedings was filed, that is 17 October 2000.[86] The court then concluded that a minister for foreign affairs enjoyed 'full immunity from criminal jurisdiction and inviolability',[87] and found, by a majority of thirteen to three, that the circulation of the warrant against Mr Yerodia Ndombasi:

> [c]onstituted a violation of an obligations of Belgium towards the Congo, in that it failed to respect the immunity of the incumbent Minister for Foreign Affairs of the Congo and, more particularly, infringed the immunity from criminal jurisdiction and the inviolability then enjoyed *by* him under international law.[88]

This finding is highly questionable, if not totally wrong in law, as 'there is no rule of customary international law protecting incumbent Foreign Ministers against criminal prosecution'.[89] The court here missed an opportunity to follow the increasing trend of recognising universal jurisdiction, even in the national fora. This is to be regretted because the Belgian law should clearly serve as a model for all states to follow in order to achieve accountability for the most serious crimes. Still, it should be pointed out that the court listed a series of exceptions to the immunity enjoyed by incumbent or former minister for foreign affairs, thus suggesting that this immunity is not absolute.[90]

As regards national fora, national courts draw a distinction between heads of states in office, who enjoy complete immunity, and former heads of states, who do not. The Pinochet case is a perfect illustration of this situation. In October 1998, General *Pinochet* was arrested in London following an extradition request by Spanish authorities regarding the

[83] See *Arrest Warrant* case, *supra* n 79, para 17.
[84] Ibid, para 21.
[85] Ibid, para 24.
[86] Ibid, paras 26-8.
[87] Ibid, para 54.
[88] Ibid, para 71.
[89] Ibid, Dissenting Opinion of Judge Van Den Wyngaert, para 10.
[90] *Arrest Warrant* case, *supra* n 79, para 61.

human rights violations committed under his military government during the period 1973-1990. Subsequently, even if they found that a former head of state could not invoke immunity for the crime of torture, the law lords concluded that a serving head of state would have enjoyed immunity *ratione personae* even for the commission of international crimes.[91]

Thus, even if this case might have seem a 'political farce'[92] due to the fact that Pinochet was subsequently released and taken back to Chile, while the extradition requests made by Spain, France, Switzerland and Belgium were rejected due to his supposedly poor health and medical condition, it still is that former heads of states do not enjoy immunity from criminal prosecution. However, the main shortcoming of the *Pinochet* case is obviously the fact that immunity of heads of state in office remains absolute[93] and, clearly, this seems to be a valid precedent.[94]

Even if it still could be maintained that, because he represents his state, a head of state should benefit from immunity, such an immunity has absolutely no legal nor moral foundation. As previously stated, international instruments now all exclude such an immunity, even if they do not expressly address the issue of whether prosecution is function of the head of state still being in exercise or not. The *Milosevice* case seems to suggest that such a distinction was not made by the Yugoslavia tribunal. In any case, such immunity has certainly no moral justification: why can someone, by virtue of his functions, be allowed to commit international crimes in complete impunity? As the Nuremberg Tribunal rightly stated:

> The principle of international law which, under certain circumstances, protects the representatives of a state, cannot be applied to acts which are condemned as criminal by international law. The authors of these acts cannot

[91] *Regina* v *Bartle and the Commissioner of Police for the Metropolis and Others ex parte Pinochet – Regina* v *Evans and Another and the Commissioner of Police and Others ex parte Pinochet*, Judgment of 24 March 1999, (1999) 38 *ILM* 581. See *infra*.

[92] Lord Lammont, former British Finance Minister, cited in O'Shaughnessy, Hugh, *Pinochet, The Politics of Torture*, Latin America Bureau Ltd, 2000, p 169.

[93] See Villalpando, Santiago, 'L'affaire Pinochet : Beaucoup de Bruit Pour Rien ? L'Apport au Droit International de la Décision de la Chambre des Lords du 24 Mars 1999', (2000) 104 *RGDIP* 393-427.

[94] For instance, in November 1998, the French government turned down the request for action against Kabila. Charles Josselin, the French minister in charge of African relations, explained that, unlike Pinochet, Kabila was invited as the Chief of State of Democratic Congo and he thus benefited from the immunity accorded to chiefs of state while in office.

> shelter themselves behind their official position in order to be freed from punishment in appropriate proceedings.[95]

It is very hard to understand why heads of states are considered differently from other hierarchical superiors, let alone other individuals. It is now time to realise once and for all that international crimes are more often than not committed by a state, and thus by a Head of State ... If heads of state are to be immune from prosecution, the whole concept of 'struggle against impunity' will fall apart. Fortunately, it seems that immunity claims, even *ratione personae*, will not impede the jurisdiction of the ICC, at least as regards nationals of States Parties.[96] Indeed, under Article 98 (1) of the Rome Statute, only nationals of a non-State Party will be able to invoke head of state or diplomatic immunity, as it provides that:

> The Court may not proceed with a request for surrender or assistance which would require the requested State to act inconsistently with its obligations under international law with respect to the State or diplomatic immunity of a person or property of a third State, unless the Court can first obtain the co-operation of that third State for the waiver of the immunity.

It is therefore to be hoped that the ratification of the Rome Statute will continue so that immunity of heads of states will definitely become an obsolete and outdated practice.

b. Responsibility for the exercise of sovereign authority

As we have previously seen, the immunity of heads of states operates *ratione personae*, which means by reason of the person concerned: in other words, by virtue of being a head of state, the person in question is inviolable. However, when the person ceases to be head of state, the principle *ratione personae* no longer applies to this individual. Immunity is then claimed *ratione materiae*, by reason of the subject matter involved. Practically, this means that immunity will then apply only to acts committed in the exercise of the official functions. Thus, the applicable test is whether the individual acted to promote the interests of the state or to pursue purely individual goals and personal gratification and benefit, while the real question here is how international crimes will be

[95] *Nuremberg* judgment 223.
[96] Article 27(2) of the ICC Statute.

qualified. While it appears that international tribunals follow the Nuremberg legacy and reject any immunity for the commission of international crimes, the situation in the domestic fora is rather ambiguous, even if it seems that there is an increasing trend to recognise international crimes as exceptions to the immunity principle.

The case of General Noriega is here interesting as, even though he was tried for non-sovereign acts, it was the first time that a United States jury convicted a serving foreign head of state of criminal charges, namely, cocaine trafficking and money laundering.[97] In his case, the court held that 'General Noriega was not recognised as a head of state and that his drug-related activities did not involve the exercise of public or sovereign authority'.[98] With this finding, the court made clear that heads of states in office could be held criminally liable, at least for non-sovereign acts.

As regards sovereign acts, the situation appears to be undergoing a crucial evolution as there is a clear trend towards recognition that international crimes, even if committed as part of official functions, are not subject to immunity. For instance, in the *Pinochet* case, the defendant's claim of sovereign immunity was unequivocally rejected by the law lords:

> International law has made plain that certain types of conduct [...] are not acceptable conduct on the part of anyone. This applies as much to heads of state, or even more so, as it does to everyone else. The contrary conclusion would make a mockery of international law.[99]

The law lords subsequently found that torture was an incrimination belonging to *jus cogens*, and that it was therefore a peremptory norm of international law. Accordingly, they concluded, by six to one, that General Pinochet was not immune for the acts of torture committed while he was head of state, and that, therefore, he could be extradited and tried.[100] It is true that this finding is limited to the crime of torture,

[97] *United States* v *Noriega*, Case No 88-0079-CR, US District Court for the Southern District of Florida, 99 *ILR* 143-94.

[98] Ibid. Cited in Decaux, Emmanuel, 'Les Gouvernants', in Ascensio et al, *Droit International Pénal*, p 198.

[99] *Regina* v *Bartle and the Commissioner of Police for the Metropolis and Others ex parte Pinochet – Regina* v *Evans and Another and the Commissioner of Police and Others ex parte Pinochet*, Judgment of 25 November 1998, (1998) 37 *ILM* 1302.

[100] *Regina* v *Bartle and the Commissioner of Police for the Metropolis and Others ex parte Pinochet – Regina* v *Evans and Another and the Commissioner of Police and Others ex parte Pinochet*, Judgment of 24 March 1999, (1999) 38 *ILM* 581.

and that it could therefore be argued that this reasoning does not apply to other international crimes. Furthermore, it was founded exclusively on the 1984 Torture Convention, and was thus limited to the States Parties to this convention. There was also a limit *ratione temporis* attached to the law lords' reasoning as the limitation of immunity was only justified by the entry into force of this particular convention. Practically, this means that Pinochet could only be tried for acts perpetrated after 8 December 1988, date on which Great Britain, in the Criminal Justice Act made torture committed in another state a crime punishable in Great Britain. In any case, notwithstanding the intrinsic limitations of the law lords' finding, this case still showed that acts of heads of states in office are not necessarily protected by immunity.

Also, in the recent French case brought against Mouammar Ghaddafi, who had been charged with murder for his complicity in a terrorist action, the French Cour de cassation, even if, relying on head of state immunity, acquitted the defendant, still issued an extremely interesting decision which suggests that such immunity is not without exception:

> [E]n l'état du droit international, le crime dénoncé, quelle qu'en soit la gravité, ne relève pas des exceptions au principe de l'immunité de juridiction des chefs d'Etats étrangers en exercice.[101]

In other words, the court found that, even if complicity in acts of terrorism is not among them, there are international crimes which are not subject to immunity from jurisdiction of heads of states in office. Thus, the Cour de cassation expressly recognised that there are exceptions to this immunity, namely, international crimes. It is true that it did not define which crimes constituted such exceptions but it is most probable that crimes against humanity and genocide were here referred to. Also, it might be argued that, since the terrorist attacks on the United States of America, acts of terrorism would also be included among these exceptions.[102]

The recent decision of the ICJ in the *Arrest Warrant* case, however, seems to be a step backwards on this issue. Indeed, the court found that a Minister for foreign affairs will no longer enjoy immunity for 'acts committed prior or subsequent to his or her period of office', and that,

[101] Cour de Cassation, No 1414, 13 Mars 2001, p 3.

[102] See generally Zappala, Salvatore, 'Do Heads of State in Office Enjoy Immunity from Jurisdiction for International Crimes? The *Ghaddafi* Case Before the French *Cour de Cassation*, (2001) 12 *EJIL* 595-612.

for acts committed during that period of office, immunity is only lifted 'for acts committed during that period of office *in a private capacity*'.[103] It accordingly emphasised that:

> [t]he *immunity* from jurisdiction enjoyed by incumbent Ministers for Foreign Affairs does not mean that they enjoy impunity in respect of any crimes they might have committed, irrespective of their gravity. Immunity from criminal jurisdiction and individual criminal responsibility are quite separate concepts. While jurisdictional immunity is procedural in nature, criminal responsibility is a question of substantive law. Jurisdictional immunity may well bar prosecution for a certain period or for certain offences; it cannot exonerate the person to whom it applies from all criminal responsibility.[104]

The legacy of such a decision is one of uncertainty as the court found that a former minister for foreign affairs of one state could be subjected to the criminal jurisdiction of another state only for acts carried out in private capacity. Such a finding seems to exclude international crimes, as it seems very unlikely that they could ever be considered as committed in a private capacity.[105] Thus, according to the court, immunity *ratione materiae* is valid even in the case of international crimes. On a practical basis, this means that a minister for foreign affairs will enjoy full immunity even for the perpetration of international criminal acts. Such a finding seems in contradiction with the increasing trend in international law not to recognise immunity *ratione materiae* as available in the case of prosecution for 'core crimes' against international law. As the ICTY stated in the *Blaškić* case:

> The general rule under discussion is well established in international law and is based on the sovereign equality of States (*par in parem non habet imperium*) [...] [E]xceptions arise from the norms of international criminal law prohibiting war crimes, crimes against humanity and genocide. Under these norms, those responsible for such crimes cannot invoke immunity from national or

103 *Arrest Warrant* case, *supra* n 79, para 61. Emphasis added.
104 Ibid, para 60.
105 See *supra* on state (or an organisational movement) involvement in international crimes. See also *supra* I on whether isolated acts could constitute crimes against humanity where it is submitted that, for this to be possible, a wider pattern of occurrence, thus necessitating some form of state or organisational policy, is still required.

> international jurisdiction even if they perpetrated such crimes while acting in their official capacity.[106]

Fortunately, the draftsmen of the Rome Statute followed this path, and, in its Article 27 (2), the Rome Statute unequivocally excludes the validity of claims based on immunity *ratione materiae*:

> Immunities or special procedural rules which may attach to the official capacity of a person, whether under national or international law, shall not bar the Court from exercising its jurisdiction over such a person.

B. The prevention of international crimes: the moral responsibility of the bystander state

The following development will concentrate on the concept of what is generally referred to as 'humanitarian intervention' or 'just wars', concepts which could be used as tools for the prevention of international crimes. Nevertheless, the doctrine of humanitarian intervention raises some serious questions in practice, and notably as regards the lawfulness of such intervention on one hand and the moral impossibility to passively witness the commission of the most heinous crimes on the other.

1. *The concept of 'just' wars*

The distinction between just and unjust wars[107] is far from being a new concept, and it may indeed be traced back to the medieval Christian times. As a matter of fact, Grotius, known as the father of international law, along with other jurists of early modern Europe, used it in order to condemn wars which were not fought in self-defence.[108] In 1758, Vattel also recognised the right of a prince to move against a neighbouring prince when the conduct of the latter towards his own subjects was

---

[106] *Prosecutor* v. *Blaškić* , Case No. IT-95-14-A, Judgment on the Request of the Republic of Croatia for Review of the Decision of Trial Chamber II of 18 July 1997, Appeals Chamber, 29 October 1997, para.41.

[107] The terms 'just wars' here refer to both wars of national liberation and humanitarian intervention. See generally, Dinstein, Yoram, *War, Aggression and Self-Defence*, 3rd edn, Cambridge University Press, 2001, pp 63-8. For the purposes of this development, 'wars of national liberation' will be understood as also including the use of force by third states in support of these wars and will be encompassed in the concept of 'humanitarian intervention'.

[108] See Grotius, Hugo, *On The Law of War and Peace*, Kessinger Publishing Co, 2004 (original 1625).

such that it might be considered as contrary to the laws of God and of humanity.[109] In other words:

> The gist of the conception of *bellum iustum*, as formulated and systematized by the medieval theologians and jurists, was that resort to violence could be regarded as a legitimate procedure of self-help only if certain requirements relating to a belligerent's authority to make war (*auctoritas principis*), and to the objective (*iusta causa*) and intent (*recta* intention) of the belligerent, were met.[110]

At Nuremberg, the International Military Tribunal took act of this 'tradition' of humanitarian intervention and Sir Shawcross, the British Prosecutor, established a direct link between the jurisdiction of the Nuremberg Tribunal over crimes against humanity and the historical right of humanitarian intervention:

> Normally international law concedes that it is for the state to decide how it shall treat its own nationals; it is a matter of domestic jurisdiction...Yet international law has in the past made some claim that there is a limit to the omnipotence of the State and that the individual human being, the ultimate unit of all law, is not disentitled to the protection of mankind when the state tramples upon his rights in a manner which outrages the conscience of mankind (...) The fact is that the right of humanitarian intervention by war is not a novelty in international law.[111]

This analogy between humanitarian intervention and the prosecution of crimes against humanity arose repeatedly in the post- Second World War proceedings. For instance, the prosecution in the *Flick* case had argued in favour of the application of the crimes against humanity provision to events occurring prior to the formal commencement of war with reference to instances of humanitarian intervention throughout history:

> This doctrine that inhumane atrocities against civilian populations are so contrary to the law of nations that a

[109] Vattel, Emmerich de, *The Law of Nations*, Ams Pr, 1975 (original, 1758), Book II, Chapter V, s 70, Chapter VI, s 72.

[110] McDougal, Myres S. and Feliciano, Florentino P., 'Legal Regulation of Resort to International Coercion: Aggression and Self-Defense in Policy Perspective', (1959) 68 *Yale L J* 1065-66.

[111] 'Concluding Speeches by the Prosecution', (1948) 19 *The Trial of German Major War Criminals, Proceedings of the International Military Tribunal Sitting at Nuremberg*, pp 471-72.

> country is rightfully entitled to interfere and endeavor to put an end to them, by diplomatic protest or even by foe, was repeatedly voiced and often acted upon during the nineteenth century.[112]

Furthermore, in the *Justice* case, the tribunal observed that the concept of crimes against humanity had its roots in humanitarian intervention as it occurred in Turkey, Lebanon, Romania and Russia in response to religious persecutions, [113] and accordingly stated that:

> The rights of humanitarian intervention on behalf of the rights of man, trampled upon by a state in a manner shocking the sense of mankind, has long been considered to form part of the recognized law of nations. Here, too, the Charter merely develops a preexisting principle.[114]

Referring to this particular case, Leo Kuper wrote that:

> Prior to the [Genocide] Convention, the right of humanitarian intervention on behalf of populations persecuted in a manner shocking to mankind had long been considered part of the law of nations. Giving judgment in one of the Nuremberg trials of Nazi war criminals, the court referred to many precedents for such international intervention. [115]

In this case, the court indeed referred to a series of previous cases of humanitarian intervention, among which: the 1827 intervention of England, France and Russia to end the atrocities in the Greco-Turkish war, to the action in 1840 of the US President who, through his Secretary of State, intervened with the Sultan of Turkey on behalf of the persecuted Jews of Damascus and Rhodes, as well as to the French intervention in 1861 to check religious atrocities in Lebanon.[116] The court

[112] *United States* v *Flick*, Case No 5, Military Tribunal IV, 6 *Nuremberg Subsequent Proceedings* 87-88. To support its argument, the Prosecution cited interventions in Greece, Turkey, Lebanon, Russia, Romania, Syria and Cuba in defence of ethnic and religious minorities. See ibid., pp 88-9.

[113] *United States* v *Altstoetter*, Case No 3, Military Tribunal III, 3 *Nuremberg Subsequent Proceedings* 981-82.

[114] Ibid, p 92.

[115] See Kuper, Leo, *Genocide – Its Political Use in the Twentieth Century*, Yale University Press, 1981, pp 19-20.

[116] See *United States* v. *Altsoetter et al*, Case No 3, Military Tribunal III, 3 *Nuremberg Subsequent Proceedings* 46-47.

also listed the various official protests made to the Governments of Russia and Romania with respect to pogroms and atrocities against Jews,[117] and to the Government of Turkey on behalf of the persecuted Christian minorities.[118]

In the post-Nuremberg era, however, the doctrine of humanitarian intervention went into decline and its understanding found itself highly limited. As a matter of fact, modern international law does not refer to 'just' or 'unjust' wars as such, but rather to 'legal' or 'illegal' wars, thus abandoning all attempt to try and defined 'just' wars. As Kunz pointed out, '[t]here are no objective criteria between "just" and "unjust" wars.'[119] In other words, the concept of *bellum legale* replaced that of *bellum justum,* and the assessment of the distinction between armed conflicts is based on the legality of the purpose rather than on the intrinsic justice of the cause.'[120]

This emphasis on legality raises a series of complex questions. Indeed, if it has to be acknowledged that one of its dramatic consequences is that it can prevent 'just' wars from being fought, it must equally be admitted that the concept of 'justice' is far from objective. As a matter of fact, what some might qualify as 'just', others will find it 'unjust'. The concept of 'just' wars relies too much on the political subjectivity of the state waging the war and of its military allies. Ultimately, the concept of 'just' wars – and thus of humanitarian intervention– can be compared with that of aggression as, in both instances, the qualification of the act depends on who actually operates this qualification. This unavoidable political and highly subjective element present in these two concepts is thus a serious impediment to their definitions. In the case of humanitarian intervention, it can also be asserted that even the criterion of legality is flawed as, again, the legality of an intervention will depend

[117] In 1902, the American Secretary of State addressed to Romania a remonstrance 'in the name of humanity' against Jewish persecutions, stating that his government could not be a tacit party to such international wrongs. In 1904, in his message to Congress, the US President, referring to the Kishniev pogrom in Russia and to the 'systematic and long-extended cruel oppression of the Armenians', stated that 'there are occasional crimes committed on a vast scale and of such peculiar horror as to make us doubt whether it is not our manifest duty to endeavour *at least* to show our disapproval of the deed and our sympathy with those who have suffered by it.' (Emphasis added.)

[118] Furthermore, on 24 May 1915, the Declaration of the Governments of France, Great Britain and Russia denounced the massacres of the Armenian population while, on 29 March 1919, the Report of the Commission of Fifteen Members of the Preliminary Peace Conference referred to the liability to criminal prosecution of all those 'guilty of offenses against the laws and customs of war or the laws of humanity'.

[119] Kunz, Josef L, 'Bellum Justum and Bellum Legale' (1951), 45 *AJIL* 531.

[120] Ibid., p 532.

on who assesses this intervention. The recent *Iraq* case and the political divisions it generated among members of the United Nations is very symptomatic of this situation: what the Americans and the British Government see as a humanitarian intervention launched with the aim of liberating a people from the oppression of a tyrant, others – and notably, as it was extensively covered by the media, the French Government – will see as an illegal violation of state sovereignty.

The acknowledged difficulties of finding an effective definitional criterion with respect to humanitarian intervention and the political controversies which might arise following such an intervention do not however change the fact that humanitarian intervention might be necessary in order to prevent human rights violations and international crimes from being committed or, if necessary, to put an end to them. Just like it must be recognised that the doctrine of humanitarian intervention has illegally been used as a pretext to wage aggressive wars, it must equally be acknowledged, and the formula is not too emphatic, that Europe – if not the world– owes its existence to the invasion of France by the liberating armies in 1944.[121] Had this humanitarian intervention never occurred or failed, civilisation and humanity would have disappeared.

2. *The doctrine of humanitarian intervention in international law: the principle of non-intervention*

There is little or no reason to believe that humanitarian intervention is lawful within the regime of the United Nations Charter and this assertion is further reinforced by the fact that no reference to a right of humanitarian intervention can be found in the text of this charter. [122] In other words, as the law currently, stands humanitarian intervention is not an exception to the charter prohibitions on the use of force. Further, it can also be noted here that Article 3 of Additional Protocol II to the Geneva Conventions expressly establishes the principle of non-intervention in cases of non-international armed conflicts:

[121] It may be recalled here that, at the time, France – led by Maréchal Pétain – was officially collaborating with the Nazis and, in this respect, the liberation was seen by the government of Vichy France as an illegal violation of France's sovereignty. Needless to say, such an argument is everything but convincing, France being at the time under the rule of the Nazi occupant and Vichy France being the collaborator of those who had illegally invaded the country.
[122] See Charney, Jonathan L., 'Anticipatory Humanitarian Intervention in Kosovo', (1999) 93 *AJIL* 836.

1. Nothing in this Protocol shall be invoked for the purpose of affecting the sovereignty of a State or the responsibility of the government, by all legitimate means, to maintain or re-establish law and order in the State or to defend the national unity and territorial integrity of the State.
2. Nothing in this Protocol shall be invoked as a justification for intervening, directly or indirectly, for any reason whatever, in the armed conflict or in the internal or external affairs of the High Contracting Party in the territory of which that conflict occurs.[123]

As previously mentioned, the reasoning behind this legal non-recognition of humanitarian intervention is due to the fact that such intervention will in practice be highly selective and will be used to serve particular political interests. In the words of Kuper, the doctrine of humanitarian intervention:

> [i]s clearly in conflict with the cardinal principles of respect for national unity, territorial integrity, and political independence. To the extent that these principles are emphasized, humanitarian intervention is excluded.[124]

Thus, according to Vargas Carreno:

> [t]he principle of non-intervention is derived from other provisions and principles of the Charter, particularly that which recognizes the sovereign equality of States, since such equality would lack any value if States could intervene in the internal affairs of other States [...] Therefore , it is not surprising that the International Court of Justice explicitly rejected, in its first Judgment with respect to a contentious case, the so-called right to intervene, as contrary to international law.[125]

[123] Article 3, Additional Protocol II.

[124] Cited in Fein, Helen, 'Genocide, Terror, Life Integrity, and War Crimes', *in* Andreopoulos, George J. (ed), *Genocide: Conceptual and Historical Dimensions*, University of Pennsylvania Press, Philadelphia, 1997, pp 41-42.

[125] Vargas Carreno, Edmundo, 'Humanitarian Intervention', in *International Law at the Eve of the Twenty-First Century – Views from the International Law Commission*, United Nations, 1997, pp 339-63 at 344.

Indeed, in the above-mentioned *Corfu Channel* case, the Court of Justice unequivocally indicated that:

> The Court can only regard the alleged right of intervention as the manifestation of a policy of force, such as has, in the past, given rise to most serious abuses and such as cannot, whatever be the present defects in international organization, find a place in international law. Intervention is perhaps still less admissible in the particular form it would take here; for, from the nature of things, it would be reserved for the most powerful States, and might easily lead to perverting the administration of international justice itself.[126]

Several years later, the ICJ reiterated the validity of the principle of non-intervention in an even wider sense, reaffirming that the said principle 'involves the right of every sovereign State to conduct its affairs without outside interference',[127] and that it 'forbids all States or groups of States to intervene directly in internal or external affairs of other States.'[128] Although the principle of non-intervention is as absent from the United Nations Charter as is the doctrine of humanitarian intervention, the court had no difficulty in finding that this principle 'is part and parcel of customary international law',[129] and in therefore reaching the conclusion that it:

> [c]annot contemplate the creation of a new rule opening up a right of intervention by one State against another on the ground that the latter has opted for some particular ideology or political system.[130]

Furthermore, it may also be noted here that, in 1949, the International Law Commission had expressly incorporated the principle of non-intervention in the draft Declaration on the Rights and Duties of States, stipulating in Article 4 that '[e]very State has the duty to refrain from intervention in the internal or external affairs of any other State'.[131] Subsequently, several General Assembly resolutions also participated in the elaboration of the principle of non-intervention. For instance, on

126 *Corfu Channel (United Kingdom of Great Britain and Northern Ireland* v *Albania)*, Merits, [1949] ICJ Reports 35 (9 April).
127 *Military and Paramilitary Activities in and against Nicaragua (Nicaragua* v *United States of America)*, Merits, [1986] ICJ Reports 106 (27 June).
128 Ibid, p 108.
129 Ibid, p 102.
130 Ibid, p 133.
131 [1948] *Yearbook of the International Law Commission* 135.

21 December 1965, the General Assembly passed the Declaration on the Inadmissibility of Intervention, which declares its deep concern as to the 'increasing threat to universal peace due to armed intervention and other direct or indirect forms of intervention threatening the sovereign personality and political independence of States' and holds that 'armed intervention is synonymous with aggression' and 'a violation of the Charter of the United Nations'.[132]

Modern international law thus expressly refutes the doctrine of humanitarian intervention by unequivocally affirming its counterpart, the principle of non-intervention. In the words of Beres:

> Ironically, the UN, which is responsible for most of the post-Nuremberg codification of the International Law of Human Rights, has sometimes been associated with increased limits on the doctrine of humanitarian intervention. [...] These limits, of course, flow from the greatly reduced justification for the use of force in the Charter system of International law, especially the broad prohibition contained in Article 2 (4). Yet, while it cannot be denied that humanitarian intervention might be used as a pretext for naked aggression, it is also incontestable that *a too-literal interpretation of 2 (4) would summarily destroy the entire corpus of normative protection for Human Rights* – a corpus that is coequal with "peace" as the central objective of the Charter. Moreover, in view of the important nexus between peace and Human Rights, a nexus in which the former is very much dependant upon widespread respect for human dignity, *a too-literal interpretation of 2 (4) might well impair the prospects for long-term security*".[133]

Interestingly, other scholars have identified the paradox of the United Nations Charter with respect to the doctrine of humanitarian intervention and to the aims set forth in the charter and found that 'the use of armed force in defence of Human Rights may be emphatically in the common interest as a mode of maintaining international peace and security'. [134] Ultimately, the prohibition of humanitarian intervention

[132] Declaration on the Inadmissibility of Intervention in the Domestic Affairs of States and the Protection of Their Independence and Sovereignty, United Nations General Assembly, 21 December 1965, A/RES/2131(XX).

[133] Beres, Louis René, 'Justice and Realpolitik : International Law and the Prevention of Genocide', (1988) 33 *AJIL* 138. Emphasis added.

[134] McDougal, Myres, Lasswell, Harold, Chen Lung-Chu, *Human Rights and World Public Order: The Basic Policies of an International Law of Human Rights*, Yale University Press, 1980, p 241. Cited in Beres, Louis René, 'Justice and Realpolitik : International Law and the Prevention of Genocide', (1988) 33 *AJIL* 138.

in international law in order to ensure good relations between states and to therefore preserve international peace is thus questionable as this prohibition could in fact defeat its aims and could generate the exact contrary results than the ones expected, notably in terms of maintaining international peace and security.

3. *The re-emerging right of humanitarian intervention*

As previously mentioned with respect to the notion of 'just' wars, the doctrine of humanitarian intervention is not a modern concept and it indeed notably finds support in the writings of Grotius and Vattel, both of whom defended the idea that a state may interfere within the territorial sphere of other states to protect innocents from their own rulers. [135] As, according to Article 38 of the Statute of the International Court of Justice, scholarly writings – of which Grotius and Vattel's are irrefutable examples – are a source on international law, it is arguable that the right to intervene actually exists in international law and has done so for centuries.

Indeed, an overview of the legal doctrine does highlight the fact that the doctrine of humanitarian intervention and its corollary, the fact that human rights issues, among which the commission of international crimes, 'are no longer strictly within the domestic purview of states',[136] are far from being completely new concepts, which is why the term 're-emerging' has been employed above in connection with the notion of humanitarian intervention.

As a matter of fact, already in 1920, Garner had acknowledged that 'violations of international law which threaten the peace and order of the community of States must be treated as a violation of the rights of all, for the law which has been broken is the law of all'.[137] Subsequently, the atrocities perpetrated during the Second World War understandably generated a revival of interest for the right of humanitarian intervention in scholarly works. For instance, in 1947, Lemkin had explained that:

> The practices of the National Socialist Government in Germany resulting in destruction of entire human groups gave impetus to reconsideration of certain principles of

[135] See Grotius, Hugo, *On the Law of War and Peace*, Kessinger Publishing Co, 2004 and Vattel, Emmerich de, *The Law of Nations*, Ams Pr, 1975 (original, 1758).
[136] Kofi Abiew, Francis, *The Evolution of the Doctrine and Practice of Humanitarian Intervention*, Kluwer Law International, 1999, p 98.
[137] Garner, *International Law and the World War*, 1920, pp 498-501. Cited in Green, Leslie C., 'New Trends in International Criminal Law, (1981) 11 *Israel Yearbook on Human Rights* 16.

> international law. The question arose whether sovereignty goes so far that a government can destroy with impunity its own citizens and whether such acts of destruction are domestic affairs or matters of international concern [...] By declaring genocide a crime under international law and by making it a problem of international concern, the right of intervention on behalf of minorities slated for destruction has been established.[138]

Adopting a similar view, Kuhn had also stressed that:

> Mass extermination of populations [...] constitutes an offense of international concern and a serious threat to the maintenance of peace [...] and security of all nations.[139]

In 1950, Lauterpacht had identified the principle that human rights were no longer falling within the restricted domestic jurisdictional sphere of individual states and had accordingly stressed that:

> [h]uman rights and freedoms having become the subject of a solemn international obligation and of one of the fundamental purposes of the Charter, are no longer a matter which is essentially within the domestic jurisdiction of the Members of the United Nations.[140]

In the same vein, Lillich had asserted that the United Nations definitely had the legal right to intervene for humanitarian reasons in the event of a state violating fundamental human rights, thus causing an actual threat to the peace.[141] He had further argued that the value of human life took precedence over legal principles:

> [t]o require a state to sit back and watch the slaughter of innocent people in order to avoid violating blanket prohibitions against the use of force is to stress blackletter at the expense of far more fundamental values.[142]

[138] Lemkin, Raphael, 'Genocide as a Crime Under International Law', (1947) 41 *AJIL* 145-51. For a similar view, see Beres, Louis René, 'Justice and Realpolitik : International Law and the Prevention of Genocide', (1988) 33 *AJIL* 139. According to Beres, humanitarian intervention is 'one way of giving effect to the enforcement of anti-genocide norms in international law', another way involving 'the use of courts, domestic and international'.

[139] Kuhn, Arthur K., 'The Genocide Convention and State Rights', (1949) 423 *AJIL* 500-01.

[140] Lauterpacht, *International Law and Human Rights*, Praeger, 1950, p 178, n 101.

[141] Lillich, 'Intervention to Protect Human Rights', (1969) 15 *McGill Law Journal* 212.

[142] Ibid.

Furthermore, this idea was also recognised in the political sphere and, speaking before the United Nations on 17 March 1977, former United States President Carter had unequivocally held that 'no member of the UN can claim that mistreatment of its citizens is solely its own business'.[143]

Consequently, the more recent interest for the right of humanitarian intervention in the legal doctrine was rather foreseeable and predictable: the international apathy with respect to the various humanitarian crises and human rights violations was bound to generate scholarly analysis.

a. The failures of the United Nations

The complete inability of the United Nations effectively to put an end to human rights violations and to international crimes may be explained by the functioning difficulties of the Security Council which can be paralysed by its permanent members through the exercise of their power of veto. In this respect, the case of Tibet is highly illustrative. In 1960, the Legal Inquiry Committee on Tibet had found that 'acts of genocide had been committed in Tibet in an attempt to destroy the Tibetans as a religious group'[144] and, in full knowledge of this report, the international community of states failed to react. If this lack of reaction is far from being exceptional, the point to be made here is that, in the case of Tibet, *there could have been no reaction*: and, indeed, even if there had been international willingness to act, China would have exercised its right of veto, thus impeding any intervention. The same can also be asserted as regards the Cambodian genocide and the inaction of the United Nations in bringing the atrocities perpetrated by the Khmer Rouge to an end. As Stanton explained, '[t]he UN was paralysed by the likelihood of Security Council vetoes by the Communist powers; at first by the Soviet Union and then by China.'[145]

More recently, the world witnessed the commission of yet another genocide and the simultaneous complete and total incapacity of the United Nations to react. In this particular case, not only did the United Nations fail in rapidly bringing an international response to the

143 Cited in Beres, Louis René, *supra* n 131, p 127.

144 International Commission of Jurists, *Tibet and the Chinese People's Republic – A Report to the International Commission of Jurists by its Legal Inquiry Committee on Tibet*, International Commission of Jurists, 1960, p 3.

145 Stanton, Gregory H., 'The Cambodian Genocide and International Law', *in* Kiernan, Ben (ed), *Genocide and Democracy in Cambodia – The Khmer Rouge, the United Nations and the International Community*, Monograph Series 41 / Yale University Southeast Asia Studies, Second impression, 1994 (original, 1993).

genocide, it was also unable to prevent the crime in the first place. As a matter of fact, it must here be recalled that, between 7 January and 21 January 1993, the International Commission on Human Rights Violations in Rwanda[146] had visited the country and had concluded in its report, published on 22 February 1993, that acts of genocide were being committed with complete impunity.[147] Subsequently, from 8 to 17 April 1993, the Special Rapporteur on Extrajudicial, Summary or Arbitrary Executions, M. Ndiaye, visited Rwanda and came to the conclusion that the Genocide Convention could be considered as applicable in this particular instance. He had indeed found – finding which he included in his report – that:

> The cases of intercommunal violence brought to the Special Rapporteur's attention indicate very clearly that the victims of the attacks, Tutsis in the overwhelming majority of cases, have been targeted solely because of their membership of a certain ethnic group, and for no other objective reason.[148]

In spite of these irrefutable evidences, the United Nations Commission on Human Rights merely decided to keep the situation in Rwanda under review.[149] This shameful inaction of all the competent – or rather incompetent – organs of the United Nations, this unwillingness of organs like the Commission of Human Rights to try and prevent the crime ended in one of the worst crimes the twentieth century has witnessed. In this particular case, the genocide was not an unpredictable outburst of violence which degenerated into genocide. It was a planned and well-prepared genocide, one that human rights organisations were predicting, one that the so-called human rights bodies of the United Nations chose to ignore, one that the United Nations deliberately and knowingly did nothing to prevent.

The case of the former Yugoslavia equally illustrated the incapacity of the United Nations in preventing international crimes, incapacity which here again was dangerously approaching the complicity zone. And indeed, although the Security Council had declared Srebrenica a 'United

[146] This Commission was composed of four humanitarian organisations, the International Federation of Human Rights, Africa Watch, the Centre international des droits de la personne et du développement and the Union inter-africaine des droits de l'homme.

[147] See Verschave, François-Xavier, *Complicité de Génocide? La politique de la France au Rwanda*, Editions la Découverte, Collection Essais, 1994, p 27.

[148] E/CN.4/1994/7/Add.1, paras 7-8 (11 August 1993).

[149] See generally Bossuyt, Marc, 'United Nations Human Rights Procedures Regarding Burundi, Rwanda and Zaire (1994-1997)', in Wellens, Karel (ed), *International Law : Theory and Practice, Essays in Honour of Eric Suy*, Martinus Nijhoff Publishers, 1998, pp 493-504.

Nations safe area', it did nothing to prevent the subsequent genocide. Worse, it knowingly abandoned Srebrenica to the hands of the Bosnian Serb genociders who, during a 12 day period in July 1995, invaded the 'safe area' and slaughtered Muslim men of military age, slaughter which was subsequently qualified as genocide by the ICTY.[150] Indeed, as Totten rightly recalled:

> The so-called safe area at Srebrenica was overrun on July 11, 1995, as the outnumbered Dutch troops watched the Serb forces divide the people within the safe area into two groups, forcing the oldest people, women, and children onto trucks and buses and removing the thousands of men and boys to secret locations. Ultimately, approximately 7,000 Muslims were slaughtered, resulting in the single, largest massacre in Europe since the Holocaust.[151]

Faced with the apathy of the United Nations, NATO decided, on 13 October 1998, to use force in Yugoslavia and subsequently implemented this decision with military actions which began on 24 March 1999. NATO's resort to force in the Former Yugoslavia was however highly controversial, and its actions were seen as inconsistent with the explicit terms of the United Nations Charter as well as with the practice of the Security Council. Furthermore, as Totten explained, this intervention might not have been as humanitarian as it seemed:

> In certain cases, even when the international community agreed to undertake an intervention, extreme efforts have been made by various nations to avoid sending in ground troops. The result has often been tragic. For example, in March 1999, a decision was made by the North Atlantic Treaty Organisation (NATO) to use air power – versus ground troops – aimed at Serb troops accused of violence, repression, and 'ethnic cleansing' against the ethnic Albanian majority in Kosovo. The controversial NATO air attack lasted for 78 days. As Alex Alvarez (2001) notes in *Governments, Citizens, and Genocide: A Comparative and Interdisciplinary Approach*, ironically and tragically, "the attacks incited the Serb leadership to speed up the policies of ethnic cleansing of Kosovar Albanians, resulting in wide-

[150] See *Prosecutor* v *Krstiæ*, Case No. IT-98-33, Judgment, Trial Chamber I, 2 August 2001, paras 595-97.

[151] Totten, Samuel, 'The Intervention and Prevention of Genocide: Where There *Is* the Political Will, There Is a Way, in Totten, Samuel, Parsons, William S. and Charny, Israel W. (eds), *Century of Genocide – Critical Essays and Eyewitness Accounts*, 2nd edn, Routledge, 2004, pp 469-90 at 483.

> spread massacres and the uprooting and dislocation of the majority of the population" (pp 139-40).[152] Had troops been on the ground, they may have been able to prevent the Serbs from carrying out their destructive aims.[153]

Nonetheless, a great number of legal scholars, although acknowledging the illegality of the intervention, still maintained that it was necessary, notably due to the inaction of the United Nations and the paralysis of the Security Council by the power of veto of its permanent members.[154] Upholding this view, Wedgwood contended that:

> It is important to acknowledge that the Kosovo intervention may represent a sea change in the responsibility of multilateral organizations to attempt to thwart ethnic slaughter – even if multilateralism takes a different form. Kosovo did not happen in isolation, but after the United Nations was unable to act effectively in Rwanda and Bosnia. The veto of the permanent members of the Security Council has often thrown a monkey wrench in the machinery of collective security, and a mature judgment is required to test whether strict proceduralism should be applied.[155]

Similarly, Slater and Nardin wrote that:

> [i]ntervention to protect human rights has moral justification but the practical constraints on armed intervention are such that it can never be more than an exceptional remedy for human rights abuses.[156]

Most interestingly, Cassese went even further in asserting that:

> NATO's action in Yugoslavia may be taken as evidence of an emerging doctrine in international law allowing the use of forcible countermeasures to impede a state from committing large-scale atrocities on its own territory, in

[152] Alvarez, Alex, *Governments, Citizens and Genocide : A Comparative and Interdisciplinary Approach*, Indiana University Press, 2001, pp 139-40. Footnote in original.
[153] Totten, Samuel, *supra* n 149, at 483-4. Emphasis in original.
[154] See, e.g., Henkin, Louis, 'Kosovo and the Law of "Humanitarian Intervention"', (1999) 93 *AJIL* 824-28.
[155] Wedgwood, Ruth, 'NATO's Campaign in Yugoslavia', (1999) 93 *AJIl* 834.
[156] Slater, Jerome and Nardin, Terry, 'Non-intervention and Human Rights', (1986) 48 *Journal of Politics* 86-96.

> circumstances where the Security Council is incapable of responding adequately to the crisis. A customary rule may emerge which would legitimise the use of force by a group of states in the absence of prior authorisation by the Security Council.[157]

Ultimately, it is ironic that one of the main reasons advanced in order to justify the right of humanitarian intervention lies precisely in the failure of the United Nations to realise its original aims. Thus, Lillich, referring to India's intervention in Bangladesh indicated that:

> [t]he doctrine of humanitarian intervention, whether unilateral or collective, surely deserves the most searching reassessment given the failure of the United Nations to take effective steps to curb the genocidal conduct and alleviate the mass suffering.[158]

b. From a right of humanitarian intervention...

As previously stressed, the incapacity of the United Nations has generated a great amount of scholarly works with respect to the doctrine of humanitarian intervention, regarding both the definition and the legality of the concept.

From a definitional standpoint, many authors have defined the doctrine of humanitarian intervention in a manner rather similar to the above-mentioned previous works. Thus, according to Bazyler, the doctrine of humanitarian intervention may be defined as 'the right of one nation to use force against another nation for the purpose of protecting the inhabitants of that other nation from inhumane treatment by their governing sovereign.'[159] Adopting a similar view, Van Schaack described humanitarian intervention as involving 'the intervention by one state into the territorial integrity of another state in order to protect individuals who are the victims of abuses of fellow citizens that the

[157] Cassese, Antonio, '*Ex iniuria ius oritur*: Are We Moving Towards International Legitimation of Forcible Humanitarian Countermeasures in the World Community?', (1999) 10 *EJIL* 23.
[158] Lillich R., Rapporteur, 'The International Protection of Human Rights by General International Law, Second Interim Report of the Sub-Committee', Report of the International Committee on Human Rights of the International Law Association, 1972, p. 54, quoted in (1973) 67 *AJIL* 277.
[159] Bazyler, Michael J., 'Reexamining the Doctrine of Humanitarian Intervention in Light of the Atrocities in Kampuchea and Ethiopia', (1987) 23 *Stanford Journal of International Law* 547-8. Cited in Fein, Helen, 'Genocide, Terror, Life Integrity, and War Crimes', in Andreopoulos, George J. (ed), *Genocide: Conceptual and Historical Dimensions*, University of Pennsylvania Press, 1997, pp 41-42.

state is unwilling or unable to prevent.'[160] Again taking the same approach, Tyagim argued that:

> The basis for a humanitarian intervention lies in the absence of a minimum moral order in the whole or a part of a state, which is inconsistent with fundamental humanitarian norms and unacceptable to other states or non-state entities.[161]

More interestingly for the purpose of the present development, many scholars have legally analysed the concept of humanitarian intervention. For instance, Kofi Abiew wrote that '[i]ntervention for human rights purposes would not contravene [the principle of non-intrvention] if it is confined within the conditions for its exercise'.[162] In this respect, Conforti wrote that

> The question whether or not a matter is within the domestic competence of a given State depends on whether this matter is regulated by customary international law.[163]

In other words, if a matter is regulated by customary international law – as it is the case for international crimes –, this matter will fall outside the domestic jurisdictional sphere of individual states to become a matter of concern for the international community as a whole.

With respect specifically to the United Nations Charter, Reisman and McDougal, analysing its purposes, indicated that its Article 2(4):

> [i]s not against the use of coercion per se, but rather the use of force for specified unlawful purposes. [...] Since a humanitarian intervention seeks neither a territorial change nor a challenge to the political independence of the state involved and is not only not inconsistent with the Purposes of the United Nations but is rather in conformity with the most fundamental peremptory norms of the Charter, it is distortion to argue that it is precluded by

[160] Van Schaack, Beth, 'The Definition of Crimes Against Humanity: Resolving the Incoherence', (1999) 37 *Columbia Journal of Transnational Law* 847-48.
[161] Tyagim, Yogesh K., 'The Concept of Humanitarian Intervention', (1995) 16 *Michigan Journal of International Law* 883-84, Cited in Van Schaack, Beth, *supra* n 158, p 848, n 289.
[162] Kofi Abiew, Francis, *The Evolution of the Doctrine and Practice of Humanitarian Intervention,* Kluwer Law International, 1999, p 93.
[163] Conforti, Benedetto, *The Law and Practice of the United Nations,* Kluwer Law International, 1996, p 136.

> Article 2 (4). In so far as it is precipitated by intense human rights deprivations and conforms to the general international legal regulations governing the use of force – economy, timeliness, commensurance, lawfulness of purpose and so on – it represents a vindication of international law, and is, in fact, substitute or functional enforcement.[164]

They further contended that individual states may undertake humanitarian interventions, based on the existence of 'a co-ordinate responsibility for the active protection of human rights: members may act jointly with the Organisation [...] or singly or collectively',[165] adding that, if such was not the case, it 'would be suicidally destructive of the explicit purposes for which the United Nations was established.'[166] Thus, even the abundance of United Nations documents on the principle of non-intervention:

> [d]oes not mean that it is an absolute principle. Even resolution 2131 (XX) and 2625 (XXV), which reproduce the final part of Article 2, paragraph 7, of the Charter, have explicitly indicated that said principle, as formulated in the above-mentioned resolutions, may not in any way affect the provisions of the Charter of the United Nations regarding the maintenance of international peace and security.[167]

It must also be stressed that the doctrine of humanitarian intervention has been recognised in a more political sphere, that of the United Nations itself. And indeed, on different occasions, different Secretaries-General of the United Nations have asserted the validity of the doctrine. For instance, former Secretary-General Javier Pérez de Cuéllar had indicated in his 1991 annual report to the General Assembly that the principle of non-intervention could not be used as a protective barrier which would allow massive or systematic violations of human rights to be perpetrated with impunity. On this occasion, he also stated:

> It is now increasingly felt that the principles of non-interference with the essential domestic jurisdiction of

[164] McDougal and Reisman, 'Response by Professors McDougal and Reisman', (1969) 3 *International Lawyer* 444.
[165] Ibid.
[166] Ibid.
[167] Vargas Carreno, Edmundo, 'Humanitarian Intervention', in *International Law at the Eve of the Twenty-First Century – Views from the International Law Commission*, United Nations, 1997, pp 339-63, at 344-45.

> States cannot be regarded as a prospective barrier behind which human rights could be massively or systematically violated with impunity. The fact that, in diverse situations, the United Nations has not been able to prevent atrocities cannot be cited as an argument, legal or moral, against the necessary corrective action, especially where peace is also threatened [...] We need not impale ourselves on the horns of a dilemma between respect for sovereignty and the protection of human rights [...] *What is involved is not the rights of intervention but the collective obligation of States to bring relief and redress in human rights emergencies.*[168]

The current Secretary-General, Kofi Annan, has also taken a stand in favour of humanitarian intervention. Thus, while calling upon the Security Council to meet future humanitarian crises, he expressly mentioned the 'developing international norm in favour of intervention to protect civilians from wholesale slaughter,'[169] and unequivocally stated:

> To those for whom the greatest threat to the future of international order is the use of force in the absence of a Security Council mandate, one might ask – not in the context of Kosovo – but in the context of Rwanda: If, in those dark days and hours leading up to the genocide, a coalition of States had been prepared to act in defence of the Tutsi population, but did not receive prompt Council authorization, should such a coalition have stood aside and allowed the horror to unfold?[170]

Furthermore, in its 1995 Report, the International Law Commission, while reiterating the importance of non-intervention as a fundamental principle of contemporary international law, has nonetheless indicated its limited scope, especially due to 'the decline in the number of situations, qualifying as internal affairs and to the emergence of situations, affecting human rights in particular, in which the internal jurisdiction exception was unwarranted'.[171]

---

[168] 'Report of the Secretary-General on the work of the Organisation', *Official Records of the General Assembly, Forty-sixth Session, Supplement No 1* (A/46/1), p 5. Emphasis added.

[169] 'Secretary-General Presents His Annual Report to General Assembly', UN Press Release SG/SM/7136, GA/9596 (20 September 1999).

[170] Ibid.

[171] 'Report of the International Law Commission on the work of its forty-seventh session', 2 May to 21 July 1995, *Official Records of the General Assembly, Fiftieth Session, Supplement No 10* (A/50/10), para.75. Cited in Vargas Carreno, Edmundo,*supra* n 165,p 347.

Ultimately, the International Criminal Tribunals for the former Yugoslavia and for Rwanda respectively established by the Security Council can be seen as a form of judicial intervention pertaining to the wider concept of humanitarian intervention. It may also be argued here that the International Criminal Court itself is a form of humanitarian intervention in the affairs of states, its purpose being precisely to prosecute these 'affairs' when they amount to international crimes.[172]

As a concluding remark on this point, it has to be noted that the purpose of this development was certainly not to advocate for the unilateral action of some states who aim at saving the world, and this in complete violation of another state's sovereignty. Rather, it was to stress the feasibility and legality of humanitarian intervention when undertaken under the auspices of the United Nations. In some particular cases, this action is not only legal it is also mandatory.

c. *... To a duty of humanitarian intervention*

It is here submitted that, in cases of international crimes, the international community of states has an express obligation to intervene to prevent these crimes from occurring or to bring them to an end. There are strong moral reasons behind this assertion, the most important one being that humanity will perish from letting these crimes happen over and over again. From a legal standpoint, if it has to be admitted that humanitarian intervention is generally not mandatory but merely legally possible, it is nonetheless submitted here that the crime of genocide is an exception to this general principle.

As regards the genocide in Cambodia, Hannum wrote that the failure of any state to institute proceedings before the International Court of Justice was an 'indefensible abdication of *international responsibility*'.[173] In fact, it can be recalled here that, not only were no complaints filed, but the Khmer Rouge actually kept their seat in the United Nations.

More technically, Judge Lauterpacht has contended that Article IX of the Genocide Convention contemplates state responsibility for genocide and that, consequently, the conventional obligations extend to the duty to prevent a state from committing genocide. According to him, there is thus 'an obligation, at any rate for a State involved in a conflict, to

[172] See Bettati, Mario, *Le Droit d'Ingérence – Mutation de l'Ordre International*, Editions Odile Jacob, 1996, p 265.
[173] Hannum, Hurst, 'International Law and Cambodian Genocide: The Sounds of Silence', (1989) 11 *HRQ* 84.

concern itself with the prevention of genocide outside its territory'.[174] In fact, this obligation to intervene in order to prevent genocide from occurring or to put an end to it was paradoxically enhanced by the United States position during the genocide in Rwanda. And indeed, the United States had continuously avoided qualifying the massacres as genocide, thus indirectly acknowledging the fact that such a qualification would necessarily entail an obligation for them to intervene. In other words, the only explanation for the reluctance on the part of the United States to use the 'g-word' is that they undoubtedly considered the perpetration of a genocide qualified as such as compulsory triggering humanitarian intervention. It is also noticeable that all cautiousness disappeared after the genocide had been committed and when, in 1998, President Clinton made public excuses for having remained a bystander, he employed the term 'genocide' no less than 11 times!

As it has been emphasised, the genocide in Rwanda is far from being the only instance in which the international community failed to intervene and to bring to an end the most atrocious crimes. But if there is a duty to intervene, which is the case with respect to genocide, if there is an obligation to carry out humanitarian interventions, there is necessarily a form of responsibility attached to the violation of this obligation, violation constituted precisely when there is a failure to intervene. Sartre thought that we were responsible for what we did not try to prevent, but, according to Revault d'Alones, there is worse: we might also be responsible for what we did not succeed in preventing.[175] Consequently, it is here contended that, at least with respect to genocide, the international community of states is under an obligation to intervene and to acknowledge the crimes committed by a given state. As regards the other international crimes contemplated in the present book, it is here submitted that such duty should also be recognised in their case and, as an exception to what has generally been advocated, the model to follow here should not be the law of crimes against humanity but that of genocide.

Even further, it is here submitted that not only do states have a responsibility before the commission of the crimes, responsibility

---

[174] *Application of the Convention on the Prevention and Punishment of the Crime of Genocide* (*Bosnia and Herzegovina* v *Yugoslavia* (Serbia and Montenegro)), Further Requests for the Indication of Provisional Measures, September 13, 1993, [1993] ICJ reports, pp. 443-44. See Schabas, William A., *Genocide in International Law – The Crimes of Crimes*, Cambridge University Press, 2000, p 494.

[175] 'Témoins de Sartre', [1990] *Les Temps Modernes*. Cited in de Saint Cheron, Michaël, *De la mémoire à la responsabilité – Dialogue avec Geneviève de Gaulle Anthinioz, Edgar Morin, Emmanuel Levinas*, Editions Dervy, Collection A vive voix, 2000, p 135.

reflected in the obligation to prevent the crimes, as well as during the commission of the crimes, responsibility here reflected in the obligation to intervene, but they also have a responsibility even after the commission of the crimes, responsibility to which is attached the concept of universal jurisdiction over international crimes. Ultimately, in the words of Christenson, there is an urge to:

> seek to hold the nation-state system of international law itself accountable to a global society whose fundamental interests are not the survival of the state system but the security and well-being of all people.[176]

The horrors committed by the Nazis and the atrocity of the genocide they perpetrated against the Jews of Europe prompted the international community to loudly and emphatically state that this would never happen again. 'Never Again' was the motto, the universal devise, but subsequent events have continuously broken this promise. The crimes have happened again, differently, in other places, against other victims, but again. In the words of the journalist Rieff:

> The failure to intervene decisively in Bosnia suggested that the rhetoric of 'Never Again' associated with Holocaust remembrance meant nothing more than that 'Never Again' would Germans kill Jews in Europe in the 1940s.[177]

[176] Christenson, Gordon A., '*Jus Cogens*: Guarding Interests Fundamental to International Society', (1988) 28 *Virginia Journal of International Law* 648.

[177] Rieff, David, *Slaughterhouse : Bosnia and the Failure of the West*, Touchstone, 1996, p 27. Cited in Fowler, Jerry, 'Out of that Darkness: Responding to Genocide in the 21st Century', in Totten, Samuel, Parsons, William S. and Charny, Israel W. (eds), *Century of Genocide – Critical Essays and Eyewitness Accounts*, 2nd edn, Routledge, 2004, pp 455-68 at 457.

Conclusion: The Practicalities of Prosecuting International Crimes: The Concept of Universal Jurisdiction

The very phrase 'crimes against humanity' connotes that it is not only a particular group that has been injured but the entire human race. Accordingly, all have a responsibility to see that justice is done. A prosecution before an international tribunal is 'Humanity vs. Radovan Karadzic' or 'The World vs. Radovan Karadzic'.

Aryeh Neier[1]

In its classical meaning, 'universal jurisdiction' is a geographical concept defined by opposition to 'territorial jurisdiction'. In practical terms, it refers to the competence of states to prosecute or to extradite perpetrators of international crimes. According to Paust:

> [i]t is the *customary duty of states* to initiate prosecution or to extradite those reasonably accused of international crime. This duty derived from a formula developed by Hugo Grotius calling for *'aut dedere...aut punire'*.[2]

Interestingly, Bassiouni has amended this maxim to '*aut dedere aut judicare*[3] since the goal of adjudication is to prosecute and not merely to punish'.[4] Thus, the universality principle allows any state jurisdiction to provide criminal or civil sanctions for violations of international law.[5] According to Paust, '[u]niversal jurisdiction is thus technically jurisdiction to enforce, and the enforcement is actually made on behalf of the international community'.[6] For Meron, 'the true meaning of universal jurisdiction is that international law permits any state to apply its

[1] Neier, Aryeh, *War Crimes – Brutality, Genocide, Terror and The Struggle For Justice*, Times Books, 1998, p 213.

[2] Grotius, Hugo, *De Jure Belli Ac Pacis*, Book II, ch XXI, para.III 8 IV, 1624, English translation by Kelsey cited in Paust, Jordan J. et al, *International Criminal Law, Cases and Materials*, Carolina Academic Press, 2nd edn, 2000, p 9. Emphasis added.

[3] See Bassiouni, M. Cherif and Wise, Edward M., *Aut dedere Aut Judicare – The Duty to Extradite or Prosecute in International Law*, Martinus Nijhoff Publishers, 1995.

[4] Paust, Jordan J. et al, *supra* n 2, p 9.

[5] See ibid, p 157. For an analysis of the doctrinal development of the universality principle, see Randall, Kenneth C., 'Universal Jurisdiction Under International Law', (1988) 66 *Texas Law Review* 785-841.

[6] Paust, Jordan J. et al, *supra* n 2, p 158.

laws to certain offenses even in the absence of territorial, nationality or other accepted contacts with the offender or the victim'.[7] The question here is thus whether, in the case of international crimes, international law merely *allows* states to exercise universal jurisdiction or if it *obliges* them to do so. In other words, is universal jurisdiction over international crimes optional or mandatory? The law on this issue underwent an evolution and it might therefore be argued that such a duty to prosecute or extradite is now part of customary international law.

A. Universal jurisdiction over international crimes in international law

The concept of universal jurisdiction can be deemed to have emerged in positive international law at the end of the Second World War with the idea that crimes against humanity were not a domestic affair and that other states than those where they were perpetrated had jurisdiction over them. Thanks to the Nuremberg legacy, crimes against humanity are thus today subjected to universal jurisdiction, and a state may thus exercise jurisdiction over offenders regardless of any nexus it may have with them, their offence or the victim. The notion behind this principle is that the nature of these crimes dictates that all states have an interest in prosecuting them. In fact, the universality principle aims at eliminating sources of refuge for offenders by permitting trials to take place even outside the state where the atrocities were committed. In practical terms, the concept of universal jurisdiction thus entails the possibility to prosecute criminals against humanity even outside the context of an international court and even when there is no effective judicial system in the state where the crimes were perpetrated. Clearly, if accountability for the most serious crimes is to be achieved, the exercise of such a jurisdiction should be made mandatory. In the words of Beres:

> [t]he Nuremberg international legal order obligates States to recognize universal jurisdiction in punishing crimes against humanity. Such punishment directly concerns each State since fundamental Human Rights have been consecrated by international law as an imperious postulate for the general community of humankind. By acting in compliance with this postulate, each State protects the interests of this entire community at the same time as it safeguards its own interests.[8]

[7] Meron, Theodor, 'International Criminalization of Internal Atrocities', (1995) 89 *AJIL* 570. Emphasis added.

[8] Beres, Louis René, 'Justice and Realpolitik : International Law and the Prevention of Genocide', (1988) 33 *AJIL* 141-42.

1. *Mandatory universal jurisdiction over international crimes*

In some cases, states have an explicit treaty obligation to penalise certain offences under domestic law and thus to have appropriate domestic criminal law statutes implementing this obligation, or a domestic law system allowing for prosecutions directly under international law. If not, they are violating their international legal commitments.[9] For instance, under the 1949 Geneva Conventions, States Parties are under an obligation to prosecute or extradite for the purpose of prosecution individuals present in their territory who are accused of grave breaches.[10] It can also be recalled here that the Torture Convention[11] and the Apartheid Convention[12] contain a similar obligation as regards the crimes they deal with respectively.

Adopting a different approach than the above-mentioned legal texts, some instruments impose on states a more indirect duty to punish perpetrators of international crimes.[13] Under these instruments, states have an obligation to take action to investigate and impose punishment on persons responsible for gross violations of the ICCPR,[14] the ECHR[15] or the American Convention on Human Rights.[16] The particularity here is that this duty derives from the obligation to ensure the rights contained in these instruments and to provide for a remedy for their violations.

Several anti-terrorist conventions, by prohibiting amnesties, also imply a duty to prosecute. Furthermore, these conventions all seek to suppress international terrorism by establishing a framework for international co-operation among states.[17] It is true that, strictly speaking, none of these conventions actually create an obligation to extradite, but they

---

[9] See Scharf, Michael P., 'Reining in Impunity for International Crimes – Report of the Rapporteur', in Joyner, Christopher C. and Bassiouni, M. Cherif (eds), *Reining in Impunity for International Crimes and Serious Violations of Fundamental Human Rights : Proceedings of the Siracusa Conference, 17-21 September 1998,* Nouvelles Etudes Pénales, Association Internationale de Droit Pénal, érès, 1998, p 129.

[10] Articles 49-50/50-51/129-30/146-47 of the Geneva Conventions and Articles 85-86 of Additional Protocol I.

[11] Article 7(1).

[12] Article IV(b).

[13] Scharf, Michael P., *supra* n 9.

[14] Article 2.

[15] Article 1.

[16] Articles 1 and 2.

[17] See Convention on Offences and Certain Other Acts Committed on Board Aircraft (Tokyo Convention); Convention for Suppression of Unlawful Seizure of Aircraft (Hague Convention); Convention for Suppression of Unlawful Acts Against the Safety of Civil Aviation (Montreal Convention); International Convention Against the Taking of Hostages; 1997 International Convention for the Suppression of Terrorist Bombings; 1999 International Convention for the Suppression of the Financing of Terrorism.

do contain an inducement to extradite.[18] Nonetheless, following the terrorist attacks on the United States of America, the Security Council's Resolution 1368 called on states 'to work together urgently to bring to justice the perpetrators, organizers and sponsors of these terrorist attacks' and stressed that: 'those responsible for aiding, supporting or harbouring the perpetrators, organizers and sponsors of these acts will be held accountable.'[19]

It is interesting to note that, with respect to the concept of universal jurisdiction, the law of war crimes seems to be more complete than that of crimes against humanity and of genocide as the 1949 Geneva Conventions provide for mandatory universal jurisdiction over grave breaches of their provisions.[20] It nonetheless appears that, more than 50 years since their adoption, only a very small number of States Parties to the Conventions have established universal jurisdiction over grave breaches.[21] Furthermore, the 'grave breaches' system created by the Conventions is hardly satisfying as it contains some serious loopholes, and notably the distinction between 'grave breaches', which are listed and individually defined, and other breaches, which consist of any conduct contrary to their provisions. In practical terms, this distinction highly restricts the scope of the compulsory universal jurisdiction as it is only in the case of 'grave breaches' that the States Parties have a duty to prosecute, and not in the case of 'other breaches'. In other words, not every violation of the laws of warfare is a punishable act.[22] According to Draper:

> [t]he system for the repression of breaches of the Conventions, with the fundamental division between

[18] See Murphy, John F., 'The Future of Multilateralism and Efforts to Combat International Terrorism', (1986) 25 *Columbia Journal of Transnational Law* 41-53.

[19] Resolution 1368 (2001), Aadopted by the Security Council at its 4370th meeting, on 12 September 2001, UN Doc S/RES/1368 (2001).

[20] See Articles 49-50/50-1/129-30/146-7 of the Geneva Conventions and Articles 85-86 of Additional Protocol I. Also, common Article 1 requires States Parties to respect and ensure respect for the provisions of the Conventions and '[t]he use of the words "and to ensure respect" was deliberate: they were intended to emphasize and strengthen the responsibility of the Contracting Parties'. Commentary to Geneva Convention I 26.

[21] See Van Elst, Richard, 'Implementing Universal Jurisdiction Over Grave Breaches of the Geneva Conventions', (2000) 13 *LJIL* 815-54.

[22] Indeed, while Article 85 (5) of Additional Protocol I states that grave breaches of both the Conventions and the Protocol 'shall be regarded as war crimes', Dinstein rightly recalled that '[t]he enumeration of grave breaches in the Geneva Conventions and Protocol I need not be regarded as co-terminous with an exhaustive roster of war crimes. But clearly, not every ordinary breach of these instruments can be viewed as a war crime'. Dinstein, Yoram, 'The Distinctions between War Crimes and Crimes Against Peace', in Dinstein, Yoram and Tabory, Mala (eds), *War Crimes in International Law,* Martinus Nijhoff Publishers, 1996, pp 3-4. Still, it might be recalled here that

Continued

> 'grave' and other breaches, does not satisfy. In their anxiety to avoid the term 'crimes', the redactors have opened a vista of uncertainty in the application of criminal justice.[23]

In spite of the shortcomings of the law of war crimes on this issue, it must however be recalled here that, in this respect, the ICTR Statute and the ICTY caselaw constituted great steps forward as they imposed individual criminal responsibility even for acts which were not 'grave breaches' but breaches of common Article 3 of the Geneva Conventions and of Additional Protocol II[24] or, to put it differently, for acts committed in both international *and* internal armed conflicts.

Furthermore, it is not entirely sure that, under customary international law, the law of war crimes is in reality the most complete. And indeed, it also seems that, even prior to the adoption and subsequent entry into force of the Rome Statute of the International Criminal Court, both crimes against humanity and genocide had been recognised as triggering universal jurisdiction. This may indeed be inferred from the 1994 final report of the Commission of Experts for the former Yugoslavia established by the Security Council which unequivocally stated:

> the only offences committed in internal armed conflict for which universal jurisdiction exists are 'crimes against humanity' and genocide.[25]

2. *The conventional exclusion of the principle of universal jurisdiction over the crime of genocide*

The law of genocide is of particular interest here, notably due to the fact that the conventional legacy with respect to the applicability of universal jurisdiction to crimes of genocide is far from clear. Indeed, the Genocide Convention fails expressly to provide for universal jurisdiction and does not therefore impose any general duty to prosecute or extradite.

... States Parties have an obligation 'to take measures necessary for the suppression of all acts contrary to the provisions of the present Convention other than the grave breaches'. See Articles 49(3)/50(3)/ 129(3)/146(3). Thus, '[t]he Contracting Parties should at least insert in their legislation a general clause providing for the punishment of other breaches'. See Commentary to Geneva Convention III 624.

[23] Draper, GIAD, 'The Modern Pattern of War Criminality', in Dinstein, Yoram and Tabory, Mala (eds), *War Crimes in International Law*, Martinus Nijhoff Publishers, 1996, p 165.

[24] See *supra*.

[25] Final Report of the Commission of Experts Established Pursuant to Security Council Resolution 780 (1992), UN Doc S/1994/674, annex, p 13.

Consequently, genocide is the only international crime not submitted to universal jurisdiction. Indeed, while war crimes, crimes against humanity, as well as the so-called *delicta juris gentium* – such as slavery, trade in children or piracy – are subject to the principle of universal repression, the crime of genocide remains under territorial jurisdiction,[26] at least according to the convention.

While the original draft of the Genocide Convention adopted the principle of universal jurisdiction, thus allowing any state to prosecute perpetrators of genocide regardless of the nationality of the perpetrator or of the victim and of the place of commission of the crime, the convention finally provided for territorial jurisdiction, most probably in order to protect state sovereignty. It was indeed argued that the principle of universal repression could cause international tension as the courts of one state would become the judge of the conduct of another state. As a result, the principle of universal jurisdiction was unfortunately deleted from the text, with the risk of allowing impunity for perpetrators of genocide. Indeed, it seems obvious that the state of commission of the crime is very unlikely to be willing to try the perpetrators, either because they are still in power or influence, or because the reconstruction of society is based on forgetting the past. As Stern rightly stated:

> The necessity to develop universal jurisdiction is even more important if one considers that quite often offenses like war crimes, crimes against humanity, or genocide have links with the state in which they were perpetrated. Without effective universal jurisdiction, the state that has normally jurisdiction over those acts is quite unlikely to prosecute them correctly, if at all. All perpetrators of international crime should know that they are 'accountable' for them, in all states throughout the world.[27]

Also, Article VI of the convention, which deals with individual criminal responsibility, does not provide for the punishment by the state of its own citizens who committed genocide abroad and found asylum in their own country. As states usually fail to extradite their own citizens, it is very likely that these criminals will never be punished…and this in complete respect of the convention. Furthermore, the principle of

---

[26] For contrary views, see *infra*, Conclusion.

[27] Stern, Brigitte, 'Better Interpretation and Enforcement of Universal Jurisdiction', in Joyner, Christopher C. and Bassiouni, M. Cherif (eds), *Reining in Impunity for International Crimes and Serious Violations of Fundamental Human Rights : Proceedings of the Siracusa Conference, 17-21 September 1998*, Nouvelles Etudes Pénales, Association Internationale de Droit Pénal, érès, 1998, pp 178-79.

territorial jurisdiction raises the question of the definition of the place where the crime was actually committed. If mass murder is easy to locate, the scenes of commission of other acts of genocide might prove difficult to determine. Indeed, it may well be that conspiracy to commit genocide, or incitement to commit genocide, does not actually occur at the place of the crime.

Such shortcomings have been acknowledged and it may be noted here that Ruhashyankiko, the Special Rapporteur on the question of Genocide, felt that 'the question of universal punishment should be reconsidered'.[28] Also, it might be recalled here that the final report of the Commission of Experts for the former Yugoslavia unequivocally stated that:

> [t]he only offences committed in internal armed conflict for which universal jurisdiction exists are 'crimes against humanity' and *genocide*.[29]

Still, in spite of the conventional silence regarding universal jurisdiction, Schabas has argued that: 'the combination of Articles I, IV, V, VI and VII might be read to imply such an obligation.' [30] In the absence of any explicit conventional provision with respect to universal jurisdiction, reading the convention so as to find indicators that universal jurisdiction could be implied from the wording of the text might be too extensive a reading. Indeed, if it had been the intention of the drafters to provide for universal jurisdiction in the convention, they would not have expressly included the territorial jurisdiction principle in its Article VI. Nonetheless, such extensive reading might not be totally ill-founded and it is here interesting to note that, in the *Jorgiæ* case, the Higher Regional Court at Düsseldorf mentioned 'the generally accepted non-exclusive interpretation of Article VI of the 1948 Genocide Convention'.[31] This finding was subsequently confirmed by the German Federal Constitutional Court[32] which 'observed that a hypothetical

---

[28] Ruhashyankiko Report, p 56.

[29] Final Report of the Commission of Experts Established Pursuant to Security Council Resolution 780 (1992), UN Doc S/1994/674, annex, p 13. Emphasis added.

[30] Schabas, William, A., *Genocide in International Law – The Crimes of Crimes*, Cambridge University Press, 2000, p 404.

[31] Nikolai Jorgić, *Oberlandesgericht Düsseldorf* (Higher Regional Court, Düsseldorf), 26 September 1997, IV-26/96, appeal dismissed: Nikolai Jorgić, *Bundesgerichtshof* (Federal Court of Justice), 30 April 1999, 3 StR 215/98F. Cited in Schabas, William A., 'National Courts Finally Begin to Prosecute Genocide, the 'Crime of Crimes'', (2003) 1 *JICJ* 39-63 at 57, n 93.

[32] Nikolai Jorgić, *Bundesverfassungsgericht* (Federal Constitutional Court), Fourth Chamber, Second Senate, 12 December 2000, 2 BvR 1290/99. Cited in Schabas, William A., *supra* n 31, p 57, n 91.

norm of customary international law forbidding the application of universal jurisdiction would be contrary to the rule prohibiting genocide, which is a peremptory norm of *jus cogens*.'[33] Furthermore, in a very recent decision of 5 October 2005, the Spanish Constitutional Tribunal expressly ruled that the Spanish courts could exercise universal jurisdiction over both genocide and crimes against humanity, regardless of their place of commission and of the nationality of the perpetrators and of the victims.[34]

In any event, and most fortunately, the Rome Statute has definitively solved the problem by clearly establishing the principle of universal jurisdiction over the crimes falling within the jurisdiction of the court, thus including genocide. Ultimately, one must not forget that universal jurisdiction, by permitting effective prosecution, is necessary from the victims' perspective. In the words of Orentlicher:

> [b]y not having a trial and not punishing Pol Pot and the Khmer Rouge over the past two decades we have, in effect, told the Cambodians that what happened wasn't a crime [...] If there was no punishment, there was no crime.[35]

By failing to provide the necessary tools for the effective prosecution of the crime of genocide, the Genocide Convention is not only counter-productive, it actually generates the ongoing perpetration of the crime through its denial. And indeed, as the absence of prosecution and punishment are collectively perceived as the absence of crime, they more often than not degenerate into denial, thus increasing the victimisation of victims precisely by denying the genocide ever took place: if there was no crime, there can be no victim. The shortcomings of the Genocide Convention thus go beyond the simple ineffectiveness of the instrument, they actually allow for the crime of genocide to continue through its denial ... We are far from the promises of prevention and punishment set forth in the title of the Convention itself!

3. *Universal jurisdiction as a customary law duty*

Apart from the explicit treaty obligations requiring that states exercise universal jurisdiction over international crimes, several other

[33] Ibid. at 57.
[34] See Chambraud, Cécile, 'L'Espagne s'autorise à juger tous les crimes contre l'humanité', *Le Monde*, 6 October 2005.
[35] Cited in Ball, Howard, *Prosecuting War Crimes and Genocide – The Twentieth Century Experience,* University Press of Kansas, 1999, p 116.

instruments stress that all states should prosecute or extradite individuals accused of war crimes or crimes against humanity under customary international law.[36] In other words, these instruments thus suggest that the exercise of such a jurisdiction is a norm of customary international law. Reinforcing this proposition is the legal status of amnesties which now seem to be prohibited in the case of international crimes.

a. United Nations resolutions

Several UN Resolutions indicate that there is an obligation to exercise universal jurisdiction and even if such resolutions are not binding, their adoption is still clear evidence of state opinion on a particular subject. For instance, at its very first session, the General Assembly unanimously adopted a resolution recommending:

> [t]hat Members of the United Nations forthwith take all necessary measures to cause the arrest of those war criminals who have been responsible for or have taken a consenting part in the above crimes, and to cause them to be sent back to the countries in which their abominable deeds were done, in order that they may be judged and punished according to the laws of those countries; [and calling upon] the governments of States which are not Members of the United Nations also to take all necessary measures for the apprehension of such criminals in their respective territories with a view to their immediate removal to the countries in which the crimes were committed for the purpose of trial and punishment according to the laws of those countries.[37]

Notwithstanding the use of the expression 'war criminals', it is arguable that this resolution, dealing with perpetrators of 'abominable deeds', also applied to 'criminals against humanity' as well as to 'genociders'.

[36] See the 1967 Declaration on Territorial Asylum, the 1970 UN Resolution on War Criminals, G.A. Resolution 2840 (1971), the Principles on the Effective Prevention and Investigation of Extra-Legal, Arbitrary and Summary Executions in G.A. Resolution 65 (1989), and the Declaration on the Protection of All Persons From Enforced Disappearances in G.A. Resolution 133 (1992). See Scharf, Michael P., 'Reining in Impunity for International Crimes – Report of the Rapporteur', in Joyner, Christopher C. and Bassiouni, M. Cherif (eds), *Reining in Impunity for International Crimes and Serious Violations of Fundamental Human Rights : Proceedings of the Siracusa Conference, 17-21 September 1998,* Nouvelles Etudes Pénales, Association Internationale de Droit Pénal, érès, 1998, p 129.

[37] G.A. Res. 3 (I), 13 February 1946. Cited in Green, Leslie C., 'New Trends in International Criminal Law', (1981) 11 *Israel Yearbook on Human Rights* 19-20.

Furthermore, in 1967, another resolution urged states not to grant asylum to anyone seriously suspected of having committed crimes against humanity, stressing that these suspects should be returned to face trial in their own countries,[38] while a 1971 resolution demanded the prosecution by all states of all war criminals and persons guilty of crimes against humanity. This resolution, passed two days after Pakistan troops surrendered to the commander of the joint India-Bangladesh forces in Bangladesh, unequivocally stated that:

> [r]efusal by states to co-operate in the arrest, extradition, trial and punishment of persons guilty of war crimes and crimes against humanity is contrary to the purposes and principles of the Charter of the United Nations and to generally recognised norms of international law.[39]

In 1973, the General Assembly also adopted a resolution which laid down principles of international co-operation in the detection, arrest, extradition and punishment of persons guilty of war crimes and crimes against humanity. Its Principle I read as follows:

> Crimes against humanity, wherever they are committed, shall be subject to investigation and the persons against whom there is evidence that they have committed such crimes shall be subject to tracing, arrest, trial and, if found guilty, to punishment.[40]

It is perfectly true that all these resolutions had little practical effect on the customs and practices of states as no national case relied upon nor cited any of them, but they still are evidence of states' understanding of the law. Furthermore, it may also be recalled here that Article 9 of the 1996 Draft Code of Crimes also contained an obligation to extradite or prosecute:

> Without prejudice to the jurisdiction of an international criminal court, the State Party in the territory of which an individual alleged to have committed a crime set out in Articles 17, 18, 19 or 20 is found *shall* extradite or prosecute that individual.[41]

[38] UN Doc A/6716 (1967).

[39] GA Resolution 2840 (XXVI), 26 UN GAOR, Supp (No 29), p 88, UN Doc A/8429, p 2 (1971).

[40] Principles of International Co-operation in the Detection, Arrest, Extradition, and Punishment of Persons Guilty of War Crimes and Crimes Against Humanity, G.A. Resolution 3074 (XXXVII), 28 UN GAOR Supp. (No 30) p 78, UN Doc A/9030, 3 December 1973.

[41] ILC 1996 Draft Code of Crimes, [1996] II (2) *ILC Yearbook* 30. Emphasis added.

Finally, the case law of the ICTY is of importance here as the tribunal has expressly emphasised the need for universal jurisdiction and for prosecution of human rights violators. Indeed, the appeals Chamber unequivocally stated that:

> [i]t would be travesty of law and a betrayal of the universal need for justice, should the concept of State sovereignty be allowed to be raised successfully against human rights. Borders should not be considered as a shield against the reach of the law and as a protection for those who trample underfoot the most elementary rights of humanity.[42]

There is therefore some evidence in international law that there now exists a customary law duty to exercise universal jurisdiction over international crimes. According to Bassiouni:

> [b]ecause these many conventions have set forth such a duty, it could be argued that the duty to prosecute or extradite, irrespective of the specific binding affect of these instruments, has become part of customary international law.[43]

b. The problem of amnesties

Amnesties may certainly be seen as a legal impediment to the prosecution of international crimes as they operate an extinction of the offence itself. As Scharf recalled:

> [t]he term 'amnesty' is derived from the Greek word 'amnestia' – meaning forgetfulness or oblivion. In the present context, amnesty is an act of sovereign power immunising persons from criminal prosecution for past offences.[44]

---

[42] *Prosecutor* v *Tadić,* Case No IT-94-1-AR72, Decision on the Defence Motion for Interlocutory Appeal on Jurisdiction, Appeals Chamber, 2 October 1995, para 58. The appeals chamber agreed that the tribunal may issue binding orders to states, since it must be able to take such steps to effectively investigate crimes, collect evidence, summon witnesses, and have indictees arrested and surrendered to the Hague. Furthermore, such authority does not apply solely to the states of the former Yugoslavia. See also *Prosecutor* v *Blaškić,* Case No. IT-95-14, Judgment, Trial Chamber I, 3 March 2000.

[43] Bassiouni, M. Cherif, 'Crimes Against Humanity', in Bassiouni, M. Cherif (ed), *International Criminal Law, Volume I: Crimes,* Transnational Publishers, Inc., 2nd edn, 1999, p 577.

[44] Cited in Paust, Jordan J. et al., *International Criminal Law, Cases and Materials,* Carolina Academic Press, 2nd, 2000, p 21.

Nonetheless, it must be stressed that, as Roht-Arriaza has noted, '[t]here is an increasing trend in international human rights bodies explicitly to condemn amnesties for certain particularly grave offenses, even those granted by successor regimes'.[45] And indeed, it is now more and more acknowledged that the granting of amnesty is either totally *prohibited* where universal jurisdiction is mandatory, or *inappropriate* where there is a customary international law duty to prosecute or extradite. In any case, amnesty is not a recommended measure in the case of international crimes and, despite inconsistent state practice, there are strong jurisprudential reasons suggesting their incompatibility with international law. In fact, the notion of granting amnesty for crimes against humanity would be inconsistent with the principles of individual criminal responsibility recognised in the Nuremberg Charter and judgment. According to Cassese:

> [t]he validity of such amnesty [to persons responsible of grave breaches of international humanitarian law and mass violations of human rights] is doubtful. Arguably, the prohibition of such crimes and the consequent obligation of states to prosecute and punish their authors should be considered a peremptory norm of international law (*jus cogens*): hence, states should not be allowed to enter into international agreements or pass national legislation foregoing punishment of those crimes.[46]

In the same vein, the Human Rights Committee held that:

> Amnesties are generally incompatible with the duty of States to investigate such acts; to guarantee freedom from such acts within their jurisdiction; and to ensure that they do not occur in the future. States may not deprive individuals of the right to an effective remedy including compensation and such full rehabilitation as may be possible.[47]

Also, it is worth noting here that, during the signature of the Lomé Peace Agreement for Sierra Leone,[48] the UN Secretary-General had

[45] Roht-Arriaza, Naomi, 'Special problems of a Duty to Prosecute: Derogation, Amnesties, Statutes of Limitation, and Superior Orders', in Roht-Arriaza, Naomi, *Impunity and Human Rights in International Law and Practice,* Oxford University Press, 1995, p.59.

[46] Cassese, Antonio, 'On the Current Trends towards Criminal Prosecution and Punishment of Breaches of International Humanitarian Law', (1998) 9 *EJIL* 6.

[47] UN Human Rights Committee General Comment No 20 in relation to Article 7 of the ICCPR.

[48] Signed on 7 June 1999.

formulated a reservation to the general amnesty provided for in the agreement, recalling that amnesty was not applicable to international crimes, crimes against humanity, war crimes or serious violations of the laws and customs of war. Subsequently, the Sierra Leone Government accepted this position and the Statute of the Special Court Tribunal for Sierra Leone[49] thus provides that amnesty will not impede legal action as regards such crimes.[50] In this respect, it is worth noting that the appeals chamber of this special court has ruled that the amnesties enshrined in the Lomé Peace Agreement did not constitute legal impediments for the court to exercise its jurisdiction over the persons and acts covered by these amnesties.[51] More specifically, while linking the concept of amnesties with that of universal jurisdiction, the appeals chamber found that the latter implied that amnesties granted by one state could not prevent another state from exercising its jurisdiction over perpetrators of international crimes and eloquently expressed this idea in the following terms:

> A State cannot bring into oblivion and forgetfulness a crime, such as a crime against international law, which other States are entitled to keep alive and remember.[52]

Finally, the preamble of the Rome Statute also implies that deferring a prosecution because of the existence of a national amnesty would be incompatible with the purpose of the court, which is to ensure criminal prosecution of persons who commit serious international crimes. Thus, the preamble:

> Affirm[s] that the most serious crimes of concern to the international community as a whole must not go unpunished and that their *effective prosecution* must be ensured [...]
>
> Recall[s] that it is the *duty of every State to exercise its criminal jurisdiction* over those responsible for international crimes.

[49] Statute signed on 16 January 2002.

[50] Article 10 of the Statute. See generally Cissé, Catherine, 'Le Tribunal Spécial pour la Sierra Leone', (2002) 4 *International Law FORUM du droit international* 7-11.

[51] *The Prosecutor* v *Morris Kallon and Brima Buzzy Kamara*, Special Court for Sierra Leone, SCSL-2004-15-AR72(E) and SCSL2004-16-AR72(E), Decision on Challenge to Jurisdiction: Lomé Accord Amnesty (Appeals Chamber, 13 March 2004). See generally Meisenberg, Simon M., 'Legality of amnesties in international humanitarian law – The Lomé Amnesty Decision of the Special Court for Sierra Leone', (2004) 86 *International Review of the Red Cross* 837-51.

[52] *The Prosecutor* v *Morris Kallon and Brima Buzzy Kamara*, Special Court for Sierra Leone, SCSL-2004-15-AR72(E) and SCSL2004-16-AR72(E), Decision on Challenge to Jurisdiction: Lomé Accord Amnesty (Appeals Chamber, 13 March 2004) para 67.

> Emphasise[s] that the International Criminal Court established under this Statute shall be complementary to *national criminal jurisdiction*.[53]

Notwithstanding the importance of the preamble,[54] it must here be pointed out that some provisions of the statute seem however to allow the court to recognise amnesty in certain given circumstances. According to Scharf,

> [t]he apparent conflict between these Articles and the Preamble reflect the schizophrenic nature of the negotiations at Rome: the preambular language and the procedural provisions were negotiated by entirely different drafting groups, and in the rush of the closing days of the Rome Conference, the Drafting Committee never fully integrated and reconciled the separate portions of the Statute.[55]

Thus, Article 16 of the statute provides that the court would be required to defer to a national amnesty if the Security Council has requested that it respects an amnesty-for-peace deal and thereby to terminate a prosecution. Still, it might be argued that, at least regarding war crimes, such an amnesty would be in direct violation of the 1949 Geneva Conventions which, as previously stated, impose a duty to prosecute.[56] This would also be in violation of Article VI of the Genocide Convention which, although not contemplating universal jurisdiction, still provides that:

> [p]ersons charged with genocide or any of the other acts enumerated in Article III shall be tried [...] by such international penal tribunal as may have jurisdiction with respect to those Contracting Parties which shall have accepted its jurisdiction.

[53] See preamble of the ICC Statute. Emphasis added.

[54] See Article 31(1) of the Vienna Convention on the Law of Treaties. The preamble may indeed serve as a source of interpretation of the treaty as it indicates both the context as well as the object and the purpose of the treaty.

[55] Scharf, Michael P., 'The Amnesty Exception to the Jurisdiction of the International Criminal Court', (1999) 32 *Cornell International Law Journal* 522.

[56] See Article 49 of Geneva Convention I. As Scharf however noted, '[a] counter argument can be made [...] that the Rome Statute codifies only the substantive provisions of the 1949 Geneva Conventions and the Genocide Convention, and does not incorporate those procedural aspects of the Conventions that require prosecution. Accordingly, the nature of the charges might constitute a significant factor to be considered, but would not necessarily be a bar to recognizing an amnesty'. Scharf, Michael P., *supra* n 55, p. 524.

In any event, a safety net is provided by Article 17 (1) of the Rome Statute itself which does not mention amnesty among the causes of inadmissibility of a particular case.

As a concluding remark on this issue, it might be asserted that, although there is uncertainty surrounding this matter, there are strong legal reasons to believe that amnesties are invalid in the case of international crimes. Furthermore, there are also important moral arguments suggesting the total inadequacy of such measures when applied to international 'core crimes'. In fact, in the words of Neier:

> the state, acting on behalf of all, should demonstrate respect for sufferers from crime, and its seriousness about its own proscriptions against criminality, by punishing the transgressors. The victims count on the state not to overlook or forgive their victimisation. They reserve this right to themselves.[57]

Ultimately, one must never forget that:

> Accountability is the antithesis of impunity, which occurs either de facto or through amnesties. But amnesty is essentially a form of forgiveness, granted by governments, for crimes committed against a public interest. How, though, can governments forgive themselves for crimes they committed against others? And how can governments forgive crimes committed by some against others? The power to forgive, forget or overlook in the cases of genocide, crimes against humanity, war crimes and torture, is not that of the governments, but of the victims[58]

... and of the victims *only*.

B. Application of the universality principle in the national fora

Although the international legal process has elaborated a corpus of law providing for international criminal responsibility for human rights violations, domestic legal systems still remain the primary fora for the application of international criminal law. Indeed, both conventional and customary international law envisage national courts

[57] Neier, Aryeh, *War Crimes – Brutality, Genocide, Terror, and the Struggle for Justice*, Times Books, 1998, p. 61.

[58] Bassiouni, M. Cherif, 'The Need for International Accountability', in Bassiouni, M. Cherif (ed.), *International Criminal Law, Volume III: Enforcement*, Transnational Publishers, Inc., 2nd edn, 1999, p. 22.

as the main arena for the trials of perpetrators of international crimes. National prosecutions will however be effective only if the judicial system is fair and impartial and this is not always the case. Moreover, states have proven very reluctant in exercising such jurisdiction, certainly due to the fact that several violations of human rights or humanitarian law are committed on behalf or with the complicity of the state itself. In this respect, Bassiouni is thus entirely correct when he qualified national prosecutions as being a system of 'selective enforcement'.[59] It is true that many individuals have been held responsible under domestic criminal laws, but there have also been a lot of cases where no prosecution took place. Such was notably – but far from exclusively – the case for the Stalin's purges or for the mass killings in Cambodia.[60] Furthermore, regarding the qualification of the crimes, it is noticeable that the great majority of domestic prosecutions for international crimes, since the Second World War, have concerned crimes linked to the war and the Axis powers and the charges were usually brought for war crimes or common crimes under national laws rather than for crimes against humanity *per se*.

In this context, the *Eichmann* and *Barbie* cases are of interest here as they both illustrated the application of the universal jurisdiction principle in the case of crimes against humanity.

On 11 May 1960, Adolf Eichmann, living under a false identity in Argentina, was abducted by the Israeli secret services and brought to Israel for prosecution purposes. The circumstances of the abduction were controversial as the Israeli action had violated Argentina's sovereignty. Consequently, Argentina lodged a complaint with the Security Council of the United Nations and, on 23 June 1960, the Security Council adopted a resolution affirming that the sovereignty of Argentina had been infringed and requesting Israel to make appropriate reparation.[61] As Wenig noted:

> The Council was 'mindful' of the concern that Eichmann be brought to appropriate justice and it is clear from the context of the resolution that there was no intent to include under the term 'appropriate reparation' any physical

[59] Bassiouni, M. Cherif, *Crimes against Humanity in International Criminal Law,* Martinus Nijhoff Publishers, 1992, p 227.

[60] However, it might here be noted that a tribunal has been set up in Cambodia to prosecute crimes committed by the Khmer Rouge. See Pejic, Jelena, 'Accountability for international crimes: From conjecture to reality', [2002] *International Review of the Red Cross* 17-8.

[61] United Nations Security Council, Res. 138, UN Doc S/4349 (1960) cited in the Eichmann Case 36 ILR 5 (1961) 277, at para 40.

> return of Eichmann to Argentina. Indeed on August 3, the Governments of Israel and Argentina issued a joint communiqué resolving to 'view as settled the incident which was caused in the wake of the action of citizens of Israel which violated the basic rights of the State of Argentina'.[62] [63]

Most interestingly for the purpose of our development, on 23 June 1960, the United Nations General Assembly unanimously adopted a resolution requesting Argentina to accept Israel's apology and, according to Heazlett:

> [t]he fact that nations of the United Nations Assembly requested Argentina to accept Israel's apology in order that Eichmann might be 'brought to appropriate justice' leads to the conclusion that the [...] view that *kidnapping does not impair jurisdiction is a principle of international law*.[64]

As Wieviorka further noted, this Resolution also provided for 'adequate reparation' to be awarded by Israel to Argentina without specifying what this reparation should be,[65] thus indirectly implying that such reparation was in fact not necessary and thereby reinforcing the idea that criminals against humanity have to be prosecuted, regardless of the means by which they are brought to trial.

In other words, no matter how valid the arguments regarding the illegality of the arrest, the international community did acknowledge the importance of prosecuting Adolf Eichmann as well as the applicability of the principle of universal jurisdiction to crimes against humanity. Ultimately, if it is true that this arrest was absolutely illegal, it was nonetheless totally legitimate. In the words of Green, if Israel 'had not expressed willingness to institute proceedings against him, Eichmann would have got away scot-free'.[66]

---

[62] Joint Communiqué of the Governments of Israel and Argentina, 3 August 1960, quoted in 36 ILR 59 (1961).

[63] Wenig, Jonathan M., 'Enforcing the Lessons of History: Israel Judges the Holocaust', in McCormack, Timothy L.H. and Simpson, Gerry J. (eds), *The Law of War Crimes – National and International Approaches*, Kluwer Law International, 1997, pp 103-22 at 112.

[64] Heazlett, 'Eichmann – International Law ?', 24 (1962) U. Pitt. L. Rev. 116 at 132. Cited in Wenig, Jonathan M., *supra* n 63, p 113. Emphasis added.

[65] See generally Wieviorka, Annette, *Le Procès Eichmann*, Editions Complexe, 1989, pp 18-22.

[66] Green, 'The Eichmann Case', 23 (1960) MLR 507 at 515. Cited in Wenig, Jonathan M., *supra* n 63, p 114.

In its judgment, the Israeli District Court confirmed the principle of universal jurisdiction and explicitly held that:

> These crimes which afflicted the whole of mankind and shocked the conscience of nations are grave offenses against the law of nations (*"delicta juris gentium"*). Therefore, so far from international law negating or limiting the jurisdiction of countries with respect to such crimes, in the absence of an international court, the *international law is in need of the judicial and legislative authorities of every country*, to give effect to its penal injunctions and to bring criminal to trial.[67]

Subsequently, the Israeli Supreme Court found that '[t]he authority and jurisdiction to try crimes under international law are *universal*',[68] and that the 'power to try and punish a person [...] is vested in every State regardless of the fact that the offense was committed outside its territory by a person who did not belong to it'.[69] By invoking the 'protective principle', which gives the victim nation the right to try any who assaults its existence,[70] the court here again acknowledged the universality principle.

The case of *Klaus Barbie* was yet another occasion for domestic courts to assert the applicability of the principle of universal jurisdiction to crimes against humanity. Klaus Barbie, after having been tried *in abstentia* and condemned to death twice in France for war crimes, was arrested in Bolivia and extradited to France. His extradition actually shared with Adolf Eichmann's abduction some rather striking similarities. Barbie had indeed found refuge in Bolivia where he was nonetheless imprisoned in 1972-73 following an extradition request by the French Government. The Bolivian law at the time prohibiting all extraditions to states with which it had no extradition treaty, as it was the case with France, this extradition request did not succeed. In 1982, following a political change in Bolivia, the Bolivian authorities decided to deprive Barbie of the Bolivian nationality he had fraudulently obtained and to expel him. By a fortunate coincidence, his plane had to stop over at Cayenne-Rochambeau, located in a French department, and once the plane had landed, Barbie was arrested by the French authorities. If it

[67] *Attorney-General of the Government of Israel* v *Eichmann* 36 ILR 26 (Israel District Court - Jerusalem, 1961). Emphasis added.
[68] *Attorney-General of the Government of Israel* v *Eichmann,* 36 ILR s. 12 (Israel Supreme Court, 1962). Emphasis in original.
[69] Ibid, 36 ILR 298.
[70] Ibid.

has to be acknowledged that Barbie's arrest was rather original, his arrest was nonetheless perfectly legal. As the Cour de cassation consequently held:

> En raison de leur nature, les crimes contre l'humanité [...] ne relèvent pas seulement du droit interne français, mais encore d'un *ordre répressif international* auquel la notion de frontière et les règles extraditionnelles qui en découlent sont fondamentalement étrangères.[71]

The *Demjanjuk* case[72] is also of a particular interest here as it represented another recognition that crimes against humanity are offences for which there is universal jurisdiction exists. The United States Circuit Court of Appeals ruled that, based on the right to exercise universal jurisdiction over offences against the law of nations and against humanity, the United States could extradite an alleged Nazi concentration camp guard to Israel or to any other nation. The court recognised that the acts committed by the Nazi and Nazi collaborators were 'crimes universally recognised and condemned by the community of nations' and that these 'crimes [were] offences against the law of nations and against humanity and the prosecuting nation is acting for all nations'.[73]

More recently, acting under the principle of universal jurisdiction, prosecutions took place for crimes committed in the contexts of the former Yugoslavia conflicts and of the genocide in Rwanda. For suspects regarding the Yugoslavia conflict, trials did lead to convictions, and thus to affirmative findings of jurisdiction, in Denmark,[74] Germany[75] and the Netherlands.[76] Other trials led to acquittals but still to affirmative findings of jurisdiction in Austria[77] and Switzerland.[78] In this respect, the finding of lack of jurisdiction by a French court is all the most disturbing, notably because, due to the fact that France has never adopted any specific legislation that provides for universal jurisdiction for grave breaches of the Geneva Conventions, things stand as if France had not even ratified them. [79]

---

[71] *Fédération Nationale des Déportés et Internés Résistants et Patriotes et Autres* v *Barbie*, cass. crim., 6 October 1983, Reprinted in (1984) 88 *RGDIP* 509. Emphasis added.
[72] *Demjanjuk* v. *Petrovsky*, 776 F. 2d 571, 582 (6th Circ. 1985), 79 ILR 545-46.
[73] Ibid., 79 ILR 535.
[74] *Sariæ* case, Danish High Court, 1994.
[75] *Public Prosecutor* v *Djajić*, Supreme Court of Bavaria, 1998.
[76] *Knesević*, Case No.3717, Netherlands Supreme Court, 1997.
[77] *Cvjetković* case, Austria Regional Court at Salzburg, 1995.
[78] *G.* case, Swiss Military Tribunal, Division I.

As regards the Rwanda genocide, it may also be noted that trials have led to convictions in Switzerland and in Belgium. Thus, Belgium has prosecuted Rwandans accused of crimes committed in Rwanda against other Rwandans.[80] Similarly, Switzerland tried and convicted Niyonteze for murder, incitement to commit murder and war crimes, but not for genocide as Switzerland had not ratified the Genocide Convention at the time of the commission of the acts.[81] Still, this conviction is extremely important as it was the first conviction following the exercise by a municipal court of universal jurisdiction under the 1949 Geneva Conventions.[82]

With respect to the genocide in Rwanda, the French caselaw is worthy of attention as, after a judicial saga, the Cour de cassation finally recognised the principle of universal jurisdiction with respect to the crime of genocide. The fact that a reluctant state such as France is beginning to acknowledge this principle represents a clear sign that universal jurisdiction is increasingly becoming mandatory under customary international law. Indeed, if the first cases regarding the Rwanda genocide were no more successful than the Bosnian complaints,[83] it then became known that a Hutu priest who had actively participated in the genocide was in France, acting as a priest in a small village. A common complaint was filed against Munyeshyaka who was arrested. The TGI of Privas declared that it had jurisdiction, but only concerning the acts of torture and cruel and inhuman treatment as defined by the Torture Convention.[84] The Court of Appeals of Nîmes reversed that decision on the astonishing grounds that jurisdiction must be established only on the basis of the 'highest', or, in other words, the most serious, offence, which in this particular case was genocide:

[79] *Javor* case, cass. crim., 26 March 1996. Reprinted in 132 *Bulletin Criminel* 379. See Stern, Brigitte, 'Universal jurisdiction over crimes against humanity under French law', (1999) 93 *AJIL* 525-29.

[80] *Ntezimana et al* case, Cour d'Assises de l'Arrondissement Administratif de Bruxelles-Capitale, 8 June 2001. It must nonetheless be stressed here that, in 2003, the Belgium law on universal jurisdiction was revised and went from the recognition of universal jurisdiction regardless of where the crimes were committed and of the nationality of the victims to the recognition of universal jurisdiction only over crimes committed by a Belgian national or by an individual residing in Belgium.

[81] *Public Prosecutor* v *Niyonteze*, Tribunal militaire de cassation, 27 April 2001. Switzerland became a party to the Genocide Convention, by accession, on 7 September 2000.

[82] See Reydams, Luc, '*Niyonteze* v *Public Prosecutor*', (2002) 96 *AJIL* 231-236.

[83] See Complaint, *Kalinda et al*, TGI Paris, filed 4 July 1994; Complaint, *Depaquier et al.*, filed July 19, 1994, TGI Paris, Order, February 23, 1995. See Stern, Brigitte, '*In re* Javor', '*In re* Munyeshyaka', (1999) *AJIL* 93, pp 525-9 at 527, n 15.

[84] TGI Privas, Order (ordonnance), *Depaquier, Kalinda et al*, January 9, 1996. See Stern, Brigitte, *supra* n 83, p 528.

> la compétence du juge doit s'apprécier uniquement au regard de la plus haute acception pénale qui est le génocide.[85]

With this ruling, the court indirectly rejected the application of universal jurisdiction to the crime of genocide and interpreted the Genocide Convention as not providing for such a jurisdiction. The court of appeals thus declared that French courts had no jurisdiction at all to deal with the events in Rwanda. Fortunately, the Cour de cassation reversed such an unusual decision, emphasising that if the criminal acts can be qualified as crimes entailing universal jurisdiction, this qualification can, on its own, trigger the jurisdiction of French court:

> [i]l suffit que les faits puissent être appréhendés sous une qualification donnant compétence même si le tribunal n'est pas compétent pour des faits recevant une qualification différente, pour que celui-ci puisse exercer sa juridiction.[86]

The Cour de cassation however failed to depart from its previous case law and maintained that French courts could only exercise universal jurisdiction over international crimes if the accused was actually present in France.[87] It is only on the basis of the passive personality principle, restricted to crimes committed against French nationals, that French courts have initiated proceedings in the absence of the accused. Two examples are that of Aloïs Bruner who was tried *in absentia* for crimes against humanity, found guilty and condemned to life imprisonment,[88] and of General Pinochet for whom France had requested extradition.

Nonetheless, the most important decision in this case was that of the Paris cour d'Appel, to which the case was remanded by the Cour de cassation, as it expressly extended the jurisdictional scope of French courts so that it now encompass crimes against humanity and genocide. The cour d'Appel based its decision on the law adopted on 22 May 1996,[89] regarding the adaption of French legislation to Security Council Resolution 955 creating the ICTR. Since the ICTR Statute and that law

---

[85] CA Nîmes, March 20, 1996. See Stern, Brigitte, *supra* n 83, p 528.

[86] *Galinier* v *Munyeshyaka* , cass. crim., 6 January 1998, Reprinted in (1998) 102 *RGDIP* 825-32.

[87] Ibid. See also Stern, Brigitte, 'Universal jurisdiction over crimes against humanity under French law', (1999) 93 *AJIL* 525-9.

[88] Cour d'assises de Paris, 2 March 2001. It may be noted here that, immediately after the Second World War, Aloïs Brunner had been tried twice *in abstentia* before a French military tribunal but, at the time, he was charged with war crimes and not crimes against humanity.

[89] Law No 96-432 of 22 May 1996, Journal Officiel, 23 May 1996, p 7695.

both provide for universal jurisdiction over genocide, the cour d'Appel was able to determine that the suspect could be tried in France for torture as well as for genocide because he was found on French territory – unlike in the Bosnian case. Because the new law is procedural, the court of appeals could apply it immediately and retroactively.[90]

Most recently, and as previously mentioned, a historical step has been taken by the Spanish Constitutional Tribunal with respect to crimes perpetrated during the dictatorship in Guatemala, and notably to the genocide of Indian Mayas between 1978 and 1986. On 5 October 2005, the Constitutional Tribunal indeed unequivocally stated that the principle of universal jurisdiction takes precedence over the existence or non-existence of national interests. Accordingly, it found that Spanish courts had jurisdiction over genocide and crimes against humanity perpetrated outside the territory of Spain by non-Spanish nationals and against non-Spanish nationals.[91]

Finally, it may be noted that, in the United States of America, under the 1789 Alien Tort Claims Act[92] and the 1991 Torture Victim Protection Act,[93] several cases upheld the right of victims of gross violations of international law to sue in United States courts whenever the perpetrator can be found in the United States. The first such case was *Filartiga* v *Pena-Irala*.[94] Since then, about two dozen cases have been filed alleging human rights abuses in countries such as Argentina, the Philippines, Guatemala, Ethiopia, Haiti, Rwanda, China and East Timor. Recently, two cases were brought against former Bosnian Serb leader Radovan Karadzić and the circuit court of appeals found that Karadzić could be found liable for genocide, war crimes, and crimes against humanity.[95] Subsequently, in both cases, the victims were awarded large financial compensation.[96] It must nonetheless be pointed out here that

[90] The case is now being tried on the merits and the length of the procedure has caused the condemnation of France by the European Court of Human Rights. See ECtHR, 8 June 2004.

[91] See Chambraud, Cécile, 'L'Espagne s'autorise à juger tous les crimes contre l'humanité', *Le Monde*, 6 October 2005.

[92] 28 USC § 1350 (1994). It provides for civil action in US courts by an alien 'for a tort only, committed in violation of the law of nations or a treaty of the United States'.

[93] 28 USC § 1350 (1994). It provides for civil action in US courts by US nationals 'against an individual who, under actual or apparent authority, or color of law, of any foreign nation' subjects another individual to torture or extrajudicial killing.

[94] *Filartiga* v *Pena-Irala*, 630 F.2d 876 (2d Circ. 1980).

[95] *Kadić* v *Karadzić*, 518 US 1002 (1996).

[96] *Kadić* v *Karadzić*, No 93 Civ. 1163, judgment (SDNY 16 August 2000), and *Doe* v. *Karadzić*, No 93 Civ. 878, judgment (SDNY 5 October 2000). See generally Murphy Sean D. (ed), 'Award of Damages against Bosnian Serb Leader Radovan Karadzić', (2001) 95 *AJIL* 143-44.

the American courts have not allowed such claims to bypass the immunity of heads of states and the protection of sovereign immunity in order to sue a foreign government or a serving foreign leader directly under the Alien Tort Claims Act. In the cases brought against Karadzić, the defendant was considered as being not entitled to such immunity as, even though he was the president of the self-proclaimed Republic of Srpska in Bosnia-Herzegovina, the United States had never recognised the legitimacy of this state.[97] In 1994, a federal court confirmed the immunity of heads of states and held that Aristide, then head of state of Haiti, was immune from suits involving a political assassination.[98] More recently, in a case against Mugabe, an American District Court found that the purpose of head of state and diplomatic immunity is not to protect human rights abusers or to condone their wrongs. Rather, 'it is in the interest of comity among nations – to safeguard friendly relations among sovereign states'.[99]

It is because of such considerations that states have proven very reluctant to exercise such a jurisdiction and, ultimately, the issue of universal jurisdiction remains highly political. There is nonetheless an increasing trend towards compulsory universal jurisdiction over international crimes and state practice is starting to show evidence of such a duty. In any event, the non-application of universal jurisdiction, leading directly to impunity, is highly immoral. In the words of Justice Jackson, 'to free [major war criminals] without a trial would mock the dead and make *cynics of the living*.'[100]

[97] See *Kadiæ* v *Karadzić*, 70 Fed 3d 232 (2d Circ. 1995).
[98] *Lafontant* v *Aristide*, 844 Fed Supp 128 (Eastern Dist NY 1994).
[99] *Tachiona* v *Mugabe*, 169 F Supp 2d 259 (SDNY 2001), para. 317. See Murphy, Sean D. (ed), 'Immunity as Head of State for Zimbabwe's President Mugabe', (2001) 95 *AJIL* 874-6.
[100] Report of Robert H. Jackson, United States Representative to the International Conference on Military Trials, London 1945, Washington Department of State Publication 3080, 1949. Cited in Cassese, A. (ed), *BVA Röling – The Tokyo Trial and Beyond, Reflections of a Peacemonger*, Polity Press, 1993, p 88. Emphasis added.

Bibliography

This selected bibliography lists the academic works which appear in the footnotes, as well as other, although not all, major works which were consulted in this study.

Books

Ackerman, John E. and O'Sullivan, Eugene, *Practice and Procedure of the International Criminal Tribunal for the Former Yugoslavia – With Selected Materials from the International Criminal Tribunal for Rwanda*, The Hague: Kluwer Law International, 2000.

Aly, Götz, *'Final Solution' : Nazi Population Policy and the Murder of the European Jews*, translated from the German by Belinda Cooper and Allison Brown, Edward Arnold, 1999.

Anders, Günther, *Nous, Fils D'Eichmann*, traduit de l'allemand par Sabine Cornille et Philippe Ivernel, Paris: Bibliothèque Rivages, 1999.

Andreopoulos, George J. (ed), *Genocide – Conceptual and Historical Dimensions*, Philadelphia: University of Pennsylvania Press, 1997.

Antelme, Robert, *Textes Inédits sur L'Espèce Humaine, Essais et Témoignages*, Gallimard, 1996.

Arendt, Hannah, *Antisemitism – Part One of the Origins of Totalitarianism*, A Harvest Book, Harcourt Brace & Company, 1958.

Arendt, Hannah, *Eichmann à Jérusalem*, traduction de l'anglais par Anne Guérin revue par Michelle-Irène Brudny de Launay, Gallimard, Collection Folio Histoire,1997 (original 1966).

Ascensio, Hervé, Decaux, Emmanuel et Pellet, Alain (eds), *Droit International Pénal*, Centre de Droit International de l'Université Paris X-Nanterre, Paris: Editions A. Pedone, 2000.

Association 'Les Fils et Filles des Déportés Juifs de France' (ed), *Discours et Messages de Jacques Chirac, Maire de Paris, Premier Ministre, Président de la République, En hommage aux Juifs de France victimes de la Collaboration de l'Etat Français de Vichy avec l'Occupant Allemand*, Paris, 1998.

Ball, Howard, *Prosecuting War Crimes and Genocide – The Twentieth-Century Experience,* University Press of Kansas, 1999.

Barbedo de Magalhaes, Antonio, *East Timor, Indonesian Occupation and Genocide,* President's Office, Oporto University, 1992.

Bassiouni, M. Cherif (ed.), *International Criminal Law, Volume I: Crimes,* New York: Transnational Publishers, Inc., 1986.

Bassiouni, M. Cherif (ed.), *International Criminal Law, Volume III: Enforcement,* New York: Transnational Publishers, Inc., 1987.

Bassiouni, M. Cherif, *Crimes Against Humanity in International Criminal Law,* Martinus Nijhoff Publishers, 1992.

Bassiouni, M. Cherif (ed.), *The Statute of the International Criminal Court: A Documentary History* , New York: Transnational Publishers, Inc., 1998.

Bassiouni, M. Cherif (ed.), *International Criminal Law, Volume I: Crimes,* New York: Transnational Publishers, Inc., 2nd edn, 1999.

Bassiouni, M. Cherif (ed.), *International Criminal Law, Volume III: Enforcement,* New York: Transnational Publishers, Inc., 2nd edn, 1999.

Bassiouni, M. Cherif, *Crimes Against Humanity in International Criminal Law,* Kluwer Law International,2nd edn (rev), 1999.

Bassiouni, M. Cherif and Manikas, Peter, *The Law of the International Criminal Tribunal for the Former Yugoslavia,* New York: Transnational Publishers, Inc., 1996.

Bassiouni, M. Cherif and Nanda, Ved P. (eds), *A Treatise on International Criminal Law, Volume I: Crimes and Punishment,* Springfield, Illinois : Charles C. Thomas Publisher, 1973.

Bassiouni, M. Cherif and Wise, Edward M, *Aut Dedere Aut Judicare – The Duty to Extradite or Prosecute in International Law,* Martinus Nijhoff Publishers, 1995.

Bernadac, Christian, *L'Ordre S.S.,* Paris: Editions France-Empire, 1996.

Bettati, Mario, *Le Droit d'Ingérence – Mutation de l'Ordre International,* Paris: Editions Odile Jacob, 1996.

Bevans, C.F., *Treaties and Other International Agreements of the United States of America, 1776-1949, Volume 2,* 1970.

Bourdon, William et Duverger, Emmanuelle, *La Cour Pénale Internationale – Le Statut de Rome,* Editions du Seuil, Collection Points Essais, 2000.

Brayard, Florent (ed), *Le Génocide des Juifs entre Procès et Histoire, 1943-2000,* Editions Complexe, Collection 'Histoire du Temps Présent', 2000.

Brownlie, Ian, *Principles of Public International Law,* 4th edn, Oxford: Clarendon Press, 1990.

Cassese, A. (ed), *B.V.A. Röling – The Tokyo Trial and Beyond, Reflections of a Peacemonger,* Cambridge: Polity Press, 1993.

Cassese, Antonio, *International Criminal Law,* Oxford University Press, 2003.

Centre de Droit International de l'Institut de Sociologie de l'Université Libre de Bruxelles (Centre Henri Rolin) et Fondation Auschwitz-Stichting (Centre d'Etudes et de Documentation), *Le Procès de Nuremberg – Conséquences et Actualisation, Actes du Colloque International, Université Libre de Bruxelles, 27 Mars 1987,* Editions Bruylant, Editions de l'Université de Bruxelles, 1988.

Chalandon, Sorj, and Nivelle, Pascale, *Crimes Contre L'Humanité – Barbie, Touvier, Bousquet, Papon,* Plon/Libération, 1998.

Chalk, Frank and Jonassohn, Kurt, *The History and Sociology of Genocide – Analyses and Case Studies,* Yale University Press, 1990.

Charny, Israel W., *How Can We Commit the Unthinkable? Genocide: The Human Cancer,* Westview Press, 1982.

Charny, Israel W. (ed), *Genocide, A Critical Bibliographic Review,* Vol 2, Mansell, 1991.

Chrétien, Jean-Pierre, *Burundi, L'Histoire Retrouvée,* Editions Karthala, 1993.

Clark, Roger S. and Sann, Madeleine (eds), *The Prosecution of International Crimes – A Critical Study of the International Tribunal for the Former Yugoslavia,* New Brunswick and London: Transaction Publishers, 1996.

Conan, Eric, *Le Procès Papon – Un Journal d'Audience,* Gallimard, 1998.

Cooper, Belinda (ed), *War Crimes – The Legacy of Nuremberg*, New York : TV Books, 1999.

Courtois, Stéphane et al, *Le Livre Noir du Communisme – Crimes, Terreur, Répression*, Paris: Robert Laffont, Collection Pocket, 1997.

Dadrian, Vahakn N, *Autopsie du Génocide Arménien*, traduit de l'anglais par Marc et Mikaël Nichanian, Editions Complexe, 1995.

De Fontette, François, *Histoire de l'Antisémitisme*, Paris: Presses Universitaires de France, Collection Que Sais-Je?, 1993.

De Saint Cheron, Michaël, *De la mémoire à la responsabilité – Dialogue avec Geneviève de Gaulle Anthonioz, Edgar Morin, Emmanuel Levinas*, Paris : Editions Dervy, 2000.

Destexhe, Alain, *Rwanda and Genocide in the Twentieth Century*, translated by Alison Marschner, London: Pluto Press, 1995.

Dinstein, Yoram, *The Defence of 'Obedience to Superior Orders' in International Law*, Leyden: A.W. Sijthoff, 1965.

Dinstein, Yoram, *War, Aggression and Self-Defence*, Cambridge University Press, 3rd edn, 2001.

Dinstein, Yoram and Tabory, Mala, *War Crimes in International Law*, Martinus Nijhoff Publishers, 1996.

Dobkine, Michel, *Crimes et Humanité – Extraits des actes du procès de Nuremberg, 18 Octobre 1945-1er Octobre 1946*, Paris: Editions Romillat, 1992.

Donnet, Pierre-Antoine, *Tibet, mort ou vif*, Paris: Gallimard, Collection Folio Actuel, 1992.

Drost, Pieter N., *The Crime of State – Penal Protection for Fundamental Freedoms of Persons and Peoples, Book II: Genocide – United Nations Legislation on International Criminal Law*, Leyden: A.W. Sythoff, 1959.

Droz, Bernard et Lever, Evelyne, *Histoire de la Guerre d'Algérie – 1954-1962*, Edition du Seuil, Collection Points Histoire, 1982.

Dworkin, Ronald, *Law's Empire*, London: Fontana, 1986.

Eluard, Paul, *Au Rendez-Vous Allemand suivi de Poésie et Vérité 1942*, Paris: Les Editions de Minuit, 1999 (original 1945).

Eluard, Paul, *Le Livre Ouvert 1938-1944*, Editions Gallimard, 2000 (original 1947).

Evans, Malcolm D., *Blackstone's International Law Documents*, London : Blackstone Press Limited, 2nd edn, 1994.

Finkielkraut, Alain, *L'avenir d'une négation – Réflexion sur la question du génocide*, Paris : Editions du Seuil, 1982.

Finkielkraut, Alain, *La Mémoire Vaine – Du Crime Contre l'Humanité*, Editions Gallimard, Collection Folio Essais, 1998.

Fouché, Jean-Jacques, *Oradour*, Editions Liana Levi, 2001.

Friedlander, Saul, *Memory, History and the Extermination of the Jews of Europe*, Bloomington and Indianapolis : Indiana University Press, 1993.

Frossard, André, *Le Crime Contre l'Humanité*, Editions Robert Laffont, 1997 (original 1987).

Garapon, Antoine, *Des crimes qu'on ne peut ni punir ni pardonner – Pour une justice internationale*, Paris: Editions Odile Jacob, 2002.

Gardam, Judith, *Necessity, Proportionality and the Use of Force by States*, Cambridge Studies in International and Comparative Law, Cambridge University Press, 2004.

Ginsburgs, George and Kudriavtsev, V.N. (eds), *The Nuremberg Trial and International Law*, Martinus Nijhoff Publishers, 1990.

Glaser, Kurt, *Victims of Politics: The State of Human Rights*, Columbia University Press, 1979.

Glaser, Stefan, *Droit International Pénal Conventionnel*, Bruxelles, 1970.

Glueck, Sheldon, *The Nuremberg Trial and Aggressive War*, New York: Kraus Reprint Co., 1971 (original 1946).

Green, Leslie C., *The Contemporary Law of Armed Conflict*, Juris Publishing, Manchester University Press, 2nd edn, 2000.

Hannikainen, Lauri, *Peremptory Norms (Jus Cogens) in International Law – Historical Development, Criteria, Present Status*, Helsinki: Lakimiesliiton Kustannus, Finnish Lawyers' Publishing Company, 1988.

Hartman, Geoffrey (ed.), *Bitburg in Moral and Political Perspective*, Bloomington: Indiana University Press, 1986.

Horowitz, Irving Louis, *Genocide, State Power and Mass Murder*, New Brunswick, New Jersey: Transaction Books, 2nd edn, 1977.

Horowitz, Irving Louis, *Taking Lives – Genocide and State Power*, New Brunswick and London: Transaction Publishers, 4th edn, 1997.

Hovannisian, Richard G. (ed), *The Armenian Genocide in Perspective*, Transaction Books, 1987.

Igounet, Valérie, *Histoire du Négationnisme en France*, Paris: Editions du Seuil, Collection XXè Siècle, 2000.

International Commission of Jurists, *The Question of Tibet and the Rule of Law*, Geneva: International Commission of Jurists, 1959.

International Commission of Jurists, *Tibet and the Chinese People's Republic – A Report to the International Commission of Jurists by its Legal Inquiry Committee on Tibet*, Geneva: International Commission of Jurists, 1960.

International Commission of Jurists, *The Trial of Macias in Equatorial Guinea: The Story of a Dictatorship*, Report submitted by Alejandro Artucio, Geneva: International Commission of Jurists, 1978.

International Commission of Jurists, *Tibet: Human Rights and the Rule of Law*, Geneva: International Commission of Jurists, 1997 (reprint 1998).

International Committee of the Red Cross, *International Law Concerning the Conduct of Hostilities, Collection of Hague Conventions and some Other International Instruments*, Geneva: International Committee of the Red Cross, 1996.

Jackson, Robert H., *The Nürnberg Case*, Cooper Square Press, Inc., 1972.

Jankélévitch, Vladimir, *L'Imprescriptible – Pardonner ? Dans l'honneur et la dignité*, Editions du Seuil, Collection Points Essais, 1986 (reprint 1994).

Jones, John R.W.D., *The Practice of the International Criminal Tribunals for the Former Yugoslavia and Rwanda*, N.Y.: Transnational Publishers, Inc., 2nd edn, 2000.

Joyner, Christopher C. and Bassiouni, M. Cherif (eds), *Reining in Impunity for International Crimes and Serious Violations of Fundamental Human Rights:*

Proceedings of the Siracusa Conference, 17-21 September 1998, Nouvelles Etudes Pénales, Association Internationale de Droit Pénal, érès, 1998.

Kiernan, Ben (ed.), *Genocide and Democracy in Cambodia – The Khmer Rouge, the United Nations and the International Community*, New Haven: Monograph Series 41/Yale University Southeast Asia Studies, 1993.

Klarsfeld, Arno, *Touvier, Un Crime Français*, Librairie Arthème Fayard, 1994.

Klarsfeld, Arno, *Papon, Un Verdict Français*, Paris: Editions Ramsay, 1998.

Kofi Abiew, Francis, *The Evolution of the Doctrine and Practice of Humanitarian Intervention*, The Hague/London/Boston: Kluwer Law International, 1999.

Ku, Charlotte and Jacobson, Harold K. (eds), *Democratic Accountability and the Use of Force in International Law*, Cambridge University Press, 2003.

Kuper, Leo, *Genocide – Its Political Use in the Twentieth Century*, New Haven and London: Yale University Press, 1981.

Kuper, Leo, *The Prevention of Genocide*, New Haven and London: Yale University Press, 1985.

Lemkin, Raphaël, *Axis Rule in Occupied Europe – Laws of Occupation, Analysis of Government, Proposals for Redress*, Washington: Carnegie Endowment for International Peace, Division of International Law, 1944.

Lipstadt, Deborah, *Denying the Holocaust – The Growing Assault on Truth and Memory*, Penguin Books, 1994.

Lord Russell of Liverpool, *The Scourge of the Swastika – A Short Story of Nazi War Crimes*, London: Cassell & Company Ltd, 1955.

McCormack, Timothy L.M. and Simpson, Gerry J. (eds), *The Law of War Crimes, National and International Approaches*, Kluwer Law International, 1997.

Melander, Göran and Alfredsson, Gudmundur (eds), *The Raoul Wallenberg Compilation of Human Rights Instruments*, Martinus Nijhoff Publishers, 1997.

Meron, Theodor, *War Crimes Law Comes of Age, Essays*, Oxford: Clarendon Press, 1998.

Mettraux, Guénaël, *International Crimes and the Ad Hoc Tribunals*, Oxford University Press, 2005.

Miller, Judith, *One by One, by One: Facing the Holocaust*, New York: Simon & Schuster, 1990.

Morris, Virginia and Scharf, Michael P., *An Insiders' Guide to the International Criminal Tribunal for the Former Yugoslavia : A Documentary History and Analysis*, Transnational Publishers, 1995.

Neier, Aryeh, *War Crimes: Brutality, Genocide, Terror, and the Struggle for Justice*, New York: Times Books, 1998.

Paust, Jordan J. et al. (eds), *International Criminal Law, Cases and Materials*, Durham, North Carolina: Carolina Academic Press, 2nd edn, 2000.

Paust, Jordan J. et al. (eds), *International Criminal Law Documents Supplement*, Carolina Academic Press, 2000.

Pictet, Jean S. (ed.), *Commentary I Geneva Convention for the Amelioration of the Condition of the Wounded and Sick in Armed Forces in the Field*, Geneva: International Committee of the Red Cross, 1995 (original 1952).

Pictet, Jean S. (ed.), *Commentary IV Geneva Convention Relative to the Protection of Civilian Persons in Time of War*, Geneva: International Committee of the Red Cross, 1994 (original 1958).

Pictet, Jean S. (ed.), *Commentary III Geneva Convention Relative to the Treatment of Prisoners of War*, Geneva: International Committee of the Red Cross, 1994 (original 1960).

Poliakov, Léon, *Le Procès de Jérusalem – Juger Adolf Eichmann*, Paris: Calmann-Lévy, 1963.

Pritchard, John R. and Zaide, Sonia Magbanua (eds), *The Tokyo War Crimes Trial: Proceedings of the Tribunal*, Garland Publishing, 1981.

Ragazzi, Maurizio, *The Concept of International Obligations Erga Omnes*, Oxford: Clarendon Press, 1997.

Ratner, Steven R. and Abrams, Jason S., *Accountability for Human Rights Atrocities in International Law – Beyond the Nuremberg Legacy,* Oxford University Press, 2nd edn, 2001.

Reisman, W. Michael and Antoniou, Chris T. (eds), *The Laws of War – A Comprehensive Collection of Primary Documents on International Laws Governing Armed Conflict,* New York: Vintage Books, 1994.

Robertson, Geoffrey, *Crimes Against Humanity – The Struggle for Global Justice,* London: Penguin Books, 2000.

Robinson, Nehemiah, *The Genocide Convention – A Commentary,* New York: Institute of Jewish Affairs – World Jewish Congress, 1960.

Roht-Arriaza, Naomi (ed), *Impunity and Human Rights in International Law and Practice,* Oxford University Press, 1995.

Sandoz, Yves, Swinarski, Christophe and Zimmermann, Bruno (eds), *Commentary on the Additional Protocols of 8 June 1977 to the Geneva Conventions of 12 August 1949,* International Committee of the Red Cross, Geneva: Martinus Nijhoff Publishers, 1987.

Sartre, Jean-Paul, *Réflexions sur la Question Juive,* Gallimard, Collection Idées, 1954.

Sassoli, Marco and Bouvier, Antoine A., *How Does Law Protect in War? – Cases, Documents and Teaching Materials on Contemporary Practice in International Humanitarian Law,* Geneva: International Committee of the Red Cross, 1999.

Schabas, William A., *Genocide in International Law – The Crimes of Crimes,* Cambridge University Press, 2000.

Schabas, William A., *An Introduction to the International Criminal Court,* Cambridge University Press, 2001.

Schwarzenberger, Georg, *International Criminal Law, Volume I,* London: Stevens & Sons Limited, 3rd edn, 1957.

Sibert, Marcel, *Traité de Droit International Public, Volume I,* Paris : Librairie Dalloz, 1951.

Stone, Julius, *Aggression and World Order – A Critique of United Nations Theories of Aggression,* London: Stevens & Sons Limited, 1958.

Stone, Julius, *Legal Controls of International Conflict – A Treatise on the Dynamics of Disputes – And War – Law*, London: Stevens & Sons Limited, Second Revised Impression, 1959.

Stone, Julius, *Conflict Through Consensus – United Nations Approaches to Aggression*, Baltimore and London: The Johns Hopkins University Press, 1978.

Terras, Christian, *Les Faussaires de l'Histoire*, Editions Golias, 1999.

Torrelli, Maurice, *Le Droit International Humanitaire*, Paris: Presses Universitaires de France, Collection Que Sais-Je?, 1985.

Totten, Samuel, Parsons, William S., Charny, Israel W.(eds), *Genocide in the Twentieth Century – Critical Essays and Eyewitness Accounts*, New York and London: Garland Publishing, Inc., 1995.

Vidal-Naquet, Pierre, *Les Assassins de la Mémoire – 'Un Eichmann de Papier' et Autres Essais sur le Révisionnisme*, Paris: La Découverte, 1987.

Wallimann, Isidor and Dobkowski, Michael N. (eds), *Genocide and the Modern Age – Etiology and Case Studies of Mass Death*, Syracuse University Press, 2000.

Weiler, Joseph H.H., Cassese, Antonio, and Spinedi, Marina (eds), *International Crimes of State – A Critical Analysis of the ILC's Draft Article 19 on State Responsibility*, Berlin – New York: Walter de Gruyter, 1989.

Wieviorka, Annette, *L'Ere du Témoin*, Plon, 1998.

Willis, James F., *Prologue to Nuremberg – The Politics and Diplomacy of Punishing War Criminals of the First World War*, London: Greenwood Press, 1982.

Woetzel, Robert K., *The Nuremberg Trials in International Law with a Postlude on the Eichmann Case*, London: Stevens & Sons Limited, 1962.

Woodhouse, Diana (ed), *The Pinochet Case – A Legal and Constitutional Analysis*, Oxford-Portland Oregon: Hart Publishing, 2000.

Chapters in Books

Brownlie, Ian, 'Crimes Against Peace', in Brownlie, Ian, *International Law and the Use of Force by States*, Oxford: Clarendon Press, 1963, pp 195-213.

Brownlie, Ian, 'Defining Aggression', in Brownlie, Ian, *International Law and the Use of Force by States*, Oxford: Clarendon Press, 1963, pp 351-58.

Brownlie, Ian, 'The United Nations Charter and the Use of Force, 1945-1985', in Cassese, Antonio (ed), *The Current Legal Regulation of the Use of Force*, Dordrecht: Martinus Nijhoff Publishers, 1986, pp 491-504.

Cassese, Antonio, 'Return to Westphalia? Considerations on the gradual erosion of the Charter system', in Cassese, A. (ed) *The Current Legal Regulation of the Use of Force*, Dordrecht: Martinus Nijhoff Publishers, 1986, pp 505-23.

Dinstein, Yoram, 'The Distinction Between Unlawful Combatants and War Criminals', in Dinstein, Yoram (ed), *International law at a Time of Perplexity, Essays in Honour of Shabtai Rosenne*, Martinus Nijhoff Publishers, 1989, pp 103-16.

Falk, Richard A., 'Ecocide, Genocide, and the Nuremberg Tradition of Individual Responsibility', in Held, Virginia, Morgenbesser, Sidney and Nagel, Thomas (eds), *Philosophy, Morality and International Affairs*, New York: Oxford University Press, 1974, pp 123-37.

Gill, T.D., 'Litigation Strategy in the Nicaragua Case at the International Court', in Dinstein, Yoram (ed), *International Law At a Time of Perplexity – Essays in Honour of Shabtai Rosenne*, Martinus Nijhoff Publishers, 1989, pp 197-224.

Greenwood, Christopher, 'Self-Defence and the Conduct of International Armed Conflict', in Dinstein, Yoram (ed), *International law at a Time of Perplexity, Essays in Honour of Shabtai Rosenne*, Martinus Nijhoff Publishers, 1989, pp 273-88.

Röling, Bert V.A., 'The Ban on the Use of Force and the UN Charter', in Cassese, Antonio (ed), *The Current Legal Regulation of the Use of Force*, Martinus Nijhoff Publishers, Dordrecht, 1986, pp 3-8.

Röling, Bert V.A., 'Crimes Against Peace', *in* Cassese, Antonio (ed), *The Current Legal Regulation of the Use of Force*, Martinus Nijhoff Publishers, Dordrecht, 1986, pp 385-94.

Röling, Bert V.A., 'The 1974 UN Definition of Aggression', in Cassese, Antonio (ed.), *The Current Legal Regulation of the Use of Force*, Martinus Nijhoff Publishers, Dordrecht, 1986, pp 413-21.

Sarooshi, Danesh, 'Humanitarian Intervention and International Humanitarian Assistance: Law and Practice', Wilton Park Paper 86, London: HMSO Publications, 1994, pp 1-11.

Shaw, M.N., 'Genocide and International Law', in Dinstein, Yoram (ed.), *International Law at a Time of Perplexity, Essays in Honour of Shabtai Rosenne,* Martinus Nijhoff Publishers, 1989, pp 797-820.

Sohn, Louis B., 'The International Court of Justice and the Scope of the Right of Self-Defense and the Duty of Non-Intervention', in Dinstein, Yoram (ed.), *International Law At a Time of Perplexity – Essays in Honour of Shabtai Rosenne,* Dordrecht: Martinus Nijhoff Publishers, 1989, pp 869-78.

Sunga, Lyal S., 'Crimes Against Peace', in Sunga, Lyal S., *Individual Responsibility in International Law for Serious Human Rights Violations,* Dordrecht: Martinus Nijhoff Publishers, 1992, pp 36-41.

White, Robin C.A., 'The Control of Intervention after the *Nicaragua* Case', in White, Robin and Smythe, Bernard (Eds), *Current Issues in European and International Law – Essays in memory of Frank Dowrick,* London: Sweet & Maxwell, 1990, pp 135-55.

Woetzel, Robert K., 'The Jus Contra Bellum', in Woetzel, Robert K., *The Nuremberg Trials in International Law – With a Postlude on the Eichmann Case,* London: Stevens & Sons Limited, 1962, pp 140-71.

Journal Articles

Akhavan, Payam, 'Enforcement of the Genocide Convention Through the Advisory Opinion Jurisdiction of the International Court of Justice', (1991) 12 HRLJ 285-99.

Aldrich, George H., 'The Laws of War on Land', (2000) 94 *AJIL* 42-63.

Alexidze, Levan, 'Legal Nature of *Jus Cogens* in Contemporary International Law', [1981] III *RCADI* 219-70.

Alland, Denis et Ferrand, Frédérique, 'Jurisprudence Française en matière de Droit International Public, Cour de Cassation, chambre criminelle, 6 janvier 1998', (1998) 102 *RGDIP* 825-32.

Alvarez, José E., 'Rush to Closure: Lessons of the Tadić Judgment', (1998) 96 *Mich L Rev* 2031-112.

Antonopoulos, Constantine, 'Whatever Happened to Crimes Against Peace?', (2001) 6 *Journal of Conflict and Security Law* 33-62.

Bassiouni, M. Cherif, 'The Commission of Experts Established pursuant to Security Council Resolution 780: Investigating Violations of International Humanitarian Law in the Former Yugoslavia', (1994) 5 *Crim L F* 279-340.

Bassiouni, M. Cherif, '"Crimes Against Humanity": The Need for a Specialized Convention', (1994) 31 *Columbia Journal of Transnational Law* 457-94.

Bassiouni, M. Cherif, 'Searching for Peace and Achieving Justice: The Need for Accountability', (1996) 59 *Law & Contemp Prob* 9-28.

Bassiouni, M. Cherif: 'International Crimes, *Jus Cogens* and *Obligatio Erga Omnes*', (1996) 59 *Law & Contemp Prob* 63-74.

Bassiouni, M. Cherif, 'From Versailles to Rwanda in Seventy-Five Years: The Need to Establish a Permanent International Criminal Court', (1997) 10 *Harvard Human Rights Journal* 11-62.

Baxter, R.R., 'Multilateral Treaties as Evidence of Customary International Law', (1965-66) XLI *BYBIL* 275-300.

Beres, Louis René, 'Justice and Realpolitik: International Law and the Prevention of Genocide', (1988) 33 *American Journal of Jurisprudence* 123-59.

Bianchi, Andrea, 'Immunity versus Human Rights: The *Pinochet* Case', (1999) 10 *EJIL* 237-77.

Binder, Guyora, 'Representing Nazism: Advocacy and Identity at the Trial of Klaus Barbie', (1989) 98 *Yale L J* 1324-83.

Bishop, William W. Jr., 'Reservations to the Convention on Genocide', (1951) 45 *AJIL* 579-90.

Boelaert-Suominen, Sonja, 'Grave Breaches, Universal Jurisdiction and Internal Armed Conflict: Is Customary Law Moving Towards a Uniform Enforcement Mechanism for all Armed Conflicts?', (2000) 5 *Journal of Conflict and Security Law* 63-103.

Bröhmer, Jürgen, 'Immunity of a Former Head of State: General Pinochet and the House of Lords: Part Three', (2000) 13 *LJIL* 229-37.

Bryant, Bunyan, 'Substantive Scope of the Convention', *in* 'Comment: The United States and the 1948 Genocide Convention, Part I', (1975) 16 HILJ 686-98.

Broms, Bengt, 'The Definition of Aggression', [1977] I *RCADI* 299-400.

Brunnée, Jutta and Toope, Stephen J., 'The Use of Force: International Law after Iraq', (2004) 53 *ICLQ* 785-806.

Bugnion, François, 'Just wars, wars of aggression and international humanitarian law', (2002) 847 *International Review of the Red Cross* 523-46.

Byers, Michael, 'Terrorism, The Use of Force and International Law after 11 September', (2002) 51 *ICLQ* 401-14.

Caron, David D., 'War and International Adjudication: Reflections on the 1899 Peace Conference', (2000) 94 *AJIL* 4-30.

Carrillo Salcedo, Juan Antonio, 'Reflections on the Existence of a Hierarchy of Norms in International Law', (1997) 8 *EJIL* 583-95.

Cassese, Antonio, 'On the Current Trends towards Criminal Prosecution and Punishment of Breaches of International Humanitarian Law', (1998) 9 *EJIL* 2-17.

Cassese, Antonio, 'The Statute of the International Criminal Court: Some Preliminary Reflections', (1999) 10 *EJIL* 144-71.

Cassese, Antonio, 'Terrorism is also Disrupting Some Crucial Legal Categories of International Law', (2001) 12 *EJIL* 993-1001.

Cassin, Vernon, Debevoise, Whitney, Kailes, Howard and Thompson, Terence W., 'The Definition of Aggression', (1975) 16 *Harvard International Law Journal* 589-612.

Chalk, Frank, 'Definitions of Genocide and Their Implications for Prediction and Prevention', (1989) 4 *Holocaust and Genocide Studies* 149-60.

Charney, Jonathan I., 'Anticipatory Humanitarian Intervention in Kosovo', (1999) 93 *AJIL* 834-41.

Charney, Jonathan I., 'The Use of Force Against Terrorism and International Law', (2001) 95 *AJIL* 835-39.

Chinkin, Christine M., '*Regina* v *BowStreet Stipendiary Magistrate, Ex Parte Pinochet Ugarte* (No.3)', (1999) 93 *AJIL* 703-11.

Chinkin, Christine M., 'Kosovo: A "Good" or "Bad" war?', (1999) 93 *AJIL* 841-7.

Christenson, Gordon A., '*Jus Cogens*: Guarding Interests Fundamental to International Society', (1988) 28 *Virginia Journal of International Law* 585-648.

Cissé, Catherine, 'Le Tribunal spécial pour la Sierra Leone', (2002) 4 *International Law FORUM du droit international* 7-11.

Clark, Roger S., 'Does the Genocide Convention Go Far Enough? Some Thoughts on the Nature of Criminal Genocide in the Context of Indonesia's Invasion of East Timor', (1981) 8 *Ohio Northern University Law Review* 321-328.

Cotler, Irwin, '*Regina* v *Finta*', (1996) 90 *AJIL* 460-76.

Cowles, Willard B., 'Trials of War Criminals (Non-Nuremberg)', (1948) 42 *AJIL* 299.

Dadrian, Vahakn N., 'A Textual Analysis of the Key Indictment of the Turkish Military Tribunal Investigating the Armenian Genocide', (1991) 44 *Armenian Review* 1-36.

Dadrian, Vahakn. N., 'The Secret Young-Turk Ittihadist Conference and the Decision for the World War I Genocide of the Armenians', (1993) 7 *Holocaust and Genocide Studies* 173-201.

Dadrian, Vahakn. N., 'The Turkish Military Tribunal's prosecution of the Authors of the Armenian Genocide: Four Major Court-Martial Series', (1997) 11 *Holocaust and Genocide Studies* 28-59.

De Hemptinne, Jérôme, 'La Définition du Crime Contre L'Humanité par le Tribunal Pénal International Pour l'Ex-Yougoslavie', [1998] *RTDH* 763-79.

De Hoogh, A.J.J., 'The Relationship between *Jus Cogens*, Obligations *Erga Omnes* and International Crimes: Peremptory Norms in Perspective', (1991) 42 *Austrian Journal of Public and International Law* 183-214.

Delmas Saint-Hilaire, Jean-Pierre, 'La définition juridique de la complicité de crime contre l'humanité au lendemain de l'arrêt de la

Chambre Criminelle du 23 Janvier 1997 (Affaire Papon)', [1997] 30th Cahier *Recueil Dalloz* 249-54.

DeWeese, Geoffrey S., 'The Failure of the International Court of Justice to Effectively Enforce the Genocide Convention', (1998) 26 *Denver Journal of International Law and Policy* 625-54.

Dinstein, Yoram, 'Crimes Against Humanity After Tadic', (2000) 13 *LJIL* 373-93.

Donnedieu de Vabres, Henri, 'Le Procès de Nuremberg Devant les Principes Modernes du Droit Pénal International', [1947] I *RCADI* 477-582.

Drumbl, Mark A., 'Judging the 11 September Terrorist Attack', (2002) 24 *HRQ* 323-60.

Dupuy, Pierre-Marie, 'Crimes et Immunités, *ou dans quelle mesure la nature des premiers empêche l'exercice des secondes*', (1999) 103 *RGDIP* 289-96.

Dupuy, Pierre-Marie, 'The Law after the Destruction of the Towers', in *The Attack on the World Trade Center: Legal Responses*, Discussion Forum, Available on the EJIL website, October 2001.

Falk, Richard A., 'Quincy Wright: On Legal Tests of Aggressive War', (1972) 66 *AJIL* 560-71.

Falk, Richard A., 'Kosovo, World Order, and the Future of International Law', (1999) 93 *AJIL* 847-57.

Falk, Richard A., 'What Future for the UN Charter System of War Prevention?', (2003) 97 *AJIL* 590-8.

Farer, Tom J., 'The Prospect for International Law and Order in the Wake of Iraq', (2003) 97 *AJIL* 621-8.

Fegley, Randall, 'The UN Human Rights Commission: The Equatorial Guinea Case', (1981) 3 *HRQ* 34-47.

Fein, Helen, 'Genocide: A Sociological Perspective', (1990) 38 *Current Sociology*, whole issue.

Fenrick, William J., 'Should Crimes Against Humanity Replace War Crimes?', (1999) 37 *Columbia Journal of Transnational Law* 767-85.

Fenrick, W.J., 'Targeting and Proportionality during the NATO Bombing Campaign against Yugoslavia', (2001) 12 *EJIL* 489-502.

Ferencz, Benjamin B., 'Defining Aggression: Where It Stands and Where It's Going', (1972) 66 *AJIL* 491-508.

Finch, George A., 'The Nuremberg Trial and International Law', (1947) XLI *AJIL* 20-37.

Finch, George A., 'The Genocide Convention', (1949) 43 *AJIL* 732-8.

Fitzmaurice, G.G., 'The Definition of Aggression', (1952) 1 *ICLQ* 137-44.

Fox, Hazel, 'The First *Pinochet* Case: Immunity of a Former Head of State', (1999) 48 ICLQ 207-16.

Fox, Hazel, 'The Pinochet Case No 3', (1999) 48 *ICLQ* 687-702.

Franck, Thomas M., 'Lessons of Kosovo', (1999) 93 *AJIL* 857-60.

Franck, Thomas M., 'Inspections and Their Enforcement: A Modest Proposal', (2002) 96 *AJIL* 899-900.

Franck, Thomas M. and Rodley, Nigel S., 'After Bangladesh: The Law of Humanitarian Intervention by Military Force', (1973) 67 *AJIL* 275-305.

Henkin, Louis, 'Kosovo and the Law of "Humanitarian Intervention"', (1999) 93 *AJIL* 824-8.

Frulli, Micaela, 'Are Crimes against Humanity More Serious than War Crimes?', (2001) 12 *EJIL* 329-50.

Gaeta, Paola, '*The Defence of Superior Orders: The Statute of the International Criminal Court* versus *Customary International Law*', (1999) 10 *EJIL* 172-91.

Gaja, Giorgio, 'In What Sense was There an "Armed Attack"?, in *The Attack on the World Trade Center: Legal Responses*, Discussion Forum, Available on the EJIL website, October 2001.

Garvey, Jack I., 'The UN Definition of "Aggression": Law and Illusion in the Context of Collective Security', (1977) 17 *Virginia Journal of International Law* 177-99.

Gomez Robledo, Antonio, 'Le *Ius Cogens* International: Sa Genèse, Sa Nature, Ses Fonctions', [1981] III *RCADI* 9-217.

Grafton Wilson, George, 'Use of Force and War', (1932) 26 *AJIL* 327-8.

Graven, Jean, 'Les Crimes Contre L'Humanité', [1950] I *RCADI* 433-605.

Gray, Christine, 'Legality of Use of Force: Provisional Measures', (2000) 49 *ICLQ* 730-6.

Gray, Christine, 'The Use and Abuse of the International Court of Justice: Cases concerning the Use of Force after *Nicaragua*', (2003) 14 *EJIL* 867-905.

Green, Leslie C., 'New Trends in International Criminal Law', (1981) 11 *Israel Yearbook on Human Rights* 9-40.

Green, L.C., 'Command Responsibility in International Humanitarian Law', (1995) 5 *Transnational Law and Contemporary Problems* 319-71.

Green, L.C., 'Enforcement of the Law in International and Non-International Conflicts - The Way Ahead', (1996) 24 *Denver Journal of International Law and Policy* 285-320.

Green, Leslie C., '"Grave Breaches" or Crimes Against Humanity?', (1998) 8 *Academy Journal of Legal Studies* 19-28.

Greenawalt, Alexander K.A., 'Rethinking Genocidal Intent: The case for a knowledge-based interpretation', (1999) 99 *Colum L Rev* 2259-94.

Greenwood, Christopher, 'International Humanitarian Law and the *Tadic* Case', (1996) *EJIL* 265-83.

Greenwood, Christopher, 'The Advisory Opinon on Nuclear Weapons and the Contribution of the International Court to International Humanitarian Law', [1997] *International Review of the Red Cross* 65-75.

Gross, Leo, 'The Criminality of Aggressive War', (1947) XLI *The American Political Science Review* 205-25.

Gross, Oren, 'The Grave Breaches System and the Armed Conflict in the Former Yugoslavia', (1995) 16 *Michigan Journal of International Law* 783-829.

Hannum, Hurst, 'International Law and Cambodian Genocide: The Sounds of Silence', (1989) 11 *HRQ* 82-138.

Harff, Barbara and Gurr, Ted Robert, 'Toward Empirical Theory of Genocides and Politicides: Identification and Measurement of Cases since 1945', (1988) 32 *International Studies Quarterly* 359-71.

Harff, Barbara and Gurr, Ted Robert, 'Victims of the State: Genocides, Politicides and Group Repression since 1945', (1990) 1 *International Review of Victimology* 23-41.

Hazard, John N., 'Why Try Again to Define Aggression?', (1968) 62 *AJIL* 701-10.

Henkin, Louis, 'Kosovo and the Law of "Humanitarian Intervention"' (1999) 93 AJIL 824-8.

Higgins, Rosalyn, 'The Legal Limits to the Use of Force By Sovereign States – United Nations Practice', (1961) XXXVII *BYIL* 269-319.

Housepian, Marjorie, 'The Unremembered Genocide', [1966] *Commentary* 55-61.

Huttenbach, Henry R., 'Locating the Holocaust on the Genocide Spectrum: Towards a Methodology of Definition and Categorization', (1988) 3 *Holocaust and Genocide Studies* 289-303.

Jessup, Philip C., 'The Crime of Aggression and the Future of International Law', (1947) LXII *Political Science Quarterly* 1-10.

Jones, Robert H., 'Jurisdiction and Extradition under the Convention' *in* 'Comment: The United States and the 1948 Genocide Convention, Part II', (1975) 16 *HILJ* 696-704.

Joyner, Christopher C., 'Arresting Impunity: The Case for Universal Jurisdiction in Bringing War Criminals to Accountability', (1996) 59 Law & Contemp Prob 153-72.

Keith, Kirsten M.F., 'The *Mens Rea* of Superior Responsibility as Developed by ICTY Jurisprudence', (2001) 14 *LJIL* 617-34.

Kelsen, Hans, 'Will the Judgment in the Nuremberg Trial Constitute a Precedent in International Law?', (1947) 1 *ILQ* 153-71.

Kelsen, Hans, 'Collective Security and Collective Self-Defense under the Charter of the United Nations', (1948) 42 *AJIL* 783-96.

Komarnicki, M. Waclaw, 'La Définition de l'Agresseur dans le Droit International Moderne', [1949] III *RCADI* 5-113.

Kritsiotis, Dino, 'The Kosovo crisis and NATO's application of armed force against the Federal Republic of Yugoslavia', (2000) 49 *ICLQ* 330-59.

Kuhn, Arthur K., 'The Genocide Convention and State Rights', (1949) 43 *AJIL* 498-501.

Kunz, Josef L., 'The United Nations Convention on Genocide', (1949) 43 *AJIL* 738-46.

Kunz, Josef L., 'Bellum Justum and Bellum Legale', (1951) 45 *AJIL* 528-34.

Lane, Eric, 'Mass Killing by Governments: Lawful in the World Legal Order?', (1979) 12 *New York University International Law and Politics* 239-80.

Lauterpacht, H., 'The Law of Nations and the Punishment of War Crimes', (1944) XXI *BYBIL* 58-95.

Law Officers' Department, Royal Courts of Justice, 'German War Trials', (1922) 16 *AJIL* 628-40.

LeBlanc, Lawrence J., 'The Intent to Destroy Groups in the Genocide Convention: The Proposed U.S. Understanding', (1984) 78 *AJIL* 369-85.

LeBlanc, Lawrence J., 'The United Nations Genocide Convention and Political Groups: Should the United States Propose an Amendment?', (1988) 13 *YJIL* 268-95.

Lemkin, Raphael, 'Genocide as a Crime under International Law', (1947) 41 *AJIL* 145-51.

Lobel, Jules and Ratner, Michael, 'Bypassing the Security Council: Ambiguous Authorizations to Use Force, Cease-Fires and the Iraqi Inspection Regime', (1999) 93 *AJIL* 124-54.

Linton, Suzannah, 'New approaches to international justice in Cambodia and East Timor', [2002] *International Review of the Red Cross* 93-119.

Lippman, Matthew, 'The Drafting of the 1948 Convention on the Prevention and Punishment of the Crime of Genocide', (1985) 3 *Boston University International Law Journal* 1-62.

Lippman, Matthew, 'Conundrums of Armed Conflict: Criminal Defenses to Violations of the Humanitarian Law of War', (1996) 8 *Dickinson Journal of International Law* 1-111.

Lippman, Matthew, 'The Evolution and Scope of Command Responsibility', (2000) 13 *LJIL* 139-70.

Luban, David, 'Just War and Human Rights', (1980) 9 *Philosophy and Public Affairs* 160-81.

Maison, Rafaëlle, 'Les premiers cas d'application des dispositions pénales des Conventions de Genève par les juridictions internes', (1995) 6 *EJIL* 260-73.

Maison, Rafaëlle, 'Le crime de génocide dans les premiers jugements du Tribunal Pénal International pour le Rwanda', (1999) 103 *RGDIP* 129-45.

Marcus-Helmons, Silvio, 'Le droit d'intervention, un corollaire des droits de l'homme?', [1992] *RTDH* 471-81.

Massias, Florence, 'La Liberté d'Expression et le Discours Raciste ou Révisionniste', [1993] *RTDH* 183-213.

McAuliffe deGuzman, Margaret, 'The Road from Rome: The Developing Law of Crimes against Humanity', (2000) 22 *HRQ* 335-403.

McCormack, Timothy L.H. and Simpson, Gerry J., 'The International Law Commission's Draft Code of Crimes Against the Peace and Security of Mankind: An Appraisal of the Substantive Provisions', (1994) 5 *Crim L F* 1-55.

McDougal, Myres S. and Feliciano, Florentino P., 'The Legal Regulation of Resort to International Coercion: Aggression and Self-Defense in Policy Perspective', (1959) 68 *Yale Law Journal* 1057-1165.

Meier Wang, Mariann, 'The International Tribunal for Rwanda: Opportunities for Clarification, Opportunities for Impact', (1995) 27 *Columbia Human Rights Law Review* 177-226.

Meisenberg, Simon M., 'Legalities of amnesties in international humanitarian law – The Lomé Amnesty Decision of the Special Court for Sierra Leone', (2004) 86 *International Review of the Red Cross* 837-51.

Meron, Theodor, 'War Crimes in Yugoslavia and the Development of International Law', (1994) 88 *AJIL* 78-87.

Meron, Theodor, 'International Criminalization of Internal Atrocities', (1995) 89 *AJIL* 554-77.

Meron, Theodor, 'War Crimes Law Comes of Age', (1998) 92 *AJIL* 462-8.

Meron, Theodor, 'The Martens Clause, Principles of Humanity, and Dictates of Public Conscience', (2000) 94 *AJIL* 78-98.

Miller, Robert H, 'The Convention on the Non-Applicability of Statutory Limitations to War Crimes and Crimes Against Humanity', (1971) 65 *AJIL* 476-501.

Moore, John Norton, 'Solving the War Puzzle', (2003) 97 *AJIL* 282-9.

Morrison, Fred L., 'Legal Issues in the *Nicaragua* Opinion', (1987) 81 *AJIL* 160-6.

Mosler, Hermann, 'The International Society as a Legal Community', [1974] IV *RCADI* 1-320.

Müller-Schieke, Irina Kaye, 'Defining the Crime of Aggression Under the Statute of the International Criminal Court', (2001) 14 *Leiden Journal of International Law* 409-30.

Münkler, Herfried, 'The wars of the 21st century', (2003) 849 *International Review of the Red Cross* 7-22.

Murphy, John F., 'The Future of Multilateralism and Efforts to Combat International Terrorism', (1986) 25 *Columbia Journal of Transnational Law* 41-53.

Murphy, Sean D. (ed.), 'Award of Damages against Bosnian Serb Leader Radovan Karadzic', (2001) 95 *AJIL* 143-4.

Murphy, Sean D. (ed.), 'Immunity as Head of State for Zimbabwe's President Mugabe', (2001) 95 *AJIL* 874-6.

Murphy, Sean D. (ed.), 'Decision Not to Regard Persons Detained in Afghanistan as POWs', (2002) 96 *AJIL* 475-80.

O'Brien, James C., 'The International Tribunal for Violations of International Humanitarian Law in the Former Yugoslavia', (1993) 87 *AJIL* 639-59.

O'Connell, Mary Ellen, 'The UN, NATO and International Law after Kosovo', (2000) 22 *HRQ* 57-89.

Orentlicher, Diane F., 'Settling Accounts: The Duty to prosecute Human Rights Violations of a Prior Regime', (1991) 100 *Yale L J* 2537-615.

Paust, Jordan J., 'The Preparatory Committee's "Definition of Crimes" – War Crimes', (1997) 8 *Crim L F* 431-44.

Pejic, Jelena, 'Accountability for international crimes: From conjecture to reality', [2002] *International Review of the Red Cross* 13-33.

Pellet, Alain, 'No, This is not War!', in The Attack on the World Trade Center: Legal Responses, Discussion Forum, Available on the *EJIL* website, October 2001.

Plattner, Denise, 'The Penal Repression of Violations of International Humanitarian Law Applicable in Non-International Armed Conflicts', [1990] *International Review of the Red Cross* 414-20.

Post, H.H.G., 'Some Curiosities in the Sources of the Law of Armed Conflict Conceived in a General International Legal Perspective', (1994) XXV *Netherlands Yearbook of International Law* 83-117.

Randall, Kenneth C., 'Universal Jurisdiction Under International Law', (1988) 66 *Texas Law Review* 785-841.

Ratner, Steven R., 'The United Nations Group of Experts for Cambodia', (1999) 93 *AJIL* 948-53.

Ratner, Steven R., 'Jus ad Bellum and Jus in Bello after September 11', (2002) 96 *AJIL* 905-21.

Reid, James J., 'The Concept of War and Genocidal Impulses in the Ottoman Empire, 1821-1918', (1989) 4 *Holocaust and Genocide Studies* 175-91.

Reydams, Luc, '*Niyonteze* v *Public Prosecutor*, Tribunal militaire de cassation (Switzerland), April 27, 2001', (2002) 96 *AJIL* 231-6.

Robinson, Darryl, 'Defining "Crimes Against Humanity" at the Rome Conference', (1999) 93 *AJIL* 43-57.

Robinson, Jacob, 'The International Military Tribunal and the Holocaust, Some Legal Reflections', (1972) 7 *Israel Law Review* 1-13.

Robinson, Mary, 'Genocide, War Crimes, Crimes Against Humanity', (1999) 23 *Fordham International Law Journal* 275-85.

Roth, Stephen J., 'Denial of the Holocaust as an Issue of Law', (1993) 23 *Israel Yearbook of Human Rights* 215-35.

Rowe, Peter, 'The International Criminal Tribunal for Yugoslavia: The Decision of the Appeals Chamber on the Interlocutory Appeal on Jurisdiction in the *Tadic* Case', (1996) 45 *ICLQ* 691-701.

Sadat Wexler, Leila, 'The Interpretation of the Nuremberg Principles by the French Court of Cassation: From Touvier to Barbie and Back Again', (1994) 32 *Columbia Journal of Transnational Law* 289-367.

Sapiro, Miriam, 'Iraq: The Shifting Sands of Preemptive Self-Defense', (2003) 97 *AJIL* 599-607.

Schabas, William A., 'National Courts Finally Begin to Prosecute Genocide, the 'Crime of Crimes'', (2003) 1 *JICJ* 39-63.

Schachter, Oscar, 'The Right of States to Use Armed Force', [1984] *Mich L Rev* 1620-46.

Scharf, Michael, 'The Letter of the Law: The Scope of the International Legal Obligation to Prosecute Human Rights Crimes', (1996) 59 *Law & Contemp Prob* 41-61.

Scharf, Michael and Epps, Valerie, 'The International Trial of the Century? A "Cross-Fire" Exchange on the First Case Before the Yugoslavia War Crimes Tribunal', (1996) 26 *Cornell International Law Journal* 635-63.

Schreuer, Christoph, 'East Timor and the United Nations', [2000] *International Law FORUM du Droit International* 18-25.

Schrijver, Nico, 'Responding to International Terrorism: Moving the Frontiers of International Law for 'Enduring Freedom'?', (2001) XLVIII *NILR* 271-91.

Schuster, Matthias, 'The Rome Statute and the Crime of Aggression: A Gordian Knot in Search of a Sword', (2003) 14 *Criminal Law Forum* 1-57.

Schwarzenberger, Georg, 'Jus Pacis Ac Belli? Prolegomena to a Sociology of International Law', (1943) 37 *AJIL* 460-79.

Schwarzenberger, Georg, 'International *Jus Cogens* ?', (1965) 43 *Texas Law Review* 455-78.

Schwebel, S. M., 'Aggression, Intervention and Self-Defence in Modern International Law', [1972] II *RCADI* 411-97.

Schwelb, Egon, 'Crimes Against Humanity', (1946) 23 *BYBIL* 178-226.

Simma, Bruno, 'NATO, the UN and the Use of Force: Legal Aspects', (1999) 10 *EJIL* 1-22.

Slater, Jerome and Nardin, Terry, 'Nonintervention and Human Rights', (1986) 48 *Journal of Politics* 86-96.

Sofaer, Abraham D., 'On the Necessity of Pre-emption', (2003) 14 *EJIL* 209-26.

Spieker, Heike, 'The International Criminal Court and Non-International Armed Conflicts', (2000) 13 *LJIL* 395-425.

Spiry, Emmanual, 'Interventions Humanitaires et Interventions d'Humanité: La Pratique Française Face au Droit International', [1998] *RGDIP* 407-33.

Starace, Vincenzo, 'La Responsabilité résultant de la violation des obligations à l'égard de la communauté internationale', [1976] V *RCADI* 263-317.

Stern, Brigitte, 'Universal jurisdiction over crimes against humanity under French law', (1999) 93 *AJIL* 525-9.

Stone, Julius, 'Hopes and Loopholes in the 1974 Definition of Aggression', (1977) 71 *AJIL* 224-46.

Symposium, 'The International Criminal Court: Consensus and Debate on the International Adjudication of Genocide, Crimes Against Humanity, War Crimes, and Aggression', (1999) 32 *Cornell International Law Journal* , whole issue.

Taft IV, William H. and Buchwald, Todd F., 'Preemption, Iraq and International Law', (2003) 97 *AJIL* 557-63.

Tomuschat, Christian, 'International Criminal Prosecution: The Precedent of Nuremberg Confirmed', (1994) 5 *Crim L F* 237-47.

Triffterer, Otto, 'Genocide, Its Particular Intent to Destroy in Whole or in Part the Group as Such', (2001) 14 LJIL 399-408.

Turlington, Edgar, 'The Settlement of Lausanne', (1924) 18 *AJIL* 696-706.

Van Elst, Richard, 'Implementing Universal Jurisdiction Over Grave Breaches of the Geneva Conventions', (2000) 13 *LJIL* 815-54.

Van Schaack, Beth, 'The Crime of Political Genocide: Repairing the Genocide Convention's Blind Spot', (1997) 106 *Yale L J* 2259-91.

Van Schaack, Beth, 'The Definition of Crimes Against Humanity: Resolving the Incoherence', (1999) 37 *Columbia Journal of Transnational Law* 787-850.

Verdirame, Guglielmo, 'The Genocide Definition in the Jurisprudence of the *Ad Hoc* Tribunals', (2000) 49 *ICLQ* 578-98.

Verdross, Alfred, 'Jus Dispositivum and Jus Cogens in International Law', (1966) 60 AJIL 55-63.

Villalpando, Santiago, 'L'Affaire Pinochet: Beaucoup de bruit pour rien? L'apport au Droit International de la décision de la Chambre des Lords du 24 mars 1999', (2000) 104 *RGDIP* 393-427.

Von Elbe, Joachim, 'The evolution of the concept of the just war in international law', (1939) 33 *AJIL* 665-88.

Von Sternberg, Mark R., 'A Comparison of the Yugoslavian and Rwandan War Crimes Tribunals: Universal Jurisdiction and the "Elementary Dictates of Humanity"', (1996) XXII *Brooklyn Journal of International Law* 111-56.

Watkin, Kenneth, 'Controlling the Use of Force: A Role for Human Rights Norms in Contemporary Armed Conflict', (2004) 98 *AJIL* 1-34.

Wechsler, Herbert, 'The Issues of the Nuremberg Trial', (1947) LXII *Political Science Quarterly* 11-26.

Wedgwood, Ruth, 'NATO's Campaign in Yugoslavia', (1999) 93 *AJIL* 828-34.

Wedgwood, Ruth, 'The Fall of Saddam Hussein: Security Council Mandates and Preemptive Self-Defense', (2003) 97 *AJIL* 576-85.

White, Robin C.A., 'Self-Determination: Time for a Re-Assessment?', (1981) XXVIII *Netherlands International Law Review* 147-70.

Wirth, Steffen, 'Immunities, Related Problems, and Article 98 of the *Rome Statute*', (2001) 12 *Crim L F* 429-58.

Wolfe, Robert, 'Flaws in the Nuremberg Legacy: An Impediment to International War Crimes Tribunals' Prosecution of Crimes Against Humanity', (1998) 12 *Holocaust and Genocide Studies* 434-53.

Wright, Quincy, 'The Legal Liability of the Kaiser', (1919) 13 *American Political Science Review* 120-8.

Wright, Quincy, 'The Concept of Aggression in International Law', (1935) 29 *AJIL* 373-95.

Wright, Quincy, 'The Law of the Nuremberg Trial', (1947) XLI *AJIL* 38-72.

Wright, Quincy, 'The Outlawry of War and the Law of War', (1953) 47 *AJIL* 365-76.

Yee, Sienho, 'The Erdemovic Sentencing Judgement: A Questionable Milestone for the International Criminal Tribunal for the Former Yugoslavia', (1997) 26 *Georgia Journal of International and Comparative Law* 263-309.

Yoo, John, 'International Law and the War in Iraq', (2003) 987 *AJIL* 563-76.

Zappala, Salvatore, '*Do Heads of State in Office Enjoy Immunity from Jurisdiction for International Crimes? The* Ghaddafi *Case Before the French* Cour de Cassation', (2001) 12 *EJIL* 595-612.

žourek, Jaroslav, 'Enfin une Définition de l'Aggression', (1974) 20 *AFDI* 9-30.

Press Articles

Cassese, Antonio, 'Créons des tribunaux internationaux!', *Courrier International* No. 583, January 2002, p 29.

Chambraud, Cécile, 'L'Espagne s'autorise à juger tous les crimes contre l'humanité', *Le Monde,* 6 October 2005.

Châtelot, Christophe, 'Devant le TPIY, un officier britannique fait état d'un plan serbe pour éliminer les Albanais du Kosovo', *Le Monde,* 19 April 2002.

Cohen, Claude, 'Après l'Affaire Touvier, Réflexions et Prolongements', *L'Arche,* 1994, pp 29-33.

Cohen, Richard, 'Killing Truth', *Washington Post,* 31 May 1983, p 81.

Conan, Eric, 'Touvier: Un profond malaise', *L'Express,* 28 April 1994.

Conan, Eric, 'Papon, Les Français et Vichy', *L'Express,* 2 October 1997, p 59.

Doucet, Ghislaine, 'Crimes contre l'Humanité, De Nuremberg à Aujourd'hui', *Le Patriote Résistant,* March 1994, pp 8-9.

Halimi, Serge et Vidal, Dominique, 'Chronique d'un génocide annoncé', *Le Monde diplomatique,* March 2000.

Johannès, Franck, 'Le général Aussaresses jugé pour "complicité d'apologie de crimes de guerre"', *Le Monde,* 27 November 2001.

Marcou, Léa, 'Ils ont déporté les Juifs de France', *La Tribune Juive,* October 1979, pp 12-13.

Moix, Yann, 'Une nouvelle ère de l'humanité', *Libération,* 14 September 2001, p 59.

Prieur, Cécile : 'Des poursuites contre Paul Aussaresses se heurteraient à plusieurs obstacles juridiques', *Le Monde,* 3 May 2001.

Samary, Catherine, 'Comparution de M. Slobodan Milosevic - Les incohérences du Tribunal pénal international', *Le Monde diplomatique,* July 2001.

Semo, Marc, 'Slobodan Milosevic inculpé de génocide - Le TPI a retenu ce chef d'accusation pour son rôle en Bosnie', *Libération*, 21 November 2001.

Thoraval, Armelle, 'Criminel de guerre ou contre l'humanité', *Libération*, 4 May 2001.

Table of Cases

Austria

Cvjetković case, Austria Regional Court at Salzburg, 1995.

Belgium

Ntezimana et al. case, *Vincent Ntezimana, Alphonse Higaniro, Consolata Mukangango, Julienne Mukabutera,* Verdict de la Cour d'Assises de l'Arrondissement Administratif de Bruxelles-Capitale, 8 June 2001.
Pinochet case, Tribunal de Première Instance de Bruxelles, 8 November 1998.

Canada

Regina v *Imre Finta,* 92 D.L.R. 4th 1, 84, Ontario Court of Appeal, 1992.
Regina v *Imre Finta,* [1994] 1 S.C.R. 701, Supreme Court of Canada, 24 March 1994.
Regina v *Ernst Zundel,* [1987] 56 C.R. 3d 1, Ontario Court of Appeal, Judgment of 23 January 1987.
Regina v *Ernst Zundel,* District Court, 1988.

Denmark

Sarić case, Danish High Court, 1994.

Equatorial Guinea

Macias case, September 1979.

European Commission on Human Rights

Request 9777/82 v *Belgium,* Decision of 14 July 1983.

France

Barbie (Klaus) case, *Fédération Nationale des Déportés et Internés Résistants et Patriotes et Autres* v *Klaus Barbie*, cass. crim., 6 October 1983. *Reprinted in* (1984) 88 RGDIP 509.
Barbie (Klaus) case, *Fédération Nationale des Déportés et Internés Résistants et Patriotes et Autres* v *Klaus Barbie*, cass. crim., 20 December 1985. Reprinted in (1986) 90 RGDIP 1024 and in 78 ILR 125.
Brunner (Aloïs) case, Cour d'Assises de Paris, 2 March 2001.
Dupaquier et al. v *Munyeshyaka*, Cour d'Appel de Nîmes, 20 March 1996.
Galinier v *Munyeshyaka*, cass. crim., 6 January 1998. Reprinted in (1998) 102 RGDIP 825-32.
Javor case, cass. crim., 26 March 1996. *Reprinted in* 132 *Bulletin Criminel* 379.
Khadaffi case, Cour de Cassation, 13 March 2001.
Le Pen (Jean-Marie) case, Tribunal de Grande Instance de Nanterres, 23 May 1990.
Papon (Maurice) case, cass. crim., 23 January 1997.
RSF v *Mille Collines*, Cour d'Appel de Paris, 6 November 1995.
Touvier (Paul) case, cass. crim., 27 November 1992, [1993-II] JCP No. 21. 977.
Touvier (Paul) case, Arrêt de la Chambre d'Accusation de Versailles, 2 June 1993.
Touvier (Paul) case, cass. crim., Jugement, 21 October 1993.
Touvier (Paul) case, cass. crim., 20 April 1994.

Germany

Djajić case [*Public Prosecutor* v *Djajić*], Supreme Court of Bavaria, 1998.
German Federal Court of Justice, 1999.
Federal Constitutional Court, 2 BvR 1290/99, 12 December 2000, *cited in Krstić Judgment* [*Prosecutor* v *Radislav Krstić*], Case No. IT-98-33, Judgment, Trial Chamber I, 2 August 2001.
Jorgić case, [Prosecutor v Nikolai Jorgić], *Oberlandesgericht Düsseldorf* (Higher Regional Court, Düsseldorf), 26 September 1997, IV-26/96.
Jorgić case, [Prosecutor v Nikolai Jorgić], *Bundesgerichtshof* (Federal Court of Justice), 30 April 1999, 3 StR 215/98F.

Inter-American Court of Human Rights

Velasquez Rodriguez case (Merits) (1988) 95 ILR 232 (29 July).

International Court of Justice

Application of the Convention on the Prevention and Punishment of the Crime of Genocide (*Bosnia-Herzegovina* v *Yugoslavia*), Further Requests for the Indication of Provisional Measures, [1993] ICJ Reports 325-50 (13 September).

Application of the Convention on the Prevention and Punishment of the Crime of Genocide (*Bosnia-Herzegovina* v *Yugoslavia*), Preliminary Objections, Judgment, [1996] ICJ Reports 595-624 (11 July).

Arrest Warrant of 11 April 2000 (*Democratic Republic of the Congo* v *Belgium*), General List No. 121, 14 February 2002. Available at: <http://www.icj-cij.org>.

Barcelona Traction, Light and Power Co. Ltd. (*Belgium* v *Spain*), Judgment, [1970] ICJ Reports 3-51 (5 February).

Corfu Channel (*United Kingdom of Great Britain and Northern Ireland* v *Albania*), Merits, [1949] ICJ Reports 4-38 (9 April).

Legality of the Threat or Use of Nuclear Weapons, Advisory Opinion, [1996] ICJ Reports 226-67 (8 July).

Legality of Use of Force (Yugoslavia v *Belgium, Canada, France, Germany, Italy, The Netherlands, Portugal, Spain, United Kingdom, United States of America),* Provisional Measures, Order, [1999] ICJ Reports 124-973 (2 June).

Military and Paramilitary Activities in and against Nicaragua (*Nicaragua* v *United States*), Jurisdiction and Admissibility, Judgment, [1984] ICJ Reports 392-443 (26 November).

Military and Paramilitary Activities in and against Nicaragua (*Nicaragua* v *United States*), Merits, [1986] ICJ Reports 14-150 (27 June).

North Sea Continental Shelf cases, Judgment, [1969] ICJ Reports 3-54 (20 February).

Reservations to the Convention on the Prevention and Punishment of the Crime of Genocide, Advisory Opinion, [1951] ICJ Reports 15-30 (28 May).

International Criminal Tribunal for the Former Yugoslavia

Aleksovski judgment *[Prosecutor* v *Zlatko Aleksovski*], Case No. IT-95-14/1, Judgment, Trial Chamber I, 25 June 1999.

Aleksovski Appeal Judgment [*Prosecutor* v *Zlatko Aleksovski*], Case No. IT-95-14/1-A, Judgment including Declaration of Judge Hunt, Appeals Chamber, 24 March 2000.

Aleksovski Appeal Judgment II [*Prosecutor* v *Zlatko Aleksovski*], Case No. IT-95-14/1, Judgment on Appeal by Anto Nobilo against Finding of Contempt including Separate Opinion of Judge Patrick Robinson, Appeals Chamber, 30 May 2001.

Blagojević and Jokić Judgment [*Prosecutor* v *Vidoje Blagojević and Dragan Jokić*], Case No. IT-02-60-T, Judgment, Trial Chamber I, 17 January 2005.
Blaškić Request Judgment [*Prosecutor* v *Tihomir Blaškić*], Case No. IT-95-14-A, Judgment on the Request of the Republic of Croatia for Review of the Decision of Trial Chamber II of 18 July 1997, Appeals Chamber, 29 October 1997.
Blaškić Judgment [*Prosecutor* v *Tihomir Blaškić*], Case No. IT-95-14, Judgment including Declaration of Judge Shahabuddeen, Trial Chamber I, 3 March 2000.
Bradjnin and Talić Decision [*Prosecutor* v *Radoslav Bradjnin* and *Momir Talić*], Case No. IT-99-36-PT, Decision on Form of Further Amended Indictment and Prosecution Application to Amend, 26 June 2001.
Čelebići Judgment [*Prosecutor* v *Zejnil Delalić et al.*], Case No. IT-96-21-T, Judgment, Trial Chamber II *quater*, 16 November 1998.
Čelebićii Appeal Judgment [*Prosecutor* v *Zejnil Delalić et al.*], Case No. IT-96-21, Judgment including Separate and Dissenting Opinion of Judge David Hunt and Judge Mohamed Bennouna, Appeals Chamber, 20 February 2001.
Čelebići Sentencing Judgment [Prosecutor v *Zejnil Delalić et al.*], Case No. IT-96-21, Sentencing Judgment, Trial Chamber II *quater*, 9 October 2001.
Erdemović Sentencing Judgment [*Prosecutor* v *Drazen Erdemović*], Case No. IT-96-22-T, Sentencing Judgment, Trial Chamber I, 29 November 1996.
Erdemović Sentencing Appeal [*Prosecutor* v *Drazen Erdemović*], Case No. IT-96-22, Appeal of Sentencing Judgment, Appeals Chamber, 7 October 1997.
Erdemović Sentencing Judgment II [*Prosecutor* v *Drazen Erdemović*], Case No. IT-96-22, Sentencing Judgment following appeal, Trial Chamber II, 5 March 1998.
Furundžija Judgment [*Prosecutor* v *Anto Furundžija*], Case No. IT-95-17/1, Judgment, Trial Chamber II, 10 December 1998.
Furundžžija Appeal Judgment [Prosecutor v *Anto Furundžija*], Case No. IT-95-17/1, Judgment, Appeals Chamber, 21 July 2000.
Jelisić Judgment [*Prosecutor* v *Goran Jelisić*], Case No. IT-95-10-T, Judgment, Trial Chamber I, 14 December 1999.
Jelisić Appeal Judgment [*Prosecutor* v *Goran Jelisić*], Case No. IT-95-10-A, Appeal Judgment, Appeals Chamber, 5 July 2001.
Karadzić and Mladić Indictment [*Prosecutor* v *Radovan Karadzić and Ratko Mladić*], Case No. IT-95-5, Initial Indictment, 24 July 1995.
Karadzić and Mladić Indictment II [*Prosecutor* v *Radovan Karadzić and Ratko Mladić*], Case No. IT-95-18, Initial Indictment, 16 November 1995.
Kordić and Čerkez Judgment [*Prosecutor* v *Dario Kordić and Mario Čerkez*], Case No. IT-95-14/2-PT, Decision on the Joint Defence Motion to Dismiss the Amended Indictment for Lack of Jurisdiction Based on the Limited Jurisdictional Reach of Articles 2 and 3, Trial Chamber III, 2 March 1999.

Kordić and Čerkez Judgment [*Prosecutor* v *Dario Kordić and Mario Čerkez*], Case No. IT-95-14/2, Judgment, Trial Chamber III, 26 February 2001.
Krnojelac Judgment [*Prosecutor* v *Milorad Krnojelac*], Case No. IT-97-25, Judgment, Trial Chamber II, 15 March 2002.
Krstić Judgment [*Prosecutor* v *Radislav Krstić*], Case No. IT-98-33, Judgment, Trial Chamber I, 2 August 2001.
Krstić Appeal Judgment [*Prosecutor* v *Radislav Krstić*], Case No. IT-98-33-A, Judgment, Appeals Chamber, 19 April 2004.
Kunarac Judgment [*Prosecutor* v *Dragoljub Kunarac, Radomir Kovac and Zoran Vuković*], Case No. IT-96-23 and IT-96-23/1, Judgment, Trial Chamber II, 22 February 2001.
Kunarac Appeal Judgment [*Prosecutor* v *Dragoljub Kunarac, Radomir Kovac and Zoran Vukovif*], Case No. IT-96-23 and IT-96-23/1-A, Judgment, Appeals Chamber, 12 June 2002.
Kupreškić Judgment [*Prosecutor* v *Zoran Kupreškić, Mirjan Kupreškić, Vlatko Kupreškić, Drago Josipović, Dragan Papić, Vladimir Santić*], Case No. IT-95-16, Judgment, Trial Chamber II, 14 January 2000.
Kupreškić Appeal Judgment [*Prosecutor* v *Zoran Kupreškić, Mirjan Kupreškić, Vlatko Kupreškić, Drago Josipović, Vladimir Santić*], Case No. IT-95-16-A, Judgment, Appeals Chamber, 23 October 2001.
Kvoèka Judgment [*Prosecutor* v *Miroslav Kvoèka, Milojica Kos, Mlado Radić, Zoran Zigić, Dragoljub Prcac*], Case No. IT-98-30/1, Judgment, Trial Chamber I, 2 November 2001.
Martić Indictment [*Prosecutor* v *Martić*], Case No. IT-95-11-R61, Review of the Indictment Pursuant to Rule 61, 8 March 1996 ; 13 March 1996.
Milošević 'Bosnia and Herzegovina' Indictment [*Prosecutor* v *Slobodan Milošević*], Case No. IT-01-51-I, Initial Indictment, 22 November 2001.
Milošević 'Croatia' Indictment [*Prosecutor* v *Slobodan Milošević*], Case No. IT-01-50-I, Initial Indictment, 8 October 2001.
Milošević et al. Initial Indictment [*Prosecutor* v *Slobodan Milošević, Milan Milutinović, Nikola Sainović, Dragoljub Ojdanić, Vlajko Stojiljković*], Case No. IT-99-37-I, Initial Indictment, 22 May 1999.
Milošević et al. Amended Indictment [*Prosecutor* v *Slobodan Milošević, Milan Milutinović, Nikola Sainović, Dragoljub Ojdanić, Vlajko Stojiljković*], Case No. IT-99-37-I, First Amended Indictment, 29 June 2001.
Milošević et al. Indictment Decision [*Prosecutor* v *Slobodan Milošević, Milan Milutinović, Nikola Sainović, Dragoljub Ojdanić, Vlajko Stojiljković*], Case No. IT-99-37-I, Decision on Application to Amended Indictment and on Confirmation of Amended Indictment, 29 June 2001.
Milošević et al. Amended Indictment II [*Prosecutor* v *Slobodan Milošević, Milan Milutinović, Nikola Sainović, Dragoljub Ojdanić, Vlajko Stojiljković*], Case No. IT-99-37-PT, Second Amended Indictment, 16 October 2001.
Nikolić Indictment [*Prosecutor* v *Dragan Nikolić*], Case No. IT-94-2, Initial Indictment, 4 November 1994.

Nikolić Indictment Review [*Prosecutor* v *Dragan Nikolić*], Case No. IT-94-2-R61, Review of the Indictment Pursuant to Rule 61 of the Rules of Procedure and Evidence, Trial Chamber I, 20 October 1995.
Sikirica Judgment [*Prosecutor* v *Dusko Sikirica, Damir Dosen and Dragan Kolundžija*], Case No. IT-95-8, Judgment on Defence Motions to Acquit, Trial Chamber III, 3 September 2001.
Sikirica Sentencing Judgment [*Prosecutor* v *Dusko Sikirica, Damir Dosen and Dragan Kolundžija*], Case No. IT-95-8-S, Sentencing Judgment, Trial Chamber III, 13 November 2001.
Sikirica Motions for Acquittal Decision [*Prosecutor* v *Dusko Sikirica, Damir Dosen and Dragan Kolundžija*], Case No. IT-95-8-T, Judgment on Defence Motions to Acquit, Trial Chamber, 3 September 2001.
Sikirica Motions for Acquittal Decision [*Prosecutor* v *Dusko Sikirica, Damir Dosen and Dragan Kolundžija*], Case No. IT-95-8-T, Corrigendum to Judgment on Defence Motions to Acquit, Trial Chamber, 20 September 2001.
Tadić Decision [*Prosecutor* v *Dusko Tadić*], Case No. IT-94-I-T, Decision on the Defence Motion, Trial Chamber II, 10 August 1995.
Tadić Interlocutory Appeal [*Prosecutor* v *Dusko Tadić*], Case No. IT-94-1-AR72, Decision on the Defence Motion for Interlocutory Appeal on Jurisdiction, Appeals Chamber, 2 October 1995.
Tadić Decision on the Form of the Indictment [*Prosecutor* v *Dusko Tadić*], Case No. IT-94-1, Decision on the Defence Motion on the Form of the Indictment, Trial Chamber II, 14 November 1995.
Tadić Judgment [*Prosecutor* v *Dusko Tadić*], Case No. IT-94-1-T, Opinion and Judgment including Separate and Dissenting Opinion of Judge McDonald, Trial Chamber II, 7 May 1997.
Tadić Sentencing Judgment [*Prosecutor* v *Dusko Tadić*], Case No. IT-94-1, Sentencing Judgment, Trial Chamber II, 14 July 1997.
Tadić Appeal Judgment [*Prosecutor* v *Dusko Tadić*], Case No. IT-94-1-A, Judgment including Declaration of Judge Nieto-Navia and Separate Opinion of Judge Shahabuddeen, Appeals Chamber, 15 July 1999.
Tadić Sentencing Judgment II [*Prosecutor* v *Dusko Tadić*], Case No. IT-94-1, Sentencing Judgment, Trial Chamber II, 11 November 1999.
Tadić Corrigendum [*Prosecutor* v *Dusko Tadić*], Case No. IT-94-1, Corrigendum to Judgment of the Appeals Chamber of 15 July 1999, 19 November 1999.
Tadić Judgment in Sentencing Appeals [*Prosecutor* v *Dusko Tadić*], Case No. IT-94-1-A and IT-94-1-A *bis*, Judgment in Sentencing Appeals including Separate Opinion of Judge Shahabuddeen and Separate Opinion of Judge Cassese, Appeals Chamber, 26 January 2000.
Tadić Judgment on Allegations of Contempt [*Prosecutor* v *Dusko Tadić*], Case No. IT-94-1, Judgment on Allegations of Contempt Against Prior Counsel, Milan Vujin, Appeals Chamber, 31 January 2000.

Tadić Appeal Judgment on Allegations of Contempt [*Prosecutor* v *Dusko Tadić*], Case No. IT-94-1, Appeal Judgment on Allegations of Contempt Against Prior Counsel, Milan Vijun, and Separate Opinion of Judge Wald dissenting from the Finding of Jurisdiction, Appeals Chamber, 27 February 2001.

Vukovar Hospital Decision [*Prosecutor* v *Mile Mrkšić, Miroslav Radić, and Veselin Šljivanèanin*], Case No. IT-95-13-R61, Review of the Indictment Pursuant to Rule 61 of the Rules of Procedure and Evidence, Trial Chamber I, 3 April 1996.

International Criminal Tribunal for Rwanda

Akayesu Judgment [*Prosecutor* v *Jean-Paul Akayesu*], Case No. ICTR-96-4-T, Judgment, Trial Chamber I, 2 September 1998.

Kambanda Sentencing Judgment [*Prosecutor* v *Jean Kambanda*], Case No. ICTR-97-23-S, Judgment and Sentence, Trial Chamber I, 4 September 1998.

Kambanda Appeal Judgment [*Prosecutor* v *Jean Kambanda*], Case No. ICTR-97-23-A, Judgment, Appeals Chamber, 19 October 2000.

Kayishema and Ruzindana Judgment [*Prosecutor* v *Clément Kayishema and Obed Ruzindana*], Case No. ICTR-95-1-T, Judgment, Trial Chamber II, 21 May 1999.

Musema Judgment [*Prosecutor* v *Alfred Musema*], Case No. ICTR-96-13-T, Judgment and Sentence, Trial Chamber I, 27 January 2000.

Musema Appeal Judgment [*Prosecutor* v *Alfred Musema*], Case No. ICTR-96-13-A, Appeals Judgment, Appeals Chamber, 16 November 2001.

Rutaganda Judgment [*Prosecutor* v *George Rutaganda*], Case No. ICTR-96-3-T, Judgment Trial Chamber I, 6 December 1999.

Serushago Judgment [*Prosecutor* v *Omar Serushago*], Case No. ICTR-98-39-S, Judgment, Trial Chamber I, 5 February 1999.

Serushago Appeal Judgment [*Prosecutor* v *Omar Serushago*], Case No. ICTR-98-39-A, Appeals Chamber, 6 April 2000.

International Military Tribunal at Nuremberg

Trials of the Major War Criminals before the International Military Tribunal (TMWC), 42 volumes, Nuremberg, 1947-1949.

International Military Tribunal for the Far East

Trial of the Major War Criminals, Proceedings of the International Military Tribunal for the Far East at Tokyo. *Compiled in* Pritchard, John R. and Zaide, Sonia Magbanua (eds), *The Tokyo War Crimes Trial: Proceedings of the Tribunal*, Garland Publishing, 1981.

Israel

Attorney-General of the Government of Israel v *Adolf Eichmann*, 36 ILR 18 (Israel District Court – Jerusalem, 1961).
Attorney-General of the Government of Israel v *Adolf Eichmann*, 36 ILR 277 (Israel Supreme Court, 1962).

Italy

Priebke case, Military Court of Rome, 1 August 1996.

Leipzig Supreme Court (German War Trials)

Llandovery Castle case, Judgment in Case of Lieutenants Dithmar and Boldt, Hospital Ship "Llandovery Castle", 16 July 1921. *Reprinted in* (1922) 16 AJIL 708-24.

National Prosecutions

Roechling case, 14 *Nuremberg Subsequent Proceedings* 1097-143.

Netherlands

Knesević case, Case No.3717, Netherlands Supreme Court, 1997.

Nuremberg Subsequent Proceedings

Proceedings by the Allied Powers held pursuant to Control Council Law No. 10. *In* [1950] Trials of War Criminals before the Nuremberg Military Tribunals Under Control Council Law No. 10, 15 volumes, Washington: US department of the Army, Government Printing Office, 1946-49.
United States v *Altsoetter et al.*, the '*Justice* case', Case No. 3, Military Tribunal III, 3 *Nuremberg Subsequent Proceedings*.
United States v *Brando et al.*, the '*Medical* case', Case No. 1 Military Tribunal I, 1-2 *Nuremberg Subsequent Proceedings*.
United States v *Flick et al.*, The '*Flick* case', Case No. 5, Military Tribunal IV, 6 *Nuremberg Subsequent Proceedings*.
United States v *Greifelt et al.*, the '*RuSHA* case', Case No. 8, Military Tribunal I, 4-5 *Nuremberg Subsequent Proceedings*.
United States v *Krauch et al.*, the '*Farben* case', Case No. 6, Military Tribunal VI, 7-8 *Nuremberg Subsequent Proceedings*.
United States v *Krupp et al.*, the '*Krupp* case', Case No. 10, Military Tribunal III, 9 *Nuremberg Subsequent Proceedings*.
United States v *Milch et al.*, the '*Milch* case', Case No. 2, Military Tribunal II, 2 *Nuremberg Subsequent Proceedings*.

United States v *Ohlendorf et al.*, the '*Einsatzgruppen* case', Case No. 9, Military Tribunal II, 4 *Nuremberg Subsequent Proceedings*.
United States v *Pohl et al.*, the '*Pohl* case', Case No. 4, Military Tribunal II, 5 *Nuremberg Subsequent Proceedings*.
United States v *Von Leeb et al.*, the '*High Command* case', Case No. 12, Military Tribunal V, 10-11 *Nuremberg Subsequent Proceedings*.
United States v *Von List et al.*, the '*Hostage* case', Case No. 7, Military Tribunal V, 11 *Nuremberg Subsequent Proceedings*.
United States v *Von Weizsaecker et al.*, the '*Ministries* case', Case No. 11, Military Tribunal IV, 12-14 *Nuremberg Subsequent Proceedings*.

Permanent Court of International Justice

German Settlers in Poland, PCIJ No. 6 (1923).

Special Court for Sierra Leone

The Prosecutor v *Morris Kallon and Brima Buzzy Kamara*, SCSL-2004-15-AR72(E) and SCSL-2004-16-AR72(E), Decision on Challenge to Jurisdiction: Lomé Accord Amnesty, Appeals Chamber, 13 March 2004.

Switzerland

G. case, Swiss Military Tribunal, Division I.
Niyonteze case, *Public Prosecutor* v *Fulgence Niyonteze*, Tribunal Militaire de Cassation, 27 April 2001.

United Kingdom

Regina v *Bartle and the Commissioner of Police for the Metropolis and Others*, ex parte *Pinochet* – *Regina* v *Evans and Another and the Commissioner of Police and Others*, ex parte *Pinochet*, Judgment of 25 November 1998, (1998) 37 ILM 1302.
Regina v *Bartle and the Commissioner of Police for the Metropolis and Others* Ex Parte *Pinochet* – *Regina* v *Evans and Another and the Commissioner of Police and Others*, ex parte *Pinochet*, Judgment of 24 March 1999, (1999) 38 ILM 581.

United States of America

Demjanjuk v *Petrovsky*, 776 F. 2d 571, (6th Circ. 1985), 79 ILR 535.
Doe v *Karadzić*, 866 F. Supp. 734 (S.D.N.Y. 1994).
Doe v *Karadzić*, No. 93 Civ. 878, Judgment (S.D.N.Y. 5 October 2000).
Filartiga v *Pena-Irala*, 630 F. 2d. 876 (2d Circ.1980).
Kadić v *Karadzić*, 70 Fed. 3d 232 (2d Circ. 1995).
Kadić v *Karadzić*, 518 U.S. 1005 (1996).

Kadić v *Karadzić*, No. 93 Civ. 1163, Judgment (S.D.N.Y. 16 August 2000).
Lafontant v *Aristide*, 844 Fed. Supp. 128 (Eastern Dist. N.Y. 1994).
Mel Mermelstein v *The Institute for Historical Review*, Superior Court of the State of California for the County of Los Angeles, pre-trial hearings, 9 October 1981.
Tachiona v *Mugabe*, 169 F. Supp. 2d 259 (S.D.N.Y. 2001).
United States v *Noriega*, Case No. 88-0079-CR, US District Court for the Southern District of Florida. 99 ILR 143-194.
United States v *Yamashita*, 327 U.S. 1, (1946).

Table of Authorities

Treaties, Conventions and Other International Instruments

Allied Control Council Law No. 10, Punishment of Persons Guilty of War Crimes, Crimes Against Peace and Against Humanity, 20 December 1945, Official Gazette of the Control Council for Germany, No. 3, Berlin, 31 January 1946. Excerpts reprinted in Ratner, Steven R. and Abrams, Jason S., *Accountability for Human Rights Atrocities in International Law – Beyond the Nuremberg Legacy*, Oxford University Press, 2nd edn, 2001, pp 350-52.

American Convention on Human Rights ("Pact of San José"), Adopted by the Organization of American States on 22 November 1969, San José, Costa Rica (Entry into force: 18 July 1978). Reprinted in *The Raoul Wallenberg Compilation*, pp 155-77.

Charter of the International Military Tribunal, Annex to Agreement for the Prosecution and Punishment of Major War Criminals of the European Axis, London, 8 August 1945, 82 UNTS 279. Reprinted in (Supp. 1945) 39 AJIL 257.

Charter of the International Military Tribunal for the Far East, 19 January 1946, *United States Treaties and Other International Acts Series* 1589.

Charter of the United Nations, 1945. Signed on 26 June 1945, San Francisco (Entry into force: 24 October 1945). Excerpts reprinted in *The Raoul Wallenberg Compilation*, pp 1-7.

Convention on the Elimination of Discrimination of All Forms of Discrimination against Women, United Nations, 1979. Adopted by the General Assembly of the United Nations, Resolution 34/180 of 18 December 1979 (Entry into force: 3 September 1981). Reprinted in *The Raoul Wallenberg Compilation*, pp 237- 47.

Convention on the Non-Applicability of Statutory Limitations to War Crimes and Crimes Against Humanity, United Nations, 1968. Adopted and opened for signature, ratification and accession by the General Assembly of the United Nations, Resolution 2391 (XXIII) of 26 November 1968 (Entry into force : 11 November 1970). Reprinted in *The Raoul Wallenberg Compilation*, pp 579-82.

Convention for the Prevention and Punishment of the Crime of Genocide, United Nations, 1948. Approved and proposed for signature, ratification or accession by the General Assembly of the United Nations, Resolution 260 A (III) of 9 December 1948 (Entry into force : 12 January 1951). Reprinted in *The Raoul Wallenberg Compilation*, pp 575-8.

Convention on the Rights of the Child, United Nations, 1989. Adopted and opened for signature, ratification or accession by the General Assembly of the United Nations, Resolution 44/25 of 20 November 1989 (Entry into force: 2 September 1990). Reprinted in *The Raoul Wallenberg Compilation*, pp 279-97.

Convention against Torture and Other Cruel, Inhuman or Degrading Treatment or Punishment, United Nations, 1984. Adopted and opened for signature, ratification and accession by the General Assembly of the United Nations, Resolution 39/46 of 10 December 1984 (Entry into force: 26 June 1987). Reprinted in *The Raoul Wallenberg Compilation*, pp 549-61.

Convention relating to the Status of Refugees, United Nations, 1951. Signed in Geneva on 28 July 1951 (Entry into force: 22 April 1954). Reprinted in *The Raoul Wallenberg Compilation*, pp.343-59.

European Convention on the Non-Applicability of Statutory Limitations to War Crimes and Crimes Against Humanity, Council of Europe, 25 January 1974, *European Treaty Series* 82.

European Convention for the Protection of Human Rights and Fundamental Freedoms, Council of Europe, 1950. Adopted by the Council of Europe on 4 November 1950 (Entry into force: 3 September 1953). Reprinted in *The Raoul Wallenberg Compilation*, pp 81-96.

European Convention for the Prevention of Torture and Inhuman or Degrading Treatment or Punishment, Council of Europe, 1987. Adopted by the Council of Europe on 26 November 1987 (Entry into force: 1 February 1989). Reprinted in *The Raoul Wallenberg Compilation*, pp 563-8.

Geneva Convention (I) for the Amelioration of the Condition of the Wounded and Sick in Armed Forces in the Field, 12 August, 1949. Reprinted in *Commentary to Geneva Convention I*.

Geneva Convention (II) for the Amelioration of the Condition of Wounded, Sick and Shipwrecked Members of Armed Forces at Sea, 12 August, 1949. Available on the ICRC website.

Geneva Convention (III) Relative to the Treatment of Prisoners of War, 12 August, 1949. Reprinted in Commentary to Geneva Convention III.

Geneva Convention (IV) Relative to the Protection of Civilian Persons in Time of War, 12 August, 1949. Reprinted in *Commentary to Geneva Convention IV.*

Hague Convention for the Peaceful Adjustment of International Disputes, 29 July 1899. Reprinted in (1907) 1 *AJIL* 107.

Hague Convention Respecting the Laws and Customs of War on Land (Convention No IV), 18 October 1907. *Reprinted in* International Committee of the Red Cross, *International Law Concerning the Conduct of Hostilities, Collection of Hague Conventions and some Other International Instruments,* Geneva: International Committee of the Red Cross, 1996, pp 13-27.

International Convention on the Elimination of All Forms of Racial Discrimination, United Nations, 1965. Adopted by the General Assembly of the United Nations, Resolution 2106 A (XX) of 21 December 1965 (Entry into force: 4 January 1969). Reprinted in *The Raoul Wallenberg Compilation,* pp 255-66.

International Convention on the Suppression and Punishment of the Crime of Apartheid, United Nations, 1973. Excerpts *reprinted in* Paust, Jordan J. et al., *International Criminal Law Documents Supplement,* Carolina Academic Press, 2000, pp 265-7.

International Covenant on Civil and Political Rights, United Nations, 1966. Adopted and opened for signature, ratification and accession by the General Assembly of the United Nations, Resolution 2200 (XXI) of 16 December 1966 (Entry into force: 23 May 1976). Reprinted in *The Raoul Wallenberg Compilation,* pp 43-60.

Protocol Additional to the Geneva Conventions of 12 August 1949, and relating to the Protection of Victims of International Armed Conflicts (Protocol I), 8 June, 1977. *Reprinted in* Sandoz, Yves, Swinarski, Christophe and Zimmermann, Bruno (eds), *Commentary on the Additional Protocols of 8 June 1977 to the Geneva Conventions of 12 August 1949,* International Committee of the Red Cross, Geneva: Martinus Nijhoff Publishers, 1987.

Protocol Additional to the Geneva Conventions of 12 August 1949, and relating to the Protection of Victims of Non-International Armed Conflicts (Protocol II), 8 June, 1977. *Reprinted in* Sandoz, Yves, Swinarski, Christophe and Zimmermann, Bruno (eds), *Commentary on the Additional Protocols of 8 June 1977 to the Geneva Conventions of 12 August 1949,* International Committee of the Red Cross, Geneva: Martinus Nijhoff Publishers, 1987.

Rome Statute of the International Criminal Court, Adopted by the United Nations Diplomatic Conference of Plenipotentiaries on the Establishment of an International Criminal Court on 17 July 1998, UN Doc. A/Conf.183/9, 1998. Reprinted in Bassiouni, M. Cherif (ed.), *The Statute of the International Criminal Court : A Documentary History,* New York : Transnational Publishers, Inc., 1998, pp 39-114.

Statute of the International Tribunal for the Former Yugoslavia, United Nations, 1993. Approved by the Security Council of the United Nations in Resolution 827 of 25 May 1993. *Reprinted in The Raoul Wallenberg Compilation,* pp 583-92.

Statute of the International Tribunal for Rwanda, United Nations, 1994. Decided by the Security Council of the United Nations, Resolution 955 of 8 November 1994. Reprinted in *The Raoul Wallenberg Compilation,* pp 593-602.

Treaty Of Peace Between the Allied Powers and Turkey, Signed at Sèvres, August 10, 1920, (Supp.1921) 15 *AJIL* 179-295.

Treaty with Turkey and other instruments signed at Lausanne, 'Treaty of Lausanne', 24 July 1924, (Supp. 1924) 18 *AJIL* 1-116.

Treaty of Peace Between the Allied and Associated Powers and Germany (Treaty Of Versailles), 28 June 1919. *Reprinted in* Bevans, C.F. (ed.), *Treaties and Other International Agreements of the United States of America, 1776-1949, Volume 2,* 1970.

North Atlantic Treaty, Signed at Washington, 4 April 1949 (Entry into force: 24 August 1949). Reprinted in (Supp. 1949) 43 *AJIL* 159-62.

Vienna Convention on the Law of Treaties, 23 May 1969, UN Doc. A/CONF.39/27 (23 May 1969). Reprinted in (1969) 63 *AJIL* 875-903.

Universal Declaration of Human Rights, United Nations, 1948. Adopted by the General Assembly of the United Nations, Resolution 217 (III) of 10 December 1948. Reprinted in *The Raoul Wallenberg Compilation,* pp 27-32.

National Legislation

Australia
Genocide Convention Act No. 27 1949.
War Crimes Statute 1988.
War Crimes Amendment Act 1989 Australian Acts No 3.

Austria
Law No. 148 Federal Law – Amendment of the Prohibition Law, 1992.

Belgium
Loi relative à la répression des infractions graves aux conventions internationales de Genève du 12 août 1949 et aux protocoles I et II du 8 juin 1977, additionnels à ces conventions, 16 June 1993.
Law on the repression of the denial of the genocide committed by the German National-Socialist regime during the Second World War, 23 March 1995.
Loi relative à la répression des violations graves de droit international humanitaire, 10 February 1999.

Canada
War Crimes Statute 1987.

China (Republic of)
War Crimes Statute, law of 24 October 1946, 14 War Crimes Report.

Costa Rica
Articulo 127 del Proyecto del Codigo Penal (14 de Abril de 1998).

Ethiopia
Article 281 of the Penal Code (1957).

France
Code de Procédure Pénale
Article 7.
Nouveau Code Pénal
Article 211-1 du Code Pénal.
Article 213-5 du Code Pénal, Loi No 64-1326 tendant à constater l'imprescriptibilité des crimes contre l'humanité, 26 December 1964.
Loi reconnaissant le génocide arménien, 29 January 2001.

Germany
Criminal Code
Article 130.

Article 131.
Article 185.
Section 78.
1985 law on the Auschwitz lie.

Israel
Nazi and Nazi Collaborators (Punishment) Law, Israel, 1950, 5710/1950. (Passed by the Knesset on 29 March 1950).
Denial of Holocaust (Prohibition) Law 5746 -1986.

Italy
Article 157 of the Penal Code.

Peru
Ley No. 26926 : Articulo 319 del Codigo Penal.

Romanian Socialist Republic
Article 356 of the Penal Code (1976).

Switzerland
Article 261b of the Penal Code.

United Kingdom
War Crimes Act 1991, c. 13, §1 (1). Reprinted in Evans, Malcolm D., *Blackstone's International Law Documents*, London : Blackstone Press Limited, 2nd edn, 1994, pp 407-408.

United States of America
Alien Tort Claims Act 1789, 28 U.S.C. § 1350 (1994). Excerpts *reprinted in* Ratner, Steven R. and Abrams, Jason S., *Accountability for Human Rights Atrocities in International Law – Beyond the Nuremberg Legacy*, 2nd edn, Oxford University Press, 2001, p 395.
Torture Victim Protection Act 1991, 28 U.S.C. § 1350 note (1994). Excerpts *reprinted in* Ratner, Steven R. and Abrams, Jason S., *Accountability for Human Rights Atrocities in International Law – Beyond the Nuremberg Legacy*, 2nd edn, Oxford University Press, 2001, p 396.

Significant Official Reports and Documents
This table only lists those official reports and documents which are recurrently referred to throughout the thesis.

European Parliament Documents
Resolution on European and International Protection for Nazi Concentration Camps and Historical Monuments, Resolution No. B3-

208, 0218, 0219, 0228 and 0283/93, European Parliament, Minutes of the Proceedings of the Sitting of 11 February 1993, Item 3.
Resolution on the Resurgence of Racism and Xenophobia in Europe and the Danger of Right-Wing Extremist Violence, No. A3-0127/93, European Parliament, Minutes of the Proceedings of the Sitting of 21 April 1993, Item 19.

Intergovernmental Reports

Commission on the Responsibility of the Authors of the War and on Enforcement of Penalties, 'Report Presented to the Preliminary Peace Conference, *March 29, 1919'*, (1920) 14 *AJIL* 95-154.

United Nations Documents

General Assembly Resolution 96 (I), UN Doc A/231, 11 December 1946.
Principles of International Law Recognized in the Charter of the Nürnberg Tribunal and in the Judgment of the Tribunal, [1950] II *ILC Yearbook* .
Report of the Secretary-General of the United Nations on the Question of Defining Aggression, UN GAOR, 7th Session, Annexes, Agenda item 54, UN Doc. A/2211, 3 October 1952.
ILC 1954 Draft Code of Offenses, [1954] II *ILC Yearbook.*
Principles of International Cooperation for the Arrest, Extradition and Punishment of War Crimes and Crimes Against Humanity, Resolution 3074 (XXXVIII), 28 UN GAOR Supp. (No.30), UN Doc. A/9030 (3 December 1973). Available at : <http://www.unhchr.htm>.
ILC Draft Articles on State Responsibility [1976] II *ILC Yearbook.*
Study of the Question of the Prevention and Punishment of the Crime of Genocide, Study prepared by Mr. Nicodème Ruhashyankiko, Special Rapporteur, United Nations Economic and Social Council, Commission on Human Rights, Sub-Commission on Prevention of Discrimination and Protection of Minorities, Thirty-first session, E/CN.4/Sub.2/416, 4 July 1978.
Review of Further Developments in Fields with which the Sub-Commission has been Concerned, Revised and updated report on the question of the prevention and punishment of the crime of genocide prepared by Mr. B. Whitaker, United Nations Economic and Social Council, Commission on Human Rights, Sub-Commission on Prevention of Discrimination and Protection of Minorities, Thirty-eighth session, E/CN.4/Sub.2/1985/6, 2 July 1985.
ILC 1991 Draft Code of Crimes, [1991] II (2) *ILC Yearbook.*
United Nations Human Rights Committee, General Comment No. 20, regarding Article 7 (15) ICCPR, UN Doc. CCPR/C/21/Rv 1/ Add 3 (7 April 1992).

Interim Report of the Commission of Experts Established Pursuant to Security Council Resolution 780 (1992), UN Doc. S/25274, Annex I (1993).
Final Report of the Commission of Experts Established Pursuant to Security Council Resolution 780 (1992), UN Doc. S/1994/674 (27 May 1994). Reproduced in Bassiouni, M. Cherif (ed.), *International Criminal Law, Volume III: Enforcement*, New York: Transnational Publishers, Inc., 2nd edn, 1999, pp 433-87.
Report of the Secretary-General Pursuant to Paragraph 2 of Security Council Resolution 808 (1993), UN Doc. S/25704 and Annex (3 May 1993). Reproduced in Bassiouni, M. Cherif (ed.), *International Criminal Law, Volume III: Enforcement*, New York: Transnational Publishers, Inc., 2nd edn, 1999, pp 519-47 (Appendix 15).
Final Report of the Commission of Experts Established Pursuant to Security Council Resolution 935 (1994), UN Doc. S/1994/1405 (9 December 1994).
ILC 1996 Draft Code of Crimes, [1996] II (2) *ILC Yearbook*.
Report on the Diplomatic Conference of the United Nations Plenipotentiaries on the Creation of an International Criminal Court, A/Conf.183/C.1/L.76, 1998.
Report of the Group of Experts for Cambodia Established Pursuant to General Assembly Resolution 52/135, UN Doc. A/53/850-S/1999/321 (16 March 1999).
Report of the Preparatory Commission for the International Criminal Court:
Part I: Finalized Draft Text of the Rules of Procedures and Evidence, 2 November 2000, PCNICC/2000/1/Add.1.
Part II: Finalized Draft Text of the Elements of Crimes, 2 November 2000, PCNICC/2000/1/Add.2.
Resolution 1368 Concerning the Threats to International Peace and Security Caused by Terrorists Acts, adopted by the Security Council at its 4370th meeting, 12 September 2001 (S/RES/1368 (2001)).
Resolution 1373 adopted by the Security Council at its 4385th meeting, 28 September 2001.
ILC Draft Articles on the Responsibility of States for internationally wrongful acts. [2001] Report of the International Law Commission on the work of its Fifty-third session, *Official Records of the General Assembly, Fifty-sixth session. Suplement No. 10* (A/56/10), Chapter IV.E.1.

About the Author

Dr Caroline Fournet obtained her Law Degree in 1997 from Université Jean Moulin – Lyon III (France), and in 1998 she obtained a Maîtrise en Droit Public (Mention Bien) from this same University. The same year, having been awarded a grant as an ERASMUS student, she also passed with distinction a Master of International Law from the Raoul Wallenberg Institute of Human Rights and Humanitarian Law in Lund (Sweden). Her Master thesis is entitled: "Nuremberg and its Aftermath: Accountability for Crimes Against Humanity – Case Study: France".

She was subsequently awarded a research grant and, in 1999, she obtained a DEA from the Institut des Hautes Etudes Européennes in Strasbourg (France), for which she wrote a dissertation on the inequities existing between States within the European conventional system of protection of human rights and fundamental freedoms.

In 2000 she was awarded a research studentship by the Faculty of Law of the University of Leicester (United Kingdom) and, in 2003, she obtained her Ph.D. Her Ph.D. thesis is entitled: "Crimes Against Humanity: *'The Accumulated Evil of the Whole'*".

After an internship at the Association for the Prevention of Torture, a non-governmental organisation based in Geneva, she has been appointed as a Lecturer at Exeter University's School of Law.